Kanuhelatuksla
Oneida Thanksgiving

Shekoli akweku. Kaik wahnislate t hetwanuhelatuh Shukwayatisu.
Hello everyone. Today we give thanks to Creator.

Ne akweku ohutsyake lawen tau I:a:yukwa' ni: kuhli:yohak.
For everything on earth he made for our good health and mind.

Ne ohnekanos okuha' a:yukwayahtaye:liste' skan ukwanikul.
For the waters that give us life, peace and our ways and beliefs

Ne ohnuhkwasuha, kahikokúha', ahs ' tekuthanutel, kaluhtesúha,
For all medicines, fruits, three sisters, all the trees,

Kutilyohsuha, Otsi'tu'suha. Ne uska ukwanikuh, Ta neh.
All animals and birds. Our minds are one, let it be so.

T hetinuhelatu lotikst hokuha' yukikalatunihe' ayakwayutehtan.
We give thanks to the Elders who teach us through stories.

N kati' tsitwalutay tho ahsé tsyukwanikuhlisane. Yawuhko.
Now we plant this new tree to renew our minds. Thank you.

–Written and translated by Grafton Antone, Oneida, Oneida of the Thames First Nation

©P

Aboriginal Beliefs, Values, and Aspirations

Author Team

Barbara Filion, Innu-Montagnais; Royal Ontario Museum Education Program

Neal McLeod, Cree/Swedish; Indigenous Studies, Trent University

Suzanne Methot, Cree, Education Consultant

Shay-Lea O'Brien, Anishinaabe/Haudenosaunee/Irish; Teacher, Toronto District School Board

Tanya Senk, Métis; York University, Faculty of Education (secondee); Instructional Leader, Aboriginal Education, Toronto District School Board

Contributing Writers

Grafton Antone, Oneida, Oneida of the Thames First Nation; Elder in Residence, First Nations House, University of Toronto

Chelsea Donaldson

Laura Edlund

Doug Gordon, Education Consultant, formerly Thames Valley District School Board

Mark Kalluak, Inuk, Elder; Advisor, Nunavut Department of Education, Arviat

Robert Leavitt, former Director of the Mi'kmaq-Maliseet Institute, University of New Brunswick

Cynthia O'Brien

Chris Paci, Manager of Education and Training, Métis Nation of Ontario

Maurice Switzer, Mississaugas of Alderville First Nation; Director of Communications, Union of Ontario Indians; Editor of the *Anishinabek News*

Shirley Williams Pheasant, Ojibwe/Odawa, Wikwemikong Unceded Indian Reserve; Professor Emeritus, Native Studies Department, Trent University

PEARSON

GoodMinds.com

Pearson Canada Inc.
26 Prince Andrew Place
Don Mills, ON   M3C 2T8
Customer Service: 1-800-361-6128

ISBN: 978 013 510651 8

Publisher: Susan Cox
Research and Communications Manager: Patti Henderson
Managing Editor: Gaynor Fitzpatrick
Project Consultants: Donna Magee, GoodMinds.com; Sheila Staats, GoodMinds.com
Coordinating Editor: Judith Scott
Developmental Editors: Laura Edlund, Cara James
Production Editor: Ann Echlin
Copy Editors: Ann Echlin, Tilman Lewis
Proofreaders: Rebecca Vogan, Heather Vogan, Jessica Westhead
Editorial Support: Christine Higdon, Kristen See, Kristiana Shin
Fact Checker: Tracy Westell
Indexer: Jin Tan
Permissions Editor: Rachel Irwin
Photo Researcher: Terri Rothman, M.L.S.
Pronunciation Guide: Dr. Marguerite MacKenzie, Dr. Carrie Dyck, Madeleine Cornthwaite, Cynthia O'Brien, Chelsea Donaldson
Supervisor, Production: Sharlene Ross
Cover Design: HandsDesign.ca
Interior Design: Alex Li
Composition: Lapiz Digital Services, India
Cover Image: iStockphoto
Manufacturing Coordinator: Karen Alley
Vice-President, Publishing: Mark Cobham
President, GoodMinds.com: Jeff Burnham

About the cover: The Council Fire represents the integrity of the words spoken in Council. The fire is considered sacred and it obligates people to speak the truth. Its flames purify the words as the two sides of the Council speak across the fire.

9 2023

Printed and bound in Canada

Program Advisors and Reviewers

Pearson Canada, in conjunction with GoodMinds.com, was commissioned by the Ontario Ministry of Education to publish resources to meet the curriculum expectations for the Grade 10 and Grade 11 Native Studies courses. These curriculum expectations are designed for both Aboriginal and non-Aboriginal students "…to increase awareness and understanding of the history, cultures, world views, and contributions of Aboriginal peoples in Canada…and to help students better understand Aboriginal issues at local, regional, and national levels." It was thanks to the commitment of everyone involved in the project that these texts truly reflect the voices of the First Nations, Métis, and Inuit peoples living in Ontario and Canada.

The first task was to identify Aboriginal and non-Aboriginal educators, educational consultants, academics, community leaders, Elders, Traditional Teachers, Senators, and other individuals throughout the province and across the country who could help provide content suggestions. Focus groups were conducted in 15 communities, revealing classroom and community challenges as well as the content these participants felt should be included in these resources. One unique aspect of this project has been the degree of consultation, review, and validation at every stage.

Pearson Canada and GoodMinds.com wish to thank their program advisors and reviewers, who helped shape this resource through their suggestions in focus group sessions, discussions, and reviews of prototype materials and manuscripts. Final content decisions have been made in consultation with our program advisors.

Advisors

Jeff Burnham, Oneida; President, GoodMinds.com

Donna Magee, Education Consultant, formerly Toronto District School Board

Sheila Staats, Six Nations of the Grand River

Vernon Douglas, Mnjikinang (Rama) First Nation; Cultural Advisor, Indigenous Studies Department, Trent University

Doug Gordon, Education Consultant, formerly Thames Valley District School Board

Keith Lickers, Seneca, Six Nations Reserve; former Education Officer, Ontario Ministry of Education

Jacqueline Moore, Cree Nation; Education Consultant, former Director, Aboriginal Teacher Education Program (1998–2009), Queen's University

Chris Paci, Métis; Manager of Education and Training, Métis Nation of Ontario

Maurice Switzer, Mississaugas of Alderville First Nation; Director of Communications, Union of Ontario Indians; Editor of the *Anishinabek News*

Reviewers

Gratien Allaire, Francophone Reviewer; Department of History and Institut franco-ontarien, Laurentian University

Cyndy Baskin, Mi'kmaq; School of Social Work, Ryerson University

Ken Beardsall, Social Studies Curriculum Coordinator, Nunavut Department of Education

Jan Beaver, Mississaugas of Alderville First Nation; Senior Education Advisor, Ogemawahj Tribal Council

Nicole Bell, Anishinaabe; School of Education and Indigenous Studies Department, Trent University

Dean Cunningham, Surrey School District, Surrey, B.C.

Lynnita Guillet, Aboriginal Education Support Teacher, Thunder Bay Catholic District School Board; Faculty of Education, Lakehead University

Jim Hollander, Weenusk First Nation; School/Student Success Leader

Laura Horton, Dene Anishinaabe, Rainy River First Nation Community Member; Director, Post-Secondary Programs, Seven Generations Education Institute

Adrian Kahgee, Anishinaabe, Saugeen First Nation, part of Saugeen Ojibwe Nation; Bluewater District School Board

Mireille LaPointe, Algonquin, Ardoch Algonquin First Nation

Robert Leavitt, former Director of the Mi'kmaq–Maliseet Institute, University of New Brunswick

John Macdonald, Teacher Consultant—Aboriginal Education, Grand Erie District School Board

Monica McKay, Coordinator, Aboriginal Student Services, Ryerson University

Neal McLeod, Cree/Swedish; Indigenous Studies, Trent University

Robyn Michaud-Turgeon, Anishinaabe; Thames Valley District School Board

Deneen Montour, Grand Erie District School Board Native Advisor, Haldimand School Support Centre

Shay-Lea O'Brien, Anishinaabe/Haudenosaunee/Irish; Toronto District School Board

Claire O'Nabigon, Education Director, Ginoogaming First Nation & Long Lake No. 58 Education Authority

Susan J. Sandau, Cree; Native Language Instructors' Program, Faculty of Education, Lakehead University

Stephen Sliwa, Superintendent of Instruction, Ottawa– Carleton District School Board (formerly with Renfrew County District School Board)

Karihwakeron Tim Thompson, Wahta Mohawk Territory, Education Consultant

Bernadette Wabie, Algonquin-Temiskaming First Nation

Kizhay Wahdizi Quay, Inuk, Baker Lake, NU, Bidassigewak Native Way School

Cynthia C. Wesley-Esquimaux, Ph.D., Odawa/ Pottawatomi/Chippewa/Mohawk, Chippewas of Georgina Island First Nation, assistant professor

Pearson Canada and GoodMinds.com would also like to thank the Elders, Traditional Teachers, Senators, and community members who participated in the focus groups that took place in Toronto (Downtown, West, East, Métis Nation of Ontario), London West/Sarnia, Woodstock/London East, Peterborough, York/Simcoe, Ottawa (Kanata and Métis Nation of Ontario), Kingston, Sudbury, Thunder Bay, Sault Ste. Marie, Collingwood.

This resource was made possible with funding by the Government of Ontario.

WC 06.12.2023 1308

©P

CONTENTS

©P

©P

CALL TO CONSCIOUSNESS

Throughout this book, you will read about beliefs, values, and aspirations of the diverse First Nations, Métis, and Inuit peoples in Canada. Aboriginal peoples in Canada today form over 50 Nations and more than 600 communities. In their great diversity, they present unique perspectives that need to be heard in this country.

Why Are Perspectives Important?

Each person's perspective reflects his or her beliefs, values, and attitudes. Why do perspectives differ and why do they matter? As Cynthia Wesley-Esquimaux says, "Where you are standing plays a big role in how you perceive the world around you." Maurice Switzer elaborates on perspectives:

Cynthia Wesley-Esquimaux
assistant professor, of Odawa/Pottawatomi and Mohawk heritage, raised in Toronto and now living on the Chippewas of Georgina Island First Nation

Different people just see things differently. It's so simple, yet so complicated... and so divisive. This is never more evident than on July 10, the anniversary of the 78-day stand-off between 63 Mohawks and over 4000 Canadian soldiers and Québec police officers.

We can't even agree on the name by which this landmark event is remembered. A generation later, journalists are still referring to the events at "Oka" instead of identifying the location as "the Mohawk territory of Kanehsatake." It was almost three centuries of denial of that fact by the governments of France, England, Québec, and Canada that led to the crisis in the first place.

What the Mohawks of Kanehsatake saw differently from most people in Canada in the summer of 1990 was that their historic occupation of that territory took precedence over plans by the neighbouring Québec town of Oka to expand an existing golf course onto a traditional Mohawk burial ground.

When he looked at that picturesque piece of land into which are rooted towering pine trees, Mayor Jean Ouellette saw golfers lining up to pay their green fees and tax assessment notices going out to dozens of ratepayers living in a new housing development. He saw dollar signs.

The people of Kanehsatake, on the other hand, saw a peaceful resting place for the remains of their ancestors.

This is a scenario that has repeated itself over and over again during the past 500 years from Baffin Island to the tip of Cape Horn... Different people just see things differently.

Maurice Switzer
citizen of the Mississaugas of Alderville First Nation in Ontario, director of communications for the Union of Ontario Indians, and editor of the *Anishinabek News*

Maurice Switzer writes that "the memorable Canadian Press photo (left) was still on the front pages...two decades after the fact. Even the keenest of Canadian history buffs would be hard-pressed to tell you that the majority of those 63 besieged Mohawks were not wearing masks or carrying rifles; they were unarmed women and children." In contrast, the two images (right) from the documentary film *Kanehsatake: 270 Years of Resistance* by Abenaki filmmaker Alanis Obomsawin show her perspective on the events.

Who Are First Nations, Métis, and Inuit Peoples?

To help you think about beliefs, values, and aspirations of the diverse Aboriginal peoples in Canada, this introduction explores big ideas about who we are, understanding, respect, what we are working toward, and what you can do.

Many different terms are used in connection with Aboriginal peoples; these variations can lead to confusion and can mean that no one term will suit everyone's ideas about appropriateness. However, clarifying what those terms mean and using them with respect and understanding can help build more just, equitable, respectful relationships. Métis student Jennifer Henry says:

Jennifer Henry

When people ask about my culture and heritage specifically, I explain that I am Métis and most people have no clue what that is. So, I try my best to explain... Being Métis in Canada today for me means pride.

Eddy Robinson, a drummer and singer who is Missanabie Cree and Ojibwe, asks:

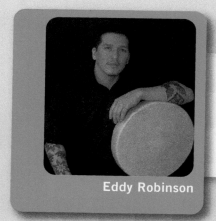

Eddy Robinson

How can we create a better society by understanding each other?... It helps our people that [non-Aboriginal] people understand who we are and where we're coming from... Who Native people are... who Inuit people are... First Nations people... Ojibwe... What does that mean?

While all Nations and communities had their own names for themselves when they first met newcomers, these newcomers often labelled specific Nations and communities with new names, including names that lumped some people together or split others apart. The act of renaming in itself was disrespectful, as it disregarded existing names. Many Aboriginal peoples and communities today are either in the process of reclaiming their inherent right to name themselves or have done so already.

In this book, we strive to use terms that are accurate, appropriate, respectful, and specific. While discussions continue about which terms are preferred, and language and spellings evolve, here are some of the key terms we have chosen to use in this book.

Aboriginal peoples—the descendants of the original inhabitants of North America. This is the term used in the Royal Commission on Aboriginal Peoples (which released its report in 1996) and the term used in Canada's Constitution Act, 1982: "In this Act, 'Aboriginal peoples of Canada' includes the Indian, Inuit, and Métis peoples of Canada." The term *Aboriginal peoples* is a very broad umbrella term; when possible, this book uses more specific terms.

First Nations peoples—a term used in preference to *Indian*, which some people consider offensive. However, *Indian* does have a legal meaning in Canada, as in *status Indian* under the federal law, the Indian Act. The term *First Nation* is often used to identify a specific people—for example, the Mississaugas of Alderville First Nation.

Inuit—the Aboriginal people indigenous to the Arctic, in northern Canada, living mainly in Nunavut, the Northwest Territories, northern Québec, and Labrador. Some Inuit live in other areas, including Ontario. The term *Eskimo* has been used for Inuit but *Eskimo* is not an acceptable term to use in Canada.

Métis—the Aboriginal people who share many of the traditions of their First Nations and European ancestors. The Métis have become a distinct people and Nation. At the same time that Métis communities east to west are diverse, the Métis have a shared history, common culture, unique language and way of life, and traditional territory. The term *Métis* is Michif (the language of the Métis) and a word derived from the French.

First Peoples—First Nations peoples and Inuit

specific Nations, communities, and peoples—When possible, more specific terms are used. You will read about the Six Nations of the Grand River Territory (in Ontario), the Métis community in Penetanguishene (in Ontario), an Inuk artist from Cape Dorset (in Nunavut), a Mi'kmaw scholar from Eskasoni (in Nova Scotia), the Haudenosaunee, and the Anishinaabe—among many others.

As you read, you will find many more words, terms, and perspectives that are new to you. Many terms will be defined in the Glossary (starting on page 324) and in marginal features such as the one at the right.

An important aspect of learning about Aboriginal peoples in Canada is understanding the diversity not only across Canada but also within regions. It is also important to understand that there are diverse perspectives among individuals, and that individuals speak for themselves. When you read someone's point of view on an issue, it's important not to lump everyone together and assume, for example, that all Aboriginal individuals see an issue from the same perspective, feel the same way, or behave the same way.

WORDS MATTER

Inuk the singular form of *Inuit*. Inuit means "the people."

Mi'kmaw the singular form of *Mi'kmaq*. The Mi'kmaq are a First Nations people in what is now Nova Scotia, New Brunswick, Prince Edward Island, the Gaspé region of Québec, and New England. The name *Mi'kmaq* is preferred over the English term *Micmac*.

Understanding and Respect

Understanding and *respect* are words you will read and hear often in studying the beliefs, values, and aspirations of First Nations, Métis, and Inuit peoples. Why? Here are some answers:

This particular project...holds the promise of a better future for Aboriginal people, and indeed, for all of Canadians, because we do live in this country together, and there needs to be a mutual understanding and respect.

Don Worme
Plains Cree lawyer from Kawacatoose First Nation in Saskatchewan

David Bouchard

Respect is one of the teachings that is common to all Aboriginal people... My Algonquin Grandmother was leery when my French Grandfather first stepped onto our Canadian shores. She was leery even though she trusted that he and his fellow newcomers would be, at the very least, respectful. Respect was an integral part of relationships between all nations, even among our enemies. It took centuries of insatiable brutality before my First Nation Grandparents finally understood these newcomers had a different understanding of what respect meant...

David Bouchard
Métis author and educator

Mary Simon

I must return to the simple wisdom that I gained from early days in northern Québec... There are many people still alive in Inuit communities who began their life as I did...in camps...among a small group of families... who valued the contributions of individuals, and shared their contributions for a higher purpose...sustaining our families... My approach to leadership in any organization draws from these early experiences of community. I treat everyone as I expect to be treated— with respect... I also encourage people to be curious—to seek out an understanding of other perspectives, and where conflicting or contradictory perspectives arise...mediate solutions.

Mary Simon
national Inuit leader, president of the Inuit Tapiriit Kanatami

©P

This brings you to *how* to gain understanding and respect. One way to learn about First Nations, Métis, and Inuit peoples is to learn about their perspectives, experiences, knowledge, and achievements. Jan Beaver (Ozhawakan Kwekwe) who is an Anishinaabe teacher, from the Bear Clan, from Alderville First Nation says:

Jan Beaver

I would want students to, first and foremost, acknowledge and be grateful for the wisdom that First Nations, Métis, and Inuit people have developed...

Larry Hill (Seneca) speaks of the importance of stories:

Our stories were us. What we knew, where we came from, and where we were going. They were to remind us of our responsibilities, to instruct, and to entertain. There were stories of Creation, our travels, our laws. There were many legends of hard fought battles, funny anecdotes—some from the smokehouse, some from the trickster—and there were scary stories to remind us of danger, spiritual and otherwise. Stories were our way of life and they still are.

Chris Paci of the Métis Nation of Ontario (Manager MNO Education and Training) clarifies that it matters to understand diversity among identities and experiences:

Chris Paci

First Nations, Métis, and Inuit peoples, while all Aboriginal, are not all the same. These are very diverse cultures and peoples with vastly different identities, histories, and experiences. Anyone hoping to understand the issues today needs to know what "identity" means from each Nation's perspective. Anishinaabe are not the same as Métis, not the same as Inuit. If all three are raised in Sault Ste. Marie, that's a different story. Where we live and our experiences shape our "identity." An Inuk raised in Toronto is different than his cousin raised in Iqaluit. Métis communities are not just a point on a map. Here in Ottawa, there is a Métis local (that means there is a historical community with continuity of the culture to now), but you won't see Métis tapping maple trees on Parliament Hill, and Métis never ran buffalo into the Ottawa River.

You and This Book

Barbara Filion

Barbara Filion (an Innu-Montagnais author and educator) says that, for relationships between Aboriginal peoples and all levels of Canadian society—from the individual to the federal government—to improve, "students learning about Aboriginal world views, perspectives, and experiences is a necessary stepping stone."

What does that mean for you? And how does this book play a role?

Don Worme offers his perspective:

If there is to be the kind of foundational and structural change in this country that we need in order for Aboriginal people to be able to take our proper place, then there needs to be a reconciliation. And part of that reconciliation means that there is a recognition of the tremendous suffering that has been inflicted, that there is a time for restitution and reconciliation.

I have every faith in young people these days, that they have the ability to be critical thinkers quite apart and quite on their own... It is up to each individual to be able to take on that enormous task of making themselves a better person, making themselves a critical thinker, of allowing themselves the opportunity to be able to accommodate ideals and visions that might be different than their own... I think it is an obligation of all of us as citizens to be able to do that, to understand other cultures and to be open minded about that and accepting that there are differences between how we might do certain things, but there's no difference between us inside. Physiologically, we're virtually all the same.

©P

Get Involved

Read about Aboriginal world views and ways of knowing throughout the coming chapters in this book, from people from a variety of communities and Nations present today in Canada. Consider multiple perspectives. Learn about communities close up.

You will not look only at the past: instead, you will learn about First Nations, Métis, and Inuit peoples in Canada today, including present realities, traditions, achievements and contributions, aspirations for the future, and experiences of the past. You will also be asked reflection questions and critical thinking questions, build your critical thinking skills, develop understandings of key words and concepts, connect to additional resources, and respond in activities to the big ideas of each chapter and unit. In doing so, you will deepen your knowledge and understanding of the diverse Aboriginal peoples in Canada today.

Don Worme

 Keep an open mind as you expand your perspectives, awareness, and understanding in your exploration of First Nations, Métis, and Inuit peoples' experiences in the land that has become Canada.

Spirit of the Land

For First Nations, Métis, and Inuit peoples, living in a close relationship with
the land and its resources affirms and defines their distinctive world views.

Today, most Inuit make a living through a variety of activities—hunting, guiding, fishing, seasonal work, and artistic endeavors are some. By the end of the 1950s, art cooperatives were in place to help Inuit market their arts and crafts to a wider audience.

Elders are recognized members of their communities who share their knowledge of history, teachings, and practices with others. Alex Jacobs is an Elder from the Whitefish Lake First Nation, near Sudbury Ontario.

The Métis are a people whose culture reflects their distinct heritage. It is in keeping in touch with their history and communities that Métis people support their identities.

SHOWING THE ENTIRE DIVERSITY of First Nations, Métis, and Inuit cultures and all of the ways individuals view the world is not possible for one book. What is offered here are examples that show how the beliefs and values of First Nations, Métis, and Inuit peoples are interconnected with their world views and ways of living, how cultures adapt, and how traditions are renewed.

CHAPTER 1

Aboriginal World Views

> In the Aboriginal world view of the four orders, the Aboriginal person is viewed as last: this is in acknowledgement of the natural superiority of Manitou, the Earthmother, Plants, and Animalkind.
>
> —Cecil King, Odawa

Whether or not you realize it, you have a world view. You express your world view in the way you think about the world, by the way you act, and by the choices you make. Like cultures, world views adapt as people exchange new technologies and ideas. The distinctive world views of First Nations, Métis, and Inuit peoples are alive and adaptive, and like the teaching from Cecil King above, have been maintained through long periods of time. This chapter will explore how the beliefs and values of First Nations, Métis, and Inuit peoples are embedded within their world views.

FIGURE 1.1 Alex Jacobs is an Elder from the Whitefish Lake First Nation. Elders are respected people who share their knowledge with others. What role might an Elder play in the continuation of world views?

INQUIRING MINDS

Use these questions to explore the big ideas in this chapter.

1. What factors influence the way a person views the world?

2. How do the traditional and contemporary beliefs and values of First Nations, Métis, and Inuit peoples influence their lives and reflect their world views?

3. How do First Nations, Métis, and Inuit peoples maintain links with traditional practices and beliefs in the modern world?

4. What challenges do First Nations, Métis, and Inuit peoples face in reclaiming and renewing their traditions and beliefs?

FIGURE 1.2 William Anthony Monague, who is from the Beausoleil First Nation on Christian Island, Ontario, created *Tranquility* (2001) for the First Nations Art Garden at the Toronto Zoo. How does art help a person express beliefs, values, attitudes, and aspirations? Do you think art is a good way to express yourself to others? Explain.

© P

5

What Is a World View?

World view affects the way people view and interpret the world around them. World view creates meaning for people by answering important questions such as

- Why is the world the way it is?
- What is the purpose of life? How do I fit in?
- What is the right way to behave?
- How do I relate to other people and the world around me?

Your world view may be influenced over the course of your lifetime depending on what you learn, the ideas you encounter, your experiences, and new views you may develop. Some of the factors that influence world view are shown in the web diagram below.

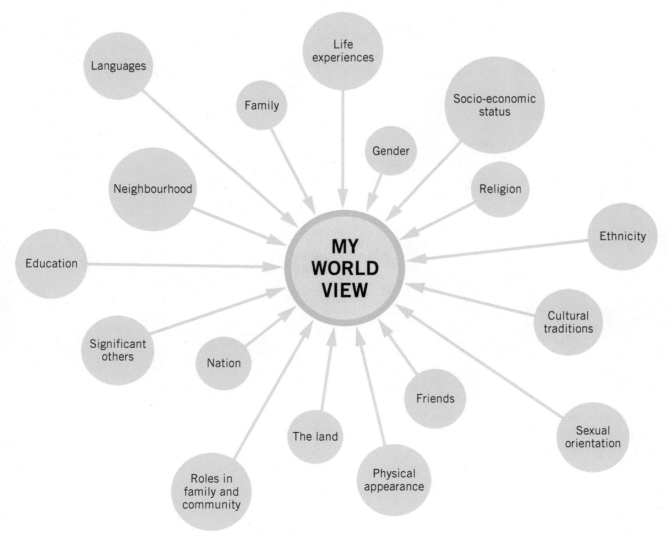

FIGURE 1.3 This web diagram shows some of the factors that may influence world view. What other factors do you think affect your world view? In your experience, are some factors more important than others? Explain.

Why Think About World View?

Everyone is born into a **community** that shapes his or her world view. Canada is made up of diverse communities, and students in your classrooms may hold many different world views. Respecting a wide range of world views is a part of being a citizen in a multicultural society. During your life, you will find that your world view may be different from those of others, but you will also be able to find things in common.

By learning about other world views, we can better understand and relate to others, and work together to solve problems. We can understand what motivates other people's actions. When we see a television news report, for example, we can go beyond the simple question "What's going on here?" We can begin to ask questions such as "Why is this happening?" "Who is reporting on this event?" "How might this person's world view affect how the event is being reported?" and "In what ways is this report biased?" **Values, beliefs, attitudes**, and **aspirations** are all aspects of world view. Here is a list of questions to consider when you look at the world views of a group or Nation.

Values	• How do members of the society think that people should act toward one another, and to people in other groups? • How is wealth valued? • How are resources distributed and used?
Beliefs	• How do people express their beliefs? • What beliefs do people share? • What spiritual beliefs guide the **culture**?
Attitudes	• What feelings do people hold toward specific persons or things? • How do people deal with challenges and obstacles?
Aspirations	• How do people gain, share, and use knowledge? • What goals do people share? • What provisions does the society make for future generations?

community a group of people organized around common values and linked together by common histories, social and political interests and structures, and/or geography

value a principle or standard that a person or a group accepts; our values guide us in thinking about what is right, what is important, what is meaningful. Values may include things such as morals, ethics, justice, and fair play.

belief what a person accepts as true or real, usually with an emotional or spiritual sense of certainty

attitude the way a person views something or tends to behave toward it; based on beliefs

aspiration a desire to achieve something; aspirations determine what we believe is possible for us and our community to do in the future

culture the way of life for a people that includes their values, beliefs, knowledge, symbols, traditions, and history and is transmitted from generation to generation

THINKING IT THROUGH

1. Choose factors from the web diagram on page 6 and describe how each factor has shaped your world view. Share your answers with a small group and discuss the following:

   a) Why are some answers in your group similar? Why are some different?

   b) Why may some aspects of your world views change throughout your lives? Why might some stay the same?

   c) How might learning about the world views of others influence both your own world view and your relationships with other people?

©P

Understanding Point of View and Perspective

WORDS MATTER

point of view a personal or collective expression of opinion on a particular issue or topic; reflects one's beliefs, values, attitudes, and world view

perspective a way of making sense of an issue or topic; perspective also reflects one's beliefs, values, attitudes, and world view

Every spoken or written word comes from a **point of view** or a **perspective**. As you continue to work with this textbook, you will read about and hear from many different people on a variety of issues. In order to gain greater understanding of a text, speech, or image, it is important to know as much as possible about the writer's or speaker's point of view. Sometimes the person will tell you, but often it will be hidden. They may even assume that you share the same point of view. The advantage of understanding the points of view and perspectives of others is that you will be able to read, listen, and ask about what you are learning in an informed way.

It is important to remember that everyone's point of view reflects his or her world view, knowledge, experiences, and culture. Consider how you view the world in order to understand what influences the way you look at something.

Asking Questions to Determine Point of View and Perspective

Exploring another's point of view or perspective on a topic requires you to ask questions. When reading an account of a specific event, you might ask questions such as

- Who was involved?
- How did what took place affect each person or group?
- Whose point of view is being expressed? Who is not represented?
- What factors might have influenced the author's point of view?
- What is not mentioned that might be important?
- What other questions should I ask?

FIGURE 1.4 Has anyone ever asked you why you think the way you do?

Apply Your Skills

1. Choose a news article (print, television, or radio) about a current issue involving First Nations, Métis, or Inuit peoples.

   a) What points of view are expressed in the article? What beliefs or attitudes are being expressed?

   b) What is the perspective of those involved? What beliefs or attitudes are being expressed?

   c) What evidence in the article shows the writer's or speaker's point of view?

   d) Does the article fairly balance points of view? What biases are there in the article?

   e) What additional points of view could be explored?

Expressing World Views

Language expresses a culture's values and beliefs, and is the main way culture is passed from one generation to the next. Because language names the world and our experiences, it reflects and shapes our world view and affects our interactions with the world. For example, in some languages, there are no words to distinguish gender. This is the case in Inuktitut, the language of some Inuit, which reflects a world view where, spiritually, people, animals, and things have equal standing.

Language is also tied to environment, and reflects experiences with the world's dynamic and cyclical nature. Because change is a part of nature, change is reflected in languages that are verb- or action-oriented. Dr. Marie Battiste explains how her language reflects her world view, below:

> [Mi'kmaq] is built around relationships, and the relationships of people to each other are more important than anything else… In Mi'kmaq, everything operates from the basis of verbs, and verbs are complicated by all of the other elements around them which show relationships. So the most important element of the language is the verb because everything is connected to it and all the other words can be shifted around because of that.
>
> There is an animate and an inanimate relationship and this inanimate relationship relates to how close we have [felt] to some things. The relationship of objects around us, those that have had an intimate relationship have an animate relationship, and those things that haven't have an inanimate relationship. But they have nothing to do with "living" and "dead."
>
> —Dr. Marie Battiste, Mi'kmaw scholar and educator, Eskasoni

First Nations, Inuit, and Métis languages capture details of natural surroundings, cycles of nature, and interrelationships. In the Algonquian languages, there is no single word equivalent to *tree*—instead, there are many words that reflect a tree's stages of life. In this way, the tree is understood to be ever-changing. Métis storytellers invent new, humorous words to create a visual image for their audience, a natural process of the Métis language, Michif. The Métis have developed as a unique Nation, distinct from both their First Nations and European parents and grandparents, but with strong ties to both. Michif varies from province to province; in the West, it is influenced by Cree, and in the North, by Dene. In Ontario, Michif is an old version of French, with English, Gaelic, Mohawk, Algonquian, and Anishinaabemowin influences.

REFLECTION

First Nations, Métis, and Inuit languages also tend to be descriptive, and are not easily translated word-for-word into a language such as English. For example, after the Northwest Resistance in 1885, Chief Big Bear was told that he was on trial for "knocking the Queen's hat off," as there was no word in his language for "treason." What do you think he might have thought about this?

VOICES OF THE PEOPLES

In our language, it is embedded, our philosophy of life and our technologies. There is a reason why we want our languages preserved and taught to our children—it is our survival.

—*Burt McKay, Nisga'a teacher and Elder*

CRITICAL THINKING

Language provides a way for us to share our experiences. Explain how differences in world view are expressed through language. Identify examples other than those cited in this text.

CRITICAL THINKING

Discuss why you think the preservation of Aboriginal languages is vital to maintaining the values, beliefs, and practices of Aboriginal peoples.

Language also describes the structures of family and society—for example, how descendents are traced. In some First Nations languages, **kinship** terms extend to the non-human realm. For instance, some Nations refer to the moon as their grandmother. In the complexities of extended Métis families, in which sons and daughters are named after fathers, mothers, and grandparents, nicknames developed as a way to distinguish one person from another. These nicknames also reflected the multiple origins of their language. For example, Chiga, or "Little Boy" comes from the French petit garçon.

Language and Identity

Language is closely tied to identity, as it allows the communication of unique aspects of culture. For many people, it is hard to distinguish between language and identity, as both are expressions of their individual and cultural realities.

A shared language provides people with a sense of belonging, in which individuals can feel secure in the continuity of the past and the passing on of their culture, beliefs, and traditions. The Royal Commission on Aboriginal Peoples (1996) recognized these important links. One of the conclusions of the report was that language preservation is essential to the health of individuals and communities.

Ways of thinking are also related to language. Language is closely linked to ceremonies, knowledge, beliefs, values, spirituality, and cultures. This means that the loss of languages spoken by First Nations, Inuit, and Métis peoples also threatens the existence of their unique world views. **Elders**, **traditional teachers**, and Wisdom Keepers play an important role in preserving and passing on their languages. Among the Métis, many Elders and **Senators** speak their languages fluently and understand how their languages convey teachings accurately. **Faithkeepers** and Elders are skilled orators who give speeches at ceremonies and celebrations. In later chapters, you will learn more about the ways in which First Nations, Inuit, and Métis peoples are working to keep their languages alive.

Changes to Language

When Europeans came into contact with First Nations, there was an intermingling of languages. Europeans often adopted First Nations words such as *toboggan* and *kayak,* and reinterpreted them, creating new words. First Nations languages acquired new words for things that were new to them, such as farm animals. When First Nations, Métis, and Inuit guided European explorers throughout Canada, they used place names in their own languages. Today, these place names acknowledge the roots of this country. For example, *Ontario* is a Wendat word meaning "beautiful sparkling water."

WORDS MATTER

kinship family relationships

Elder a person who has gained significant wisdom and understanding of Aboriginal history, traditional teachings, ceremonies, and healing practices. Elders are recognized by their communities, who have acknowledged their wisdom and granted them permission to pass on knowledges and give guidance.

traditional teacher a person who carries the traditional teachings and ceremonies of his or her community and Nation

Senators persons elected by their Métis communities as leaders and advisors

faithkeeper a person responsible for learning ceremonies, songs, and stories from their community. A faithkeeper maintains these teachings by ensuring that all aspects of ceremonies are followed according to protocol. Faithkeepers are expected to continue learning and to share what they learn.

Naming Ceremonies

How many names do you have? Why do you have different names? Who gave you these names? Why were these names chosen for you? Do you know what they mean or where they come from? In many cultures around the world, names have many meanings and are chosen or used for specific reasons. This significance is reflected in naming ceremonies, which make up an important part of a culture's social structure. For many Aboriginal peoples, it is not unusual for individuals to be given several names in their lifetime. Allowing an individual to acquire new names is considered to be reflective of his or her growth and experiences.

Naming ceremonies vary depending on the culture. A person might be given the name of an ancestor, in which case he or she is expected to uphold the values held by that ancestor. Some names are meant to acknowledge a person's new relationship to the community or the spiritual world. Some cultures believe that having a name in your own language is necessary in order for the Creator to recognize you.

Naming ceremonies are also seen as significant rites of passage. Some First Nations of the Northwest Coast, for example, hold potlatches in order to mark the naming of a child. Some Inuit cultures give the newborn an atiq, meaning both name and spirit or soul, within a few days after the baby's birth. The name usually comes from a relative who has passed away. After receiving an atiq, the child is considered a full person, embodying both his or her own personality and that of the deceased. If, for example, a father gives his newborn son the name of his grandfather, then the son can later call his father "grandson."

To the Haudenosaunee, a person's name or names are an integral part of his or her identity. Clan Mothers are responsible for keeping track of a pool of names that belong to their clan. Whenever someone passes away, the name can be returned to the pool a year after his or her death. Sharing names within the clan creates a connection between the ancestors and later generations.

Haudenosaunee naming ceremonies usually take place during the Mid-Winter Ceremony, which signals the beginning of a new year. Depending on the moon cycle, the ceremony is held sometime in January, and lasts for six to eight days. The naming ceremonies usually occur on the fourth day. During this time, babies, children, adults, and Elders can all receive a new name. Prior to the ceremony, the Clan Mother will work with the head of the family to ensure that the name is suitable for the person. The Clan Mothers then take the name(s) to the head faithkeeper, who will make a short speech and announce the name(s) to those attending longhouse or to the community.

QUESTIONS

1. With a partner, discuss your name or names. What do your names mean and how were these particular names chosen for you? Do you have a nickname? How did you get it?

2. Compare the traditions of name-giving in your family or culture with those of a partner.

FIGURE 1.5 How do your names reflect your identity?

Aboriginal Stories and World View

Cultures around the world practise storytelling as a way to share beliefs, teach lessons, entertain, and inform. Among First Nations, Métis, and Inuit peoples, teachings that are passed on in **oral tradition** often take the form of stories. These stories teach truths about people and how they should behave and relate to each other, as well as the nature of the physical world and people's relationships with it. Stories are considered significant and sacred, and are an essential part of tradition and world view.

FIGURE 1.6 This sculpture, *Raven and the First Men* (dedicated April 1, 1980) by Haida artist Bill Reid, depicts the story of human creation according to the Haida Nation. Raven, who is lonely and wants company, coaxes the first men out of a giant clam shell he found on the beach. Do you know any creation stories? What values are told through these stories?

First Nations, Métis, and Inuit peoples value the close connection they feel with their environment. There are **spiritual** as well as material connections with the environment, which are reflected in the diverse **creation stories** of different Nations. Creation stories tell how the world began, how people came to be, and how they came to have their present relationship with the natural world. These stories contain the core values and original teachings of the culture.

Through oral traditions, the beliefs, values, customs, and history of a people are recorded. Oral traditions also contain concrete skills and knowledges, such as where to hunt or how to prepare medicines. Sharing stories also brings people together. Some take hours or even days to tell. Keep in mind that some stories in this textbook are short versions, and that even the same story can have variations depending on the teller.

WORDS MATTER

oral tradition a way of remembering the past through stories and spoken explanation, rather than in writing; objects to aid memory can also be used

spiritual relating to the sacred essence of the soul or spirit. *Spiritual* is often contrasted with *worldly*, which relates to the things we see in the world.

creation stories accounts or series of accounts that tell about the beginnings of time, the structure of the earth and the universe, and the establishment of the social order

©P

Creation Stories

The Mother of the Sea Mammals

This Inuit story tells of Nuliajuk (also called Sedna), the Mother of the Sea Mammals. This version of the story was recorded in the early 1900s.

Once in times long past people left the settlement at Qingniertôq in Sherman Inlet. They were going to cross the water and had made rafts of kayaks tied together. They were many and were in haste to get away to new hunting grounds. And there was not much room on the rafts they tied together. At the village there was a little girl whose name was Nuliajuk. She jumped out on to the raft together with the other boys and girls, but no one cared about her, no one was related to her, and so they seized her and threw her into the water. In vain she tried to get hold of the edge of the raft; they cut her fingers off, and lo! as she sank to the bottom the stumps of her fingers became alive in the water and bobbed up round the raft like seals. That was how the seals came. But Nuliajuk herself sank to the bottom of the sea. There she became a spirit, the sea spirit, and she became the mother of the sea beasts, because the seals had formed out of her fingers that were cut off. And she also became mistress of everything else alive, the land beasts too, that mankind had to hunt.

In that way she obtained great power over mankind, who had despised her and thrown her into the sea. She became the most feared of all spirits, the most powerful, and the one who more than any other controls the destinies of men. For that reason almost all taboo is directed against her, though only in the dark period while the sun is low, and it is cold and windy on earth; for then life is most dangerous to live.

—**Kappianaqtut: Strange Creatures and Fantastic Beings from Inuit Myths and Legends, Volume 1**

Crow Creates the World

This Tagish story tells of the creation of the world by Crow. This version of the story was told by Angela Sidney.

A long time ago the world was water. Crow saw that Sea Lion owned the only island in the world. The rest was water. Sea Lion was the only one with land. The whole place was ocean.

Crow is resting on a piece of log. He's tired. He sees Sea Lion with that little island just for himself. He wants land too. So he stole that Sea Lion's kid.

"Give me back that kid," said Sea Lion.

"Give me some beach, some sand," says Crow. So Sea Lion gave him sand. You know how sand in water floats? Crow threw that sand around the ocean.

"Be world!" he tells it. And it became the world.

—**I Have Lived Here Since the World Began**

Métis Creation Stories

The Métis share stories that were passed down from their First Nations and European ancestors. Métis creation stories depict the coming together of worlds, resulting in culturally rich coexistence.

The central figures of Métis creation stories include beavers and wood smoke, canoes and buffalo, sturgeon and the palisades of forts. These stories include teachings about the restorative rest of winter, the renewed life and hope of spring, the berries of summer and gratefulness for the harvest, and the slowing pace of fall.

The shared motif of Métis creation stories is the sash, which weaves together different colours. Patterns emerge and attract the eye. The sash symbolizes the strength of coming together. Métis stories also have their own soundtrack; the fiddle has a rhythm which resonates in the heart.

When people reconnect with their Métis culture, they often describe it as "coming home." They feel it and live it, and at last have a name to describe how they think, hear, see, and believe. Lessons of caring for others in our communities, respect, and having the unique ability to walk harmoniously between two cultures are themes innate to the very fabric of Métis culture.

—**The Métis Nation of Ontario** ◆

Trickster Stories

Humour is an important aspect of storytelling. It can be a powerful tool when used to deliver difficult messages. Laughing and sharing a funny story can bond people together, relieve stress, and help people get through hard times. For First Nations, Métis, and Inuit peoples, humour has been an important part of the resiliency of their cultures.

Some Aboriginal stories involve a trickster figure teaching humans or others (such as animals or birds) certain lessons, often using humour. The trickster is a common figure, but takes many forms, depending on the Nation. For example, the Abenaki have Azeban, the Swampy Cree have Wee-sah-kee chak, the Anishinaabe have Nanabush, the Métis have Chi-Jean, and so on. Many Nations have more than one trickster figure and their roles are varied; some, such as the Haudenosaunee, have no trickster figure in their stories, although they do use humour. The trickster can also be a creator, as you saw on page 13.

The name *trickster* comes from the idea that these figures are meant to trick the learner into understanding a teaching, giving the impression that things are not as they seem, until the lesson is understood. Humour is often used to convey the lesson. Many contemporary First Nations, Métis, and Inuit authors use trickster characters in their work. How might humour in stories and art reflect world view?

VOICES OF THE PEOPLES

In legend, the Trickster steals, betrays, kills. But this is a Hero as well, because in other stories he is a creator, an inventor, he brings light to the world. I began to remember that the Trickster is the two faces of life, the noble and the base, the dream and the chaos. He represents you and me. He brings confusion, and doubt, but in the end, there is the fire of awakening, the light of understanding.

—Aaron Paquette, Cree, Cherokee, and Norwegian artist

FIGURE 1.7 *Trickster* (2007). Compare Aaron Paquette's description of the trickster to his painting above.

©P

The Arts and World View

Art has been used throughout human history to express thoughts, beliefs, hopes, feelings, and world views. Different art forms also serve to record history and tell stories. Art connects people to the spiritual realm and to their communities, reflects identity, and shows the distinct and diverse forms of expression of First Nations, Métis, and Inuit peoples. Today, art continues to play these important roles, while also providing income for many artists. Some artists practise traditional art forms, some mix traditions with new ways, and others use completely new materials and techniques.

Many First Nations and Inuit languages do not have a word for art, although art has always been present in their cultures and is a part of everyday activities. Every aspect of daily life is imbued with art. The role of artist is not reserved for specific individuals, since everyone is involved in artistic endeavours—dance, song, and other regular tasks. Métis women, for example, are well known for the colourful and complex beadwork on the clothing they make. Some individuals have particular talents, but they are considered artists in the same way as are other community members who participate in creative acts. In many ways, this consideration is a reflection of the talent and skill of the entire family.

Communal creative acts, such as songs, dances, and drum circles, not only connect people through shared experience, but bring individuals closer to the Creator. Artists often say that their creative processes involve a spiritual connection.

FIGURE 1.8 Even everyday items are made with care and artistic expression. This Ojibwe box, made of birchbark and sweetgrass, has been decorated with porcupine quills. What items in your life reflect your culture? How do they express your world view?

COMMUNITY CLOSE-UP

The Collective Spirit: Exploring the Identity of Urban Aboriginal People

Ojibwe photographer Nadya Kwandibens lives in Toronto and is the creator of a photographic series entitled *Concrete Indians*. The series is an exploration of individual and collective Native Identity. Kwandibens encourages First Nations people to submit portrait ideas that visually convey their thoughts regarding what *Native Identity* means and how it is affected as a result of living in urban centres.

Concrete Indians is also an online social network where people can upload photos and discuss the concept of the series.

FIGURE 1.9 How might this series support a feeling of collective identity in an urban environment?

Symbolism

First Nations, Métis, and Inuit peoples have always used images rooted in their spirituality and in their close connection to the environment. Everyday objects are decorated with designs that represent stories and spiritual relationships, and celebrate the achievements of community members. For the Métis, decorative arts reflect a blend of European and First Nations symbols and forms, shown, for example, in their beadwork and embroidery, which reflects First Nations, French, and English patterns. In this sense, symbols reflect a cultural, social, and individual identity. Specific symbols are often repeated on a variety of objects, because they have meaning for every community member.

The symbols used in Aboriginal art often reflect spiritual connections. For instance, in a ceremony involving a pipe, the pipe is often decorated with symbolism representing the spiritual realm. In this way, creative expression becomes a medium through which people connect with and pay tribute to the spiritual world.

FIGURE 1.10 The Métis are famous for the wild rose patterns in their beadwork and embroidery, which is used to decorate clothing, pouches, and other items. This "octopus pouch" was used to carry flint, pipes, and tobacco.

Art in a Changing World

The lifestyles, experiences, and world views of First Nations, Métis, and Inuit peoples have changed drastically over time, and their art has taken on a wider array of styles and forms. Aboriginal artists contribute nationally and internationally as musicians, performance artists, visual artists, actors, sculptors, architects, designers, and in many other creative roles.

Web Connect • • • • • • • • • • • • •

To learn more about Métis beadwork, visit our website.

VOICES OF THE PEOPLES

Annie Pootoogook is an Inuk artist born in Cape Dorset, Nunavut. She is the granddaughter of artist Pitseolak Ashoona and daughter of artists Napachie and Eegyvudlu. Like her family before her, she documents her world and experiences by drawing the things that surround her. Her work illustrates her personal stories and those of her community. Her experiences and art reflect the geographic remoteness of her community, and she comments on how external economic, social, environmental, and cultural factors have an impact on life there.

FIGURE 1.11 *Holding Boots* (2004). Inuk artist Annie Pootoogook's work speaks to social, cultural, and physical changes happening in her home community of Cape Dorset. How do you think this artwork reflects some of the changes in her community?

©P

Shirley Cheechoo: Art and the Community

Shirley Cheechoo, a Mushkegowuk, is an award-winning filmmaker, director, writer, actor, and visual artist, and is a leader in the arts community. "What I do is my life, it's my breath, it's my way I communicate, it's how I express love, anger, it's my social responsibility, and it's the blood flowing through my veins and I suppose if I wasn't doing this I would evaporate," she says. It was through her creative vision that Cheechoo gathered like-minded artists and founded De-ba-jeh-mu-jig Theatre Group. ["De-ba-jeh-mu-jig" means "storytellers."] This touring company has become one of the foremost and respected independent Aboriginal theatre companies in the world. It is located on Manitoulin Island.

Realizing she could ease a pain or raise an issue with her film work, Cheechoo enrolled in writing classes, directors' labs, acting workshops, and film schools, and entered film festivals where she worked with some of the best in the industry.

Shirley Cheechoo is now a mentor and leader for many in the Aboriginal arts community. She is co-owner of the Kasheese Studios art gallery,

promoting Aboriginal artists. She is also the president of Spoken Song film production company and founded the Weengushk Film Institute on Manitoulin Island, which trains, develops, and guides independent filmmakers.

FIGURE 1.12 An actor with the De-ba-jeh-mu-jig Theatre Group

THINKING IT THROUGH

1. Read the creation stories on page 13. Choose one and reflect on how it illustrates the world view of the people who tell it. What are the values, beliefs, or cultural traditions in the story you have chosen?

2. Research a First Nations, Métis, or Inuit artist and create a photo essay of his or her work. In your essay, explore the following questions: How does the work reflect the artist as an individual? How does the artwork reflect the Nation or community of the artist? What are some of the messages? Describe any recurring themes. How does the artist use symbolism?

3. How would you express your own world view through art? Choose an art medium such as photography, video, painting, or collage and create an image that explains an aspect of your own culture, values, beliefs, or attitudes.

Common Threads in Aboriginal World Views

Before the arrival of Europeans in North America, the First Nations and Inuit had developed distinct world views, ways of thinking, spirituality, economies, governance, and social structures. The potlatch ceremony of the Pacific Nations, the sacred ceremonies of the Plains Nations, the political structures of the Haudenosaunee and Wabanaki Confederacies of Eastern Canada, and the intimate spiritual ties between Inuit and the animals of the Arctic are unique to the peoples of those regions. As the Métis Nation grew, it too developed a distinct world view.

The creation stories and oral traditions of First Nations, Métis, and Inuit peoples are diverse. Aboriginal peoples have their own ways of relating to the land, and each year they conduct unique ceremonies and celebrations. Of course, there have always been exchanges of ideas and practices among neighbouring Nations, across the country and within urban areas. Yet each Nation's culture remains distinct today.

Still, values such as respect, responsibility to others, sharing, and reverence for the sacred are held by many groups and can be seen as common threads. This is because the world views of First Nations, Métis, and Inuit peoples have some fundamental things in common:

- There is sacredness in all things. Everything has a spiritual side.

- Everything in the world, both living and non-living, is interconnected and forms a single whole. Humans need to live in balance with the Earth and with all of Creation.

- The world is constantly changing in recurring cycles.

As you further explore these common threads in the following pages, keep in mind that the ways in which these beliefs are expressed have sometimes changed in response to a changing world.

All Things Are Sacred

What do First Nations, Métis, and Inuit peoples mean when they say that everything is **sacred**? Their traditional spirituality (which is different from spirituality influenced by Christianity or other world religions) reflects the belief that everything the Creator made—humans, animals, plants, and objects such as rocks and the land—is invested with spirit and is therefore sacred. People are thought to have a personal relationship with all that has been created, because everything contains spirit. There is no separation between the **temporal** and the spiritual.

FIGURE 1.13 In Timmins, Ontario, the Métis Nation of Ontario keeps a community freezer. Moose meat kept in the freezer is made available to the Elders and the rest of the community, exemplifying the value of sharing held by the Métis. What values are central to your culture? How are these values expressed?

FIGURE 1.14 Teddy Boy Houle, Ojibwe Elder from Manitoba, speaks to students in 2007 about the Métis sash. Explain why you think the sash can be a symbol of interconnectedness.

WORDS MATTER

sacred regarded with reverence; entitled to veneration or respect by virtue of a connection to divinity or divine things

temporal related to the physical world of matter, time, and space

What Is Spirituality?

Spirituality is not the same as religion; the practice of spirituality is not always written in a book or practised in a special place of worship. Spirituality is being mindful of the sacred. It considers the meaning of existence and relationships in and with the natural world. Spirituality involves feelings of awe and reverence toward that which is not understood in physical terms, but rather as life force or spirit. The spirit of something is its life force; the Inuit call this anirniq, or "breath."

When we want to understand people's ideas about the sacred or the spiritual, we might ask them what they believe and how their beliefs affect their lives. The beliefs of First Nations, Métis, and Inuit peoples relate to the natural world, and the effects of the powers or processes that they accept as true. Of course, individuals have their own ways to express their spirituality. As you will see later in this chapter, the spiritualities of First Nations, Métis, and Inuit peoples have also been influenced by Christianity and other world religions since the time of first contact.

One way to express respect for the spiritual is through prayer. Prayer often takes the form of giving thanks, as you can see in Christi Belcourt's personal prayer, below.

REFLECTION
Consider what aspects of your life and your world you would include in a message of thanksgiving. Create a short piece of writing or a visual representation that expresses your personal message of thanksgiving.

VOICES OF THE PEOPLES

I thank the Creator, Grandfather Sun, Grandmother Moon, Mother Earth and all the waters for giving us life. I thank the plants, our first family, for giving the earth life and sustaining all the creatures, including us, on this earth. I thank them for the inspiration they give me for my paintings and what they have taught me about life. I thank all the creatures, the animals, the birds, water creatures and insects, for keeping the earth moving and for giving of themselves so we can live. I pray for human beings, that we will be kind and generous towards each other. I thank the spirits of the four directions for giving us gifts. And I thank the Creator for this precious and rare gift of life that we've been given. Miigwetch.

FIGURE 1.15 Métis artist Christi Belcourt created this painting, called *Prayer* (2007), to remind herself and her daughter of what they wanted to remember in their prayers. What connections can you make between the words in Christi Belcourt's prayer and the images in her painting?

Distinctive Aspects of Aboriginal Spirituality

The sacredness that First Nations, Métis, and Inuit peoples see in all things is reflected in their belief that in order to lead healthy and balanced lives, people must attend to all aspects of their being. They must nurture not only the needs of the body but also those of the mind, the heart, and the spirit—the physical, mental, emotional, and spiritual.

Just as people have four parts to their being, so too do the animals on which people depend. This is why Inuit, for example, have elaborate ways of spiritually connecting with the animals they hunt to ask for their cooperation in providing food for the people.

VOICES OF THE PEOPLES

Song for Calling the Caribou
Wild caribou, land louse, long legs,
With the great ears,
And the rough hairs on your neck,
Flee not from me.
Here I bring skins for soles,
Here I bring moss for wicks,
Just come gladly
Hither to me, hither to me.

—*Orpingalik, Netsilik Inuit, 1921*

FIGURE 1.16 Caribou run across a frozen lake in the Northwest Territories

VOICES OF THE PEOPLES

I remember my grandmother sprinkling tobacco on the wood stove as an offering and then going to Mass on Sunday. Obviously she felt the pull of both spiritual influences.

—*Métis Senator Roland St. Germain*

For the Métis, their distinctive spirituality springs from the traditions and beliefs of their ancestors, and therefore reflects both First Nations and European cultures. Often called "having hearts in two worlds," the Métis spirituality is rooted in family experience, which varies a great deal between communities and families. Over time, attitudes and values were influenced by a number of forces, including the Catholic Church, the creation stories of their First Nations ancestors, and the stories of the Bible.

The reverence First Nations, Métis, and Inuit peoples have for the land, as well as love for family and for community, is aligned with the values of many world religions. Today, there is a growing appreciation that spiritual diversity is acceptable, and that it is important to be both mindful and respectful of different faiths.

©P

What Are Sacred Places?

The shape of the land and the characteristics of the animals are not accidental. They are the result of meaningful events long ago in which a powerful sacred figure, such as the Creator, played a leading role. This being was considered to be an ancestor, who also gave the people the practical and spiritual knowledge required for living on the land. This world view is reflected in the identification of certain places as sacred. These places are where Nations have direct contact with spiritual beings and their ancestors. For example, the Serpent Mounds at Hiawatha First Nation near Keene, Ontario, are considered sacred and give the Mississauga First Nations a connection to their ancestors.

Sacred places are also areas in which Aboriginal peoples can gather for celebrations and ceremonies. Cypress Hills Interprovincial Park in southern Alberta and Chapel Island in Nova Scotia are two examples.

FIGURE 1.17 The Serpent Mounds in Ontario consist of nine burial mounds. The largest mound has a zigzag or serpentine appearance. This park is the only one of its kind in Canada.

ABORIGINAL WORLD VIEWS CLOSE-UP

Kinomagewapkong: The Teaching Rocks

Located north of Peterborough in Eastern Ontario are Kinomagewapkong—the Teaching Rocks. Considered a sacred place, the Teaching Rocks are made up of over 900 petroglyphs, symbols and pictures carved in solid rock. The site is one of the largest known collections of Aboriginal carvings in North America. The carvings show turtles, birds, rabbits, trees, fish, people, symbols, and shapes.

The site of the Teaching Rocks is now Petroglyphs Provincial Park, which opened in 1976 and is under the supervision of Curve Lake First Nation, for whom the park is a sacred place.

The carvings are housed in a high glass-walled building to protect them from erosion. An elevated walkway allows visitors to view the carvings from every angle.

Dorothy Taylor, a citizen of Curve Lake First Nation, explains to visitors that the rocks themselves are a living body possessed with spirit. First Nations people pray, meditate, and hold ceremonies at the site year-round.

FIGURE 1.18 How does the maintenance of this site and guidance by the Curve Lake First Nation support and express their world view?

Everything Is Interconnected

The understanding of **interconnectedness** forms an essential dimension of First Nations, Métis, and Inuit world views. Aboriginal peoples continue to be connected to the land and each other. In the past they relied more on their own ingenuity for basic needs such as food and shelter, as well as for emotional and spiritual needs. Today, those living in cities tend to be more sheltered from the seasons and do not rely on the land for food, while those living in rural or isolated communities still depend in part on the land. The survival of all is dependent on the health of the environment. People are connected within a social structure and by the various roles and responsibilities they fulfill in their families and in their community. Past, present, and future connections are also seen across the generations. The belief in interconnectedness across generations is also expressed in the Seven Generations Teaching, which will be further explored in Chapter 2.

How Are People Interconnected?

Today, interconnectedness is expressed in the responsibilities people have for one another, in the respect they show to Elders, Senators, Wisdom Keepers, traditional teachers, and children, and in the ways they manage community resources cooperatively.

No single person knows all there is to know, so within any community, individual men and women specialize in certain knowledges and skills. For example, a grandmother may teach younger women how to harvest, prepare, and use medicinal plants. In many ways, older community members impart knowledge to young people so that all societal roles are fulfilled.

FIGURE 1.19 Powwows are spiritual and social gatherings that take place among First Nations every year. Dances held during powwows may be social or competitive. Here fancy shawl dancer Deanne Morrison from Temagami First Nation dances at the Strawberry Moon Festival in Peterborough, Ontario, in 2009. What events or gatherings does your community have to bring people together?

©P

The words *n'dalgommek* (Abenaki) and *indinawemaaganidog* (Anishinaabe) express the belief that everything is related—that all things in the universe are related. This belief is expressed by many Nations in many ways. Below are some examples.

Language	"We are all related"
Cree	niw_hk_m_kanak
Lakota Sioux	mitayuke oyasin
Anishinaabe	indinawemaaganidog
Mi'kmaq	msit No'kmaq
Abenaki	n'dalgommek
Métis	tous familes
Inuit	illamareit, illageit

FIGURE 1.20 Edward Benton-Banai

WORDS MATTER

Three Fires Midewiwin Lodge a specific set of spiritual beliefs and practices followed by certain peoples, such as the Anishinaabe; while there is no direct English translation for Midewiwin, it is sometimes translated as "the way of the heart"

We are all related or *all my relations* encompasses not only family and community, but embraces all things. "All my relations" extends kinship ties to animals, plants, and all things both visible and invisible. In some Nations, a family connection to the land is expressed by the term *Mother Earth,* which you will read more about in Chapter 2. These ties are expressed in many ways—through language, stories, ceremonies, and social organizations. In some Nations, the Seven Grandfather Teachings are a way of expressing and passing down these values.

Ways of Knowing

The Seven Grandfather Teachings

These spiritual teachings, or gifts, are part of the Anishinaabe tradition and have been adopted by other Nations. By practising these gifts, people bring harmony and balance to their own lives and to their relationships with others and the land. This is how Edward Benton-Banai, an Ojibwe author, teacher, and Grand Chief of the **Three Fires Midewiwin Lodge**, expresses the teachings.

1. Nbwaakaawin — To cherish knowledge is to know **wisdom**.

2. Zaagidiwin — To know **love** is to know peace.

3. Mnaadendiwin — To honour all of creation is to have **respect**.

4. Aakde'win — **Bravery** is to face the foe with integrity.

5. Gwekwaadziwin — **Honesty** in facing a situation is to be brave.

6. Dbadendizwin — **Humility** is to know yourself as a sacred part of creation.

7. Debwewin — **Truth** is to know all these things.

Life was seen as a great circle; each person had a place on that circle and was related to everyone and everything.

—*Joseph Bruchac, Abenaki writer and storyteller*

Everything Is Part of a Never-Ending Circle

When all things are interconnected, they form a single, continuous whole that must be respected. For many First Nations, Métis, and Inuit peoples, the circle is a powerful symbol of this concept and can be seen in the repetition of changes in nature: the migration of birds, the cycle of the seasons, the waxing and waning of the moon. All of these patterns are cyclical, predictably turning and returning. Even life itself takes the form of a cycle. For example, plants grow from the earth and produce seeds. The plants then return to the earth when they die. Finally, new seedlings spring from the soil.

How Do Aboriginal Peoples Experience Life as a Cycle?

Among some First Nations, Métis, and Inuit peoples, the members of a community share responsibilities by assuming new and different roles. A woman, for example, may be a teacher in the elementary school for a

Ways of Knowing

The Medicine Wheel

The medicine wheel is a symbol in the form of a circle or hoop. The word *medicine* indicates the sacred nature of the symbol and its connection to spiritual powers and healing practices. The circular shape of the medicine wheel expresses belief in the endless cycle of life. The medicine wheel can convey many lessons and there is diversity among different Nations. For the Anishinaabe, the medicine wheel represents all of creation, and it shows the circle of life. The wheel is often divided into four sections, which show not only the stages in a cycle, but also the different parts of a person or the natural world:

- spirit, heart, body, mind

- childhood, adolescence, adulthood, old age

- east, south, west, north

- spring, summer, fall, winter

- earth, air, water, fire

- red, yellow, black, white (the sacred colours)

The medicine wheel shows the importance of balance and harmony among all parts of the circle.

When one or more of these parts overshadow the others or are neglected, a person must restore balance in order to regain spiritual, emotional, physical, and mental health. Because the medicine wheel conveys values commonly found in teachings, many Nations and organizations across Canada have adapted the medicine wheel for their own use in teaching and healing.

FIGURE 1.21 Zoey Wood-Salomon, an Odawa-Ojibwe artist from Manitoulin Island, has included many circles in her painting *Meeting with the Chiefs* (1993). What elements in nature could the circles represent?

©P

number of years, and then become a mother, before becoming a healer in her community. A university student may research his community's land rights, then work as a lawyer before taking time to make a film about fishing with his grandfather.

Each person sees their path through life as a cycle of responsibilities to family, community, and the wider world. Living life in this way provides many opportunities for gaining new knowledge and for teaching others. As time goes on, the accumulation of individual contributions to knowledge becomes the foundation of the whole community's culture. Culture is kept alive and is constantly changing because individuals continue their personal journeys in a cycle of renewal and revitalization.

Ceremonies Representing Cycles and Change

The annual cycle of First Nations, Métis, and Inuit ceremonies and communal celebrations nourishes the bonds among individuals and within families. People gather together at home or away to learn sacred and spiritual teachings, to hear and speak their languages, and to revisit and reconnect with the places where they feel at peace.

For some, a way of sharing knowledge and ideas is the **talking circle**, in which participants each have an opportunity to speak in turn. Talking circles show how people value individual contributions and cooperation as they share ideas, feelings, and insights. Talking circles are used for many types of discussions, from sharing spiritual teachings to planning community projects and resolving conflicts. A sentencing circle, a type of talking circle, is sometimes used for lesser crimes within the Canadian justice system. You will read more about sentencing circles in Chapter 8.

WORDS MATTER

talking circle a structured discussion used by many Nations to share and solve problems

VOICES OF THE PEOPLES

This morning we greeted the new light of the day. Our purpose for doing that ceremony was to start fresh with the beginning, the arrival of the sun and the breaking of the dawn. That is the most powerful time of day to say our guiding prayer and request for that day. The sun spirit is the one that comes out to acknowledge us and to watch us. So the song that was used today was one that we refer to as the Sun Spirit Song. In our Ojibwe language what the words are saying is that the sun spirit is coming out to watch us, to look at us. While it is difficult to translate it into English, it means that the sun spirit is taking ownership of his relationship with us and with all things in creation.

—*Paul Nadjiwan, Chippewas of Nawash Unceded First Nation*

FIGURE 1.22 In Timmins, Ontario, National Aboriginal Day 2010 started with this sunrise ceremony at the Hollinger Park.

The Talking Circle

A talking circle is a structured discussion in which everyone has a chance to speak and to be heard. Participants sit in a circle so that everyone can see each other. A symbolic item such as feather, talking stick, or stone is passed around the circle from one person to the next. Participants speak only when it is their turn and must listen respectfully to other speakers without interrupting. What is said in a talking circle is considered confidential: what is said in the circle stays in the circle. The only exceptions are in cases where crimes such as child abuse are disclosed.

The purpose of a talking circle may be to share feelings or thoughts. It may be a healing circle, helping people to deal with a personal or community problem. Often it helps people reach agreement on an important issue or helps to solve a conflict.

The talking circle ensures that everyone's voice can be heard. Many people say that the powerful effect a talking circle has on its participants comes from the knowledge that their words are truly being heard—people often share deep insights or are moved to tears.

FIGURE 1.23 Volunteers for Aboriginal Ganootamaage Justice Services of Winnipeg take part in a healing circle. In what ways does the talking circle address the various aspects of an individual (physical, mental, emotional, and spiritual)?

Rites of Passage

Every culture has ceremonies that mark important events in life, such as birth or marriage. Men and women pass through stages—childhood, adolescence, adulthood, and old age—and these stages are repeated with each generation. The passage from one stage of life to another is celebrated in many cultures. Men and women, boys and girls, each group has its own ways of acknowledging the important stages in life. Generally, female Elders or Wisdom Keepers guide the ceremonies of girls and women, while male Elders or Wisdom Keepers lead those of boys and men. In many First Nations, Métis, and Inuit cultures, the transition from youth to adulthood is an important one and is marked with special ceremonies and practices. These can include a first hunt, such as among Inuit, or a vision quest, among First Nations such as the Algonkian and the Nêhiyaw Cree. Not all young people follow these practices, but those who do may find opportunities to learn more about themselves and their culture.

Fruit of Self-Knowledge: Getting in Touch with My Cultural Roots

By Sophie Bender Johnson as told to Jessica Yee

In February 2007, I did something not a lot of girls my age would do. I started a berry fast. I am Anishinabe, Ojibwa, and berries are a very important food in our culture. The strawberry is the leader of all the berries: it is the ode-imin, which means heart berry. For one year I didn't eat berries of any kind.

There are many reasons why young women choose to go on a berry fast. It was important for me to do this because I wanted to tap into my roots to help me form my own identity. Many young women decide to go on a berry fast when they begin their menstrual cycle. It's interesting because mainstream society has made having your period a bad thing, but in my culture, it's one of the times when women are strongest.

We also believe that women are naturally powerful because they are able to produce life. That doesn't have to be taken literally: when I am motherly to my friends, it is recognized as a strength, even though I am not a mother. But that belief also means that our bodies are sacred: it's our job to make sure that we take care of our bodies and that people around us respect that power.

During the fast, my focus was on learning how to take care of myself. So I chose not to date, wear makeup, or carry babies unless they could walk.

You may think that's ultra-conservative, but my reasons were far from that. Women have so much to do in this world, and it's important for us to take the time to work on just ourselves. I had a lot of help from my mother's cousin, Diana, and my aunt, Joanne: they both gave me advice on how to remain strong and helped me through the difficult points.

Some parts of my fast were harder than others. It wasn't hard for me to not wear makeup since I don't think I need it to be pretty. But there were times when I really wanted to eat some blueberries or I would see a cute baby that I wanted to hold.

Instead of thinking "I can't do that," I tried to see the significance of why I wasn't doing it. There are a lot of women who feel they are ready to have babies at a young age or face unhealthy situations where they make decisions that put themselves last.

I spent a lot of time reflecting on the different pressures we face as teenagers and as young women, and my ability to complete my fast showed me that I have the strength to make a decision and stick to it. My most powerful defence is right inside me; the word *empowerment* makes a lot more sense now.

I came off my berry fast in May and attended a ceremony where I feasted with other women who were also coming off their fasts. When I ate a strawberry, I appreciated it much more. I am so proud to be Anishinabe, and I'm really proud to be a woman.

THINKING IT THROUGH

1. Research Aboriginal artists who depict an aspect of First Nations, Métis, or Inuit world view. Choose an artist whose work you particularly like and give a short presentation to a small group describing the artist and his or her work.

2. How is interconnectedness expressed in Orpingalik's song (page 20)?

3. Research pictographs or petroglyphs of different First Nations in Canada. Present your findings using visual images and text.

REFLECTION

How have you, your family, and your community marked different stages in your life?

©P

Health and Aboriginal World Views

First Nations, Métis, and Inuit peoples have perspectives on health that are often different from beliefs in which health is classified as physical or mental, and illnesses are treated separately. Although there are diverse approaches to health and healing in First Nations, Métis, and Inuit communities, also evident is a common world view that health and healing are to be approached from a holistic perspective. In order for good health to be achieved, an individual must balance their physical, mental, emotional, and spiritual sides. The diagram below shows an Ojibwe-based approach to the Four Sacred Medicines, which are viewed as essential to all aspects of health.

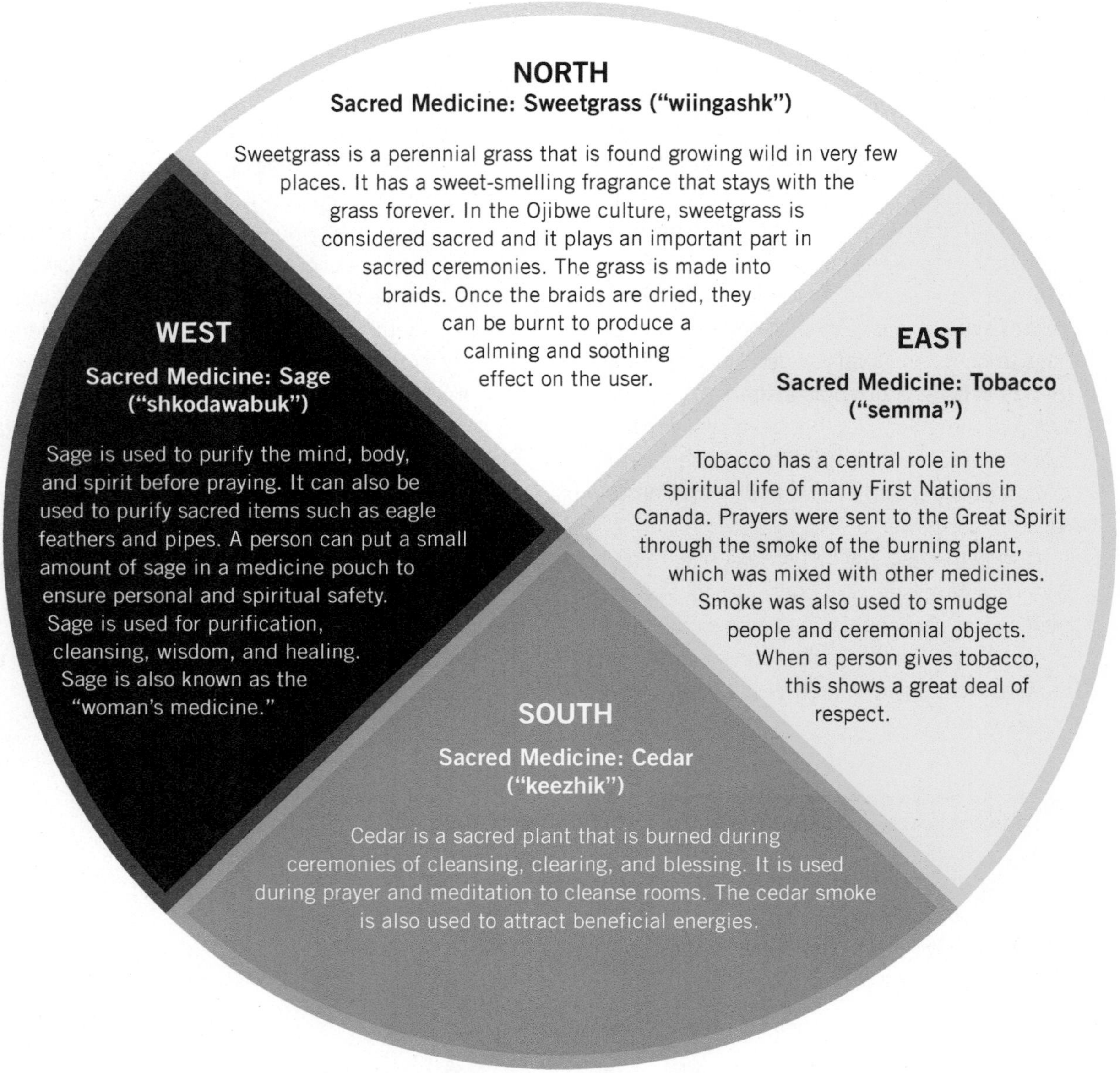

NORTH

Sacred Medicine: Sweetgrass ("wiingashk")

Sweetgrass is a perennial grass that is found growing wild in very few places. It has a sweet-smelling fragrance that stays with the grass forever. In the Ojibwe culture, sweetgrass is considered sacred and it plays an important part in sacred ceremonies. The grass is made into braids. Once the braids are dried, they can be burnt to produce a calming and soothing effect on the user.

WEST

Sacred Medicine: Sage ("shkodawabuk")

Sage is used to purify the mind, body, and spirit before praying. It can also be used to purify sacred items such as eagle feathers and pipes. A person can put a small amount of sage in a medicine pouch to ensure personal and spiritual safety. Sage is used for purification, cleansing, wisdom, and healing. Sage is also known as the "woman's medicine."

EAST

Sacred Medicine: Tobacco ("semma")

Tobacco has a central role in the spiritual life of many First Nations in Canada. Prayers were sent to the Great Spirit through the smoke of the burning plant, which was mixed with other medicines. Smoke was also used to smudge people and ceremonial objects. When a person gives tobacco, this shows a great deal of respect.

SOUTH

Sacred Medicine: Cedar ("keezhik")

Cedar is a sacred plant that is burned during ceremonies of cleansing, clearing, and blessing. It is used during prayer and meditation to cleanse rooms. The cedar smoke is also used to attract beneficial energies.

FIGURE 1.24 Consider what you have learned about the medicine wheel. How does this diagram of the Four Sacred Medicines reflect the meanings behind the medicine wheel?

©P

Approaches to Healing

The terms healer, medicine man, and medicine woman cover a broad range of roles, but generally speaking, they are understood to be those who look after the spiritual and physical health of the community. Some may be given the responsibilities of a healer, while others may have a gift and take on the role. Some may specialize in particular knowledges or conditions while others may be generalists. In some Nations, these roles are gender-specific. Medicine people can treat illness and can enter the spirit world in order to gain knowledge and power to help with the healing process. Among the Inuit, healing may involve a combination of approaches, including dance, song, medicine, ceremony, words, and much more. Healers and medicine people are also considered to be responsible for safeguarding and restoring the health of the community as a whole.

The Sweat Lodge

For the Anishinaabe, the sweat lodge ceremony is part of ceremonial life. On a spiritual level, sweat lodge ceremonies are held with good intent. This means that traditions surrounding the ceremony, as well as the construction of the sweat lodge itself, are done with care and respect. Sweat lodges are also considered gateways for communication between humans and the spirit world. A connection with the spirit world may help guide a person in the right direction in life.

Today, many First Nations and Métis use sweat lodges for spiritual and physical cleansing, and to achieve and maintain good health and well-being. For example, Anishnawbe Health Toronto offers sweat lodge ceremonies as part of their services to the urban Aboriginal community in Toronto. Sweat lodges are usually made with a turtle-shaped frame, which is covered with tarps or blankets. A pit inside the lodge is filled with hot rocks, which are heated in a spirit fire outside. Only wood, along with tobacco, cedar, sage, or sweetgrass, is used in the spirit fire.

Medicinal Plants

Knowledge of medicinal plants allowed Aboriginal peoples to treat illnesses and make antiseptics and painkillers. Many of today's medicines were originally discovered and used by First Nations and Inuit peoples, including aspirin. Nations who lived in areas where willow trees grew used willow bark to treat pain and other ailments. Willow bark contains salicin, one of the principal ingredients in aspirin. First Nations and Inuit peoples were also open to sharing their knowledge with newly arrived European explorers, traders, and settlers. Those who accepted the help offered by First Nations medicine people were much more likely to recover.

It should be noted that the tobacco described in the diagram on page 28 is locally grown for ceremonial use, and is different from the tobacco used to make cigarettes. Commercial tobacco is processed and has chemical additives. Many Aboriginal people are working to educate others about the differences and the hazards of commercial tobacco.

FIGURE 1.25 Mohawk healer and Elder Janice Kahehti:io Longboat feels that healing is a balance of all things: "My suggestion is to turn off the TV and computer. Technology won't do it for us; we have to do it for ourselves." What do you think she means?

VOICES OF THE PEOPLES

Sweetgrass Song
by Michelle Comeau

Along the blue breeze breath
lights a perfume prayer on air,
my slow sung sweetgrass
song.
Smell the air,
mmm-mmm!
mouth-watering medicine
song.
Rise and drift
by currents lifted
on blue-grey wings
in tiny
tender
thought
spirals
Swirling melodic messengers
Whirling like my spirit mini-
sun-kissed
moon bathed and thunder
shaken.
Awaken, my Mind!
Heal, my Heart!
in the gift of a cleansing bath,
my slow sung sweetgrass
song.

©P

Ways of Knowing

Peer Leaders Spread Message of Traditional Way

By Laura Stevens, Wikwemikong
Ontario Birchbark, 2006

This summer, eight peer leaders employed by the Youth Action Alliance of Manitoulin (YAA-MAN) set out on a canoe excursion through the North Channel to raise awareness of tobacco misuse and to encourage First Nation communities to return to traditional tobacco use. The YAA-MAN participants range in age from 14 to 18.

Alanna Trudeau is a youth advisor at the Waasa Naabin Community Youth Services Centre, the organization coordinating the YAA-MAN project. Alanna said the idea behind YAA-MAN isn't to lecture First Nation communities; it's to help them realize the dangers of smoking and chewing tobacco.

Although this was a part-time job for the eight peer leaders, Alanna said they all worked really hard in the fight against tobacco misuse and the promotion of traditional use. The YAA-MAN leaders tried to get the concept of the sacredness of tobacco across to their audiences.

They spoke about the basics of tobacco such as how to use it, what it looks like and that you hold it in your left hand because it's closest to your heart.

"They talked about how the Creator gave us tobacco and we need to understand that tobacco is our link to the Creator. That's our way to make an offering and to be thankful for this wonderful life that we have," she said.

If the funding continues for this program, 16-year-old Vince Migwans said he would probably apply to be involved again because of what he was able to promote.

"We talked about the harmful effects of smoking and chewing tobacco, like what it can do and the stuff that's in it," said Vince, a Grade 11 Manitoulin Secondary School (MSS) student. "The kids think it's normal to smoke and they see their parents doing it and their friends do it so they think they might as well do it too, so we were there to talk about what it should be really used for."

QUESTIONS

1. Explain the differences between tobacco used by Aboriginal peoples for ceremony and commercial tobacco used for smoking.

2. How do you think this campaign will influence attitudes toward tobacco use?

THINKING IT THROUGH

1. Research the use of traditional medicines in the region in which you live. Ask an Elder, talk to a healer, or read about the plants used in teas, lotions, or other forms of traditional medicine used by Aboriginal peoples. Describe to a small group how one such plant is harvested, prepared, and used.

2. Explain how methods of healing and beliefs about health are practised today. Your research can include speaking to an Elder or a healer, or visiting an Aboriginal health centre. Give one example of a method that is still used for healing.

©P

Challenges to Aboriginal World Views

First Nations and Inuit peoples have been living in what is now called North America since time immemorial. Contact with Europeans came to First Nations and Inuit peoples across Canada at different times and in different ways. Early relationships were often reciprocal; trade was welcomed, languages were learned, and new technology was explored by both sides. The timeline on this page shows only a few of the recorded encounters that took place.

Trade and settlement by Europeans, and the introduction of unfamiliar technology, religious beliefs, customs, and attitudes, would have profound effects on the world views of First Nations, Métis, and Inuit peoples in North America. Some of these effects are still evident today.

The Impact of Contact

The North American fur trade lasted from the early 1600s to the mid-1800s. Trade relations between the First Nations and the European traders were at first balanced and reciprocal. The Wendat, for example, insisted that their own language be used for trade. As the fur trade became more lucrative, more Europeans began to arrive and settlement increased. Permanent settlement meant a need for land and resources, and the balance of power began to shift. Although every First Nations, Métis, or Inuit community experienced the influences of contact and settlement differently, the effects were often similar.

REFLECTION

How might interactions between cultures shape or alter world views?

Contacts Between Europeans and Aboriginal Peoples in North America	
10th century	possible Viking settlement in what is now Newfoundland
1497	John Cabot explores northeastern coast. Cod resources attract fishers from Spain, England, France, and Portugal; contact with Beothuk, Inuit, and Innu
1534	first contact by Jacques Cartier with the Mi'kmaq and Haudenosaunee
1576	Martin Frobisher conducts first search in the Arctic for the Northwest Passage
1604–07	Samuel de Champlain in Acadia; contact with Mi'kmaq and Malecite
1608	Champlain establishes Québec settlement; contact with Montagnais, Innu, Wendat, and Algonquin. Fur trade and settlement begin
1609	Henry Hudson of the Dutch India Company arrives in Hudson River (Manhattan) followed by more Dutch and German settlers
1626	arrival of the first Jesuits, including Father Brébeuf, at the shores of Lake Huron
1742	La Vérendrye extends his explorations as far as Manitoba
1778	Captain Cook arrives in Nootka Sound in what is now British Columbia; contact with Nuu-chah-nulth
1819	Franklin's first voyage into the Arctic
1885	completion of Canadian Pacific Railroad across Canada; settlement in the West increases
early 1900s	increased presence of missionaries, traders, whalers, and RCMP in the North
1953	Canadian federal government becomes more active in the North

FIGURE 1.26 This timeline gives a brief overview of contacts between Europeans and Aboriginal peoples in North America.

The Wendat

After the establishment of a settlement on the St. Lawrence River, Samuel de Champlain created trading partnerships with local First Nations, in particular the Wendat Confederacy. At that time, the Wendat had communities in Central Ontario, between Lake Huron and Lake Simcoe. They also managed a trade network reaching north to Sault Ste. Marie and south to the Mississippi River.

Missionaries began to live in Wendat villages as early as 1615. The Récollet and Jesuit missionaries attempted to enforce European and Christian beliefs and customs, which had a profound social, cultural, economic, and political impact on the Wendat. Some took on Christian beliefs and practices, some combined Christian and traditional ways, and others refused conversion. The long-term experiences of the Wendat people were unfortunately very common for Aboriginal peoples.

The population of the Wendat had numbered between 30 000 and 45 000 people before contact with the French. Within a few decades, there were fewer than 10 000 left, mostly due to exposure to European diseases. Many Elders died, leaving villages without their teachers, leaders, and healers. Communities became divided, and tensions rose between those who chose to convert and those who did not. The remaining Wendat dispersed.

COMMUNITY CLOSE-UP

Wendake

Many Wendat settled near Québec City. Their community is now known as Wendake. Tourism is an important part of the local economy, and Wendake village offers many activities, including snowshoeing. There is a reconstructed historical village site, complete with presentations of arts and crafts by local artists and artisans. The community hosts a powwow every year.

Recently, Wendake inaugurated a new cultural complex that includes a museum, a hotel, and a restaurant offering a menu based on traditional foods. As the community continues to flourish, future plans include building an outdoor amphitheatre for ceremonies, concerts, and more. The amphitheatre will be situated near the Saint-Charles River and Kabir Kouba Falls.

The survival of the Wendat Nation today is a testimony to their strength and resilience as a people.

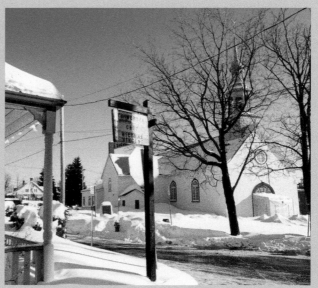

FIGURE 1.27 In 2010, members of Wendake, a Wendat reserve near Québec City, number about 3000. The Ontario-Michigan Wyandot Nation has about 800 Wendat members. A few thousand Wyandotte also live in Oklahoma and Kansas.

The Exchange of Technology and Ideas

As a trading economy developed between Aboriginal peoples and Europeans, there was a substantial exchange of technology and knowledge, which affected the world views of both sides. Some Europeans considered their world views and technologies to be superior to those of Aboriginal peoples. However, it was quickly evident that early traders and settlers who adopted Aboriginal technologies and food were more likely to survive.

In some cases, these experiences led Europeans to value the knowledge of Aboriginal peoples, who shared information about clothing, transportation, and food. Haudenosaunee peoples taught English settlers how to companion-plant corn, squash, and beans. Some European traders married First Nations women, improving the men's quality of life, gaining connections and skilled partners who acted as interpreters, fur processors, and clothing-makers.

As more settlers arrived, they brought ideas and philosophies from Europe, including notions of racial and gender hierarchies. Cooperation between First Nations and Europeans became increasingly difficult. Colonial governments established laws meant to **assimilate** and eventually eradicate First Nations, Inuit, and Métis beliefs, values, languages, and ceremonies. These laws included the creation of residential schools and day schools, which forcibly turned Aboriginal children away from the cultures of their families. These actions had a profound effect on the world views of Aboriginal peoples.

Reclaiming and Adapting Traditions

As Canada grows increasingly diverse, what is considered to be "mainstream" or the "norm" with respect to world view continues to evolve. Many First Nations, Inuit, and Métis people have adapted their own practices and beliefs in ways that reflect or incorporate some aspects of mainstream world views. The efforts of Christian missionaries to convert Aboriginal peoples have had lasting effects. Some Aboriginal peoples follow the Christian faith, while others combine European religious beliefs with their own traditional spiritual beliefs. Some completely reject European faiths, while others follow Baha'i, the Native American Church, or other belief systems.

FIGURE 1.28 Christian Pilon, a Métis, recreated a fur-trading expedition. In 2005 he paddled from Montréal to Thunder Bay, and continued for a full 100 days to finish in Winnipeg. Why do you think Pilon would do this?

WORDS MATTER

assimilate to absorb one group of people into another by causing them to adopt the customs, beliefs, culture, and attitudes of the majority group

CRITICAL THINKING

In what other ways have First Nations, Métis, and Inuit peoples adapted in order to maintain their traditions?

FIGURE 1.29 Métis rap artist Samian performs in Michif and French. He speaks about his life in his poetry and music.

©P

Contemporary Beliefs and Values: the Métis

In the past, First Nations mothers and grandmothers taught their Métis children the beliefs and ceremonies of their people, while many fathers brought the influences of Christianity to their children. Today, spirituality continues to be at the heart of the cultural events and activities of the Métis; rendezvous and meetings often begin with a Métis prayer.

While the influences of different religions, urbanization, and new technology may seem to eclipse spirituality, Métis always return to what it is that they were meant to do. There are many Métis who draw upon their traditions for strength, staying connected to their great grandmothers, who were physically, emotionally, mentally, and spiritually strong. There are also Métis who are devoted parishioners in the various religions of Canada. As Senator Roland St. Germain notes, "I offer tobacco and prayers to the Creator. I participate in ceremonies whenever I can and end my Métis prayers with Amen, Merci and Megwetch, to honour all of my ancestors from both traditions."

THINKING IT THROUGH

1. Explain how modern technology can affect cultural traditions and beliefs. Use an example from your own life if applicable. Do you believe this influence to be beneficial or damaging? Explain.

Conclusion

In this chapter, you have learned about world views and how your world view can influence how you interpret and interact with the world. You have also come to know more about the world views of Aboriginal peoples, and how these world views are expressed.

Throughout this textbook, you will continue to see examples of the diverse ways in which First Nations, Métis, and Inuit peoples live and reflect their world views. You will see the vibrancy of traditions as they continue and are revitalized in new ways. Keep in mind that it is impossible to completely cover the diverse beliefs, values, and ways of knowing of all Aboriginal peoples in Canada. Even within Nations, there are those who may or may not follow the world views presented here. We hope that you will discover the many voices of people who live their world views in different ways, and find respect and understanding for the beliefs and values of Aboriginal peoples.

CRITICAL THINKING

How are the beliefs and values of First Nations, Métis, and Inuit reflected in their world views?

End-of-Chapter Activities

1. Examine this painting by Oji-Cree artist Moses Beaver (Amik) and discuss the concepts of First Nations world views that you see reflected in it. Consider and describe the subject matter, the colours, and how the different beings within the work relate to each other.

FIGURE 1.30 *Knowledge Quest* (2004) by Moses Beaver (Amik)

2. Consider the teachings on page 18 about how all things are sacred and are connected. Using an art form you like, create a piece that communicates the value of these teachings. This can include poetry, visual art, or a performance piece. Make sure the work reflects your own viewpoint on the teachings.

3. Contact a traditional teacher, an Elder, or a grandparent and interview him or her about how one can be healthy in our modern world. Prepare for the interview by writing a list of questions. Remember to include the physical, emotional, intellectual, and spiritual aspects of health. Keep in mind that the person you speak to may decide to tell you things that he or she feels you should learn.

4. Look at the Seven Grandfather Teachings on page 23. Choose one of the teachings and reflect on what it means to you. Think about your own life and relate the teaching to a personal experience. Then write a short story or essay explaining how you value this Grandfather Teaching.

5. Research First Nations, Métis, or Inuit musicians, artists, or storytellers who use their own culture in their art, but who also use contemporary media or styles. Present a song, artwork, story, or video clip from your research and explain how the artist fuses their culture with their chosen form or style.

6. Do some research on an Aboriginal language by interviewing someone who speaks that language, by looking online, or by reading books. Find words that illustrate how that language shows ties to the land, traditional knowledge, world views, or spiritual beliefs.

7. Read the information about the medicine wheel (page 24) and the Four Sacred Medicines (page 28). Using the medicine wheel to organize your material, find other examples of healing plants and show how they are used. Remember to address the balancing aspects of the medicine wheel. You could speak to an Elder or a healer to help with your research.

CHAPTER 2

Relationships with the Land

These are our times and our responsibilities.
Every human being has a sacred duty to protect
the welfare of our Mother Earth... We must begin
with ourselves... We must live in harmony with
the Natural World... We cannot trade the welfare
of our future generations for profit now...
See your sons and daughters...and see your sons'
and daughters' children and their children's
children even unto the Seventh Generation.

—Leon Shenandoah, a former Onondaga Nation Tadadaho (Chief)

In this chapter, you will learn how living in close relationship with one's natural environment for millennia influences and shapes the world views of First Peoples. You will also explore examples of First Nations, Métis, and Inuit peoples living closely connected with the land, of the beliefs that the land is sacred and that everything is connected, and of how the land has changed and continues to change. In finding out more about Aboriginal peoples, you will also build skills in evaluating sources.

FIGURE 2.1 This environment near Hazelton, British Columbia, is home to the Gitxsan people.

INQUIRING MINDS

Use these questions to explore the big ideas in this chapter.

1. What significant relationships do First Nations, Métis, and Inuit peoples have with the land?

2. How have Aboriginal peoples taken on roles to respect, protect, and care for the land?

3. For First Nations, Métis, and Inuit peoples, how are their links to the land and to a sustainable environment part of their cultural identity?

©P

FIGURE 2.2 Santee Oglala Sioux artist Maxine Noel was born in the Birdtail First Nation in southwestern Manitoba. What relationship between people and the environment does her painting *The Sea's Protection* (2008) suggest?

The Land Is Sacred

When we hunger, Mother Earth nourishes us… When we need to clothe our bodies from the sun, wind, rain, snow, and insects, Mother Earth provides the means to cover our bodies… When we are sick and need care, Mother Earth's meadows, forests, and shorelines are lush with berries, plants, roots, seed, and resins that bear the elixir of life and health… When our spirits flag and are burdened with cares, worries, losses, and sorrows, Mother Earth comforts us.

—*Basil H. Johnston, Anishinaabe linguist and educator*

To First Nations, Métis, and Inuit peoples, the word *land* refers not only to the ground or earth, but also to the entire environment, including plants, animals, bodies of water, and air. First Nations, Métis, and Inuit peoples have developed different ways of expressing the relationships they have with the land, but there are two common themes, which you explored in Chapter 1:

1. There is sacredness in all things. Thus, the land is sacred and is to be cared for and respected because it maintains all life on this planet.

2. Everything is interconnected. Thus, humans, animals, plants, the land, and the water are all connected. The land is the Earth's life-support system, not just for humans, but for all life. (Starting on page 39, you will consider connections to the land in greater depth.)

Life-Sustaining Force

Among First Nations, Métis, and Inuit peoples, the concept that the Earth is a sacred and life-sustaining force is a deeply held belief. Referring to the planet as "Mother Earth" is one way in which some First Nations peoples express their relationship to the land. In the same way that a mother gives life, and nurtures and sustains that life, the Earth nourishes both physical and spiritual life. The land is seen as a living being, fulfilling the same role as a mother.

Even in the technologically developed world that we live in today, every human being still depends on the Earth to meet their needs and live a good life. For people living in cities or towns, the connection to the Earth may seem less obvious; going to a supermarket for food, the hardware store to build homes, and a shopping mall for clothes does not directly show a reliance on the Earth. However, among peoples who have always lived off the land, this connection is seen and lived daily. Even for First Nations, Métis, and Inuit people living in towns and cities, there is still a profound respect for these teachings, which are expressed in countless ways depending on each person's specific cultural heritage.

CRITICAL THINKING

Think about your daily life. In what specific ways do you depend on the Earth to meet your needs and live a good life?

FIGURE 2.3 This photograph shows the Moose River. Métis writer Joseph Boyden says, "This stretch of water between James Bay and the Onakawana is where I bring my son when we need to reconnect again. When the trouble of his teenage years threatens to unground him, and me. There's magic in this stretch of river, magic on the shores. …These rivers, and the lowlands around it, are part of Mushkegowuk, the Moose Cree homeland." What do you think Joseph Boyden means by *unground*? What are some ways to *ground* yourself?

©P

Sacred Connections

The sacredness of the Earth and connections to it can be expressed in many ways—such as through dance, language, drumming, and ceremonies.

Women's Traditional Dance

The women's traditional dance is one of the dance categories at a powwow. The dance calls for great stamina, concentration, and grace as the dancer slowly bends her knees to the beat of the drum and slightly turns her feet. The dancer must always have one foot on the ground in order to stay connected to Mother Earth. During the dance, the dancers will raise their feathers or fans as tribute to the drum and to Mother Earth when "honour beats" are played (page 40) or "honour words" are sung.

Naming the Land

With over 50 Aboriginal languages in Canada, First Nations, Métis, and Inuit peoples express the concept of the *land* or *nature* in many ways.

In major First Nations and Inuit languages in Canada, the expression *Mother Earth* is not found. For example, in the language of the Mushkegowuk Cree of James Bay, animate nouns (for example, *mother*) and inanimate nouns (for example, *earth*) cannot be combined. When expressing themselves in English, some Aboriginal communities and individuals choose the term *Mother Earth* and others do not. Some consider *Mother Earth* to be unduly influenced by European colonizers. However, some use *Mother Earth* because it seems better than *nature* or *planet Earth* or *land* at expressing in English a sense of kinship, reverence, and the spiritual aspects that sustain life, relationships, and responsibilities.

Nation	Word for "land"
Cree and Innu	aski
Dene	digeh
Anishinaabe	aki
Cayuga	o-heh-dí-yo
Mi'kmaq	maqamigew
Inuit	nuna
Tlingit	tl'atk
Métis	note terre

FIGURE 2.4 This photograph was taken at Curve Lake First Nation in 2008. Anishinaabe teacher Pauline Decontie describes the women's traditional dance: "It is a very sedate dance, where their feet touch the Earth very gently. The reason [for this] is that the women are the mothers of the Nation, just as the Earth is the mother to us all. Our relationship to the Earth is very special in that way. We both give life. So the dance is very gentle, stepping very lightly on the Earth to be respectful of that attachment we have with Mother Earth."

Spirit of the Drum

I was always told that when you hit the drum, you open the path of communication between us and the spirit world. [The beat] signifies the heart beat of the people and of the Nation and our people, our people's connection to the spirit world and animals and creation, our original family.

The original style of drumming was giving thanks to the spirits. During the song, you'll hear the down-beats, as we call them. The honour beats are the harder beats.

We were always told from our Elders and our teachers that you treat that drum like you would treat a person. You have to acknowledge that sacred object as not just an instrument. It's a part of you and it takes care of you so you need to take care of it.

—Eddy Robinson, Ojibwe/Cree, drummer and singer with Morning Star River

FIGURE 2.5 Eddy Robinson has been drumming and singing for over 20 years.

The Gift of the Creator

Creation stories tell how the world began, how the people came to be who they are, their relationship to and responsibilities on this Earth, and much more. Among First Nations and Inuit peoples, creation stories often explain how particular landmarks and features came into being. One Dene story, for example, tells how the southern shore of Lake Athabasca got its striking white sand dunes: a giant hunted a beaver and threw it on the south side of the lake, assuming it was dead. However, the beaver was not dead, and it thrashed around in pain with such force that it ground the surrounding soil into white sand with its strong tail.

Stories such as these confirm the ties between the original inhabitants and the land that is their home; the land was a gift from the Creator to that particular Nation, and it is considered to be an essential aspect of the Nation's identity as well as the birthplace, birthright, and burying place for its members. Many stories also underline the importance of never taking the land and its resources for granted.

Connected and Sacred

Many practices and examples of traditional knowledge express
the concepts that the land is sacred and all things are connected.
In Haudenosaunee culture, berries are food, they grow in the cycle
of the seasons, and they are sacred:

> *The strawberry is the leader of the berries because it is the first
> one to ripen. All of the other berries follow in their time. The
> strawberry is food, but it is also a medicine. The strawberry is
> also known as the Big Medicine. Eating strawberries or drinking
> strawberry water is very healthy. The strawberry, all of the
> berries and all of the medicine plants are part of the web of
> life and so are important in making sure that life as we know
> it can continue. The strawberry, all of the berries and all of
> the medicine plants are greeted and thanked each day by the
> Haudenosaunee... In the Thanksgiving Address it is specially
> thanked as a hanging fruit, growing among the grasses, just
> above the earth. It represents beginnings—the beginning
> of warm weather and a productive agricultural season.
> Strawberries are said to grow along the road to the Sky World
> which is reached by the Milky Way.*
>
> —*Iroquois Indian Museum*

FIGURE 2.6 This basket honours
the strawberry. Because berries are
fruit that hang, they are neither on
the ground nor in the sky, so they
represent the space between the
Earth and the sky, the entry way
between the Earth and the Sky World.

FIGURE 2.7 The sunrise ceremony involves people gathering before sunrise to greet the sun
and give thanks for the new day. This ceremony varies among the Nations and communities
that practise it. In the above photograph, Lawrence Houle performs a sunrise ceremony at
Fort Wyte in Winnipeg to start Earth Day 2000. In Toronto, the urban First Nation and Métis
community have gathered for a sunrise ceremony to give thanks for the special day honouring
Louis Riel. The city of Toronto holds a sunrise ceremony every year to welcome the summer
solstice on National Aboriginal Day.

VOICES OF THE PEOPLES

Métis continue to follow the
teachings about land from
both sides of their ancestors.
First Nations influences taught
Métis to honour all relations
and the European influences
taught the Métis the value of
holding title to the land. Métis
who took up the voyageur life,
quickly learned ecological
knowledge that was necessary
to traverse and live a good life
on the land.

—*Chris Paci, the Métis
Nation of Ontario*

Giving Thanks

WORDS MATTER

protocol established rules for respectful behaviour

Many practices that express the beliefs that the land is sacred and that everything is connected involve expressions of thanks. Cultures all over the world have ways of expressing gratitude for what they have, and First Nations, Métis, and Inuit peoples are no exception. Expressing thanks is considered a personal and collective responsibility, and **protocols** have been put in place so that ways of expressing thanks are practised and passed forward:

- Each spring, ceremonies are held to celebrate and thank the Creator for the opportunity to rejuvenate after winter and for new life.

- In the Cree tradition, hunters may offer tobacco in thanks to the Creator and to the hunted animal's spirit; share the meat with family, neighbours, or other community members; and place some meat in the fire where the smoke will take it up to feed the spirits.

- Some cultures, such as the Anishinaabe, put out a spirit plate at feasts and other ceremonial occasions.

- One reason that Haudenosaunee people play lacrosse is to please and thank the Creator; just as parents enjoy watching their children play a sport or game, so does the Creator.

Tabaldak: An Abenaki Story

A very long time ago, Tabaldak (the Creator) was walking on the Earth He had built. This was a nice place to live. However, the Earth felt empty and He wanted to hear laughter and song. Instead of using clay, as He had done until now, He took stones that He shaped into human beings and brought to life with his breath. Soon, these creatures began to move about but Tabaldak noticed with sadness that they were careless. They moved in an awkward and slow fashion, squashing the plants with their heavy feet. Their spirits were rigid and their hearts cold and hard because such was their nature. In order to reduce their damage, Tabaldak decided to crush them. Because they were filled with the breath of the Creator, however, they took the form of small beings called "Manogemassek" or little men. Tabaldak commanded them to protect Nature against those who would do her wrong.

So Tabaldak looked around Him for the best way to make humans. He saw some magnificent ash trees, straight and tall. He carved the shapes of men and women in the trunks of these trees. Then, He shot arrows into each of the trunks, so giving them life. These humans were able to dance gracefully in the wind as the great ash trees did. They were beautiful and proud. Their hearts, like the trees, were warm, big and full of life. These were the first Abenaki.

The Manogemassek did not trust the Abenaki. The Abenaki would pick fruit from the tree and gather the plants they said had the power to heal. They would also kill the animals of the forest. In order to ensure that peace reigned over the forest, the Abenaki offered tobacco to the small beings with the guarantee that the Abenaki would take no more than what they needed to live. The small beings were very fond of tobacco and that's how it came to be that before entering the forest, an offering of tobacco is always placed on the ground in order to remind and assure the small beings of the pact made with them. ◆

—Traditional Abenaki story from the archives of the McCord Museum of Canadian History

©P

Sacred Tobacco

Some expressions of gratitude involve gifts of traditional tobacco. Along with sweetgrass, sage, and cedar, tobacco is a sacred medicine and it is used by such Nations as the Anishinaabe, the Potawatomi, the Mi'kmaq, and the Haudenosaunee to express gratitude and honour, to pay respect, and to heal. Some people use tobacco on a daily basis, laying it on the Earth in thanks to the Earth for providing them with everything they need. Tobacco can also be offered before ceremonies, before a hunt or picking berries, or as an offering before seeking advice. In many Nations, someone asking something of an Elder or Wisdom Keeper (for example, to participate in an event or ceremony) will offer sacred tobacco.

FIGURE 2.8 Gifts of tobacco, making offerings, and playing lacrosse to please and thank the Creator are all ways to give thanks. In this photograph from May 2009, college teams Herkimer Generals and Alfred State play lacrosse.

The Giveaway

Another sacred way of expressing thanks is to give something away ceremonially. In the Anishinaabe tradition, the ceremonies are called giveaway ceremonies. These ceremonies might be held after a young hunter's first successful hunt. If a giveaway is held in honour of someone who has died, the belongings of the deceased will be given away so that those receiving the items will remember that person. Giveaway feasts are often held after another celebration. For example, at a wedding, the couple getting married will give presents to their guests, laying the groundwork for sharing in their future. There are many other ceremonies of which giveaway feasts are a part. Giveaway feasts may end with honour songs or circle hugs.

At the core of the giveaway feast lies gratefulness to the Creator for bestowing blessings upon the people. The gifts thank others for their support, acknowledge each guest as a witness to the event, allow others to see how they are respected and cared for, and show that a fulfilling spiritual life is more important than material belongings.

The Thanksgiving Address

One of the most revered addresses among the Haudenosaunee is the Ganohonyohk. The Ganohonyohk (Opening Address) varies in length and from speaker to speaker. Here is one section of an address recounted by George Beaver:

> *We are happy and thankful to see this large gathering and to see each other in good health. We have travelled over dangerous roads and have arrived safely, so let that be in our minds.*
>
> *Now let us be thankful to our Mother, the Earth. We come from the Earth. The food we eat comes from the Earth. When we die, our bodies will return to the Earth, so let that be in our minds.*
>
> *Now we will be thankful and remember the many kinds of plants that cover the Earth. Beautiful flowers make us happy, grasses feed the animals and medicine plants keep us healthy and well, so let that be in our minds…*

CRITICAL THINKING

Karihwakeron Tim Thompson of Wahta Mohawk Territory describes Ohenton Karihwatehkwen (literally "that which comes before all other matters") as a "means of acknowledging all of creation, from the earth to the sky, both the seen and the unseen." After reading the section at left, discuss in a group what else you think a full Thanksgiving Address would acknowledge.

©P

A Caribou Hunting Story

One of the most important spirits among the Innu is the Master Caribou, or Kanipinikassikueu. He was a man who, after marrying a female caribou, was himself transformed into a caribou, giving this precious resource to the Innu. This story describes the established ways of respecting the caribou after killing it.

Pashin burst into Shanut's tent where she was busy scraping the flesh from a beaver pelt. "My cousin," he exclaimed, a great smile of pride on his face, "I killed my first caribou today, at the ushakatik." (Ushakatik refers to a place where there is always caribou.)

Shinipesht, Pien, and Mishen arrived at the camp on Pashin's heels. Each of them carried a heavy load of caribou meat in his backpack. "Lots of meat to carry us through the fall," said Pien, "and we've left eight caribou on teshipitakan." (Teshipitakan are platforms built a couple of metres off the ground. They are still important to the Innu—every camp has at least one—because they keep food away from the dogs and other scavengers.)

For most of the next week, all the women and girls at the camp were busy drying caribou meat, and pounding it into niuekanat (powdered dried caribou meat) with a mitunishan (pestle). The flesh and fur had to be scraped off of the caribou hides with a mitshikun (scraper) and pishkuatshikan (another tool). Shanut knelt beside her grandmother as she worked the fur off of one of the hides. "Granddaughter, I learned how to do this from my own grandmother, and it is she who gave me this pishkuatshikan. I can't remember how many caribou hides I've cleaned with this tool," she said. "One day, it will be my gift to you."

All of the caribou leg bones had been set aside on the large teshipitakan in the centre of the camp, to keep them away from the dogs. The caribou master, Kanipinikassikueu, must be shown respect. The idea of respect is extremely important in traditional Innu culture. The animal masters in particular had to be shown great respect at all times through the proper treatment of the caribou bones, meat, and fat.

Early one morning, Mishen gathered all the bones together carefully on a large canvas sheet on the floor of his tent. Here, he spent the entire morning crushing the leg bones with a mitunishan. The tender white marrow and the small pieces of crushed bone all went into a large pot of boiling water on the stove.

At one point, all the young people gathered in the tent. "I am being careful not to waste any of the marrow," Mishen told them. "However, if any piece of marrow, bone, or meat falls on the ground, I put it in the stove immediately out of respect for Kanipinikassikueu."

Later in the day, Mishen took the boiling broth off the stove. He added a cup of snow to the broth to cool it and to get the atiku-pimi (fat) from the bone marrow to solidify at the top. Using a mishtiku emikuan (ladle), he scooped the fat from the surface and pressed it into wax-like cakes. "Tonight we will have makushan. (Makushan is the traditional Innu feast involving atiku-pimi.) "We will eat the atiku-pimi and caribou meat that Kanipinikassikueu has given us. I will drum, and everyone who can will dance."

And that is what happened. A great feast was held, and everyone rejoiced. ◆

—Traditional Innu story from the archives of the McCord Museum of Canadian History

Maintaining and Revitalizing Connections

First Nations, Métis, and Inuit peoples live all across Canada, in rural areas, towns, and cities. Ties to the land remain strong, and ceremonies are often adapted to maintain this bond and recognize the land as sacred. The sunrise ceremony (page 41) is an example. Many contemporary First Nations, Métis, and Inuit peoples who practise the ceremonial ways of their ancestors also conduct their own daily personal ceremonies.

Sometimes Aboriginal individuals and organizations also have the chance to declare their connections to the land and their concerns at special events and in ways that raise awareness. First Nations in Canada and the United States have been participating in a Peace and Unity Tour since 1986. A different Nation takes responsibility for running the tour in a four-year cycle. At a summit of the Six Nations in 2004, it was decided that youth would lead the tour. As a result, the Spirit of Youth group led the tour and delivered a Youth Declaration to the United Nations in New York City.

FIGURE 2.9 On the Peace and Unity Tour during 2007, these runners carried sacred staffs as the tour travelled through traditional territories from Ontario to Virginia. Melissa Elliott (Ojistari:yo) is a co-founder of Young Onkwehonwe United (YOU), a rising youth group at Six Nations. At age 17, she was a member of the Spirit of Youth group and took part in the trip to the UN. She says that the environment was an important point in their declaration: "Our connection to it, and how we don't want any more destruction of it. We're its protectors[;] we should be protecting it and keeping that connection open."

THINKING IT THROUGH

1. In what ways do the stories on pages 42 and 44 illustrate gratitude and show the Earth as sacred?

2. Research one sacred site and explain why it is considered sacred.

3. Choose one practice, ceremony, or spiritual belief that connects a First Nation, Métis, or Inuit people to the land and summarize it in writing.

WORDS MATTER

Aboriginal Affairs and Northern Development Canada In June 2011, the name of the federal department of Indian Affairs and Northern Development was officially changed to Aboriginal Affairs and Northern Development Canada.

Living on the Land

Reduced Land Base

First Peoples once spanned all of what is now Canada. Now, however, the land base for Aboriginal peoples is greatly reduced. One report from Indian and Northern Affairs Canada (now named **Aboriginal Affairs and Northern Development Canada**) notes that 2267 First Nation reserves total 2.6 million hectares or 0.2 percent of the total land area in Canada. What does 2.6 million hectares look like? It is a little larger than Lake Erie.

Growing Populations

Well over one million First Nations, Métis, and Inuit people live in Canada. Many First Nations, Métis, and Inuit organizations believe that the numbers below (from Statistics Canada) underestimate the reality for a variety of reasons. However, Aboriginal populations in Canada are growing, and increasing numbers (more than half) are living in urban areas.

This shift to urban areas and other changes in ways of living (for example, when a hydroelectric dam disrupts rivers and food supplies) present challenges to maintaining connections to the land.

Population Reporting Aboriginal Identity in Canada, Provinces and Territories, 2006

Area	Total Population	Self-Identified as Aboriginal People	
		Population	As Percentage of Total Population
Canada	31 612 897	1 172 790	3.8
Newfoundland and Labrador	505 469	23 450	4.6
Prince Edward Island	135 851	1730	1.3
Nova Scotia	913 462	24 175	2.7
New Brunswick	729 997	17 655	2.4
Québec	7 546 131	108 430	1.4
Ontario	12 160 282	242 490	2.0
Manitoba	1 148 401	175 395	15.3
Saskatchewan	968 157	142 045	14.7
Alberta	3 290 350	188 215	5.7
British Columbia	4 113 487	196 075	4.8
Yukon Territory	30 372	7580	25.0
Northwest Territories	41 464	20 665	49.8
Nunavut	29 474	24 890	84.4

FIGURE 2.10 Which area reports the highest population identifying as Aboriginal people? What area reports the highest proportion identifying as Aboriginal people? Do these numbers surprise you? Why or why not?

Interconnectedness and the Land

The concept that everything is connected is expressed in many ways, such as through language, stories, and visual art.

In the North, the term meaning the Inuit region in Canada was recently changed to Inuit Nunangat. Previously, the region's name was the Greenlandic term for land only; the new name, Inuit Nunangat, includes the land, sea, and ice. The Inuit Tapiriit Kanatami explains:

> [Because we] consider the land, water, and ice of our homeland to be integral to our culture and our way of life it was felt that "Inuit Nunangat" is a more inclusive and appropriate term to use when describing our lands.

Another example of interconnectedness is found in many First Nations (especially Nations in Eastern Canada and the United States) where the turtle plays a central role and is considered sacred. In the creation stories of the Haudenosaunee and the Anishinaabe, for example, a turtle makes a great sacrifice by offering its back for humans and other life forms to live on. This is why some First Nations peoples refer to North America as *Turtle Island*.

Among the Oji-Cree, the Six Nations Confederacy, and some other Nations, the people have a system of clans, each named for an animal. Traditionally in Anishinaabe culture, people of the Bear Clan have responsibilities that include keeping the community safe.

The connection between animals and humans is also expressed in language. In the Anishinaabe language, animals and humans are viewed as equals, not in a hierarchy. Alex McKay, an Anishinaabe language teacher and a professor of Aboriginal Studies at the University of Toronto, explains:

> Does it confuse you when I refer to animals as people? In my language, this is not confusing. You see, we consider both animals and people to be living beings. In fact, when my people see a creature in the distance, the thing they say is: Awiiyak (Someone is there). It is not that my people fail to distinguish animals from people. Rather, they address them with equal respect. Once they are near and identify the creatures' shadows, then they use their particular name.

FIGURE 2.11 This print, titled *Unity* (1995), by Kinta-Way, expresses the concept that "beings of the land, sea, and air—we are all related." What beings can you identify in the artwork? According to this concept, what beings in your environment are related?

Diverse Nations and Relationships

First Nations, Métis, and Inuit peoples vary widely across Canada, as do their relationships to the land, traditional knowledge, and current practices. On pages 48, 49, and 50, you will read profiles of communities across Canada. For each profile, note what you can about land features and the relationships between people and the land. Each community is located on the map below, which also shows the different **geocultural zones** in which the communities are found.

Sandy Lake First Nation Dodems

The Sandy Lake First Nation in Ontario has a clan system that links each family with an animal. If members of the same dodem ("clan" in Oji-Cree) meet, they greet each other as brothers and sisters. In Sandy Lake First Nation, the main clans and the corresponding last names are as follows:

The Suckers	Fiddler, Goodman, Harper
The Pelicans	Meekis
The Cranes	Kakegamic, Kakepetum
The Caribou	Linklater, Rae
The Sturgeon	Mamakeesic

FIGURE 2.12 This photograph was taken near Gjoa Haven. With information from the area hunters, researchers will be able to create an overview of polar bear populations, their movements, and diet.

Gjoa Haven, Cambridge Bay, and Taloyoak Hunters

Inuit hunters from Gjoa Haven, Cambridge Bay, and Taloyoak in Nunavut partnered with researchers at Queen's University in Kingston, Ontario, to track polar bears. The Inuit hunters located bears; noted their sex, age, and size from footprints; and set hair traps to gather hair samples (for DNA analysis). The goals are to better understand the effects of climate change on polar bear populations and to support local economies.

FIGURE 2.13 What geocultural zone do you live in? What First Nations live closest to you? As you read about communities from different geocultural zones on this map, make connections between the land, plants and animals, peoples, and current practices. What animals are probably a big part of the culture found in each zone? What relationships to the land are evident?

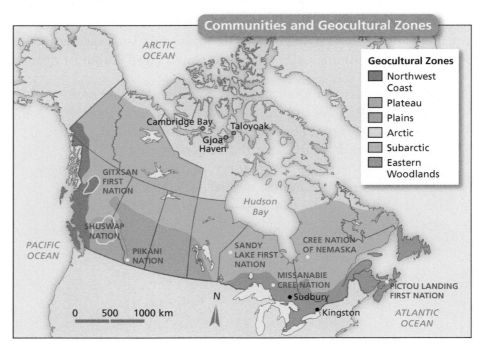

Communities and Geocultural Zones

ARCTIC OCEAN

Geocultural Zones
- Northwest Coast
- Plateau
- Plains
- Arctic
- Subarctic
- Eastern Woodlands

Cambridge Bay
Taloyoak
Gjoa Haven

GITXSAN FIRST NATION

Hudson Bay

SHUSWAP NATION

PACIFIC OCEAN

PIIKANI NATION

SANDY LAKE FIRST NATION

CREE NATION OF NEMASKA

MISSANABIE CREE NATION

PICTOU LANDING FIRST NATION

N

Sudbury

Kingston

ATLANTIC OCEAN

0   500   1000 km

©P

Pictou Landing First Nation Waters

Pictou Landing First Nation is a Mi'kmaq First Nation in northern Nova Scotia—a coastal environment that includes fisheries. One Nation member, Andrea Dykstra, has combined her knowledge of the land with scientific research and studies to earn a Bachelor of Science from St. Francis Xavier University, spearhead a study of the impact of industrial thermal disturbance around freshwater streams, and work for environmental protection, both in the Atlantic region and in Ottawa.

Gitxsan and Northwest Coast Feasting

Dolly Watts and her daughter Annie, from the Gitxsan First Nation (the Nation shown in the photograph on page 36), have published a cookbook that focuses on local ingredients of the Northwest Coast. The book, *Where People Feast: An Indigenous People's Cookbook,* includes stories (which provide a cultural context) and recipes—for example, smoked oolichan, spawn on kelp, wild rice pancakes, seaweed and salmon roe soup, wild huckleberry glazed duck, and Pacific macaroni and cheese.

Stories of the Shuswap Nation

The people of the Shuswap Nation are participating in a project with CBC Radio to record their stories. The recordings are in the Secwepemctsin language and in English, and the recordings combine narrators, performers, music, vocalizations, and sounds from the natural environment. One of the stories is "Spider's Gift," which explains how the first human learned from all animals how to live off the land. These recordings—and those by other First Nations and Inuit peoples—are broadcast across the country and made available on compact disc. The aim is to support the preservation of ancestral languages.

FIGURE 2.14 Andrea Dykstra, at home in Pictou Landing First Nation, continues her work to ensure that Aboriginal peoples are consulted on federal activities and projects that could have an impact on their rights, including the right to practise activities such as fishing, hunting, and gathering.

FIGURE 2.15 The Shuswap Nation is in the Plateau geocultural zone. This photograph shows the reserve often called the "Sugar Cane"—the village of Williams Lake Band—T'exelc, east of Williams Lake, B.C.

©P

The Métis Nation of Ontario's Captains of the Hunt

FIGURE 2.16 These Métis hunters harvested this moose in 2007 near Sudbury.

Métis people in Ontario harvest berries, hunt, and trap both for food and to have a good quality of life. The Métis Nation of Ontario's system ensures effective natural resource management; the Chief Captain of the Hunt (who is also the president of the Métis Nation of Ontario) appoints special people as Captains of the Hunt. These individuals have accumulated a deep knowledge of the Métis way of life; they live in the Métis traditional territories across Ontario, and they are important sources of knowledge in Métis communities.

Niskee Peesim: the Canada Goose Moon

For most Mushkegowuk (Cree) communities, Niskee Peesim (the Canada Goose Moon) in the spring announces the return of these geese to the North. The traditional April goose hunt is a significant part of Cree culture; it marks the change to warmer seasons and honours the geese for all they provide. At this time of year, extended families traditionally get together, celebrate, and hold ceremonies. Many Cree people today still gather for the spring goose hunt. The Cree Nation of Nemaska offers tourists a chance to participate in the spring hunt and learn about this important practice. Unfortunately, in some Cree communities, such as the Missanabie Cree First Nation, climate change is having an impact on the goose hunt. Global warming is causing the ice to thaw sooner, making it unsafe for hunting. This climate change also affects the nesting success of waterfowl and, in turn, their populations.

Piikani Nation Powwow

Powwows flourished with Plains Nations such as the Lakota, the Piikani, and the Siksika. Now, powwows take place in many areas of North America and have changed over time and with local adaptations. The Piikani Nation powwow takes place each summer and includes dance competitions, a youth rodeo, and many kinds of food. The Piikani rodeo reflects the Piikani Nation's history as a people who followed the bison, then turned to agriculture and ranching when the bison were depleted (you will read more about this in Chapter 3).

FIGURE 2.17 In 1991, the Alberta government dammed the Oldman River (which runs through the Piikani Nation) for irrigation and electricity production. Here and on other traditional lands, what impact would dam construction have on land use by Aboriginal peoples?

©P

Learning from the Land

Indigenous peoples across Canada have been living on and learning from the land since the beginning of time. The resulting **Indigenous traditional knowledge** is deep and complex. This knowledge embodies all of a community's expertise, skills, inventions, and ingenuity, coupled with communal wisdom, beliefs, and practices. Indigenous traditional knowledge is shaped by the local environment and can adapt to change over time.

Plant Wisdom

Over time, people of diverse Nations have learned what and when to pick, and how to use the plants found in Canada. When thinking of plants for healing, many people might think of acetylsalicylic acid, developed from salicin and found in the bark of certain willow and aspen trees. Another plant called kinnikinnick (Cree for bearberry) can be made into a tea for bladder and kidney problems, used for skin rashes, and added to meats and stews.

Timekeeping

Traditionally, the Innu needed to keep track of time to know when to meet up with extended family at the start of summer or when to travel for berry-picking at its end. For the Haudenosaunee, time-keeping has meant tracking a six-season cycle to plant, harvest, and rotate the core crops (corn, beans, and squash). These crops are often called the Three Sisters, but the Haudenosaunee call them *our sustainers*. The turtle calendar (page 52) is a timekeeping method used by some First Nations.

Passing Knowledge Forward

Nations have developed ways to retain certain knowledge.

- Inuit in the Nunavut Land Claim have established the Inuit Heritage Trust to safeguard customs— for example, by recording place names, involving Elders with students, and through archaeological sites.

- In Anishinaabe culture, wiigwaasabakoon (birchbark scrolls) etched with complex designs and shapes are one way to memorize and retain knowledge. The scrolls contain information about astronomy, medicines, migration routes, ancestry, and ceremonies.

- Nations such as the Piikani, Siksika, and Dakota used winter counts—animal hides with sometimes hundreds of images. One person would memorize the community's history and add a new image each winter. Each image was a memory aid to the historian.

FIGURE 2.18 In 2010, the Métis Nation of Ontario released a study of traditional plant uses in southern Ontario. Arnica (above) is one of the plants documented in the study.

The Turtle Calendar

The shells of most turtle species found in Canada have 28 outer scutes (sections) and 13 inner scutes. Among the Anishinaabe people, a turtle's shell has been used as a calendar: while the 28 outer scutes can be used to track the days (and nights) in the cycle of the moon, the 13 inner scutes can be used to track each lunar month in the year.

In Anishinaabe culture, the names of the lunar months carry local information about natural cycles or phenomena, animal activities, and practices and beliefs. So, the turtle calendar can be used for tracking time and for knowing what happens when.

However, note that Indigenous traditional knowledge is necessarily local and diverse across Canada. So, for example, the Mushkegowuk (Cree) of James Bay do not use a turtle calendar and do not use the term *Turtle Island* because turtles are not part of the Mushkegowuk world view.

FIGURE 2.19 Snapping turtles (such as the one above) live as far south as Ecuador. In Canada, they live primarily in southern Ontario but can be found from Saskatchewan to Nova Scotia. The turtle calendar is an important symbolic reminder of the connection to the land.

FIGURE 2.20 The jak'wun have been affected by environmental damage. Eden Robinson (above) writes: "I hate to think of thousands of years of tradition dying with my generation. Because if the eulachon don't return to our rivers, we lose more than a species. We lose a connection with our history, a thread of tradition that ties us to this particular piece of the Earth, that ties our ancestors to our children."

Educating Children

Passing knowledge forward to the younger generation is also a way to educate each child. Until formal education in schools was established, education was always within the family, in the community, and on the land. In Ojibwe, learning by observation is called gikinawaabi.

Many young people continue to learn in traditional ways. For example, on the West Coast, in the Haisla territory, Eden Robinson writes about recently fishing with her father for the Haisla food, jak'wun (a small fish, also called eulachon or oolichan). Later, he taught her how to smoke the jak'wun so that they could have a family get-together celebrating spring's beginning.

©P

VOICES OF THE PEOPLES

My English name is Jan Beaver. My Anishinaabe name is Ozhawakan Kwekwe. I am Bear Clan, and I am from Alderville First Nation.

For First Nations people, the importance of place is a reminder to us that our first relationship is with Creation, with our mother, which is the Earth, and that comes before all other relationships.

When we acknowledge place and the first inhabitants of the land, it's a demonstration of respect. It also serves as a reminder of the Nation-to-Nation aspect of the relationship between the first inhabitants of the land and those who came later. I truly believe that visitors should follow the protocol of place. So it is when you are visiting someone else's home, there is a need to ask permission to be there, to let others know the purpose of your visit, to acknowledge the territory or the land that you're on. I believe also that it's a responsibility for visitors to go beyond that surface

FIGURE 2.21 Jan Beaver says that following the seasonal cycles and the moon cycles can help people maintain their connection to the land: "Nature itself constantly reminds us about what we should be doing now, the important events that happen within these natural cycles."

relationship; it's a responsibility to learn about the community that you're visiting, their history, their culture, their ways of being in the world so that there is a deepening of the understanding and relationship with the people and the land that you're visiting.

THINKING IT THROUGH

1. Research one example of how a First Nations, Métis, or Inuk person is using Indigenous traditional knowledge to promote connectedness to the land.

2. Research a plant native to Canada that was used as a medicine prior to the arrival of Europeans and is still used today. In a visual presentation, present your findings about the plant and explain its characteristics and uses.

3. For one specific First Nation, Métis, or Inuit community in Canada:

   a) Gather information about the present-day community, its environment, and its history.

   b) Note your findings, your unanswered questions, and sources. For example, what could you learn about Indigenous traditional knowledge in the community? What photographs might provide information?

   c) Examine your information for connections.

   d) Post your information as a community profile on a wall map.

Recognizing and Evaluating Sources

Perhaps you belong to a First Nation, Métis, or Inuit community or you would like to know more about the Aboriginal peoples who live closest to you. Or maybe, in this chapter, you read about a Nation you knew nothing about before, and you are curious to know more. Where would you look for information?

Locating and Recognizing Sources

To learn more about a people, their way of life, or a certain time period, you can use a variety of sources, some of which can be described as primary and some of which can be described as secondary.

FIGURE 2.22 This child is learning from an Elder in the In-SHUCK-ch Nation in British Columbia. From what sources might you find out more about this Nation?

1) **Primary sources** are original first-hand accounts or items that have survived from the past. These can include

   - accounts in the oral tradition. The knowledge encompassed in oral traditions has come from the past and has been maintained from one generation to the next. As you will read in Unit 3, oral tradition is greatly valued among First Nations, Métis, and Inuit peoples, and it has been recognized recently in the Canadian court system as a valid testimony.

   - written items such as letters, diaries, records, and journals

   - visual items such as photographs, paintings, maps, diagrams, and other drawings

   - sites, monuments, and artifacts or objects from the past, such as clothing, tools, furniture, or jewellery

   All of these primary sources are used to gain a first-hand account of people or events in the past. Primary sources can be hundreds of years old or date back only to yesterday. Primary sources need to be considered in the context of the time in which they were created.

2) **Secondary sources** are accounts that are literally second-hand and are written after the fact. This textbook is an example of a secondary source. Other secondary sources might include media profiles, editorials on issues, websites, and magazine articles.

Evaluating Sources

It is important to distinguish what kind of source you are using—primary or secondary. This can help you evaluate how reliable the source is and if you need it.

Check the Origin of the Source

- Find out anything you can about those who created the source and why they did so. What point of view (or perspective) and world view do they have? What **biases** might they have? Is the source a first-hand account (primary source) or a second-hand account written afterward (secondary source)?

- If it is a book, examine the front pages, which usually contain its publication information. Who is (are) the author(s)? When was it published?

- If it is another type of written source (for example, a newspaper or magazine) find publication information about it.

- If the source comes from the oral tradition, seek information about the story and the context in which it was told.

- If it is an artifact, try to find who made it and when. Where is the artifact now and how did it get there—for example, was it stolen or found and then placed in a museum or was it entrusted to the current holder? Why should you be careful about making assumptions based on a particular artifact?

- If it is an electronic source (a CD-ROM or a website), try to find out who compiled the information and when. Is the material borrowed or original?

Look for Clues Within the Source

- Primary sources often show clues of the time they come from. For example, a very old primary source may use antiquated language.

- Some primary sources, letters or journals, have a personal feeling to them, using first-person words "I" or "we." Records typically do not.

- Secondary sources are typically in the third person and use formal language.

- Just as students are expected to cite their sources, secondary sources usually use quotation marks or credit lines to note sources. Check for clues.

Evaluate for World View, Point of View, and Bias

Every person has a world view. All authors, speakers, and artists have a point of view about a subject. People can have very different evaluations of the same event. When using and evaluating sources based on point of view, ask the questions in the Critical Thinking box in the margin.

Apply Your Skills

1. Choose a topic about Aboriginal peoples and gather a range of sources about it—for example, through the Internet or at the library.

2. Identify each source as primary or secondary, then evaluate its point of view, world view, possible biases, and potential usefulness.

CRITICAL THINKING

What is the source? Is it authentic? In what context was it created?

Who wrote or created it? How can you be certain? What is his or her point of view? What knowledge, experience, and bias does this person bring to the subject?

When was it created? How can you tell its age?

Where was it created?

Why did the person create this material? What is the purpose of the material?

So what? What is the significance of this source? How can you interpret it?

The Living Earth

The land—both within Ontario and across Canada—changes. At the same time, even though not all First Nations, Métis, and Inuit people today still live off the land, the connections between land, community, and culture are still present. Some communities and individuals retain a relationship to the land that is very similar to the one that their ancestors had. In other cases, communities and individuals must work hard to maintain these ties, renew them, or reshape them. In some cases, these connections have grown weaker as a result of displacements and other moves, loss of traditional lands, and changes in resource availability because of development or resource extraction. Sometimes, what was once a hunting ground has become an urban community. As you read on page 46, land bases have been reduced.

Naming and Renaming Connections

For all the above reasons, some communities are working to highlight their ties to the land, revitalize connections, and revert to original names for lands and territories. Original place names not only highlight the diversity of Nations across the country, but also give valuable insights into relationships with the land and can help explain why a certain area is highly valued. Certain areas might be appreciated for the resources found there or because of a special spiritual, cultural, or historical connection. When these place names were changed by colonizers, some of these ties were severed, and some derogatory names were introduced. Iqaluit ("many fish" in Inuktitut) was changed to Frobisher Bay and then back to Iqaluit. In Ontario, M'Chigeeng on Manitoulin Island was once named West Bay but has reclaimed its name of M'Chigeeng (village enclosed by stepped cliffs). Squaw Bay, near Thunder Bay, remains as an example of derogatory terminology.

FIGURE 2.23 The Kahonitake Kitikan Garden serves as a place to conduct ceremonies, find serenity, grow indigenous plants and medicines, and teach.

While maintaining a strong relationship with the land can be difficult in an urban context, First Nations, Métis, and Inuit peoples across Canada find ways of sustaining their connections to the land. The Native Students' Association at the University of Toronto has planted a sacred medicine garden on campus. Kahonitake Kitikan Garden (which translates as "garden" in Oneida and Ojibwe respectively) honours First Nations, Métis, and Inuit cultural values and teachings and recognizes the Mississaugas of the New Credit Nation, who were the most recent First Nations people to occupy this territory.

The Changing Land

Changes in the land and how it is perceived can be shown in how the land is mapped. Métis artist Christi Belcourt was born in Scarborough (now a part of Toronto) and has lived in Edmonton, Ottawa, the Manitoulin Island region, and recently the Lake of the Woods region.

Before you look at the impact of contact with Europeans, exploration, and settlement on the land, have a look at this artwork by Christi Belcourt.

FIGURE 2.24 This painting is part of Christi Belcourt's series *Mapping Roots: Perspectives of Land and Water in Ontario*. The artist says: "This piece has about 300 original Indigenous/Native place names on it. It is the culmination of two years of research into original place names. It is titled *A Work In Progress* (2007) because this in no way represents the totality of existing Native place names. The work of re-naming and re-claiming is being done by people and communities across Ontario and Canada." The detail of this large painting (122 cm x 122 cm) is not visible here, but if you could read the place names closest to your home, what names and languages do you think you would find?

Mapping Perspectives on the Land

After contact with Europeans and during the periods of exploration and then settlement, relationships with the land changed. Christi Belcourt states:

> *Historical maps reveal a great deal about how Europeans and their descendants viewed and continue to view the land—as a property to be owned and exploited... When Europeans first began mapping North America, they believed the land was a series of vast, empty and nameless territories, save for a few small pockets of people who dotted the land here and there.*

Starting in the late 1700s, as European immigration increased and expansion moved westward, Aboriginal peoples were continually displaced from their lands. The government set aside small sections of land for them to live on, but the sections were too small to allow for each Nation's own self-sustaining practices. As more new settlers arrived, they farmed and exploited lumber resources. These activities drastically altered the landscape and increased pressures on the diminishing resource base of Aboriginal peoples. As Christi Belcourt observes, over time, territories

> *...once indicated with markers such as "This land belongs to the Seneca" or "Six Nations Territory" are now entirely dotted with towns with such names as Caledonia, Sarnia, London, Essex, etc. ... During the fur trade era, many Métis communities emerged adjacent to the forts and trading posts of the Hudson's Bay Company or North West Company. The sites of the forts were recorded on various maps of the day, but burgeoning Métis communities more often than not, weren't acknowledged whatsoever... Although there are some Native place names that have managed to survive to this day, the vast majority of places—the lakes, the rivers, the streams, the hills, the valleys, the mountains, the islands, the lands, the sacred sites—places that all had significance to us, became renamed into English or French names and have lost their meaning. Places like Bauwiting became Sault Ste. Marie; Gichi Gumme became Lake Superior; etc. To a large extent the original names have now been lost even to our own people.*

As you think about the above quotations and look at the maps opposite, recall what you have learned about the history of First Nations and Inuit peoples, contact with Europeans, then the periods of exploration, the fur trade, the emergence of the Métis people, and the waves of settlement across what became Canada. Compare and contrast how lands are represented on the maps. What do you think your observations tell you about the ways in which land was viewed by the different people who made the maps?

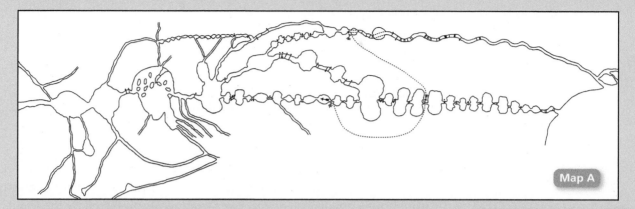

Map A

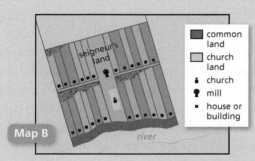

Map B

seigneur's land

river

common land
church land
church
mill
house or building

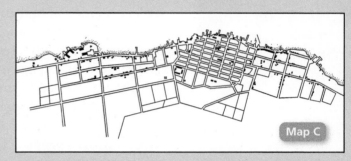

Map C

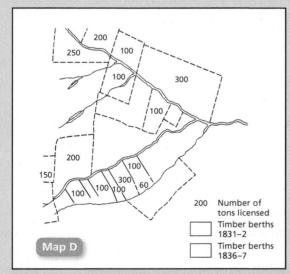

Map D

200   Number of tons licensed

Timber berths 1831–2

Timber berths 1836–7

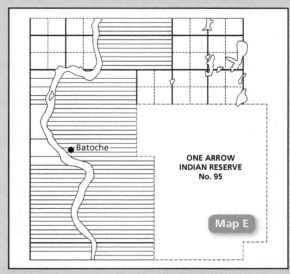

Batoche

ONE ARROW INDIAN RESERVE No. 95

Map E

FIGURE 2.25 Map A copies one drawn in the 1700s by Auchagah (Ochagach), an Assiniboine map maker, to show a river route and surrounding territories. **Map B** shows the French settlers' seigneurial system of land division; the seigneuries were usually divided into rangs (lots) for habitants. The land divisions allowed for multiple points of river access and easy ways for neighbours to mingle and cooperate. **Map C** shows the city street layout for Halifax in 1784. **Map D** delineates timber licences in the Tracadie River area in the 1830s. **Map E** shows the area of Batoche (about 1884 to 1930), including a reserve, Métis river lots, and grid parcels laid out by English surveyors.

Displacements, Dislocations, and Restrictions

When ties to the land run so deep, displacements, dislocations, and restrictions are traumatic. Aboriginal peoples have been and continue to be displaced from their lands as newcomers arrive. You will explore these subjects again in Chapter 7; however, here are some examples.

Batoche

The map of Batoche (Map E on page 59) indicates the conflicting perspectives on the land and some results of displacement. One Arrow Indian Reserve is named for Chief KÜPEYAKWÜSKONAM (Chief One Arrow or Une Flèche). KÜPEYAKWÜSKONAM and his people had hunted bison, but by the 1870s, the bison were depleted. Treaty 6 was to reserve land and provide farm equipment, instruction, and supervision.

By the early 1800s, many Métis farming communities were established throughout Canada, often with river frontage as preferred by the French settlers. A group of homesteads formed an extended family complex, providing social relations. Seasonal activities for the families included harvesting furs or other resources according to ancestral ways. Because land title offices had not yet been set up in the West, most Métis in the Batoche region lived on unregistered lands. As colonization continued westward, the English began imposing their own township system of dividing lands into grid patterns. In 1872, the government attitude regarding Métis people ("Halfbreeds" in the following) and the land they considered "unoccupied" was the following:

> These people can found no claim upon their being Halfbreeds. It's only as Settlers that any indulgence can be [shown] them... Anybody who goes to the Saskatchewan to settle has just as much right to go there and enter on unoccupied lands as those had who went before them...
>
> —from A.G. Archibald, Lieutenant Governor, Fort Garry to W.J. Christie, Fort Edmonton, January 11, 1872

The Residential School System

As you will read in Chapter 5, many generations of First Nations, Métis, and Inuit students went to residential schools. Most of these schools were shut down in the 1970s, but their impact continues to be felt. In many cases, children were taken hundreds of kilometres from their homelands, families, and communities for the entire school year or for years at a time.

VOICES OF THE PEOPLES

Ernie Crey tells about his father's separation from the land and its rich resources in the Sto:lo Nation, in British Columbia:

From their dormitory windows, Sto:lo children like my father would grieve for parents and home, pining for the life on the river they had left behind... [He recalled] school where children had to rise at 5 a.m. every day, say prayers on their knees for hours and eat thin gruel three times a day. Porridge, porridge, and more porridge was his abiding memory of the school's fare, particularly galling to Sto:lo who thrived on the Fraser River's rich salmon and sturgeon resources.

—Ernie Crey, Sto:lo author

©P

The High Arctic Relocations

In the 1950s, Canada's claim to the Arctic was being challenged by other countries. When people live in an area, a country can reinforce its claim to the land, so in August 1953, over 80 Inuit were transported from Inukjuak to Grise Fiord and Resolute Bay. The families had been promised better living and hunting opportunities at a time when their traditional hunting grounds were severely depleted. And, although they were told that they were going to live together, the families were dropped off on separate islands.

In this and other examples, displacements caused suffering and undermined traditional ties to the land.

Land Harvest Restrictions

Trapping and hunting are important activities for many First Nations, Métis, and Inuit peoples. Trapping provides food and other materials for household needs, and the sale of furs and leather goods provides income and stimulates local economies. Trapping is considered a link to the past and a vital part of the economic health of Aboriginal communities.

Since the early 1900s, trappers have operated under strict provincial and federal guidelines regulating seasons, quotas, and registrations.

When trapline registrations began, First Nations, Métis, and Inuit peoples were told that they would benefit, and registrations would ensure the proper management of wildlife. However, First Nations, Métis, and Inuit trappers saw the system as a way to legalize the presence of non-Aboriginal people on their lands, a breach of their treaty rights, and a way to control land use and restrict traditional economies and cultures.

The registration system also highlighted different views of the land. First Nations, Métis, and Inuit trapping territories did not have fixed boundaries; they were based on Indigenous traditional knowledge and part of a system of ever-changing relationships with the land and among people. In contrast, settlers saw the land as something they could claim and use exclusively.

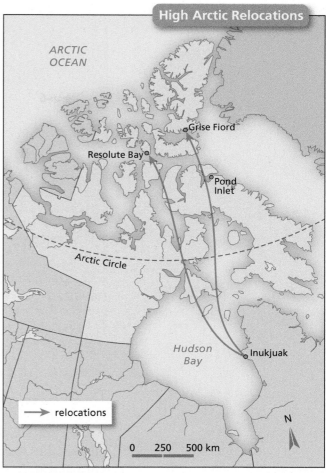

FIGURE 2.26 Families were relocated from Inukjuak in Northern Québec to two islands north of the Arctic Circle. For the relocated families, the environment was so unfamiliar that families from Pond Inlet came to teach them how to live in the High Arctic. For example, the relocated families had never before faced weeks without any sunlight.

CRITICAL THINKING

Describe the impact of changes that have affected or are affecting First Nations, Métis, or Inuit connections to the land. These might be disruptions to livelihoods, environments, or other changes.

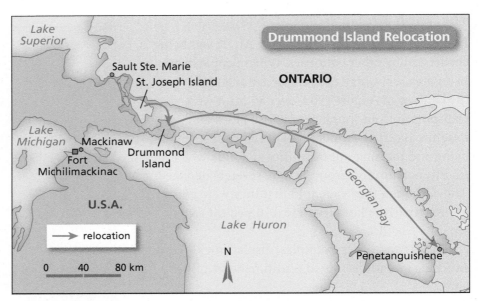

FIGURE 2.27 Near where Lake Huron and Lake Michigan meet, Drummond Island was a traditional First Nations gathering point. The area was also key for the British controlling the fur trade, in both the American War of Independence and the War of 1812.

Drummond Island Relocation

The fur trade played a significant role in the settlement of Canada in the 18th century, and many historical Métis communities formed at or near trading posts. Communities also formed where independent traders or missionaries were active. In Penetanguishene, Métis did not follow the normal pattern, as the community's roots are largely military.

In 1796, the British moved their garrison to St. Joseph Island. When the United States declared war on Great Britain in the War of 1812, the area became a key battleground. A force of 160 Métis and French Canadian voyageurs and 30 British soldiers took Fort Michilimackinac from the Americans. The American forces burned Fort St. Joseph.

After the war, all territory was returned to each country, and surveys were to be done. With Fort St. Joseph burned down, the British chose Drummond Island as an alternative military post. Most Métis and Canadian voyageurs chose to relocate under the British flag to Drummond Island. After the Hudson's Bay and North West Companies merged, Drummond Island became the hub for voyageurs from Mackinaw and numerous posts west.

However, in 1822, the surveys required by the peace treaty were complete, and Drummond Island was declared American territory. In 1828, the main British military establishment on the Upper Lakes moved to Penetanguishene. As part of the move, families of Métis and French-Canadian fur traders, voyageurs, boatmen, and pensioners were enticed to relocate with liberal allotments of land, 20- to 40-acre (8- to 16-hectare) lots in the region around Penetanguishene Bay. The journey by bateau, canoe, and sailboat took roughly two weeks, and one schooner was lost during the treacherous late-autumn journey.

FIGURE 2.28 These paddlers are arriving in Sudbury for the Métis Nation of Ontario general assembly in 2005—combining Métis heritage with present-day activities.

©P

Oujé-Bougoumou

The Cree community of Oujé-Bougoumou ("where the people gather") in Northern Québec is a place where people have hunted, fished, trapped, and raised their families for over 5000 years. Over the past few decades, the community was constantly forced to relocate as mining, dams, and forestry developments devastated the environment and pushed people out of the territories where their ancestors had always lived. As a result, people have been marginalized, living in impoverished conditions. Yet they have prevailed and created a model of a sustainable Aboriginal community, which has set in motion a healing and renewal process for the people of Oujé-Bougoumou.

The goal of the renewal project was to find a way to combine traditional ways of life within the framework of contemporary facilities and institutions. The housing program aimed to provide community members with affordable and energy-efficient housing, drawing on local resources and labour.

Since the project's completion, the health of this community has improved, and in 1995, the United Nations selected Oujé-Bougoumou as one of 50 model communities worldwide.

FIGURE 2.29 The community hired distinguished Métis/ Blackfoot architect Douglas Cardinal (who also designed the Canadian Museum of Civilization). Mr. Cardinal was the principal designer of the master plan for Oujé-Bougoumou, designing the complete site as well as the major public buildings.

THINKING IT THROUGH

1. With a partner, look back to the maps shown on page 59 and the last paragraph on page 58. With your partner, discuss your ideas about the maps. What conclusions and questions do you have about maps and contrasting perspectives on the land? How would your own relationship to land be expressed on a map?

2. In a group, discuss the impact of displacements from the land. What impact would a forced relocation or the building of a dam have on an Aboriginal community and its ties to the land?

3. a) Research Aboriginal place names.
   b) How do you think using, or reverting back to, Aboriginal places names affects the perceptions of various people toward those places?

4. How do First Nations, Métis, and Inuit people combine respect for the land and technical innovation in specific practices today? Research to find an example and present it to your class.

Aspirations for the Land

In this last section, you will consider how many First Nations, Métis, and Inuit peoples today are acknowledging, expressing, reclaiming, rejuvenating, or reinforcing their connections to the land as well as working toward healing the land.

Reclaiming Connections to the Land

Experiencing or re-experiencing connections to the land can take many forms. These include the following:

- maintaining access to the land's resources
- identifying burial grounds
- taking legal action
- gathering sacred medicines and safeguarding traditional knowledge
- holding political protests
- expressing a relationship to the land through art

FIGURE 2.30 Darlene Johnston (above, at her ancestral home in Cape Croker) has been involved in her community's court battle over fishing and land rights, has worked with the Mayan people in Belize, and is now a professor of law at the University of British Columbia.

Taking Legal Action

Many organizations and individuals today are working to reclaim lands that were never ceded or to rectify land rights that have not been honoured. This work is central to maintaining connections with ancestors and cultural practices that are tied to the land.

VOICES OF THE PEOPLES

Legal battles over land are often lengthy and require leaders with strength and determination in order to pursue their rights. Darlene Johnston was inspired to study law by her community in Cape Croker, home to the Chippewas of Nawash First Nation. She became the first member of her family to attend university and the first female Aboriginal law student at the University of Toronto. She then went on to become a professor of law.

First Nations peoples are indigenous to this land and they identify with it as the land identifies with them. When the children are here, the land comes alive; the berries are bigger and wild apples grow, but when the children are not here, the apples will not grow. This is First Nations land; this is home. You do not sell something that is sacred… It is not only the burial sites that are sacred and in need of protection, but plants, medicines, stories and the location of stories as well.

—Darlene Johnston, in a February 2005 meeting on the Ipperwash Inquiry

Recognizing Traditional Knowledge

Indigenous traditional knowledge is deep, interconnected, local knowledge that has been built up for millennia. Through observation, experimentation, and daily practice over generations, systems of knowledge have flourished that include information about the Earth's cycles, resources, techniques to survive and thrive, and how to live in harmony with many diverse environments. This knowledge is collective (not belonging to an individual person, but rather to everyone in the community) and is passed forward from one generation to the next. In many communities, certain people are responsible for learning particular knowledges and using them for the good of the entire community. In that sense, there is a tradition of **stewardship**, to safeguard knowledge, as well as customary laws that guide its use.

Experience and increasing worldwide interest in Indigenous traditional knowledge raise the question of who *should* benefit. Because the knowledge belongs to no specific individuals, some people and companies have treated the knowledge as though it is free for the taking. Unfortunately, Indigenous traditional knowledge continues to be disrespected, **appropriated**, and exploited.

People and organizations around the world are working to recognize and protect Indigenous traditional knowledge and to ensure that the communities themselves benefit from their knowledge. For example, the United Nations has begun a project to document Indigenous traditional knowledge by audio-recording it. In North America, scholars such as Marie Battiste and James Youngblood Henderson are exploring questions about Indigenous traditional knowledge and legal protections.

FIGURE 2.31 Maple syrup has been found to have many health benefits—including a low calorie count relative to its sweetness, plus zinc and manganese (which help the immune system), and antioxidant compounds.

FIGURE 2.32 Visual artist and lecturer Jane Ash Poitras (born in Fort Chipewyan, Alberta) earned degrees in microbiology and printmaking at the University of Alberta and a Master of Fine Arts in Painting and Sculpture from Columbia University. In her series *Consecrated Medicines*, she brings together explorations of science, art, and her Cree/Chipewyan heritage. At the series' outset, she said, "What can I do to ensure the continued survival and abundance of our precious plant resource? I, as an artist, would like to embark on a journey into ethnobotany—growing, studying, tasting medicinal plants; exploring not only their scientific importance, but also their spiritual significance to various cultures." This artwork is *Buffalo Seed, 2004.*

Web Connect • • • • • • • • • • • •

To learn more about Indigenous traditional knowledge and its protection, visit our website.

Expressing Connections to the Land

The art of First Peoples came from the land, using materials from the environment and reflecting the dynamic relationship between the land and its peoples. According to tradition, everyone has creative capacities, and art brings you closer to the Creator because creativity comes from the Creator.

Today, First Nations, Métis, and Inuit artists continue their Nations' traditions while exploring new directions, showing again their people, their cultures, their innovations, and their connections to the land. Throughout this chapter, what connections to the land do you see in contemporary writing and visual art?

FIGURE 2.33 Rick Beaver is an Anishinaabe artist from Alderville First Nation. His paintings, prints, and designs often include images from nature. About this work entitled *Current Connections* (2010), he says that fish are perfect representatives for the human connection with all things, and for millennia peoples have celebrated and relied on the seasonal migrations of fish.

Healing the Land

First Nations, Métis, and Inuit cultures in Canada have teachings and stories that address looking after the lands provided by the Creator. The common principles of being stewards of the land, of not harming the Earth with wastefulness, and of leaving enough for other living things and future generations are important beliefs that have allowed First Peoples to live in harmony with nature for millennia.

Philip Kevin Paul, of the W̱SÁNÁĆ Nation from the Saanich Peninsula on Vancouver Island, is a poet, instructor in the University of Victoria Writing department, and a researcher in the Linguistics department. He is working to ensure the preservation of the SENĆOŦEN language. After you read the poem, think about what it says about languages and the "world" we live in.

Doorways to a Younger World
by Philip Kevin Paul

Nephew dropped carrot, corn, pole-bean seed into my ear while I slept. When I woke he told me so, smiling into a tall, fat book. He said it was a good harvest and that my ears must be very fertile.

We've finished the trees and tomorrow we'll start on the fruit-bearing plants. He tries to stay ahead of me by reading books he's hidden. I overhear him whispering the Latin and English names in the TV room.

But it's the Indian names that quiet him. He says the most peculiar thing after I tell him the secret names of salal and the story-trail they lead us to.

You know what, Uncle? Everything I was thinking, except your voice, went away when you were saying the story.

Our survival depended on our wise use of game and the protection of the environment. Hunting for pleasure was looked upon as wasteful and all hunters were encouraged to share food and skins. Sharing and caring for all members of the society, especially the old, the disabled, the widows, and the young were the important values of the Mi'kmaq people. Without these values, my people would not have survived for thousands of years as a hunting, fishing, and gathering culture.

—Kep'tin John Joe Sark, Mi'kmaq Grand Council

From the deep relationships with the land, and rooted within an ethical system that is tied to personal and collective responsibility, comes the holistic concept that the health of the land is directly linked to the well-being of communities and peoples.

Today, the Earth is in the midst of major environmental crises, suffering from climate change, over-population, and pollution of its lands and waters. In response, many First Nations, Métis, and Inuit individuals and organizations are applying traditional knowledge and practices—and developing new ways—to help restore the well-being of the Earth. For example, Andrea Dykstra (page 49) has combined traditional knowledge as a Mi'kmaw and scientific study.

REFLECTION

As you read specific examples and reflect back on the chapter, think about what relationships to the land are expressed. What choices are being made, and what responsibilities are being taken?

Seven Generations Teaching

On page 36, you read about the Seventh Generation. This phrase comes from a teaching that many Aboriginal peoples and Nations use today to guide their decisions and actions on many levels, whether individual, family, community, social, economic, or political.

The Seven Generations Teaching is based on the world views that everything is related and that the Earth is sacred, given as a gift from the Creator. Hence every generation must preserve the delicate balance among all things by making individual and communal decisions based on the implications for the next seven generations. Making decisions with this teaching requires wisdom, humility, and care; the impact of each decision will go beyond what we can even fully imagine. This teaching also bonds people and communities by recognizing connections among people now, from people now to past generations and decisions, and forward from the current generation to future generations.

This teaching reflects a deep conception of time; it requires long-range planning in the extreme—thinking ahead hundreds of years into the future. Decisions are not made based on material wealth but to ensure that what is here for us now will be here for our children, grandchildren, great-grandchildren, and on, for seven generations.

FIGURE 2.34 Many organizations and Nations apply the Seven Generations Teaching to decision making. For example, the Assembly of First Nations developed its position on nuclear waste disposal with the teaching. The In-SHUCK-ch Nation of British Columbia (the photograph above was taken in their territory) also applies the teaching in its Land Stewardship Plan. However, the teaching has also become mainstream, with many companies and products using *Seven Generations* in their names. What products or companies use this phrase? Why do you think they have chosen to? What is the impact of removing the words *Seven Generations* from their original context?

VOICES OF THE PEOPLES

Water is precious and sacred. It is one of the basic elements needed for all life to exist.

—*Grandmother Josephine Mandamin*

It's important to bring awareness to people of the state of our water and that we have to do something about it.

—*Grandmother Irene Peters*

The Water Walkers

In the Great Lakes region, a group called the Water Walkers has taken up the cause of pollution in a cross-border effort. Started by Anishinaabe grandmothers and Anishinaabe women and men, the group completed a walk around the perimeter of Lake Superior in 2003. They have since completed walks around Lakes Michigan, Huron, Ontario, and Erie, and along the St. Lawrence River. Each walk started in spring—the time of renewal, regrowth, and rebirth—and the walkers averaged 50 kilometres per day. During the 2005 Water Walk, when she was 63, Grandmother Josephine Mandamin wore out six pairs of shoes. Traditional teachings talk about the role of women as water carriers.

©P

FIGURE 2.35 This photograph from 2009 shows the Water Walkers during the St. Lawrence River walk. Grandmother Mandamin is in front, wearing the black hat.

Sherrole Benton writes about joining the Water Walkers:

On Mother's Day of 2008, I was called to join a caravan of Anishinaabe people who were walking around Lake Michigan from Ontario... I asked my youngest son to join me on this walk. The walkers needed both men and women to join the walk: the men to stand guard and carry the eagle staff, and women to carry the water... The head water walker, Josephine Mandamin, is from the Wikwemikong Unceded Indian Reserve No. 26 located on Manitoulin Island in Lake Huron...

As local walkers joined the caravan, they were smudged with cedar and cleansed of all other worries except the mission of the water walk. The women were instructed to wear long skirts and be mindful of the women's teachings. The men were instructed to carry the eagle staff high and protect the women as they carried a copper pail of water down the road. The Anishinaabe people always point out how important it is for men and women to work together. They tell young men and women that they each have their own roles and responsibilities not only for themselves, but for others, including the Earth and the environment.

Throughout the day, several groups of people joined the water walkers including: Oneida, Ojibway, Hochunk, Menominee, Navajo, Kwaguilth, and others...

The water walkers' war is against big corporations, and their mission is to save fresh, clean water for future generations. The corporations are polluting the Great Lakes and nearby waters with chemicals, disease-causing organisms, exotic species, mercury, and other harmful substances. Corporations are also trying to bottle and sell spring water, even as local communities protest. That Sunday, it was appropriate that men and women gathered together to walk for clean water and environmental justice on Mother's Day.

Sheila Watt-Cloutier

Sheila Watt-Cloutier is an Inuk woman who has energetically represented Inuit interests regionally, nationally, and internationally. Born in Kuujjuaq, Nunavik, in Northern Québec, Sheila Watt-Cloutier grew up on the land and understands the important connections between the health of the people and the land. She has been involved with reviewing the Nunavik educational system, with the Makivik Corporation (an Inuit land-claim organization related to James Bay and Northern Québec), and as elected president of the Inuit Circumpolar Council (which represents Inuit in Canada, Russia, the United States, and Greenland).

Sheila Watt-Cloutier advocated for banning the manufacture and use of harmful pollutants such as PCBs and DDT, pollutants found in high concentrations in many Inuit communities because of bioaccumulation in the food chain. Recently she has focused on climate change—for example, diminishing sea ice and risks to traditional Inuit hunting. As a result, she filed an international legal petition backed by 62 Inuit Elders and hunters to the Inter-American Commission on Human Rights. The lawsuit shone the spotlight on climate change and human rights.

FIGURE 2.36 Sheila Watt-Cloutier has described the environment of the Arctic as the early warning system for the globe. She has received many awards, including the Rachel Carson Award, a United Nations Human Development Award, and the Order of Canada.

VOICES OF THE PEOPLES

Jessica Simpson is from the Tlicho First Nations from Wha Ti and grew up in Somba Ke (Yellowknife), Denendeh. She co-founded the Arctic Indigenous Youth Alliance, completed a degree at Mount Allison University in Sackville, N.B., and works as Community Liaison Officer for the Mackenzie Valley Environmental Impact Review Board. While working with the Alliance, she wrote:

As young people, the words we use are new, but the concepts have been important to Indigenous people for thousands of years. But what we've managed to do is translate these sacred beliefs into the discourse of sustainability and climate change... Curing the effects of colonization can be simplified. All we need to do is change one mind at a time and then start all over again— it's called perseverance.

In what ways are the words new but the concepts very old?

Living the Teaching

There are numerous examples in communities across Canada where the Seven Generations Teaching is being applied by individuals, organizations, and businesses to guide their decisions and actions. The endeavour undertaken by the Water Walkers (page 68) is a living expression of the teaching.

Jim St. Arnold (Great Lakes Indian Fish and Wildlife Commission specialist at a summer science camp for students in the Lake Superior region) puts it another way:

> *Traditional use of natural resources for the Anishinabeg and other native peoples always reflected the philosophy called The Seventh Generation. The concept is simple, and culturally ingrained. When you do things, you don't just do things for today, you do things for the future. Resources should be protected not for your children or their children, but for children seven generations down. With that goes some other simple beliefs. People have their place within the natural systems and there is a give and take within that circle. When you take something, you always give something back.*

Isabelle Knockwood remembers from her childhood in Shubenacadie in Nova Scotia the lessons of everything being related and how to live harmoniously:

> *The stories were ancient... One of the principal ways of teaching young children was through the telling of [stories] that embodied thousands of years of experience in living off the land. The story-tellers emphasized living harmoniously with the two-legged, the four-legged, the winged ones, and those that swim in the waters—all our relations. Even the plants are said to have a spirit and are our relations.*

FIGURE 2.37 Kevin Lee Burton (Swampy Cree) and Caroline Monnet (Algonquin/French) collaborated on an exhibition that included this photograph from God's Lake Narrows First Nation in Manitoba. They state, "Native people have adapted to the ever-changing world while keeping pride intact, languages alive, and diverse cultural distinctions. Yet a homogenized and uniform image of Native people remains in the general public eye."

1. Define the words *steward*, *protector*, and *custodian* as they relate to the land and the environment. In what different ways have individuals and organizations taken on those roles? In what other ways might they? Summarize your ideas in a poster, essay, or web page.

2. Research other First Nations, Métis, or Inuit organizations, communities, or individuals that apply traditional knowledge to contemporary environmental issues. Share your findings with the class.

CRITICAL THINKING

How is *the land* defined and what relationships to the land do First Nations, Métis, and Inuit peoples generally have?

Conclusion

In this chapter, you have explored big ideas about relationships to the land experienced by many First Nations, Métis, and Inuit peoples, as well as commonly held beliefs about the interconnectedness of all living things and the sacredness of the land. By looking at changes to the land, different perspectives on the land, and displacements from the land, you have examined challenges to relationships to the land. Finally, you have looked at aspirations for the land, including reclaiming connections and healing the land.

Activities in this chapter have engaged you in locating and evaluating sources for research, tracing relationships to the land, and more.

©P

FIGURE 2.38 In April 2006, Kashechewan First Nation in Ontario was in the news. In this photograph, Janell Carpenter, 11, paddles down a street before being evacuated. Her home was flooded after the barrier protecting the Cree community from rising waters on the James Bay coast began to leak. The community faced a water crisis: substandard drinking water, flooding, and evacuation.

1. How does the quotation on page 36 reflect a relationship to the land? In a group, discuss the quotation and brainstorm its implications.

2. **a)** Review the chapter and then summarize your understandings of First Nations, Métis, and Inuit relationships to the land. Note any common themes you see and any differences among Nations, communities, and individuals.

   b) Consider your own relationship to the land and the relationships to the land that you see in your family and community. What similarities and differences do you see when you compare these observations to the summary notes you made earlier? How does your family or community maintain or weaken ties to the land? How do you relate to the natural world?

3. Imagine you have been asked to join a Senate committee to discuss outside institutions (for example, pharmaceutical companies, governments) wanting to use specific Indigenous traditional knowledges.

   a) In a group, develop recommendations for guidelines on the use of traditional knowledge by outsiders, and how outsiders could give back to communities that are sharing their knowledge.

   b) As a group, present your recommendations to the Senate committee (your other classmates) and receive their feedback on your recommendations.

4. Collect and examine current news stories from both mainstream and First Nations, Métis, and Inuit sources that illustrate beliefs about the land. To what extent do the news stories illustrate the concepts of the land as sacred, of interconnectedness, of change, and/or of stewardship? Which source would you recommend as a useful source of information and perspectives?

5. Research one community's history of place names and settlement in order to

   a) locate, evaluate, and use a variety of primary and secondary sources, using Building Your Skills on pages 54 and 55 as your guide.

   b) learn as much as you can about the subject and report your findings in an oral presentation, essay, or display incorporating visuals and written text.

   c) reflect on the process and challenges of evaluating sources.

CHAPTER 3

Economy, Trade, and Resources

> Our Elders and ancestors have passed the responsibility to protect our lands and way of life on to us. It is not possible for us to agree to the destruction of the land that sustains us.
>
> —*Chief Marilyn Baptiste, Xeni Gwet'in First Nation, 2009*

There are many successful businesses owned and operated by First Nations, Métis, and Inuit peoples across Canada today. Each has contributions to make and challenges to face. As you read through this chapter, keep the concept of world views in mind. How do these businesses meet the challenges of trade, economy, and the use of resources while also respecting the land and satisfying the need to make a living? What efforts are being made to ensure sustainability for future generations?

FIGURE 3.1 Anne Marie Sam (Nak'azdli First Nation) spent her childhood learning how to fish and gather medicines. Her family's traditional lands are near a proposed mine in British Columbia. The community of Nak'azdli feels a responsibility to protect the area. How can the community share their value of the land with others?

Use these questions to explore the big ideas in this chapter.

1. In what ways can trade and the use of resources reveal the relationships between First Nations, Métis, and Inuit peoples and the land?

2. How are economy, trade, and resources connected to the values, beliefs, and aspirations of First Nations, Métis, and Inuit peoples?

3. What challenges to their values and beliefs would First Nations, Métis, and Inuit peoples face regarding trade, resources, and their economic well-being in the past, present, and future?

©P

FIGURE 3.2 Cree guide Gordon Moar at his camp in the Ashuapmushuan Game Reserve, Québec. Tourists from around the world come to Moar's camp to experience canoeing, snowmobiling, trapping, and camp life. How does Moar's business sustain his beliefs, values, and knowledge of the land?

FIGURE 3.3 Goulais Bay, home to the Batchewana First Nation, is on the eastern shore of Lake Superior, about 56 kilometres north of Sault Ste. Marie. What do you think are some of the modern pressures facing remote communities in terms of resource development?

REFLECTION

How would a world view that involves being part of the land affect your personal economic choices?

CRITICAL THINKING

Consider what you have learned about the Seven Generations Teaching. How does it reflect world views about the land and its resources? How is this teaching reflected in modern resource development?

Economy and Trade Before Contact

The land now known as North America is vast and diverse. It contains life-sustaining resources such as air, fresh water, plants, and animal life. First Nations, Métis, and Inuit peoples occupied every geographic region of the continent, and their values and ways of life kept them close to the land. However, with the arrival of European settlers came new economic pressures, the loss of land, and increased use of resources. This in turn meant stresses on values and ways of life. How can values be balanced with the use of resources both today and in the future?

Values and Trade

Although there are diverse, distinct, and evolving world views among all Aboriginal peoples, there are also some common threads within these world views, especially in relation to valuing and respecting the land. Diversity is reflected in how various First Nations, Métis, and Inuit peoples relate to and use the land for food, shelter, and trade.

The Land as a Gift

A common belief among many First Nations, Métis, and Inuit peoples is that the land does not belong to any one person, group, or organization. The land is considered to be a gift from the Creator. Since all things are interconnected, all things on the land, in the sky, and in the waters— people, plants, animals—rely on one another and contribute to the cycle of life.

Elders and Wisdom Keepers continue to be responsible for passing along teachings about the land, how to harvest resources, and how the land is to be respected and regarded. The value of the land and resources is also taught by Elders and Wisdom Keepers, including how trade can ensure sharing of resources.

In Chapter 2, you read about the concept of Seven Generations. The principles of the Seven Generations Teaching show that all people are to honour and consider the needs of the seven generations that have come before them as well as the seven generations that will come after them. This teaching creates a sense of communal stewardship and encourages sustainable use of the land.

Respect and Care for the Land: Inuit Perspectives

A relationship to the land is of profound importance to Inuit, and most Inuit are still hunters. Hunting is considered not only a part of cultural identity, but also a link to the past. Inuit value hunting because they believe it provides

- independence, self-esteem, and respect
- physical and emotional well-being
- food and a healthy lifestyle

"Going out on the land" renews the spirit. Providing food for your family and sharing with others create pride and support traditions of sharing. Although hunting techniques and harvesting patterns have changed with modern technology and settlement in permanent communities, Inuit maintain their beliefs and still practise traditional knowledge about the land.

In the early 1970s, an organization called the Inuit Tapirisat of Canada was formed to voice Inuit concerns over mining and drilling for oil and gas. Its efforts would eventually contribute to the creation of Nunavut. The Nunavut Act also created five committees to co-manage land, water, and wildlife.

Nunavut is divided into three regions: Kitikmeot, Kivalliq, and Qikiqtani (Baffin). Inuit rely on the animals unique to each region to survive, and each region has different challenges for hunting and fishing. For this reason, Inuit members of the committees are appointed by region. Committees work with local hunters and trappers to ensure that resources are managed in a sustainable way. Each committee uses traditional knowledge to measure and manage the effects of resource use and development on both the people and the land. This approach includes giving guidance and direction to mining, oil, and gas companies. In this way, the well-being of the land is controlled by Inuit themselves.

Local control is now more important than ever. Global warming has caused higher sea levels, loss of pack ice, sudden changes in weather, and changes in patterns of migration—all of which deeply affect day-to-day Inuit life. Activities as basic as hunting, fishing, and travelling are becoming increasingly difficult.

In Inuktitut, avatitinnik kamatsiarniq—which means "respect and care for the land, animals, and environment"—outlines the Inuit philosophy of environmental stewardship, a balanced approach to the way the land, water, wildlife, and other resources are used.

Although there have been many changes to Inuit life, avatitinnik kamatsiarniq continues to be applied. Today, it is understood as preserving and protecting habitat, minimizing waste, and sharing harvests with the community. When these principles are applied, for example, Inuit rely less on goods shipped from the South.

Today, Inuit Tapirisat of Canada is called the Inuit Tapiriit Kanatami (ITK). It is a national advocacy organization representing over 50 000 Inuit in Canada. ITK conducts studies on climate change and actively voices concerns about increased shipping and the effects of potential oil spills on the fragile Arctic environment.

QUESTIONS

1. How have Inuit in the North maintained connections to the land and how are their current lifestyles tied to values about the land?

2. How do Inuit advocate for sustainable resource development in the North?

3. Research how Inuit are working to prevent and deal with climate change.

Trading Practices

Resource	Use
amber	beads
silica	arrowheads
obsidian	cutting tools
copper	cutting tools, hooks, jewellery

Well before the fur trade, First Nations and Inuit peoples distributed a wide range of resources through extensive trade networks. The area of trade was far-ranging and diverse, and in fact was larger than that of the Roman Empire. Archaeologists in Missouri, in the central United States, have found such items as shells from both the Pacific Ocean and the Gulf of Mexico, and copper from the Great Lakes. Items traded by Inuit included amber, obsidian, and iron, which were eventually traded to peoples in the Great Lakes region and Labrador. On the west coast, trade routes wound their way through the mountain ranges. One trade item, oolichan oil, was so commonly traded that the routes would later be called "grease trails."

The ancient city of Cahokia, in what is now Illinois, once had a population nearing 20 000. Situated where the Mississippi, Missouri, and Illinois Rivers join, the city was the centre of a network of trade routes reaching to the Great Lakes.

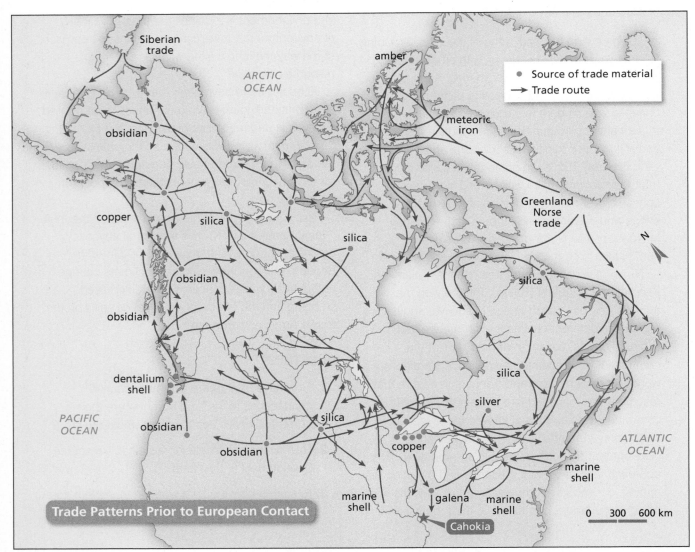

FIGURE 3.4 This map shows some of the trade routes of First Nations and Inuit peoples prior to the arrival of Europeans. Rivers and lakes enabled Aboriginal peoples to trade across vast distances. Compare these trade routes with a road map of North America. What differences and similarities do you see?

©P

Kay-Nah-Chi-Wah-Nung: The Manitou Mounds

Kay-Nah-Chi-Wah-Nung translates to "the place of the long rapids" and consists of over three kilometres of shoreline along the Rainy River in northwestern Ontario. The area is also known as the Manitou Mounds. Close to the headwaters of the Mississippi River, it was an ideal meeting place for First Nations peoples in North America.

Declared a national historic site in 1970, Kay-Nah-Chi-Wah-Nung was the centre of a continent-wide trading network. People gathered to trade, share, celebrate, and mourn at this site, which also served as a ceremonial burial ground. Artifacts found at the site reflect a diverse trading network that brought items such as copper, shells, and stone from across North America. The site has likely been in use for about 8000 years.

Kay-Nah-Chi-Wah-Nung has a rich heritage and deep spiritual and cultural meaning for First Nations across North America. It is treasured for its beauty and as a sacred place, and it continues to be a significant ceremonial centre. Visitors come every year to share the oral and physical history of the land. Tours are offered, and there is an interpretive centre on site. Areas are set aside for ceremonies, dances, and spiritual practices. The site is

FIGURE 3.5 Kay-Nah-Chi-Wah-Nung today. Why is it important to preserve national historic sites?

maintained by the guardians of the land, the Ojibwe people of the Rainy River First Nation.

QUESTIONS

1. Research Kay-Nah-Chi-Wah-Nung and its location. Why was this location important for trade?

2. What evidence is there that many First Nations came together at this site?

3. How is the history of these mounds maintained and shared with people today?

Economic Practices

The economic practices among the First Nations and Inuit were centred on a resource-based economy. Although frequently described as a **subsistence economy**, that term implies a difficult hand-to-mouth existence, with little surplus for trade. However, trade among First Nations and Inuit was active, thriving, and far-reaching well before the arrival of Europeans and the **market economy.** In fact, the economic practices of the First Nations and Inuit were in tune with the concept of **supply and demand.** The Algonquians in areas such as Ontario and parts of Québec, for example, supported themselves with resources obtained from hunting, the harvesting of plants, and fishing. Food and other items were usually shared within the community, but items were also traded. A demand for certain animals, plants, and other items existed in areas where they were scarce or could not be found, and the Algonquians could trade what they did not need with other First Nations. In the same sense, Inuit would exchange whale and seal products for items such as soapstone and wood.

Trading would occur at regular times throughout the year, typically at gathering places such as Kay-Nah-Chi-Wah-Nung. More than just items were exchanged; knowledge was also shared and alliances were created. Trade languages such as Chinook Jargon developed in British Columbia. These languages further forged ties between Nations.

Trade was an integral part of life for the First Nations and Inuit, so in the 1600s it was natural for them to trade with the newly arrived French, English, and Spanish, who were very interested in the resources that First Nations and Inuit peoples had to offer.

Ways of Knowing

Dentalium Shells

Dentalium shells are harvested from deep waters around the Northwest Pacific Coast of North America. The shells were and still are highly valued by First Nations peoples as an international trade item.

Dentalium shells were traded by First Nations living in the Northwest Pacific Coast region, and into the Great Plains, central Canada, and Alaska. In exchange, First Nations would accept various items such as foods, decorative materials, dyes, hides, macaw feathers from Central America, and turquoise from the southwest United States.

Although dentalium shells are sometimes equated with money, these shells were mainly used for ceremonial clothing (also called regalia) and jewellery, and are valued for their strength and unique appearance.

Today, dentalium shells still hold great value, and their use in jewellery and ceremonial clothing honours the past in the present. Regalia have special and personal meaning to those who wear them, and often the items found on regalia are treasured gifts from others. Dentalium shells are still used in all parts of Canada, and are traded and sold across the country. The shells can often be found at artists' functions, at powwows, and in craft stores.

FIGURE 3.6 Dentalium shells used as decoration on a dress. In what ways are dentalium shells still used in the present to honour the past?

©P

The Fur Trade

The arrival of Europeans dramatically altered the lives of First Nations and Inuit peoples. First encounters in the 1500s evolved into alliances, trade, and political relations. Trade increased with the fur trade, which would eventually involve thousands of people over the next 300 years.

Furs were first traded with First Nations and Inuit peoples in exchange for European goods such as tools and weapons. In the decades that followed, an organized fur trade began as French and English organizations such as the North West Company and the Hudson's Bay Company created trade networks and built forts across the continent. They traded mostly for beaver fur, which was a vital component in the fashionable fur hats of the era—and anything fashionable in Europe was very profitable. The companies employed First Nations and Inuit people as mapmakers and guides, and traded with them for food and clothing as well as for furs.

FIGURE 3.7 Étienne Brûlé (1592–1633) was a French explorer and trader who lived with the Wendat and learned their language.

The Métis

As trade expanded, more and more First Nations and Inuit peoples came into contact with the French and English traders, and communities began to form around trading posts. Some of the European traders married First Nations women, and their children would come to be known as the Métis.

The Métis played a number of roles in the fur trade, and between the late 1700s and the 1900s, they worked as independent traders, voyageurs, trappers, guides, and suppliers. Over time, these different roles would lead to a rich diversity among the Métis of different regions.

The Decline of the Fur Trade

As fashion changed, the demand for furs decreased. European traders and settlers moved on to mining, lumber, land buying, and railroad building. The role of First Nations, Métis, and Inuit peoples in the economy diminished as the 1800s came to a close. The decline of the fur trade also meant an end to the income brought by employment and trade. In many cases, this change created the need to adapt to other ways of making a living, such as harvesting wild rice or blueberries, selling crafts and art, fishing and hunting, or establishing cooperatives.

FIGURE 3.8 A competitor at the Voyageur Games in Sudbury, Ontario, 2005. Métis voyageur games include endurance and strength challenges related to Métis voyageur life. This woman is carrying milk jugs, which in the past would have been 50-pound sacks of flour or beaver pelts. She must carry them a certain distance without putting them down. Why might these games be important to Métis?

Challenges to Values and Practices

The end of the fur trade, the building of railroads, and the depletion of the bison in the West had an enormous impact on the lives of many First Nations and Métis. Loss of land, restrictions on hunting and fishing, and forced relocations would also change the economies of Aboriginal peoples across Canada.

First Nations, Métis, and Inuit peoples would have to balance their core values of respect and sharing with the need to provide for themselves. Some did build their personal wealth and property. Family members had to be concerned about personal survival at a time when collective sharing of personal fortune or wealth was not allowed.

In addition, new laws restricting practices such as the potlatch were introduced by the federal government, placing further pressure on the beliefs and values of First Nations, Métis, and Inuit peoples.

Distribution of Wealth: The Potlatch

The potlatch is practised among most First Nations of the Northwest Coast of Canada, binding communities together in a celebration of sharing, distribution of wealth, and confirmation of the positions within the community. In 1884, the potlatch was banned by the Canadian government. The potlatch was seen as an obstacle to government policies of the time, which were focused on the assimilation of First Nations peoples. Officials and missionaries believed that banning ceremonies and other practices was one way to encourage assimilation. However, many First Nations continued to conduct potlatches in secret. The law was finally repealed in 1951.

A potlatch gathering was a feast hosted in a family's home. The reason for holding a potlatch varied, depending on the Nation. Sometimes a potlatch was held for a rite of passage, a wedding, or a funeral. Winter was a popular time for potlatches, as the other months of the year were busy with trade and harvesting activities. Potlatches also established relations among Nations and clans, as status was based upon who distributed the most resources.

Potlatches still hold an important place in First Nations societies. They can be big events, with hundreds of guests, or they can be celebrated on a smaller, more local, or family scale. In contemporary potlatches, food is served, songs and dances are performed, and gift-giving patterns are followed. Artwork, blankets, and money are often given to Elders, community leaders, and honoured guests. Potlatches have changed over time—a reminder that cultures are adaptable. Although beliefs and values may change and adapt to external influences, they can still be maintained; in modern powwows, for example, there are giveaways of items to dancers, singers, Elders, and other participants.

FIGURE 3.9 A modern potlatch in Alert Bay near Vancouver Island. Can you name a modern law that bans a cultural practice? How would your family's values, beliefs, and world views be affected if you were forbidden to practise your family celebrations?

©P

The Inuit Seal Hunt

Inuit have always hunted and used seals in a sustainable way. Today, there is a great deal of controversy over hunting seals in Canada, mainly over the commercial seal hunt that takes place on the country's east coast. In 2006, the European Commission called for a ban on the import, export, and sale of all harp and hooded seal products worldwide. Inuit seal hunting, which accounts for three percent of the total hunt in North America, was excluded, but many Inuit worry that further sanctions against seal hunting will prove harmful to their ways of life.

Seal is still used by many Inuit for food, clothing, fuel, and tools. Today, some seal products are also distributed through companies and co-ops to be sold to others. Inuit hunters, designers, and craftspeople also take part in the fashion industry in Canada, using traditional products and styles to create clothing made of fur, leather, and sealskin.

Inuit hunt adult seals and use the entire animal. They do not hunt the seals in massive numbers, which would cause depletion. In fact, the Nunavut Wildlife Management Board monitors the hunting of seals as well as other wildlife in Nunavut.

However, animal rights groups such as the International Fund for Animal Welfare (IFAW) draw little distinction between commercial seal hunts and Inuit hunts. While these groups focus their protest on the hunt of baby seals on Canada's east coast, the protests encourage the ban of all seal products, including those produced by Inuit.

THINKING IT THROUGH

1. One reason given for banning the potlatch was that it was "wasteful." What world view might that be from? How does this differ from the world views of those practising the potlatch?

2. How can values about sustaining the environment be accommodated in modern industries?

3. Do some web research on the controversy of the Inuit seal hunt. Find several articles by different publications with different perspectives on the hunt. What economic consequences are there for Inuit, even if they are not included in the ban? Why do you think the use of fur in fashion creates controversy? What is your viewpoint regarding the Inuit seal hunt?

FIGURE 3.10 Designer Karliin Aariak models one of her sealskin jackets.

Asking Questions

As a student, you are probably more familiar with answering questions than asking them. However, asking questions is a way to focus your study and to apply critical thinking skills. There are many different types of questions that you can ask.

Factual Questions	Factual questions usually require simple, straightforward answers.	Example: Who is affected by this mine?
Opinion Questions	Opinion questions can have more than one answer. They may ask someone to provide expert judgement and can bring out different perspectives on a topic.	Example: Which option is better: a road blockade, or a protest march?
Research Questions	Research questions will help you find answers more quickly.	Example: What are some of the issues regarding the use of resources in Canada today?
Critical Thinking Questions	Critical thinking questions can help you see beyond what you are reading on the page. These types of questions will also help you understand different perspectives. You will begin to form your own point of view and learn to defend it while discovering what you think and why.	Example: How can some of the values that Aboriginal peoples hold regarding the land help address environmental concerns?

Apply Your Skills

1. Choose a person or topic you have read about in this book. Write six questions for which you would like to know the answers.

   a) What types of questions would you find most useful?

   b) Which question do you consider to be the most important? Explain.

2. Use the questions you created in Question 1 to do some additional research on the person or topic. Make short journal entries to explain how the questions helped guide your research. Did the questions change as you went along? Why or why not?

The Modern Economy

The Dominion of Canada was created in 1867, and consisted of the provinces of Québec, New Brunswick, Nova Scotia, and Ontario. More settlers began to arrive, and the economy moved away from the fur trade and into farming, commerce, and manufacturing. As the focus shifted from the fur trade, the situation of Aboriginal peoples was also altered. First Nations people were placed on reserve lands during the treaty process, which you will learn more about in Chapter 7. The Métis lost their lands as what would become the provinces of Manitoba, Saskatchewan, and Alberta were settled by newcomers. And beginning in the 1950s, many Inuit were relocated from their traditional lands to permanent settlement in small communities in the North. These events reduced access that Aboriginal peoples had to the lands that supported their lives and their economies. The questions of who owned the lands and who had the right to harvest natural resources would also be complicated by expanding treaty agreements, changing federal and provincial policies, and different world views. Unquestionably, as Canada moved into the 20th century, the economic activities of Aboriginal peoples would undergo great change.

WORDS MATTER

mixed economy an economy in which income derives from a variety of sources, including private enterprise, government assistance or subsidies, and activities such as hunting and fishing (which provide food and other materials)

Changing Economies

Now facing a more limited land base and fewer resources, Aboriginal peoples sought new ways to support themselves, and for the most part, First Nations, Métis, and Inuit peoples across Canada took part in **mixed economies.** Economic activities such as agriculture, trapping, hunting, fishing, and harvesting wild rice were mixed with newer sources of income such as seasonal employment, the production of crafts or other products such as canoes, and, when necessary, social assistance. Other sources of income included the commercial fishery, guiding, high-steel work (on bridges or skyscrapers) and mining. Some Aboriginal men joined the Canadian army or the navy. As Aboriginal communities developed, residents also worked to improve their economic situation by lobbying governments about land use, or asking for compensation for resource extraction on their lands.

Most First Nations maintained their rights to hunt and fish on the land after signing treaties with the government of Canada. They were able to hunt and fish on Crown lands, but these areas were constantly being reduced as new settlers bought land. When the Natural Resources Transfer Act was passed in 1930, it transferred the management and revenue of natural resources from the federal government to the provinces. The provinces had no treaty agreements on hunting and fishing with First Nations peoples, and new game laws resulted in challenges to hunting rights or in some cases legal action. As you read in Chapter 2, First Nations trappers would also be required to get licenses for their trap lines, although they and their families had trapped in those areas for generations.

FIGURE 3.11 A Mohawk iron worker connector climbs a steel beam for a new skyscraper.

The Development of Communities

The British North America Act, 1867 and the Indian Act, 1876 outlined ways in which the First Nations were to be treated by the Crown. The Indian Act did not include the Métis and Inuit, however, so First Nations, Métis, and Inuit communities developed in different ways.

Métis Communities

The Métis regarded themselves as a Nation, a blending of two cultures that incorporated economies such as farming, bison hunting in the West, and the fur trade. The Métis were not granted land or support through treaties, resulting in many cases of poverty and the disintegration of farming communities. Eventually some land in the West was set aside and allocated under a **scrip** system. This system was by most accounts abused by land speculators who bought scrip for a fraction of its real value, then sold the land to settlers at a profit. In the end, only about one quarter of the land set aside within the scrip system was actually occupied by Métis.

Many Métis remained in areas that later developed into towns or cities. In Ontario, these communities included Sault Ste. Marie, Penetanguishene, and Timmins. They and their descendants would make a living through seasonal work, fishing and hunting, employment in forestry or mining, or operating their own businesses.

In 1896, the federal government set aside 37 000 hectares of farm land for Métis people near St. Paul, Alberta. Each family was to receive 32 hectares as well as livestock and equipment. Thirty Métis families from across Alberta and Saskatchewan moved to Saint Paul des Métis in the first year. However, the promised livestock and equipment did not arrive. Families drifted away, and rather than continue as farmers, the Métis went north to hunt, trap, and fish again.

Farming Communities

Farming had long been a way of life for First Nations such as the Wendat and the Haudenosaunee, who grew crops such as beans, corn, and squash.

FIGURE 3.12 Wahta Mohawk Territory was first developed as a farming community in the 1880s. It is now home to the Iroquois Cranberry Growers, Ontario's largest cranberry farm.

The Mississaugas of the New Credit

The Mississaugas of the New Credit originally lived on the northern shore of Lake Huron, moving closer to fishing grounds from early spring until late fall, and living in urban centres in the winter months.

From the mid- to late 1600s, the Mississaugas allied with the French. During this period, the Mississaugas also allied with the Ojibwe, Odawa, and Potawatomi in order to resist Haudenosaunee attempts to take over their lands. This alliance was later known as the Three Fires Confederacy. The Mississaugas later split into two groups, one going east to the Bay of Quinte, and the second south, to land near the Holland and Humber Rivers. The southern group then split again, with one group moving toward the Trent River, and the other moving west toward Toronto and Lake Erie, to become the direct ancestors of the present Mississaugas of the New Credit.

Between 1700 and 1800, the French built fur-trading posts and extended trading credit to the Mississaugas, giving the name "Credit River" to the main river in the area. As European settlement expanded, the Mississaugas were forced to move further inland to hunt and fish, and some of their lands were given to the Six Nations by the British colonial government.

In the 1800s, the British government gave exclusive fishing and hunting rights to the Mississaugas, who then added a prosperous salmon fishery to their successful farming operations. From the late 1820s to the 1840s, the community was almost entirely self-sufficient. However, it became more and more difficult for the Mississaugas to thrive among the growing settlements, and they were eventually forced to accept an offer of land from the Six Nations at Grand River.

Today, the Mississaugas of the New Credit live on the tract of land offered to them by the Six Nations and in the townships of Oneida and Tuscarora. There are approximately 1788 band members, but nearly half of the population lives off-reserve due to an inadequate land base, lack of available housing, and lack of employment opportunities. In 2010, the Nation voted to accept a $145 million settlement for lands lost 200 years before, land now within the Greater Toronto Area.

- Research the 2010 settlement reached by the Mississaugas of the New Credit and the government. What does the deal involve? Speculate what the deal might mean to this community and other communities in southern Ontario in the future.

In the 1800s and 1900s, the federal government began promoting farming as a means of support for First Nations living on reserve lands. This plan met with mixed success.

In many cases, farm equipment and livestock were part of treaty agreements, as First Nations leaders recognized the need for new sources of income and food for their peoples. For example, in Treaty 6, which covered lands in Alberta and Saskatchewan, the government agreed to deliver farming equipment, supplies, and livestock. However, many First Nations farmers in the West were not successful due to lack of proper equipment, rules that limited the sale of their crops, and other factors.

In southern Ontario, farming became an important economic activity in communities such as Wahta Mohawk Territory, near Georgian Bay. Mohawk families had moved to the area from Kanehsatake, Québec, in the

1880s. They cleared the land and established small farms from three to eight hectares in size. They grew crops such as corn, and raised livestock, including cattle and chickens.

Urban Settings

First Nations, Métis, and Inuit people living in urban areas typically have more employment and educational opportunities. Life expectancy is also higher. Across Canada, urban Aboriginal populations are growing. Statistics Canada indicates that in 2006, 54% of First Nations, Métis, and Inuit people in Canada lived in an urban centre, which was an increase from 50% in 1996. However, populations of Aboriginal people within urban areas are also very mobile, and numbers are constantly changing as

COMMUNITY CLOSE-UP

Alert Bay

The community of Alert Bay is on Cormorant Island, off the northeast coast of Vancouver Island, within the territory of the 'Namgis First Nation. In 1870, two settlers, Wesley Spencer and Aulden Huson, established a small fish saltery in Alert Bay. They convinced many 'Namgis to relocate in order to provide labour for the saltery. A community of both settlers and First Nations people soon developed. By 1896, Kwakwaka'wakw women also worked for the Alert Bay Canning Company.

Fishing was and still is the mainstay of the community. Salmon and halibut, herring roe, rockfish, crab, urchin, geoduck, prawns, and clams are harvested. Fishing for a living, as well as fishing for food, has been at the core of the culture and economy of the 'Namgis for thousands of years. However, new developments in the fishing industry have created long-term challenges for the 'Namgis First Nation.

Bill Cranmer, Chief Councillor and Hereditary Chief of the 'Namgis First Nation, has been a leader in the battle against open-net fish farms since the 1980s. The primary concerns of the 'Namgis include the increase of transport traffic in the waterways, overfishing, and pollution. They also want sustainable livelihoods in the local fishing industry under their own management and care.

FIGURE 3.13 Chief Cranmer delivers an eviction notice to fish-farm owners as part of a First Nations demonstration against aquaculture in 2003.

QUESTIONS

1. Discuss the pattern of growth for the community of Alert Bay. What was the driving force behind settlement? Is this the case for all urban communities? Explain.

2. Why are the 'Namgis opposed to open-net fish farms? What alternatives could help solve the problems associated with fish farms?

©P

people move around within urban areas or between urban areas and reserves. This can make it harder for Aboriginal peoples to access services for housing, health, and education.

Urban communities also have a need for organizations that help revive and revitalize Aboriginal cultures within diverse populations. While there are advantages to living closer to schools and jobs, there are also challenges related to loss of connections to the land, to languages, and to traditions. Organizations such as friendship centres can help Aboriginal people living in urban areas across Canada to meet those challenges. These centres nurture community renewal, providing First Nations, Métis, and Inuit people access to cultural and recreation programs, language training, and skills training. Some centres also organize community events throughout the year.

Remote Communities in the North

Remote northern communities present unique challenges to economic development. The federal government had very little presence in the North until the mid-1900s, with the construction of radar lines (the DEW line) during World War II and the subsequent Cold War. Prior to this time, contact was limited to the RCMP, missionaries, whalers, and traders.

When change came, it came very quickly. Inuit families accustomed to travelling and gathering at specific times were now encouraged to settle in permanent towns. Within a few decades, many Inuit were living in prefabricated "matchbox" houses shipped in from the South. Schools, nursing stations, and churches were also built. Electricity and equipment such as snowmobiles were introduced.

Faced with a sudden change in their way of life, many Inuit looked for new ways to support themselves and their families. Occasional employment with the RCMP or in resource development augmented trapping, hunting, and fishing. In the late 1950s, cooperatives began to form in various Inuit communities as a way for local people to share resources and make a living. Inuit-owned and -operated cooperatives were (and still are) very successful. The first cooperative was the George River Eskimo Fishermen's Cooperative, which supported the local fishing economy by renting a freezer and marketing to the South. Within 10 years, the cooperative had expanded into timber and the arts and crafts industries, and had also built a co-op store where local people could purchase goods, gasoline, and other items.

Changes to Transportation

The First Nations, Métis, and Inuit peoples of Canada had provided means of travel for early explorers and traders, who quickly adopted the birchbark canoe, the toboggan, and the snowshoe. Prior to the 1870s, the main mode of long-distance transportation for both people and goods was by water. Canoes and boats were an integral part of the fur trade, carrying furs, goods, and people across the continent. However, developing economies needed new infrastructure. Canoes and boats were

FIGURE 3.14 Bison bones gathered in a train yard in Saskatchewan. How did changes in transportation affect the bison in the West?

replaced by steamships, then by trains. The advent of the car resulted in road-building, and air transportation also became more common into the 20th century. As with other technological advances, new modes of transportation came with great cost.

The Railway

The creation of railways in Canada was a major contributor to economic growth and settlement. Railways meant that resources and goods could be transported more quickly and they opened up remote areas to forestry and mining. Railways also linked isolated settlements to major cities and towns, and populations boomed.

However, railway building in Canada had major impacts on First Nations and Métis peoples. Land used for the construction of railways was often taken without the consent of Aboriginal peoples. Railways also brought more settlers, increasing conflicts over land. On the Prairies, the railways expanded the trade of bison meat, hides, and bones. Traders no longer had to rely on Plains Nations and Métis to process and transport bison hides. Larger numbers of bison were killed, and overhunting devastated the ways of life of many Plains Nations and the Métis. In British Columbia, the construction of the railway along the Fraser and Thompson Rivers damaged or destroyed rivers, affecting those First Nations that relied on fishing.

The transcontinental railway was built to connect the east and west coasts of Canada, increasing the country's political and economic powers. The government gained greater control of land and resources and increased trade. For settlers, the railway represented civilization, progress, and a new life in the West. For First Nations and Métis, it represented the loss of their lands and their ways of life.

Air Travel

For the First Nations, Métis, and Inuit peoples who live in remote communities, transportation is vital. Air transportation has been beneficial in many ways, as it provides access to even the most rural and remote communities. It also enables these communities to bring in supplies and services that were previously inaccessible to them. Several small airlines operate in northern areas, such as Air Creebec (page 102).

However, air travel to and from remote communities is very expensive, and is therefore not available to everyone; goods shipped in by air are also highly priced.

Accessibility to goods and services has had an impact on ways of life. In the North, some communities have struggled with health problems related to a diet of processed "southern foods." Hunters who once used dogsleds may now opt to use snowmobiles to travel, which in turn means paying for expensive gas and repairs.

VOICES OF THE PEOPLES

The Métis dominated all parts of the western transportation system. They were the teamsters and harness makers. They were the contractors and employees of the first northwestern postal system. They carried the mail by canoe, by cart, by dog sled, and on horseback. They were the riverboat pilots, stevedores, and crewmen on the great river systems of the Northwest. Almost every ferry across the western rivers was Métis-owned and operated. Gabriel Dumont, although better known as a great buffalo hunter and military general, operated a ferry at Gabriel's Crossing.

—*Lawrence Barkwell,*
Métis author

©P

Modern Industrial Development

The scale and pace of change brought about by **industrialization** have had both positive and negative effects on the economies of First Nations, Métis, and Inuit peoples in Canada. Modern industrial development was aided by several factors, including developing mines, lumber operations, fish canning, and farming, aided by advances in technology.

While industrial development also meant the creation of jobs and further economic opportunities for Aboriginal peoples, the negative effects of large-scale resource extraction were soon felt. Pollution, cutting roads through hunting territories, and lack of consultation with Aboriginal peoples regarding activity on their lands created lasting social, economic, and health issues. Some communities faced industrial development on a large scale, and for many it suddenly became difficult to live in that kind of environment. In 1970, the Anishinaabe community of Grassy Narrows First Nation, Ontario, hit the news after it was revealed that a nearby pulp and paper mill had dumped mercury-contaminated effluent into the Wabigoon River. Residents of Grassy Narrows began experiencing neurological problems. These problems are still present today.

WORDS MATTER

industrialization the increased development of industry such as large-scale manufacturing, forestry, or mining

CRITICAL THINKING

In your view, do people living in remote northern communities gain or lose quality of life when economic developments such as mining happen in their community?

Web Connect • • • • • • • • • • • •

To learn more about Grassy Narrows, visit our website.

FIGURE 3.15 Sea lifts, which are ocean-going freight vessels, and barges, such as this one on the Mackenzie River, are still used to ship goods to northern communities. Will developments in northern industries change this in the future? Explain why or why not.

THINKING IT THROUGH

1. What effect do you think the rapid change brought by development has had on the world views of Aboriginal peoples?

2. First Nations, Métis, and Inuit peoples are not well represented in planning and managing jobs in resource industries such as mining and forestry. How might this lack of input from Aboriginal peoples affect the choices made by companies in these industries? How might more Aboriginal people become involved in these leadership roles?

Aboriginal Resurgence

Rapid industrial development and increased harvesting of resources have resulted in First Nations, Métis, and Inuit peoples becoming more involved in not only what happens on their lands, but also how they may benefit fairly from those developments. Aboriginal peoples have begun to stand up for their rights to good health and a fair share of wealth from lands and resources, using the courts, the media, and the Internet to make their voices heard.

At the same time, Aboriginal peoples have begun to take control by creating their own businesses, fighting for agreements to share resource benefits, and applying their beliefs and values to their own economic development.

FIGURE 3.16 Lucien Wabanonik, Grand Chief of the Tribal Council of the Algonquin Nation, delivers a speech after representatives of the Algonquin Anishinaabe marched on Parliament Hill in Ottawa, April 21, 2010, disputing property and land rights with the federal government.

> We...the Lubicon Lake Nation, are tired. We are frustrated and angry... Our children have nothing—they can't breathe—even that has been taken... When we were young and lived in the bush—it was a good life. Now, we have no traplines, nothing to hunt. There are no jobs, no money to live a decent life... We are people just like you. We are equal. We have every right to be here... We have lost more...than you can imagine, our way of life that we loved, our culture, our beautiful land, our health, our happiness. What else can we lose?... We demand an end to the invasion and devastation to all spheres of our lives... We demand control over our lives once again.
>
> —*Lubicon Lake Nation Women's Circle (1992)*

Sector Development

In the 1970s and 1980s, thriving sectors attracted workers across Canada. There was an oil boom in Alberta, greater forestry exports in British Columbia, and increased fishing exports in Nova Scotia. This expansion drove population growth, which in turn boosted the production of goods and services. Some First Nations, Métis, and Inuit communities also underwent rapid development, commercialization, and change.

Many First Nations, Métis, and Inuit people have sought employment in emerging sectors, usually through seasonal or yearly contracts. However, lack of professional training for Aboriginal people has resulted in limited involvement at management levels. Although the number of First Nations, Métis, and Inuit people with formal education has increased, most still work as labourers or seasonal workers. Increasingly, specialized training and mentoring programs have become part of agreements negotiated between Aboriginal peoples and corporations. These programs can include job shadowing, firefighting and truck-driving courses, and medical training.

©P

Becoming more involved in sector planning gives Aboriginal communities more opportunities for communication and cooperation, including increased protection of their traditions, beliefs, values, and lands.

Business Development

Many Aboriginal people own and operate businesses involving resource development and sustainability. Respect for the land does not disallow making a living from the land—but it should be done responsibly.

The challenges involved in developing various resources while maintaining rights to the land and its resources are complex. Still, First Nations, Métis, and Inuit peoples insist on being consulted on projects, especially those that involve **ecological concerns**. Many support the creation of partnerships among Aboriginal peoples, corporations, and governments. By making these challenges public and by being proactive, Aboriginal peoples are trying to ensure the success of their communities both in the present and in the future.

WORDS MATTER

ecological concerns pollution, displacement of species, soil erosion, loss of natural habitats caused by industrial growth and development

Ways of Knowing

Traditional Practices in a Modern Economy: Wild Rice Harvesting

Traditionally, harvesting wild rice was a very social activity. Families would set up camps along waterways where the rice grew, and everyone helped with the gathering and storing of the rice, which is actually the seed of a wild grass. The Ojibwe name is kagiwiosa manomin (good berry).

To harvest the time-honoured way, one person is in charge of manoeuvring the canoe through the tall grasses, while the other person uses two sticks to collect the rice—one to gently bend the stalk over the canoe and the other to tap the stalks and gently loosen the ripe kernels. This process must be done carefully in order not to break the stalks, which will continue to yield more rice. The wild rice must be dried soon after the harvest to prevent mould. Once it is dry, the rice is hulled to remove the chaff from the kernel. The methods of hulling are thrashing the kernel with a stick, churning, or treading on the kernels. Before storing the rice, the harvesters must separate the broken pieces of chaff from the kernels.

The rice could be stored in animal-skin bags, birchbark containers, or woven baskets.

In contrast, non-traditional rice harvesting involves collecting the rice mechanically while a boat is driven at about 20 kilometres per hour through the grass. This method allows a single person to harvest more rice at a faster rate.

FIGURE 3.17 Harvesting wild rice using traditional methods. Based on this photograph, describe the sustainability of this method.

Sustainable Development

Sustainable development advocates the use of resources in a way that meets human needs while also preserving the environment—so that needs can be met both in the present and the future. This idea became popular in the 1970s, and is still widely used today. However, this concept has been around since the beginning of time for many Aboriginal peoples, and is the Seven Generations Teaching of the Anishinaabe and Haudenosaunee.

For First Nations, Métis, and Inuit peoples, sustainable development considers the following key aspects:

- Earth is a life-giving force that is to be respected.

- There is a time and season for all activities.

- Take only what you need.

- Balance is needed among the four basic elements of nature: air, which provides life; earth, which provides life-sustaining resources and food; fire, which provides heat and light; and water, which makes life and growth possible.

- Everyone and every thing has a place and a role, and no person, animal, or thing is to be taken for granted.

These aspects of sustainable development are essential in creating a world that can provide for everyone—now, and in the future.

VOICES OF THE PEOPLES

The Tsilhqot'in Nation is neither against development nor against the responsible use of natural resources. In fact, as traditional keepers of the land for thousands of years, we have successfully balanced the need for sustainable harvesting with long-term preservation. To the Tsilhqot'in people, the destruction of Teztan Biny is an unacceptable use of land and water, incompatible with modern principles of sustainability, and an ill-conceived and short-sighted attempt to inject an industrial project into the heart of our pristine watershed.

—*statement from the Tsilhqot'in Nation*

FIGURE 3.18 Teztan Biny, also known as Fish Lake, is located in southwestern British Columbia. It is home to 80 000 genetically unique wild lake trout. It is currently under threat due to the development of a mine.

Pikangikum First Nation

Pikangikum is an Anishinaabe community north of Kenora, Ontario. With a population of about 2300, it has one of the highest rates of first language use of any First Nation in Northern Ontario.

The Whitefeather Forest Initiative is an economic development program focusing on renewal and resource stewardship. With the province of Ontario, Pikangikum manages the Whitefeather Forest— 12 200 square kilometres of Crown land in the Pikangikum land-use area.

The community completed its Land Use Strategy, entitled "Keeping the Land," in 2006. The strategy was created to provide guidance for the management of commercial forestry, protected areas, and **eco-cultural tourism**. Rooted in the traditional ecological knowledge of the people of Pikangikum, the "Keeping the Land" strategy is made up of three parts:

- Stewardship Strategy—an obligation to respect all living beings

- Customary Activities—the physical, mental, and spiritual states of well-being necessary to support oneself on the land

- Economic Development—activities adapted to customary stewardship approaches in order to provide for the Pikangikum people

This initiative is an example of how Aboriginal communities are taking part in current development

FIGURE 3.19 Alec Suggashie is the Senior Translator for Whitefeather Forest Management Corporation.

projects, while at the same time providing for sustainable practices that respect the land and maintain core values.

QUESTION

1. Do the three key components in the "Keeping the Land" strategy fit with what you have learned about how Aboriginal peoples value the land and the environment? Why or why not?

Conflicts Over Resources

While in some cases Aboriginal perspectives and rights have been acknowledged, various levels of government in Canada, large corporations, and private enterprises continue to exploit resources on lands meant for the sole use of First Nations and Inuit peoples.

Oil, Gas, and Timber on Lubicon Land

The Lubicon Lake Cree Nation, near Peace River, Alberta, has a population of about 500. The Nation's culture is based on hunting and trapping. The

WORDS MATTER

eco-cultural tourism responsible and sustainable travel to natural areas and places of cultural interest

FIGURE 3.20 A protest outside the TransCanada Pipeline annual general meeting in Calgary, 2008. A rally was held against a new pipeline that would cross Lubicon land.

CRITICAL THINKING

Many judges in Alberta's provincial courts are former oil-company lawyers. How do you think this fact could affect the ability of the Lubicon Lake Cree Nation to stop development on its territory?

federal government admits that the Lubicon were overlooked when Treaty 8 was signed in 1899; as a result, the Lubicon have never given up the rights to their land.

Since the 1970s, oil and forestry companies have removed oil, gas, and timber from Lubicon land without the band's consent, seriously affecting the Lubicon way of life. Income for the average trapper has dropped to only $400 per year, and the number of moose killed for food has also dropped. As a result, 90 percent of the Lubicon are on welfare.

In 1990, the United Nations charged Canada with a human rights violation, stating that the government's treatment of the Lubicon "threatens the way of life and culture of the Lubicon Lake Cree" and violates Article 27 of the International Covenant on Civil and Political Rights. In a 1998 court case, a judge stated that the Lubicon situation was "intolerable." Still, oil, gas, and logging companies continue to operate on Lubicon land while the Lubicon wait for a land-rights settlement and continue to oppose development on their land.

The "KI Six"

In 2008, six residents of the northwestern Ontario community of Kitchenuhmaykoosib Inninuwug ("KI")—Chief Donny Morris, Jack McKay, Sam McKay, Darryl Sainnawap, Cecilia Begg, and Bruce Sakakeep—were given six-month jail sentences for protesting against mining explorations on KI lands. A multinational company called Platinex had obtained a mining permit from the provincial government to explore for platinum, even though the residents of KI had protested against it and demanded to be fairly consulted.

The "KI Six" remained in jail in Thunder Bay for several months. Their case was eventually appealed, and they were released. However, the issue of mining rights and who has the right to grant them had been brought to the forefront. Proposed amendments to the Ontario Mining Act in 2010 would include a system of legislated consultation, requiring mining companies to advise First Nations of their activities, consult with them, and in some cases acquire permission from First Nations to proceed.

Diamonds in the North

The Ekati Diamond Mine, north of Yellowknife, is North America's first commercial diamond mine and the world's third-largest. To mine the diamonds, Broken Hill Proprietary (BHP) drains water from a lake, excavates the rock underneath, and transports the rock to a plant where it is crushed. Over 18 000 tonnes of rock are excavated per day. After the rock is crushed, the diamonds are extracted.

Over 800 people work at the Ekati mine, half of them from First Nations and Inuit communities. However, communities remain divided. For some, employment is the way toward a better future. Others say that drained lakes, roads cutting through caribou migration paths, and pollution will destroy the ecosystem. They believe that the loss of hunting and trapping territories will mean an end to their way of life.

Current Hunting and Fishing Rights

Donald Marshall Jr., a Mi'kmaw from Nova Scotia, was released from prison in 1982 after being wrongfully convicted of murder in 1971. Marshall, who died in August 2009, was fully exonerated in 1990 when a Royal Commission concluded that racism had contributed to his wrongful imprisonment. Marshall then became an advocate for the rights of Mi'kmaq people.

After Donald Marshall was arrested and convicted of fishing for eels out of season in 1996, he petitioned the courts in protest, stating that his Mi'kmaq treaty rights allowed him to catch and sell fish. In 1999, in a landmark ruling, the Supreme Court of Canada ruled that First Nations treaty rights guaranteed First Nations peoples the right to fish and hunt. The ruling also acknowledged and confirmed that Mi'kmaq and Malecite in Nova Scotia and New Brunswick have the right to hunt, fish, and gather in order to earn a living.

Donald Marshall's stand for treaty rights and the Supreme Court of Canada ruling that recognized and guaranteed these rights for First Nations peoples were instrumental in assisting other Nations in securing their rights to continue their way of life in relation to the land.

In 1993, Steve Powley and his son, Roddy, shot a moose outside Sault Ste. Marie. They tagged it with a Métis card and a note: "Harvesting my meat for winter." When the moose was found by conservation officers, the Powleys were charged with harvesting without a licence and "unlawful possession of moose."

The Métis Nation of Ontario decided to take the charges against the Powleys as a test case in establishing Métis hunting rights, and provided political and financial support to the Powleys. In 1998, a trial judge ruled that the Powleys had a right as Métis to hunt—a right protected under Section 35 of the Constitution Act. Charges were dismissed, but the Crown appealed the decision to the Supreme Court of Canada. In a unanimous decision in 2003, the Supreme Court confirmed the existence of Métis communities in Canada and the constitutional protection of their existing Aboriginal rights.

The courts determined that these rights existed not just for hunting, but for any number of historical cultural activities that Métis continue to practise. Since the Powley decision, governments across Canada cannot continue to deny or ignore the existence of Métis rights, and are constitutionally obliged to consult Métis in any instance in which Métis rights may be affected.

FIGURE 3.21 Donald Marshall Jr. also held survival camps in which youth could go onto the land and learn Mi'kmaq cultural ways. How do you think this fits with his defense of fishing rights?

FIGURE 3.22 Steve Powley. How do you think court decisions such as this affect the cultural survival of the Métis?

Values and Business

In the past few centuries, First Nations, Métis, and Inuit peoples have faced many dramatic changes to their ways of life, including the introduction of the concept of personal wealth. Sharing with others has always been an important part of Aboriginal belief systems. The Creator made nature's bounty available to all Aboriginal peoples, to share what they could grow, hunt, or gather from the lands and waters with one another. When newcomers came to the continent looking for wealth and resources, First Nations, Métis, and Inuit became involved in the fur trade. Trade of furs and other products, land, forests, minerals, and other resources soon became sources of wealth for traders and settlers, while First Nations, Métis, and Inuit peoples grew increasingly marginalized in what had once been their exclusive domain.

Today, First Nations, Métis, and Inuit communities and organizations across Canada are working to resolve outstanding land-rights disputes and taking steps to regain control over resources within their traditional territories. This is especially important to First Nations, Métis, and Inuit who have been excluded from economic activities such as forestry and mining on their lands. Some provinces have legislated consultation and resource sharing, which means that companies must first negotiate with First Nations, Métis, and Inuit peoples before conducting activity on their traditional lands, as well as share the profits from those activities. This is a positive sign for future efforts by Aboriginal peoples to gain a foothold in economic activities from which they have previously been excluded.

There are some economic activities from which Aboriginal peoples have not been marginalized or excluded—such as organized gaming. Games of chance have always played a role in Aboriginal cultures, even before contact. These games involved guessing or using dice. Wagers were often made on the outcome, but these were generally made for entertainment rather than for monetary gain. The modern development of casinos and other gambling establishments on several reserves has resulted in considerable revenue for some First Nations communities. Those who support it see it as a source of revenue to obtain much-needed monies for community services. Gambling, however, is seen in a negative light by many other people. One way or another, people often feel very deeply about gambling, and it is important to consider the range of perspectives that people have on the subject.

In Canada, gaming is regulated by provincial and territorial governments, so each province and territory is unique in regard to what it will allow. The governments also negotiate particular agreements with charities and First Nations to allow gaming. In Ontario, bingos, lotteries, betting, and casinos are legal. Casino Rama, based on Rama First Nation near Orillia, generates millions of dollars in revenue every year. In 2010, Rama First Nation and the Ontario Lottery and Gaming Corporation signed a 20-year agreement that will take effect in 2011. Under this deal, the provincial government will receive 20 percent of gross revenues (hundreds of millions of dollars) from all casinos in the province, including Casino Rama. Ontario First Nations will share the net profit from Casino Rama (about $500 million since it opened in 2006), plus 1.7 percent of revenue from all provincial gaming revenue in Ontario, including revenue from other casinos and lotteries.

As a result, millions of dollars will be made available to First Nations in Ontario to fund recreational facilities, cultural centres, education, and health services. Revenue sharing from gaming brings a source of income separate from the funding provided by the federal government. First Nations will be able to choose how and when to spend the money without the oversight in place over federal funding. Needed services and facilities are provided, and jobs are created. Casino Rama alone is one of the largest employers of Aboriginal people in Canada.

Some critics say that, in supporting gaming facilities, provincial governments have made Aboriginal peoples partners in an unsavoury business. Many people—including many First Nations, Métis, and Inuit people—object to gambling on moral or social grounds. They believe that the ends do not justify the means. They point out the problems associated with gambling and the negative impacts on individuals, families, and communities—addictions, depression, loss of property, and lost savings. Small local businesses are also affected. Gambling is also particularly offensive to those who adhere to traditional values of sharing and who shun the accumulation of wealth for its own sake. As well, some see First Nations communities that have casinos as being complicit with the government, enjoying large revenues from an activity that is not sustainable in the traditional sense.

They see economic activities that draw on traditional ecological knowledge as being healthier and more sustainable for their communities.

Similar concerns have been raised about the sale of cigarettes and tobacco products on reserves, which, for some people, goes against traditional values regarding tobacco.

Activities such as gambling, the sale of cigarettes, forestry, and mining all have impacts—sometimes positive, sometimes negative. Many people feel very strongly one way or another. Is it possible to find a "win–win" situation? Can people find a balance between the pros and the cons? For First Nations, Métis, and Inuit peoples in Canada it is also important to find ways to balance their values and beliefs with economic choices.

1. Read the perspectives on gambling on these pages. Then discuss with a partner why you think gambling operations have become a source of revenue and employment for some Aboriginal peoples in Canada. Take into consideration issues surrounding trade, economy, and the use of resources for Aboriginal peoples, which you have already studied in this chapter.

2. Describe the social effects that gambling might have on First Nations communities that have on-reserve gambling establishments. Do the benefits of gambling operations, such as funding for programs or jobs, offset the costs? How might a community offset the negative effects and maximize the return to the community? Explain.

3. Research a First Nations community that has been affected by a large-scale economic activity such as a casino, the cigarette trade, a mine, a factory, or forestry. Explore how that community has dealt with the effects of the activity. Are there more sustainable alternatives? Explain.

4. What might First Nations communities do to ensure the health and well-being of people and communities while still participating in the local, provincial, or national economy?

Web Connect • • • • • • • • • •

To learn more about the Canadian Council for Aboriginal Business, visit our website.

First Nations, Métis, and Inuit Businesses

Many First Nations, Métis, and Inuit people across Canada operate a wide variety of businesses. There are over 27 000 Aboriginal entrepreneurs in Canada. Many of these business owners strive to be inclusive of their community's beliefs and values in relation to the land and the environment. Like all entrepreneurs, they work long hours and face challenges such as developing a customer base and finding skilled employees. However, many face obstacles that are unique to Aboriginal peoples, and some businesses do fail as a result.

Obstacles to Aboriginal Entrepreneurship

Many of the challenges faced by Aboriginal entrepreneurs are unique to their situation. Perhaps they live in an isolated area with a very small customer base, or in an area with few resources and not enough skilled workers. One of the greatest obstacles is difficulty in finding enough money to start a business. Many Aboriginal people are not considered for bank loans because they have few assets and no credit history. If they live on a reserve, they cannot use their property as security for loans, as other business owners can, because under the Indian Act the Crown owns reserve lands and homes. Other obstacles include:

- lack of community support and difficulty finding mentors
- lack of information and training in how to run a business
- complex legal and financial relationships with the government or with their community
- lack of a clear vision or economic plan from their community leaders.

However, these obstacles are not present in every case. There are many programs in place, such as the Canadian Council for Aboriginal Business, that help encourage and educate those interested in starting a business. Many banks now provide a variety of services specific to the needs of First Nations, Métis, and Inuit customers. These include loans, customized services, and flexible solutions for Aboriginal entrepreneurs. There are also banks owned and operated by Aboriginal peoples. The First Nations Bank of Canada, for example, is 80-percent owned by First Nations, Métis, and Inuit shareholders. These and other programs and services are helping to increase the rate of success for Aboriginal entrepreneurs. The examples on the following pages are only a small sample, but illustrate the diversity and success of some Aboriginal enterprises.

FIGURE 3.23 The Business Development Bank of Canada sponsors E-Spirit, an internet-based business plan competition for Aboriginal youth in Canada. Winners of the 2009 E-Spirit competition were these students from Saugeen District Secondary School. What sort of business plan would you like to create?

Birch Bark Canoes by Mahigan

Métis businesses in Ontario often start out as practical solutions to problems or as ways to provide culture-specific services to a wider audience. Self-sufficiency and community are key characteristics of Métis economic development. Many businesses begin as small enterprises meant to sustain the family. Trapping and guiding might evolve into seasonal work, but also into small enterprises that provide a good living. There are many small businesses that start out as a vehicle to share and promote Métis culture.

Marcel Labelle is a proud Métis whose personal business, Birch Bark Canoes by Mahigan, has been in operation since 2004. The Métis Nation of Ontario helped Labelle get his business started with a Métis Culture-Based Economic Development Grant. While the core of his business is about reconnecting with the craft of building birchbark canoes, it also demonstrates the ingenuity, simplicity, and beauty of Métis culture.

Labelle comes by his entrepreneurial spirit honestly, as part of a long line of trappers and fur buyers in the Mattawa area, north of what is now Algonquin Park. An education with his family on the trapline taught him to be a responsible steward of the land and water. As important as these lessons in sustainability were, it also gave him a deep spiritual connection to the concept of living a good life. As an adult, this spiritual connection took him from employment on a factory floor to an epic journey across the land. It was not a decision made lightly. He had a family to care for, and he would have to leave a well-paying, secure union job. However, the job "didn't feel right." Labelle travelled from Ontario to British Columbia as part of a vision quest to leave tobacco in the mountains he had dreamed about.

The story of Birch Bark Canoes by Mahigan is one of being true to yourself and finding a way to move from talking about doing something to actually doing it. Labelle's business is a product of his experience as a trapper, as president of the Mattawa and Area Trappers Council, and as one of the founders of Fur Harvesters Auction Inc., based in North Bay—the only fur auction jointly owned by Aboriginal and non-Aboriginal people. It is this variety of experience that has shaped his views on what makes a successful business. According to Labelle, "It isn't the money." After a presentation he sees "that glow in the eyes of children as they listen to the wood speak as it splits." He enjoys talking to the children afterwards and "having them come up…and ask me for a hug." After all, he says, "When I grew up it wasn't popular to be Métis." Labelle is passing on his craftsmanship to his family, and in 10 years he hopes to train enough people to build a 10-metre canoe and perhaps paddle with the Haida.

FIGURE 3.24 Demand for Marcel Labelle's canoes comes from around the world. While birchbark canoes are his business, Labelle also speaks at schools about the importance of Métis and First Nations cultures.

REFLECTION

The motto of the Great Spirit Circle Trail is "Experience the past and enjoy the present." How does this show harmony between values and the tourism business?

FIGURE 3.25 Albert Diamond, former president and CEO of Air Creebec

FIGURE 3.26 Dawn Madahbee, of the Aundeck Omni Kaning First Nation on Manitoulin Island, is General Manager of the Waubetek Business Development Corporation. This organization provides business financing to Aboriginal entrepreneurs and 27 First Nations throughout northeastern Ontario. She first gained business experience in her family's store, and is the first Aboriginal woman in Canada to lead a regional financial lending institution.

Tourism: The Great Spirit Circle Trail

Owned and operated by eight First Nations communities on Manitoulin Island and in the Sagamok region in northwestern Ontario, the Great Spirit Circle Trail offers nature-based cultural tourism through retreats, cruises, theatre, and hikes. The experiences reflect the First Nations history and culture of the region. The organization has been recognized as one of the 28 Significant Aboriginal Tourism Organizations by the Canadian Tourism Association and Aboriginal Tourism Canada.

Air Creebec

Originally a partnership between the Cree Nation of Québec and Austin Airways, Air Creebec began operation in 1982, providing air transportation to the people of Eeyou Itschee within the region and to southern communities. An original workforce of 17 people has now grown to almost 200. The airline provides freight transportation and passenger flights, and is offering charter flights to take advantage of growing tourism in the area. Air Creebec is now wholly owned by the Cree Nation.

Inuit Communications Systems Ltd.

Inuit Communications Systems Ltd. (ICSL) has provided audio and video production services for government, industry, and education sectors since 1982. Staff in Iqaluit and Ottawa provide audio files, video editing, video production, television production, and camera crews for clients from Canada, Japan, Britain, and the United States. Operating in English, Inuinaqtun, and Inuktitut, ICSL has created commercials and documentaries for major television networks. It also provides stock footage of political events, northern communities, people, and aspects of northern life. ICSL is 100 percent Inuit-owned, and profits are reinvested into northern economic and cultural development. Its mandate is to adapt the latest communications technologies to link northern communities to each other and the world.

THINKING IT THROUGH

1. Using research if necessary, make a list of Aboriginal-run businesses that relate to the land and have a sustainable approach (for example, wind power, eco-tourism, food products from the land).

2. In your own Nation or community, could you envision businesses that use resources without being destructive to the environment? Explain.

3. How could businesses be developed that fit with First Nations, Métis, or Inuit values and identity?

©P

Trading on the Arts

One of the most significant aspects of economic industry involving First Nations, Métis, and Inuit people is the art industry. Paintings, prints, soapstone sculptures, as well as cultural items such as dream catchers, masks, and mukluks are valuable **commodities** today.

Some of these items have become available in retail stores, and both Aboriginal and non-Aboriginal people make a profit from the sales. Some stores sell products that look like Aboriginal items, but are not actually made by Aboriginal people and may not be authentic at all. Some are even made in other countries by people who are only copying Aboriginal crafts.

Some significant cultural items are sold without the full teachings that should accompany them. Many gift shops, for example, sell drums. Drum teachings vary from Nation to Nation, but many First Nations believe that the drum was brought to the people by a woman and that this gift helps First Nations men remember and respect their connection to the earth. People who purchase drums may not receive these teachings.

The positive side to the popularity of cultural items is the promotion and sharing of First Nations, Métis, and Inuit cultures and practices. While some Aboriginal people sell their products at gatherings, such as powwows, others have contracts with retailers, and many have created websites to promote and sell their products. Others have organized cooperatives, which provide the artists with a way to control their own products and their economic choices. Some cooperatives, such as the one in Belcher Islands, not only sell the soapstone carvings of their artists, but also mine and process the soapstone.

FIGURE 3.27 Does the mass-production of objects such as dream catchers lessen the importance of the objects?

COMMUNITY CLOSE-UP

Cape Dorset

Cape Dorset is an Inuit community on Baffin Island. The self-declared "Capital of Inuit Art," Cape Dorset is also home to the West Baffin Eskimo Co-operative (WBEC). Art cooperatives are owned and operated by their members. Cooperatives such as the one in Cape Dorset support a community of artists.

In Cape Dorset, the WBEC is locally known as Kinngait Co-operative and is unique among cooperatives in the Arctic for its sustained focus on the arts. There are two printmaking studios for stonecut and lithography, as well as a carving operation. The cooperative's most enduring contribution to both the community of Cape Dorset and the world beyond has been the prints and carvings produced by its extraordinary artists.

FIGURE 3.28 Kenojuak Ashevak is an internationally acclaimed Inuk artist in Cape Dorset. The cooperative has been producing the work of local artists since the 1950s. How do art cooperatives encompass and honour the art and artists?

Music and Literature

Cultural items are not the only things being created and distributed by Aboriginal peoples. Literature written, published, and sold by Aboriginal peoples can be found in friendship centres, online, and at bookstores all across the country, including large chain stores. First Nations, Métis, and Inuit people also publish magazines, newspapers, and journals in English, French, and their first languages.

First Nations, Inuit, and Métis music flourishes in today's music industry. Singing and drumming have always been used in social events, in ceremonies, for personal recreation, and for healing. Festivals and powwows showcase artists, Métis fiddlers, Inuit throat-singers, drummers, country music artists, pop artists, and hip-hop artists. The diversity within their work has a wide appeal to many different audiences, and Aboriginal music has become very marketable. Prominent Aboriginal singers, songwriters, and musicians include Buffy Sainte-Marie, Kashtin, Robbie Robertson, Susan Aglukark, and Tom Jackson.

The Canadian Aboriginal Music Awards is currently developed and managed by Aboriginal people across Canada. It has a mission not only to showcase and develop Canadian Aboriginal artists, but also to acknowledge and honour the keepers, teachers, promoters, creators, and performers of Aboriginal music.

FIGURE 3.29 Two books from Pemmican Publications, a publisher in Winnipeg, Manitoba. Pemmican produces books in Michif, English, and French. Why is it important to produce books about cultures and languages?

FIGURE 3.30 Buffy Sainte-Marie (left) continues to contribute to the music scene, winning an Aboriginal Music Award in 2009. First Nations folk and blues group Digging Roots (right) has toured Europe and North America, and won a Juno Award in 2010.

1. Some Aboriginal people object to having their cultural items sold as products for decoration or entertainment, without the proper cultural teachings that usually accompany the items. What do you think about this issue?

2. Many companies sell copies of Aboriginal cultural items for profit. Sometimes these products are not made in a way that honours traditions. Do you think that Aboriginal peoples should have control over the use of their cultural traditions and the use of their cultural imagery? How could this be done?

3. Canadian artists have copyright over the images and objects they create. Aboriginal artists may discover that their objects have been copied and sold without their permission. Should copyright laws be enforced when the rights of Aboriginal artists are being violated in such a way?

Conclusion

In this chapter you have read about economy, trade, and resource use from Aboriginal perspectives. You have also learned that First Nations, Métis, and Inuit peoples have made and continue to make significant contributions to the Canadian economy. Aboriginal peoples in Canada now own successful businesses, help to sustain and manage their lands, and continue to seek control over their lands and resources. Aboriginal peoples also continue to face the challenge of maintaining traditional values and beliefs while being competitive in the economy and making a living.

The relationships that Aboriginal peoples have with the land are contributing factors in trade, resource use, and economic practices. These relationships sustain them in many ways, and are based on respect. But they are also continually challenged by the demands of modern industrial economies, which typically operate in ways contrary to the values and beliefs held by First Nations, Métis, and Inuit peoples.

Still, there are positive changes. Aboriginal peoples are being consulted more and more for their expertise in sustainable practices and environmental knowledge.

CRITICAL THINKING

How can economic growth, trade, and resource development be balanced with the values, beliefs, and aspirations of First Nations, Métis, and Inuit peoples in Canada today?

End-of-Chapter Activities

1. Do you think businesses should consider future generations and their need to have safe and clean water, food, and air? How can businesses operate in a more sustainable way? Explain your thoughts in a short opinion piece.

FIGURE 3.31 The Conserve the Light Gathering in 2009. How do activities such as this connect to some of the key aspects of sustainable development? Give two examples to support your answer.

2. Research the current fur trade in Canada. How does lobbying from animal-rights groups and organizations such as the European Commission affect practices such as seal hunting? Do you think Aboriginal people should continue to sell products made from what they harvest from the water and the land? Explain your views.

3. Research businesses that are owned and operated by a First Nations, Métis, or Inuk person. For example, you could examine businesses in tourism, farming, manufacturing, communications, or consultation. Choose one business and present its products or services by creating a promotional item such as a web page, a flyer, or an advertisement.

4. Research a current conflict over resources and land use such as those found in this chapter. Find different perspectives on the issue and write a set of questions (use the Building Your Skills on page 84 as a reference). Then find the answers to your questions. Consider concepts such as the Seven Generations Teaching, values, and sustainable practices. Summarize how you think this issue could be resolved.

5. There are several dozen art cooperatives in the North. Why do you think art cooperatives are a good model for promoting Aboriginal cultures while creating income for First Nations, Métis, and Inuit people? Research one cooperative and the products produced by its members. Create a presentation about this cooperative.

6. Create a profile of one First Nations, Métis, or Inuk artist who makes his or her living from painting, writing, singing, crafts, architecture, design, or the performing arts. Perhaps it is someone in your community, in a book, or on the Internet. Create a profile of that person and his or her creative work.

©P

Unit 1 Rich Performance Tasks

Choose one or more of the following tasks:

Analyze a Story or Teaching

1. Using available resources—an Elder or Wisdom Keeper, a family member, writings of a First Nations, Métis, or Inuk author, or a reliable website—find one story or teaching that conveys information that you find valuable.

   a) As you search, consider the following: Is the storyteller presenting a First Nations, Métis, or Inuit story? If the storyteller is non-Aboriginal, what perspectives might he or she be bringing to the story? Are there other versions of the story you could consider?

   b) Next, listen to or read the story and think about the information it conveys. What can the story teach you? What does it show about First Nations, Métis, and Inuit world views? Does it tell you anything about First Nations, Métis, or Inuit Identity? Analyze and communicate your findings about the story. Present your analysis in written form, create a visual image, or make a video that communicates the information you can gather from the story.

Write a Report

2. Research a contemporary issue in Canada concerning First Nations, Métis, or Inuit relations with a government or corporation. The issue could, for example, involve mining or forestry on the territory of an Aboriginal Nation, or a partnership between an Aboriginal Nation and a business interest.

   Start by collecting information. Consider the perspectives of your sources. Are the perspectives balanced or can you identify bias? Is the source factual, or does it rely on statements not supported by evidence? After reading at least four sources of information, write an analysis of the issue that clearly states

   a) the issue and who is involved in it

   b) the First Nations, Métis, or Inuit values, beliefs, and aspirations that are affected

   c) the factual information that is available

   d) your opinion on the issue based on your own values about the land, economic factors, and sustainable environmental practices. Use your findings to create a balanced report on the facts.

   Create an outline for a report on the topic and show it to another student for feedback. Next, write a rough draft and have someone proofread it for you before you complete the report.

Make a Visual Presentation

3. Look at initiatives that reconnect First Nations, Métis, and Inuit students with the land (for example, land-based teaching camps). Also look at urban initiatives that reconnect First Nations, Métis, and Inuit peoples with Elders and Wisdom Keepers who pass on traditional knowledge and survival skills (programs in friendship centres, for example). Choose one of these initiatives and think about the following: How could youth be re-engaged with teachings about the land? How could they learn from Elders and Wisdom Keepers? How could the community ensure that Aboriginal perspectives about the land are available to its youth?

   Once you have decided which initiative in your community works, write a one-paragraph description of the program. Then make a visual presentation using a poster, pamphlet, or magazine spread to promote the initiative. Ensure that the perspectives of First Nations, Métis, and Inuit peoples are highlighted in your visual.

Diverse Identities

Young Métis and the Métis Youth Council are a growing part of the Métis Nation. What do you think the Youth Council means to council members and to other Métis? What role might the youth play?

©P

What ideas about Inuit identities does this artwork suggest to you?

Diane M. Kelly's roles have included lawyer, Grand Chief of Treaty 3, member of the Midewiwin, and pipe carrier.

IDENTITY IS AN EXPLORATION of the questions "Who am I?" and "Who are we?" For First Nations, Métis, and Inuit peoples, identity takes into account individual identity, identity in family and community roles, identity in Nations, past and present challenges to identity, and both the great diversity and the great resilience of Aboriginal identities.

CHAPTER 4

Identities: Realities and Perceptions

When you no longer go around accounting for yourself, making yourself understood, justifying your existence, when you no longer feel an alien anywhere, you've come home. You know who you are.

—*Wilfred Pelletier, Odawa educator, 1973*

FIGURE 4.1 What stereotypes about Aboriginal peoples do you recognize in this image?

In this chapter, you will learn what identity is, and how identities are formed. You will study complex aspects of the identities of First Nations, Métis, and Inuit peoples, the impact of laws on identity, how identity is expressed, stereotypes, and media portrayals. You will also read about how Aboriginal peoples honour and celebrate their identities through their cultures.

Use these questions to explore the big ideas in this chapter.

1. What influences how we see ourselves and our sense of identity?

2. How do culture, traditions, and the arts influence the various identities of First Nations, Métis, and Inuit peoples?

3. How are the diverse identities of First Nations, Métis, and Inuit peoples expressed?

4. What challenges do Aboriginal peoples encounter related to their identities?

FIGURE 4.2 This photograph of Monica Ethier-Clair is called *Perception*. Discuss what you think the photographer is saying with this image.

What Is Identity?

REFLECTION

Describe who you are in 10 words or less. What do you feel is the most important aspect of your identity? Why? What do you want other people to know about you?

What do we mean by *identity*? How do you decide who you are, and what your place is in the world? How do you feel about how others define you? What factors shape how you see yourself? The easiest way to explain the concept of identity is this: identity is what you think, know, and believe about yourself.

Many factors are involved in determining identity. Some are internal and others are external. Connections to other people, whether through ethnic background, religion, or geography, are very important to identity. You can have a sense of yourself as an individual and also have an identity as a member of a community. You may see your identity as a teenager or student as being different from your identity at home or in your cultural group. Your identity may alter as you grow older, shaped by both experience and knowledge.

Although many factors can influence your sense of who you are, how you **self-identify** is up to you. If you happen to grow up in two different parts of Canada, you may feel more connected to one region than to the other. Your family members may have different cultural backgrounds, and throughout your life, you may identify with one culture more than the other.

What are some of the factors that have influenced your identity? Below are some examples to consider.

WORDS MATTER

self-identification the traits, groups, or people that you consider your own

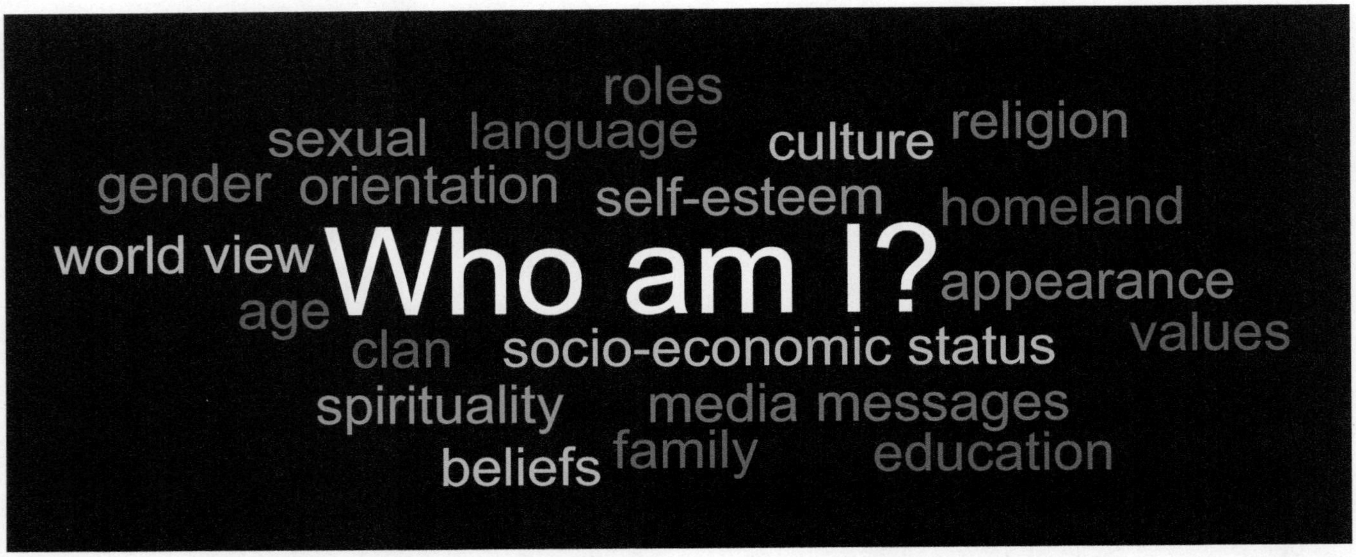

roles
sexual language culture religion
gender orientation self-esteem homeland
world view **Who am I?** appearance
age clan socio-economic status values
spirituality media messages
beliefs family education

FIGURE 4.3 Would you add anything to this list? How might this list be different for you in 10 or 20 years? Select 10 factors from the above. Describe how each of these relate to you and your identity.

©P

Expressions of Identity

Expressing their identity helps people reinforce who they are and where they feel they belong. Identity can be expressed through individual creative acts, such as poetry, journal keeping, blogs, or filmmaking. It can also be expressed within a community, through the sharing of language or celebrations. Perhaps your family celebrates certain times of the year, or has special celebrations and ceremonies for significant times in life. Perhaps you speak your first language when at home with your family or at social gatherings. Many cultures and communities have their own ceremonies and celebrations that help to express their identity and bring the community together. Expressing identity in these ways can be vital not only to form identity, but to support it, to make it stronger, and to reinforce a sense of place in the world.

Outside Influences on Identity

What do you think of when you see how young people are depicted in the media? What do you think about yourself when you are drawn to a certain type of music, or to a movie or television show? How do you feel when you are told, "We don't behave that way"?

Many factors influence your identity as you grow and change throughout your life: religion, ethnic background, language and cultural practices, family members and the values they support, expected social behaviours, views about gender, and the laws of the land. All of these aspects contribute to who you are as an individual, but they can also challenge your sense of self as you journey through life.

Think of how you view the roles of men and women, and how you view the roles of children, teenagers, adults, and senior members of your community. Think of how you are expected to behave on public transit, in school, at the movie theatre, or at a family function. What outside influences or experiences have changed or challenged your identity and how you think about yourself?

FIGURE 4.4 Two young women pose with dried fish at a camp for teens in Fort Good Hope, Northwest Territories. The camp is run by Sahtú Dene Elders, who pass on their knowledge about the land. Discuss what you consider to be the greatest outside influence on your identity right now. Do you think that influence might have more or less importance in the future? Explain.

THINKING IT THROUGH

1. Think about how other people influence you. How does what others think of you or say to you influence how you think about yourself?

2. How does the place you are from affect who you are?

Aboriginal Identities

In this section, you will learn about some of the unique and diverse aspects of First Nations, Métis, and Inuit peoples, who in the 2006 Census of Canada accounted for 1 172 790 people (only those who self-identified). The following section focuses on how identities may be determined. It also discusses some issues that First Nations, Métis, and Inuit peoples encounter in establishing their identities.

The Canadian Constitution states:

> In this Act, "Aboriginal Peoples of Canada" includes the Indian, Inuit and Métis peoples of Canada.
>
> —The Constitution Act, 1982

Although First Nations, Métis, and Inuit peoples in Canada have distinct and unique cultures and histories, they are often lumped together under the umbrella terms *Aboriginal* or *Native*. These terms are used to talk about the three peoples that the government recognizes as indigenous to Canada. However, the use of these terms can contribute to a lack of understanding of the diversity found among and within First Nations, Métis, and Inuit peoples.

How are Aboriginal identities defined? Who defines who is and who is not First Nations, Métis, or Inuit? This is a complex question that Aboriginal communities and government officials continue to debate. Establishing citizenship or membership can happen either through informal or formal processes, and how this happens may differ depending on the individual's situation.

Identities by Choice

Complex factors affect identity for many First Nations, Métis, and Inuit people. Some individuals feel that they have always known their identity: they have always known who they are, their family, their community, and their Nation—and their community and Nation have always considered them to be members and citizens. In other situations, identity is more complex and difficult for a variety of reasons, which we will explore throughout this chapter and the next. For example, a person who self-identifies in one way but whose identity is not recognized in law may constantly feel the need to justify his or her identity. Frequently, people who are part First Nations, Métis, or Inuit feel pressured into having to "choose" one identity over the other. This need to choose can leave people without a sense of belonging or purpose and with feelings of being disconnected from others. How do you establish your place in the world and determine your responsibilities to others without a community to identify with?

©P

Identities by Law

Part of the difficulty for First Nations, Métis, and Inuit peoples in establishing identities is the involvement of the government, which is under certain obligations to some Aboriginal peoples because of treaties. *Status Indians* are given identification cards by the government, but some First Nations people choose to identify themselves by Nation, clan, family, land, or name. Being identified as *non-status* can result from mistakes in membership records, bureaucratic errors, or early Indian Act definitions of status. Ancestry, or **blood quantum**, is also used to determine First Nations membership. Without status, a person may also be excluded from treaty and other Aboriginal rights.

While legal issues related to status as an "Indian" might seem to have an impact only on First Nations peoples, all Aboriginal peoples can be affected by discriminatory policies. The imposition of the Indian Act separated Aboriginal peoples and communities when it was first introduced and made it clear that one was either "status Indian" or not. For example, in 1939 a court ruled that Inuit should be considered as though Indian and subject to the Indian Act. Some Métis in Ontario were told, from 1850 to 1982, to identify themselves as either "Indian or White." After 1982, Métis could once again assert they were Métis and neither "Indian" nor "White."

FIGURE 4.5 A sample of a status card issued by the Canadian government. Organizations such as the Métis Nation of Ontario also issue membership cards to certify citizenship within their Nation.

First Nations Identities

There are approximately 756 700 First Nations people living in more than 630 First Nations communities across the country, in both rural and urban areas. There are regional differences, cultural and language differences, unique customs and spiritual beliefs, and various governance structures found in every First Nation.

VOICES OF THE PEOPLES

While there are many differences, there are similarities in beliefs, values, and aspirations, as set out by the Assembly of First Nations:

We the Original Peoples of this land know the Creator put us here.

The Creator gave us laws that govern all our relationships to live in harmony with nature and mankind.

The Laws of the Creator defined our rights and responsibilities.

The Creator gave us our spiritual beliefs, our languages, our culture, and a place on Mother Earth which provided us with all our needs.

We have maintained our Freedom, our Languages, and our Traditions from time immemorial.

We continue to exercise the rights and fulfill the responsibilities and obligations given to us by the Creator for the land upon which we were placed.

The Creator has given us the right to govern ourselves and the right to self-determination.

The rights and responsibilities given to us by the Creator cannot be altered or taken away by any other Nation.

—*Assembly of First Nations*

Web Connect ● ● ● ● ● ● ● ● ●
To view a map of the First Nations of
Ontario, visit our website.

Some of the Nations in Ontario include the Oneida, Algonquin, Cree, Ojibwe, Oji-Cree, and Mohawk. There are differences among cultures and traditions in different areas. For example, Ojibwe is spoken in northern and southern communities, but the dialects vary depending on the area. Many cultural differences exist among various First Nations, such as in political systems and spiritual practices. For example, men in Anishinaabe societies designated leaders, and among the Haudenosaunee, women fulfilled this role.

The Legal Term "Indian"

The term *Indian* appears in the Canadian Constitution Act and has been used to describe those peoples defined as *Indian* in the Indian Act. Section 6 of the Indian Act states who is entitled to register with the government as *Indian,* therefore, who is regarded as a *status Indian.* What makes First Nations distinct in the Indian Act is their relationship with the government through the Royal Proclamation of 1763, which includes

- the establishment of a nation-to-nation relationship between the Crown and Indian peoples
- a recognition that Indian peoples have rights to the land
- the establishment of a treaty-making process
- a recognition of the existence of First Nations rights, which include rights to land; rights to hunt, fish, and gather; and rights to self-government

Not all First Nations people register with the government, for various personal reasons. The issues surrounding First Nations membership are complicated by a system that recognizes the existence of only First Nations people who qualify for status under the terms set out by the government.

In the next pages, we will look at how the Indian Act has undergone many amendments, but remains a controlling force in the lives of First Nations individuals and communities today. You will consider sovereignty and self-determination in later chapters, but here we look at the Indian Act and what it means for First Nations identities.

VOICES OF THE PEOPLES

When I fought to protect my land, my home, I was called a savage. When I neither understood nor welcomed this way of life, I was called lazy. When I tried to rule my people I was stripped of my authority... Shall I thank you for the reserves that are left me of my beautiful forests? For the canned fish of my rivers? For the loss of my pride and authority, even among my own people?

—*Chief Dan George, actor and author, chief of the Tsleil-Waututh Nation, 1967*

FIGURE 4.6 After reading the quotation by Chief Dan George, what do you think he values? What do you think contributes to his sense of self?

The History of the Indian Act and Status

Before the arrival of Europeans, First Nations defined for themselves who was a citizen. Some Nations, such as the Haudenosaunee, the Wet'suwet'en, and the Tsimshian, were **matrilineal**. The fact that First Nations defined their own citizenship and that some Nations were matrilineal conflicted with the settlers' views during the 1800s. The prevailing attitudes among settlers valued men over women and asserted the notion of the settlers' "superiority" and thus the notion that settler governments had the right to determine what happened to people considered to be inferior.

How Is Status as an "Indian" Determined?

One outcome of the attitudes above was that the federal government decided it should determine and control First Nations citizenship, rather than each Nation controlling its own citizenship.

From the beginning, the Indian Act discriminated against women in three ways:

1. The Act used a **patrilineal** system in order to trace ancestry; a First Nations man or woman would have to prove his or her father to be First Nations in order to have Indian status.

2. The Act ruled that a woman who had Indian status but married someone without Indian status ("marrying out") would lose her Indian status. Her children were also denied status. Men with status as Indians kept their status when they married women without Indian status.

3. Until 1951, the Act also prevented women from voting in band council elections.

Since the first Indian Act was created, there have been many amendments. However, the impact has been that Nations are not, ultimately, allowed to decide for themselves who are citizens, and women have been discriminated against. What was the difference between having status as an "Indian" and losing status? In general, the difference could mean being able to live on reserve, vote for the band council and chief, share in band resources, and own and inherit property on the reserve—or not being able to do any of those things.

Seeking Change in "Indian" Status

Many individuals and organizations have sought change. Sandra Lovelace Nicholas (page 118) took up the challenge after she tried to return to her community with her children after her marriage to an American man ended. She and her children were refused housing, health care, and education in the community because of her lost Indian status. The timeline on the next page shows some highlights and people involved in challenges to the Indian Act and gender discrimination.

These challenges raise many questions—about how Nations define citizenship, about expectations of citizens, about possible restrictions on whom one marries, and about the impact on children.

WORDS MATTER

matrilineal based on kinship with the mother; the female line in a family tree

patrilineal based on kinship with the father; the male line in a family tree

VOICES OF THE PEOPLES

At the beginning, when the "others" first came here, we held our rightful positions in our societies, and held the respect due us by the men, because that's the way things were then, when we were following our ways. At that time, the European woman was considered an appendage to her husband, his possession. Contact with that...and the imposition of his ways on our people, resulted in our being assimilated into those ways.

—Osennontion (Marlyn Kane, Cree/Saulteaux) and Skonaganleh:rá (Sylvia Maracle, Bay of Quinte Mohawk, from Tyendinaga)

Bill C-31 and After: Controlling Citizenship

Throughout the existence of the Indian Act, there have been many arguments against the Act. One key outcome of those arguments was Bill C-31, which was passed into law in 1985 (described in the timeline below). Some male First Nations leaders argued that allowing First Nations women to keep their status if they "married out" would bring about assimilation and further encroach upon First Nations' sovereignty. Some argued that reserves do not have the land, housing, and money to include more citizens. The Six Nations band council opposed striking down one section of the Act because it believed the entire Act needed changing. Other critics believe that, flawed as it is, the Indian Act is protection for First Nations.

Once Bill C-31 passed as legislation, about 40 percent of the bands decided to take control over their citizenship. Some bands refused to restore Indian status to women who had "married out." However, some say that First Nations women wanted to see Bill C-31 implemented in order to achieve inclusiveness, fairness, and respect in their Nations.

Although legal identity under the Indian Act remains an issue, the legacy is clear. The difference in how "Indian" status has been assigned and passed forward has affected First Nations women for generations.

FIGURE 4.7 Sandra Lovelace Nicholas, a Wolastoqiyik (Malecite) woman, was appointed Senator in 2005. In 1979, she and her children took part in a walk from Oka, near Montréal, to Ottawa, to raise awareness of discrimination against First Nations women. In what ways have you seen people raise awareness of a cause?

1967	Mary Two-Axe Earley leads a delegation to the Royal Commission on the Status of Women.
1970	The Royal Commission concludes that the Indian Act does discriminate on the basis of gender and should change.
1970s	Women who have lost status by "marrying out" take their battles to court. Jeannette Corbiere Lavell and Yvonne Bédard take their cases to the Supreme Court of Canada, but the court rules that the Indian Act does not discriminate on the basis of gender because women who lose status as Indians gain the legal rights of non-Indian women in Canada.
1977	Sandra Lovelace Nicholas appeals to the United Nations Commission on Humans Rights.
1981	The UN Commission rules that the Indian Act is discriminatory and violates Aboriginal women's human rights.
1982	Canada enacts the Canadian Charter of Rights and Freedoms, putting human rights in Canada in the spotlight.
1983	Mary Two-Axe Earley asks to speak at the Canadian Constitutional Conference but is denied. Québec Premier René Lévesque gives up his seat so that Mary Two-Axe Earley can speak.
1985	The federal government passes Bill C-31 into law, giving First Nations the option of determining their own citizenship. The government's rules allow that women who had "married out" can regain status and their children can obtain status.
1985	Mary Two-Axe Earley becomes the first woman to regain status.
1993	Three First Nations leaders from Alberta launch a court case to gain complete power in determining Nation citizenship.
1997	The Supreme Court of Canada rules that the Canadian government has the final say in Nation citizenship.
2009–2010	A 2009 court decision leads to the government proposing changes to the Indian Act in 2010, to extend the option of status to the grandchildren of women who lost their status by "marrying out."

FIGURE 4.8 This timeline gives a brief overview of milestones in challenging the Indian Act.

©P

Mary Two-Axe Earley

Mary Two-Axe Earley founded Equal Rights for Indian Women (later the national organization known as Indian Rights for Indian Women). A Mohawk woman from Kahnawake in Québec, Mary Two-Axe Earley felt compelled to fight when the government refused to let her deceased friend be buried with her family in the community cemetery because she had lost her status. Mary Two-Axe Earley herself had lost her status after "marrying out" and faced losing the log cabin her grandmother had left to her. She saved family ownership of the cabin by putting it in the name of her daughter, who had gained status by marrying a Mohawk man. After regaining status in 1985, Mary Two-Axe Earley said:

> Now I'll have legal rights again. After all these years, I'll be legally entitled to live on the reserve, to own property, die and be buried with my own people.

FIGURE 4.9 Mary Two-Axe Earley said that her reserve had one cemetery for Catholics, one for Protestants, and one for dogs, but Mohawk women who married non-Indian-status men could not be buried on the reserve. Issues of housing and Nation citizenship still present challenges on many reserves. Why do you think these issues persist?

Meghan McGill

My name is Meghan. I'm a Grade 11 student who loves Broadway, *Star Trek*, and history class. I'm an avid writer and I'm very outgoing. I also can't feel the right side of my body due to a stroke I had when I was born. However, no one can see any difference between me and anyone else in the way I move, walk, or act, because I've adjusted. When people find out I've had a stroke they are very surprised, but they don't doubt me for a second. They don't ask me for medical papers or MRI scans to prove that I've had a stroke; people just believe me.

On the other hand, when people find out I am Aboriginal, they still act surprised, but it is obvious that they don't believe me. It makes me wonder sometimes why people are so quick to understand my medical issue, yet so reluctant to believe my cultural background. I've been told it's because I don't "look Native," but what does "Native" really look like? Is it that image of Indian people in old Western movies? I admit, I don't look like that, but just because I'm not out of a Western doesn't mean I'm not Aboriginal.

FIGURE 4.10 Meghan McGill is a high-school student in Ontario. She has a status card, was born in Toronto, and grew up in Grand Bend. What are the challenges she faces with respect to her identity? Do you think these challenges are common to all teenagers? Why or why not?

I am Aboriginal, though I don't really know much about my history or culture, because my grandmother, who was from Timiskaming First Nation, was in a residential school for eight years of her childhood. She wasn't allowed to practise her culture or language there, and as a result it wasn't passed on in our family. I'm just starting to learn about being Aboriginal, and through this learning process I've come to realize that being Aboriginal doesn't change who I am, or label me as an Indian from a Western movie. It adds to my identity, and helps me define myself as a proud member of my cultural community.

©P

FIGURE 4.11 This graffiti artwork was created by two young Inuit artists for the Alianait Arts Festival in Iqaluit in 2006.

Web Connect • · · · · · · · · · · · ·

To view an interactive map about Inuit, visit our website.

FIGURE 4.12 This photo shows a sunrise festival in Inuvik. How might events such as this relate to identity?

Inuit Identities

Inuit live throughout Canada, but their lands are in the Arctic, which they refer to as Inuit Nunaat. About 55 000 Inuit live in 53 communities in Nunatsiavut (Labrador), Nunavik (Québec), Nunavut, and the Inuvialuit settlement region of the Northwest Territories; these four regions cover one-third of the land mass of Canada. The Inuit Tapiriit Kanatami (ITK), founded in 1971, is the national Inuit organization in Canada, representing the four Inuit regions.

Inuit have their own unique histories, languages, cultural practices, and spiritual beliefs. The Inuit language has many dialects, one of which is called Inuktitut. Inuktitut is used in many parts of Inuit Nunaat, within Canada, and across international borders.

What sets Inuit apart from First Nations peoples in the eyes of the Canadian government is the fact that many Inuit communities did not sign treaties, retaining much of their political power in their lands. These lands include the self-governing territory of Nunavut. Still, Inuit were included in the Indian Act in 1939, and were then considered to be wards of the government, just as First Nations peoples were. After being registered, Inuit were given identification numbers and were not recognized by name. This experience troubled many people, because a person's name is tied to who the person is and to his or her place in the

©P

Traditionally, it was up to Elders to name babies after relatives or favourite people, and many given names had long been used—names like Aniqmiuq, Annogakuluuk, Annogaq, Arnaquq, Kimalu, Aitii, Maatu, Quvianatukuluk, Ikilluaq, and thousands more. When the missionaries came, some could not pronounce these ancient names properly. They gave our people names from the Bible—Joanasie, from John, Jamiesie (James), Olutie (Ruth), Miali (Mary), Jonah, Ilisapie (Elizabeth), and so on. Among ourselves, we always used our ancient names. So when I was baptized, I became Annie, but to my parents and Elders, I was Lutaaq, Pilitaq, Palluq, or Inusiq.

To the Canadian government, however, I was Annie E7-121! In the early 1940s, Inuit had to be counted and identified for government records so that our parents or guardians could receive family allowance. E stood for east and W stood for west. We were given a small disc looped on a sturdy string, brown with black lettering. I only learned about last names when I went to school in Toronto in the early 1960s. My foster parents let me use their family name, so in Toronto I went by Annie Cotterill—E7-121 was not a very attractive name for a young girl! And when I came back home, I certainly did not want to be Miss E7-121 as a secretary in a government office, so I took my father's first name, Meekitjuk, as a surname.

By the late 1960s, Simonie Michael, our first elected Inuk member of the Northwest Territories legislative assembly, stated that he no longer wanted to be known by his E7- number. Thus, Project Surname was created. Abe Okpik, a respected Inuk from the western Arctic, headed the project. Between 1968 and 1970, Abe visited every Inuit home and asked the families to choose a name. The head of the family picked a surname—often a relative's given name—and we were no longer known by numbers.

—from *Nunavut 99*, by Inuk author *Ann Meekitjuk Hanson*

FIGURE 4.13 The photographs above show both sides of an identification disc. What was Ann Meekitjuk Hanson's reaction to having a number attached to her name?

family and the community. Project Surname (above) was very important in that families were able to choose their surnames and have names of their own language.

One very important aspect of Inuit identity is one's atiq (namesake). In Inuit culture, when a child is named after someone, that child is treated as if he or she is that person. You may hear someone calling a small boy "grandpa" because he is named after that person's grandfather.

REFLECTION

If you were forced to change your name from the one given to you by your family to one given by a government official, how would you respond? What do you think would be the impact on your sense of identity?

Métis means a person who self-identifies as Métis, is of historic Métis Nation ancestry, is distinct from other Aboriginal peoples and is accepted by the Métis Nation.

—*The Métis Nation of Ontario, 2002*

CRITICAL THINKING

Some people think that an individual who loses legal status as an "Indian" is necessarily Métis. That is not the case. The original word *métis* means "mixed," and most people around the world have mixed heritage; so-called "pure blood" is very rare. However, *Métis* defines a people and a Nation, and the characteristics of being Métis are outlined on this page. How do you define your heritage?

WORDS MATTER

nationalism the belief that a people who share a common language, history, and culture constitute an independent nation

Métis Identities

If you ask any Métis person what makes them Métis, they will probably give you a long answer. Just as for First Nations and Inuit, Métis identity is more than genealogy or the rules of citizenship. However, these factors cannot be ignored, because they are the basis for how the Métis defend their rights. Being part of a community and being recognized and accepted by that community are key factors in understanding Métis identity today.

The Métis became a Nation during the fur trade, before Canada formed as a Dominion. Under both French and English rule, the Métis developed identities that both included and became distinct from their First Nations and European ancestors. The Métis have their own language, Michif, which varies in different regions; in Ontario, there are French influences. The Métis have a rich cultural life with traditions such as fiddle music and jigging (a type of social dancing) and with symbols such as a flag and a sash. The Métis sash is a symbol of identity for the Métis. The story of the sash begins with the woven belts worn by habitants in Québec in the late 1700s. Its practical uses as a belt, tourniquet, towel, or rope made it popular among the voyageurs and the coureurs de bois. The Métis adapted it with their own styles and colours. The sash now symbolizes how the lives of the Métis are interwoven through traditions, beliefs, and cultures.

In the 2006 Canadian Census, 390 000 people identified as Métis, most of them living in British Columbia, Alberta, Saskatchewan, Manitoba, and Ontario. The majority of Métis live in urban areas. In Ontario, there are approximately 73 610 Métis people. The Métis Nation of Ontario represents, serves, and provides programs to Métis in Ontario, and is part of the Métis National Council.

Métis **nationalism** formed in large measure because of the marginalization the Métis experienced due to Canada's "Indian policies" from the 1850s onward. Before Louis Riel and the Métis in Manitoba fought for their rights, the Métis in Ontario opposed the exploitation of resources at Mica Bay and sought to secure rights to land and resources. These struggles continue to be negotiated peacefully to this day, sometimes through the court system.

The year 2010 was the Year of the Métis, and this is a source of pride for all Canadians. The existence of the Métis across Canada testifies to the strength and tenacity of Métis identity. It is an identity celebrated at annual rendezvous, in community hunts, and in ongoing partnerships with First Nations, and with provincial and federal governments.

©P

We Are Métis

Creator, we thank you for many blessings you have given these many years.

We are Métis, with roots and rights that extend hundred of years into this continent.

We are neither First Nation, Inuit, nor European immigrants to this land. We are the middle ground between two camps, the compromise between differences and the dawn that separates night from day. We are not Half Breeds but the children born of a marriage between two different worlds.

We are descendants of the English, the French, the Scots, the Algonquins, the Cree, and the Ojibwe to name a few. Dark or fair hair, brown or blue eyes, we are an invisible minority.

See our sash we so proudly wear? It is a mix of different elements like the life of we Métis. We speak English, French, Michif, and Maskegon.

To be Métis is to be blessed with the fruit of not one but two family trees. Not half but doubled being, twice blessed. We are a strong, proud Nation, we are Métis.

Creator, for all of this we give you thanks.

—*Métis prayer*

FIGURE 4.14 These young Métis dancers are performing at Saskatoon Folkfest in 2008. The boys have Métis sashes tied around their waists. What does the phrase *invisible minority* mean to you? How might feeling like an invisible minority affect a Métis person's identity?

THINKING IT THROUGH

1. In a group of three, one student summarizes key information about First Nations identities, one about Métis identities, and one about Inuit identities. Share and compare your summaries in your group. Then note your outstanding questions and where you might find answers.

2. Reread Delbert Majer's words on page 114. In what ways are his ideas reflected in other examples in pages 114 to 123? Give your answer in two to three paragraphs.

Expressions of Identity

Art is a powerful way of expressing beliefs, hopes, and values. It is also a way for individuals to explore identity for themselves and others. Imagine creating a portrait of yourself, either in writing or with images. What would show who you are? Why would it be important for you to show certain aspects of yourself to others?

First Nations, Métis, and Inuit art is deeply connected to the artists' beliefs and world views, and Aboriginal artists frequently use their art as a way to express their diverse and unique identities. Art is a way to show what they know, what they believe in, and what they value. It is also a way to pass on those beliefs and values to the following generations. Art can also stand in for language and therefore become an effective method of communication between the artist and the audience.

Art in its many forms is also a way for First Nations, Métis, and Inuit people to connect within their communities, strengthen community ties, and express hopes for the future. Artists and art events increase public awareness and contribute to public understanding of First Nations, Métis, and Inuit cultural contributions. They also increase pride in each culture, challenge assumptions, and express a Nation's distinctive identity in multicultural Canada.

Artists may choose from different artistic forms—writing, painting, or photography, for example—and Aboriginal artists may also choose more traditional forms of expression or create new ones. In many ways, being an artist is a part of identity for the First Nations, Métis, and Inuit men and women who choose to express themselves through art.

VOICES OF THE PEOPLES

My people will sleep for 100 years, and when they awake, it will be the artists who give them back their spirit.

—Louis Riel, Métis leader

Web Connect

Some artists combine traditions of their ancestors with new forms and techniques. Artist Michael Nicoll Yahgulanaas (born 1954) combines Indigenous design from Haida Gwaii with manga, a comic narrative form from Asia. To learn more about this artist, visit our website.

VOICES OF THE PEOPLES

My shyness during most of my childhood and adolescence prevented me from opening up to people around me, even to my own dear mother, Napatchie. She will never know just how much I wanted to be frank with her about my feelings. And this is also true with some of the people I grew up with in Iqaluit.

My art, and especially my writings, are the major reasons why I have gradually broken the ice—so to speak—that shielded me from dealing with humans around me... What really helped me to open up was the desire to somehow express the silent voice of our people when so many changes were happening to our lives and over which we still did not have any control.

—Alootook Ipellie, Inuk author and illustrator, 1951–2007

FIGURE 4.15 What does Alootook Ipellie reveal about himself in this statement? What outside influences and circumstances have affected his sense of identity?

©P

FIGURE 4.16 Reddnation, a rap group made up of five First Nations men from Edmonton and Regina, has received numerous Aboriginal Peoples Choice Music Awards. Reddnation tours Canada conducting youth workshops to promote cultural values.

The Artists and Their Arts

In the past and the present, many First Nations, Métis, and Inuit have become accomplished artists. They are actors, writers, musicians, sculptors, painters, and filmmakers. Some are listed here and you will read about many more in this and other chapters.

- Kenojuak Ashevak: one of the first women in the Inuit community of Cape Dorset to begin drawing professionally.
- Christi Belcourt: Métis painter, craftsperson, and writer. She is known for her acrylic paintings that depict floral patterns.
- Neil Diamond: Cree filmmaker. His 2009 film *Reel Injun* tackled Hollywood stereotypes of Aboriginal peoples and was widely acclaimed at various film festivals.
- Tanya Tagaq Gillis: Inuk singer and artist who has developed a unique solo version of throat-singing. She won Best Female Artist at the 2005 Canadian Aboriginal Music Awards.
- Alanis Obomsawin: Abenaki documentary filmmaker, singer, educator, and activist. A member of the Order of Canada, she is considered one of Canada's most distinguished filmmakers.
- Bill Reid: Haida artist. Several of his sculptures are displayed at the Canadian embassy in Washington, D.C., at the Vancouver International Airport, and at the Canadian Museum of Civilization.
- Robbie Robertson: Mohawk singer, songwriter, and guitarist who has worked with Bob Dylan and Eric Clapton. He is an inductee of Canada's Walk of Fame.

Literature written by First Nations, Métis, and Inuit authors of all ages provides authentic representations and accounts of Aboriginal peoples. The diversity among styles, prose, and topics is endless, and it is clear that First Nations, Métis, and Inuit authors are well established on the literary scene. Writing is a powerful means of communication, and Aboriginal voices are represented and published by mainstream publishers as well as by Aboriginal publishers such as Pemmican Publications, the Gabriel Dumont Institute, Theytus Books, and Kegedonce Press.

FIGURE 4.17 This young woman is weaving a Métis sash. Many Aboriginal youth today maintain their identities by using their cultures to express themselves. Why do you think that it is important for First Nations, Métis, and Inuit youth to have connections with their traditions?

The Influence of Technology

Technology has had an impact on artistic creations, the exposure of Aboriginal artists, and the connections among artists as well. Architect Douglas Cardinal (left) is known for his early use of computer-assisted design. Artists such as Rick Beaver (below) are combining media with technical and artistic innovation. As well, an increasing number of artists are using the Internet to publish their works.

Art and literature can now be shared across great distances with audiences not only in Canada, but around the world. Technology such as the Internet can now provide instant messaging, viewing, and listening to music and films online, and teleconferencing bridges gaps between artists and their audiences. Technology, financial support, and promotion during international events such as the Vancouver 2010 Olympic Winter Games have showcased Aboriginal artists from around the world, connecting artists in ways never before experienced.

Art and First Nations, Métis, and Inuit Lives

Whether using traditional means or newer technologies, the arts can also be a way for individual artists to express what their lives are like and a way to hone their skills. Works by blog writers and filmmakers, playwrights, contemporary visual artists, and others are also opportunities for audiences to experience authentic accounts of the diverse lives and communities of First Nations, Métis, and Inuit people.

FIGURE 4.18 Douglas Cardinal, of Métis and Blackfoot heritage, is an internationally recognized architect. His designs include the Canadian Museum of Civilization in Gatineau, Québec.

Web Connect • • • • • • • • • • • •

To learn more about First Nations, Métis, and Inuit artists, visit our website.

FIGURE 4.19 Rick Beaver is an Anishinaabe artist from Alderville First Nation, whose work *Current Connections* you saw in Chapter 2.

©P

FIGURE 4.20 Jules Koostachin started a blog about developing a film project and reflecting on her home community of Attawapiskat First Nation on James Bay (above), her life in Toronto, and her Cree language classes. In what ways could you learn about life on a First Nations reserve, in a Métis settlement, in an Inuit community, or among First Nations, Métis, and Inuit people in an urban community?

COMMUNITY CLOSE-UP

Manitoulin Island

In Anishinaabemowin, the language of the Anishinaabe, Manitoulin Island means "the dwelling place of the spirits." The island is the largest freshwater island in the world and has long been a sacred place to the Anishinaabe "People of the Three Fires"—the Ojibwe, the Odawa, and the Potawatomi. This special place of lakes and limestone, on the northern end of Lake Huron, is home to about 12 000 permanent residents, six First Nations communities, and eight non-Aboriginal communities.

One community on the island, Wikwemikong Unceded Indian Reserve, has officially hosted powwows since 1960, although powwows date back further. The Wikwemikong powwow, one of the major powwows in North America, draws together thousands of people.

Manitoulin Island also has a thriving visual arts community. The Manitou Arts Foundation was founded in 1966, and its summer school has hosted artist mentors including Daphne Odjig, Carl Ray, and Gerald Dokis. Leland Bell, Shirley Cheechoo, Randolph Trudeau, Blake Debassige, and Martin Panamick were among the students who participated in this camp. All five went on to develop and express their own distinctive styles and visions and have become internationally renowned.

Demonstration and observation have often been used by artists to share their techniques. The artists' community grew as everyone shared insights and techniques. As Blake Debassige recalls, "All of us worked together as a group, as opposed to as individuals… Listening to Elders and researching legends was my schooling." The art grew "exactly the same way grandmothers taught their children: by experience, by oral history."

The De-ba-jeh-mu-jig Theatre Group, which you read about in Chapter 1, is also located in Wikwemikong.

FIGURE 4.21 Sandra Laronde (left) is the founder of Red Sky Theatre. She is of the Teme-Augama-Anishinaabe in Temagami, Ontario. As artists involved in theatre, people such as Sandra Laronde and Carlos Rivera (right, in *Raven Stole the Sun*) can present their artistic vision to large audiences.

Reaching Wide Audiences

Many artistic activities, including stage performances, are taking expressions of First Nations, Métis, and Inuit identities to wide audiences. The Inuk singer Elisapie Isaac is one example. The Métis celebration called Rendezvous connects Métis communities, just as the cultural and musical celebration La Nuit sur l'étang unites Franco-Ontarians. Other examples include plays, such as *Raven Stole the Sun*, and films by filmmakers such as Gil Cardinal and Alanis Obomsawin.

Another play that contributes to promoting Aboriginal identities and understanding among Aboriginal peoples and non-Aboriginal peoples is the play *L'Écho d'un peuple*. This outdoor evening play, two and a half hours in length, recounts in 12 scenes 400 years of Francophone presence in Ontario. The first four scenes are dedicated to Aboriginal peoples and the relationships, alliances, challenges, and successes.

Language and Identity

Language is a reflection of a person's world view, and is an active link to a person's culture. Language connects people to one another through shared experiences and by building a sense of community. Language is the key to identity, giving people a way to express and share their beliefs, values, and experiences. Thus, First Nations, Métis, and Inuit languages (which you will consider again in later chapters) are expressions of identity.

COMMUNITY CLOSE-UP

Language Promotes Cultural Pride

by Brent Wesley, Wawatay News Online

Simply put, language immersion programs have a common goal. "To make children proud of who they are," says Saul Williams, chairperson of the District Education Planning Committee (DEPC) in the Sioux Lookout district.

The Kwayaciiwin Anihshiniimowin Immersion Program run by the DEPC strives to prepare students for the academic world through the use of their Native language. The hope of the program is to develop students who are able to speak, read, and write in Anihshiniimowin and English.

The immersion program not only fulfills the need to prepare students academically, but also serves the purpose of instilling cultural knowledge. "What we're modelling after is a Native way of teaching," Williams says.

This is the goal of such programs: to make children proud of their culture and heritage. In doing so, students become confident and are more likely to succeed.

Art Programs and Support for Artists

Many Aboriginal artists are very successful, marketing their work to audiences worldwide. There are also programs and organizations that support artists and their work. The Canada Council for the Arts supports individual Aboriginal artists, arts groups, collectives, and organizations through the Aboriginal Peoples Collaborative Exchange. Through this program, artists from all disciplines travel to other Aboriginal communities, share artistic practices, and develop their own techniques. Networks and artistic relationships are formed through these collaborative exchanges. Other programs and grants for Aboriginal people in Canada also support the arts, including crafts such as regalia making, which encourage expressions of self-identity and cultural knowledge. The Métis Nation of Ontario administers a grant to support Métis culture–based economic activities. Many provinces have their own arts councils that provide specific funding to First Nations, Métis, and Inuit people, status and non-status, for artistic endeavours.

The Ontario Arts Council has specific programs that support a wide range of Aboriginal artists and organizations. Programs such as Aboriginal Arts Projects help develop and strengthen relationships within Aboriginal communities. Aboriginal Arts Education Projects supports Aboriginal artists who work with students, educators, youth, and adults. Activities for Aboriginal Arts Education Projects are diverse and can include workshops, arts camps, and other opportunities to create new works that pass on knowledge, languages, and skills.

FIGURE 4.22 The play *L'echo d'un peuple* honours Aboriginal peoples and demonstrates the continued relationships between Aboriginal and Francophone communities.

CRITICAL THINKING

Aboriginal art or symbols are often used to advertise and promote Canada to people around the world. A recent example is the image of the Inuksuk used to promote the 2010 Olympic Winter Games. Why do you think this is done? Why might using the Inuksuk image in this way be considered "cultural appropriation"?

THINKING IT THROUGH

1. Why do you think it is important for people to represent and express their own cultures and identities?

2. Choose one of the artists featured in this section, or do some research to find a First Nations, Métis, or Inuk artist, playwright, author, or musician whose work appeals to you. Choose one piece of work by that artist—a painting, photograph, essay, poem, play, or song—and discuss how this work expresses the artist's identity.

Analyzing Images

Images are used to convey information, but it is important to remember that even an image represents a point of view and could be biased in some way.

A useful way to "read" an image is to identify what is in the foreground or centre. This is probably the main subject and the most important part. Next, examine the background and the edges of the image. These parts tell you the setting or context. Reading foreground and background will help you draw information from the image. Think as well about what is not in the image. A photograph can be cropped or altered to emphasize or delete a certain part of the image. Artists depicting a scene in a painting may leave out part of what they see if it does not add to the message they want to give through their work, or if they think this part will not appeal to their audience.

Look closely at the image on the next page. Determine the artist's point of view by asking some questions:

- What does the image show?

- Who created the image, when, and why?

- Is the image accurate? How can you find out?

- What is the artist trying to express?

- What was the purpose of the image?

- What is the context of the image? How is the image being used? Does this particular use change the artist's original purpose?

- Is the artist's point of view current or out of date? Do you agree with it or not?

- What biases are present in the image?

FIGURE 4.23 This painting by Paul Kane is entitled *Big Snake, Chief of the Blackfoot Indians, Recounting His War Exploits to Five Subordinate Chiefs*. It was probably painted between 1851 and 1856.

Paul Kane was born in Ireland in 1810 and grew up in York, Upper Canada (now southern Ontario). He travelled for years in western Canada, living with and sketching Métis and First Nations peoples, and finishing his paintings when he returned home. His work was very popular among eastern Canadian and European people, the majority of whom had never been to western Canada. While Kane's sketches provide us with many insights into the lives of First Nations and Métis peoples, he sometimes added incorrect cultural information or exaggerated details to enhance their appeal to European audiences.

Apply Your Skills

1. How are First Nations people portrayed in the painting? Consider all aspects of the image in your answer, including the background.

2. How would this image contribute to a stereotypical view of First Nations peoples in the minds of Paul Kane's audience? How might a person see this painting today?

3. In your view, how would Paul Kane's images be useful to the study of North American history?

4. Write two short captions for the image: one that might have been written by Paul Kane for his audience, and one for a contemporary history textbook.

The Problem with Stereotypes

We have something they do not know about—we have our teachings, our value systems, our attitudes, our clan systems and on and on and on... Let's educate them.

Right now, they think they do not want to know about us. They look at us in a mystical way. They think we worship smoke. They think we are in a dream world. They fund us so they can continue to look at us as unreal. They educated us to a point where we almost forgot who we are. Now it is time we educate them, people to people. We are different. We have a different perspective on life and all creation. We have many wonderful things to share. We have different and wonderful teachings to share that are simple to live by, reasonable, sensible, for the good of all within the community, full of respect. These have remained a mystery to mankind until now.

—Merle Assance-Beedie, Ojibwe, Christian Island First Nation

We live in a world that thrives on **stereotypes.** We are consistently given statements about people or images that have become so ingrained in our culture that we often forget they are stereotypes; in fact, we frequently accept these statements and images as truths.

As part of critical thinking, it is important to be aware of stereotypes. Stereotypes are generalizations that reflect incorrect, oversimplified, or exaggerated views. They can be both negative and positive. If you have heard a phrase such as "teenagers are lazy," "men love action movies," "women are bad drivers," or "all First Nations people are great artists," you have heard a stereotype.

Stereotypes can undermine a person's sense of identity. The next time you turn on your television or read a newspaper article, look for stereotypes. At the same time, look for challenges to stereotypes, and think about the role that the media and society play in creating, sustaining, and changing stereotypes.

Stereotypes and Identity

Stereotypes can have a powerful effect on a person's identity. Trying to find out who you are can be difficult for anyone, especially in the face of media portrayals that seem to define what is "normal."

Although many stereotypes about First Nations, Métis, and Inuit peoples have been challenged, they still exist, and they affect the way Aboriginal peoples are viewed. You may have been taught about First Nations, Métis, and Inuit peoples in the past tense, as though they existed only in the past. For Aboriginal peoples, these past-tense references can create a feeling of being made invisible, or of being left out of contemporary reality. Feeling that the world thinks you do not exist can naturally have a profound effect on identity.

FIGURE 4.24 The 2009 Canadian documentary film *Reel Injun* explores the portrayal of North American Aboriginal peoples in movies. How have you seen First Nations, Métis, and Inuit peoples portrayed in films? What stereotypes are presented?

©P

Stereotypes in the Media

Stereotypes of First Nations, Métis, and Inuit peoples continue to exist partly because of the way Aboriginal peoples are represented in stories, textbooks, newspapers, film, television, and newscasts. Common stereotypes present First Peoples in the times before contact with Europeans or early during contact; these stereotypes include the "noble savage" and the "Indian princess." You may be familiar with the story of Pocahontas, the princess warrior who "saves" a European man and is then taken to England and given the possessions and education valued by women in Europe. However, this story is largely untrue. Not only are the depictions of the "noble savage" and the "Indian princess" inaccurate, but they present Aboriginal peoples as needing values imposed on them by others. Their own values, already in place and well established, are ignored.

FIGURE 4.25 *Avatar*, a successful movie released in 2010, was criticized by some as a portrayal of the "ecological Indian" stereotype. This stereotype presents Aboriginal peoples living in perfect harmony with nature, in contrast with destructive colonizers.

How do these stereotypes come to be, and how have they survived for so long? Stereotypes of Aboriginal peoples have become ingrained in part due to inaccurate textbooks, some of which repeat fictional accounts. Contemporary issues and stories are for the most part ignored, and Aboriginal peoples are relegated to the past or examined only in terms of their interactions with settlers or explorers, as though they had no independent history prior to or since contact with Europeans.

Many non-Aboriginal novels, films, and art also contribute to the stereotyping of First Nations, Métis, and Inuit peoples. Authors and filmmakers often present what they think represents the lives of First Nations, Métis, and Inuit peoples. Audiences generally accept the authority of these storytellers, even when the tellers have no authority. Films and fiction commonly depict First Nations as being a homogeneous people and rarely acknowledge the diversity of Aboriginal peoples across North America. First Nations are often featured in historical stories as lacking in language and technology—almost "frozen in time."

Even when Aboriginal people are depicted as contemporary, the images are often stereotyped. How often do you see a First Nations, Métis, or Inuk individual on the nightly news dressed in jeans and talking about something other than treaties, taxes, land rights, crime, powwows, or road blockades? First Nations, Métis, and Inuit peoples too frequently appear wearing regalia, or are shown in the midst of a crisis brought about by unemployment, poverty, alcoholism, or pollution. They are too often portrayed as warriors or victims. Such representations do not reflect the real world or who Aboriginal peoples really are. The impact of these representations is negative, but there are some ways to combat stereotypes, as you will read.

REFLECTION

After reading this section, revisit the image on page 111. Has your understanding of this image changed? Explain why or why not.

CRITICAL THINKING

Why does a newspaper, magazine, television program, or website choose to discuss particular stories or events? What factors are involved in its decisions? Do you think these factors lead to better or worse reporting?

Negative Impacts

The mainstream media—what you see on major television channels, in magazines, in newspapers, or on websites—exists to inform an audience about issues and events on local, national, and international levels. In what ways can the reporting of mainstream media be biased? Historically, the media has relied on **skewed** images of First Nations, Métis, and Inuit peoples and the issues that affect them. The mainstream media represents a mainstream audience, writing and broadcasting stories and opinions that target that audience. Crises always get attention, and when the media adds bias and sensationalism to this fact, it perpetuates some negative stereotypes of Aboriginal peoples.

These negative stereotypes have an impact not only on the mainstream audience but also on the people portrayed. Cayuga actor Gary Farmer says that negative portrayals in many media make it hard for Aboriginal youth to have positive self-images. Susan Swan (Ojibwe from Lake Manitoba First Nation) says that First Nations youth she talks to in communities have the impression from media that most other Aboriginal youth are in gangs, but in fact, only about three percent are in gangs.

Combatting Stereotypes

Making the News

One solution to the problem of stereotypes in the media may be greater inclusion of Aboriginal people in producing major television, radio, news, and Internet media services:

> These days, more mainstream news media outlets are beginning to realize the importance of having a more diverse workforce working in their newsrooms. Canadian cities are becoming more diverse, and media outlets in print and broadcast are recognizing the need to attract readers, listeners, and viewers from those diverse communities. But for me, diversity in newsrooms needs to be more than just hiring people of colour to cover mainstream issues. Diversity also means providing coverage that is reflective of issues and events important to those diverse communities. And the coverage needs to increase and be consistent. Only then will diversity be meaningful in mainstream newsrooms.
>
> —*Maureen Googoo, Mi'kmaw journalist*

FIGURE 4.26 What is your first impression of this front-page headline?

There are now media outlets owned and operated by Aboriginal peoples telling their own stories. The Aboriginal Peoples Television Network (APTN), Aboriginal Voices Radio, *Turtle Island News*, and *Windspeaker* (also available online) are a few examples. Aboriginal people are delighted to see news items that focus on their community's issues within these media forms. It is important for audiences to be able to recognize that there are a variety of perspectives on an issue.

©P

Telling Our Own Stories

There are many contemporary authors, artists, filmmakers, and historians who recognize the inaccuracies and stereotypes in the media. Many are First Nations, Métis, or Inuit, and they work to tell their own stories—in other words, to share authentic stories and accurate information with their audiences. The artists whom you read about on pages 124 to 129 are examples of First Nations, Métis, and Inuit people expressing their identities. Audiences are becoming more open to the realities of First Nations, Métis, and Inuit peoples; perspectives are broadening, and sources are being viewed more critically. Presenting First Nations, Métis, and Inuit peoples in contemporary contexts; honouring their diversity; acknowledging their beliefs, values, and aspirations; and learning from authentic sources are ways to represent the identities of Aboriginal peoples as they see themselves—not as others see them.

Web Connect • • • • • • • • • • •

To listen to a song by First Nations musician Angus Jourdain called "Warriors," visit our website. What stereotypes does Angus Jourdain sing about breaking down?

FIGURE 4.28 A promotional poster for the imagineNATIVE Film + Media Arts Festival, held annually in Toronto. In what ways could a festival of many works by Aboriginal artists help combat stereotypes?

FIGURE 4.27 Maurice Switzer (of the Mississaugas of Alderville First Nation and whose writing about perspectives you read on pages viii–ix) is the director of communications for the Union of Ontario Indians and editor of the *Anishinabek News*. Maurice Switzer has been inducted into the Nipissing District Human Rights Hall of Fame for his development of public education initiatives to create greater awareness of First Nations cultures, traditions, and contemporary issues. What other individuals and organizations do you know about who are combatting stereotypes?

indian enough

by kateri akiwenzie-damm

i have felt the sting of accusation
from non-Natives who say i am "not Native enough"

i have been told countless times
i "don't look Indian"

i have been encouraged to forget
rise above
leave behind:
destroy my
self

i have seen the disappointed looks
at my fair skin shining
natural blond streaks of hair glistening
and not even a feather
buckskin
or jingle dress
to redeem me

i have read the dismay on tightly held faces
when i speak in complete English sentences
none of which begin "many moons ago"
none of which are spoken in telltale sing-song
    speech pattern
expected from a "Native speaker"

as i speak
i have felt a cold martyred patience
blasting from those who want to hear
"Native storytelling"
for as long as the words shall flow

    to them i am not "colourful" enough in reality

and I have been told
by a Native woman
an elder
that I am "not a very good Indian"
because I can't speak Ojibway

I have been held suspect

because I have endured with no noticeable scars
(and even some success)
in the "White" school system

because working with the federal government
was interpreted as a change in loyalties
(though I struggled there too for being
too outspoken
to know my place)

because I have lived most of my life in cities
on quiet tree lined streets

because my skin pales in comparison

because I am a C-31 Indian

i have felt myself splinter into pieces

1. kateri akiwenzie-damm is a writer with Anishinaabe, Polish Canadian, Potawatomi, English, and French ancestry. What stereotypes has she faced?

2. What do you think the poet means by her last line, "i have felt myself splinter into pieces"?

©P

Sports Logos

One of the factors perpetuating stereotypes of Aboriginal peoples is the use of Aboriginal images and names for sports logos. Peoples from diverse cultural heritages come to live in Canada alongside Aboriginal peoples and the descendents of the settlers who came to Canada hundreds of years ago. Today's emerging Canadian identity is one that embodies a vision of Canadians living in harmony and respect. Racism is regularly challenged. However, sports logos seem to be the exception to this positive trend.

In popular sports such as hockey or baseball, it is common to see both amateur and professional athletes wearing logos or using mascots that depict Aboriginal peoples as **caricatures**. Characters' features are often distorted, their faces are painted, or they wear buckskins and crowns of turkey feathers. Feathers, in fact, are seen as sacred by many First Nations. The Chicago Blackhawks hockey team, for example, accepted the 2010 Stanley Cup wearing sweaters showing an imaginary "Indian warrior" wearing four feathers. Such stereotypical images are considered offensive and insulting by many First Nations people.

Still, a number of universities and schools have made changes to their team logos and names, adopting more acceptable symbols. In 2010, the student council of Chippewa Intermediate and Secondary School in North Bay agreed to replace its school mascot—a stereotypical First Nations man named Joe Raider—after meeting with representatives from Nipissing First Nation. In British Columbia, the Vancouver Board of Education recommended a province-wide ban on school team names or mascots that depict Aboriginal stereotypes.

CRITICAL THINKING

Is it okay for First Nations, Métis, or Inuit teams to use Aboriginal names and images in their logos? Why or why not?

WORDS MATTER

caricature a picture or description that comically exaggerates the peculiarities or defects of persons or things

FIGURE 4.29 A 1979 cartoon by Everett Soop, a political cartoonist and writer for the *Kainai News* newspaper. What point is he making in this cartoon? How do the images help make his point?

THINKING IT THROUGH

1. Look at textbooks, news sources, movies, children's books, and websites to gather examples of stereotypes about First Nations, Métis, and Inuit peoples. What are the similarities and differences in the portrayals?

2. Find a news story that deals with an issue affecting an Aboriginal person, Nation, or community. Next, find two news sources that cover this issue: one in the mainstream press and one in an Aboriginal-operated media organization (APTN, *Windspeaker,* etc.). Analyze how the story is covered in both media sources. Do the sources give balanced perspectives? What evidence of bias is present in each source?

3. Research local, regional, and national sports teams that have either refused to change or have changed their logos or names. What were the results of their actions? Write a letter to the editor explaining what you have discovered, and suggesting a way to resolve any future disputes.

Honour and Recognition

On a local, national, and international level, more and more First Nations, Métis, and Inuit people are being recognized and honoured for their achievements and contributions. In many instances, what they do connects to their identity, what they believe in, what they value, and what they aspire to for themselves and others.

Sports and Games

Sports and games are an important part of First Nations, Métis, and Inuit communities. Sports help bring communities together. Individuals often play sports and games that are associated with their traditions, and that ultimately contribute to their sense of self-worth. In First Nations, Métis, and Inuit communities, beliefs and values are emphasized through sports, which are seen as part of a holistic approach to finding balance in life. Sports and games are also an important part of leisure time. They are often derived from aspects of daily life, such as games of skill associated with hunting or wrestling, and games of precision such as "ring and pin," canoe racing, archery, and horseshoes.

Recreation and sports in various First Nations, Métis, and Inuit communities are maintained by organizations such as the Ontario Aboriginal Sport and Wellness Council, which promotes the spiritual, physical, emotional, and mental health of Aboriginal youth. Community support helps strengthen the identity of individuals by showing them they are strong, proud contributors to the community. Aboriginal athletes also provide First Nations, Métis, and Inuit people with positive role models.

An important game to First Nations peoples is lacrosse, one of the oldest team sports in North America.

FIGURE 4.30 These photographs show pentathlete Monica Pinette, Paralympic athlete Richard Peter, and NHL hockey player Jordin Tootoo. Why do you think that Aboriginal athletes such as these can be such strong role models for young people? Investigate to find other sports heroes of Aboriginal ancestry and report to your class.

©P

Lacrosse—the Creator's Game

For the Haudenosaunee, the game of lacrosse is considered to be a gift from the Creator and is called the Creator's game. The Haudenosaunee creation story tells of the instructions the Twins received from the Creator on how to play the game with the purpose of reaching peaceful solutions to major disagreements without resorting to war. The lessons of the game include fair play, honour, courage, respect, generosity, and strength—characteristics that demonstrate how to interact with each other to reach peaceful decisions. The game of lacrosse, now played around the world, is recognized as Canada's national sport and is a proud contribution of Aboriginal peoples to the world of sports.

The National Lacrosse League's games have become popular events in sports arenas across Canada and the United States in recent years. Eleven teams, three of which are based in Canada—the Calgary Roughnecks, the Toronto Rock, and the Edmonton Rush—make up a professional league of lacrosse players.

First Nations players such as Ross Powless, a Mohawk from the Six Nations of the Grand River reserve, have been inducted into the Canadian Lacrosse Hall of Fame.

FIGURE 4.31 Today, lacrosse is played around the world by both men and women.

In addition to lacrosse, First Nations peoples in North America have contributed greatly to that other "national game"—hockey. Long before the arrival of Europeans, First Nations men and women ice skated using the bones of animals as blades. Many consider this activity to be the origin of modern hockey. Notable players such as Jordin Tootoo add a sense of pride and honour to the identity of First Nations, Métis, and Inuit peoples in Canada.

Web Connect • • • • • • • • • • • •

To watch videos and listen to radio programs about lacrosse, visit our website.

FIGURE 4.32 The medals for the 2010 Olympic Winter Games were based on an image of an orca whale by Corrine Hunt, a designer and artist of Komoyue and Tlingit heritage. Some First Nations peoples had serious concerns about the way that First Nations were involved in the Olympics. What might their concerns have been about?

The Four Host First Nations

Recognition on an international scale came through contributions of the Four Host First Nations to the Vancouver 2010 Olympic and Paralympic Winter Games. The Games were held within the territories of the Lil'wat, Musqueam, Squamish, and Tsleil-Waututh Nations. The Chiefs and Councils of these Nations agreed to work together to host and support the 2010 Winter Games. As a result, the Four Host First Nations Society became one of the official hosts of the games.

The Protocol Agreement stated that the Four Host First Nations would

- increase opportunities to showcase art, language, traditions, history, and culture
- promote skills development and training related to the Games
- build lasting social, cultural, and economic opportunities and benefits
- improve health, education, and the strengthening of the communities through sport and cultural involvement
- create a youth sport legacy
- increase participation in arts festivals, events, and in the Opening and Closing Ceremonies

The Four Host First Nations were active participants in planning for the Games, ensuring that their traditions and practices were acknowledged and respected. This event marked the first time in history that Indigenous peoples had been recognized by the International Olympic Committee as official partners, evidence of how relationships have come a long way since the experience of the First Nations runners at the 1967 Pan Am Games.

FIGURE 4.33 In 1967, 10 First Nations young men were selected to carry the Pan Am torch from Minnesota to Winnipeg for the opening of the Pan Am Games. They ran a relay of 800 kilometres, only to have the torch taken from them outside the stadium; a non-Aboriginal runner made the final lap of honour with the torch. A film titled *Niigaanibatowaad: FrontRunners* tells their story. Compare this event with the status given to the Four Host First Nations at the 2010 Olympic Winter Games.

©P

Awards

Since 1993, the National Aboriginal Achievement Foundation has recognized individuals who have excelled in their community. Each year, the accomplishments of 14 individuals in areas ranging from health, law, and political science to culture, arts, education, youth achievement, and lifetime achievement, are recognized. The awards are presented at the televised National Aboriginal Achievement Awards (NAAA) ceremony. The awards are seen as one of the highest honours the Aboriginal community can give.

First Nations, Métis, and Inuit individuals are also recognized by the Order of Canada, which is the highest civilian honour awarded by the Governor General of Canada. Actress Tantoo Cardinal entered the Order of Canada in 2010, as did Judy Gingell of Whitehorse. Judy Gingell, the first Aboriginal commissioner in the Yukon, was recognized for more than 40 years of work advancing First Nations' rights and self-governance in the Yukon. Also awarded the Order of Canada in 2010 was Joan Glode, a Mi'kmaw woman from Nova Scotia, recognized for her contributions as a human rights officer, administrator, policy maker, negotiator, and fundraiser.

Other notable recognitions have been made in the arts. Graham Greene (Oneida) and Adam Beach (Saulteaux) have been nominated for Academy Awards. Cree musician Buffy Sainte-Marie won an Academy Award in 1984. Joseph Boyden, a Métis author, won the Scotiabank Giller Prize for his novel *Through Black Spruce*. Inuk musician Susan Aglukark has won three Junos, and Inuk Jessie Oonark, an internationally renowned artist, was elected into the Royal Canadian Academy of the Arts.

FIGURE 4.34 William Commanda, an Algonquin Elder, was inducted into the Order of Canada in 2008. He is shown here with Michaëlle Jean, Canada's governor general at the time.

VOICES OF THE PEOPLES

Jessica Yee

At age 12, Jessica Yee started volunteering at a women's shelter. Since then, she has formed the Native Youth Sexual Health Network (the only organization working in the full spectrum of sexual and reproductive health by and for Indigenous youth in North America), organized several United Nations conference forums, started a letter-writing campaign, written books and blogs, and more. Jessica Yee has a Mohawk mother and Chinese father, and makes her home in Toronto and on the Oneida Indian Reservation in Wisconsin. One of her distinctive qualities as a leader and activist is her ability to make connections between issues: "We try to incorporate everything, from environmental justice to violence prevention, that you wouldn't typically see within a sexual reproductive health mandate."

FIGURE 4.35 In 2009, Jessica Yee won the Toronto YWCA's Young Woman of Distinction Award.

FIGURE 4.36 Sylvia Maracle (of the Tyendinaga Mohawk Territory in Ontario) was honoured with a 2008 National Aboriginal Achievement Award. For many years, she has been executive director for the Ontario Federation of Indian Friendship Centres.

THINKING IT THROUGH

1. How can sports and games contribute to your own identity? What sort of benefits do you gain through playing sports and games that help shape who you are and your sense of yourself?

2. What are the positive contributions of sports and games to Aboriginal peoples' sense of identity?

3. Research Aboriginal and mainstream media to identify a recent award to a First Nation, Métis, or Inuit person or group for achievements. Create a profile of the achievements to share with your class in a presentation combining writing and visuals.

CRITICAL THINKING

For each of the following, describe the impact on identities as positive, negative, or possibly mixed: artistic expressions, legal definitions, stereotypes, recognition of and awards for achievement. Explain your answers.

Conclusion

In this chapter, you have studied some factors that influence identity. For First Nations, Métis, and Inuit peoples, the formation of identity has been made complex by the legacy of government policies and by stereotypical representations of Aboriginal peoples. You have also learned about expressions of identity, honours, and recognition of First Nations, Métis, and Inuit peoples. As well, you have developed the skill of analyzing images.

©P

End-of-Chapter Activities

1. Read the song "E5-770, My Mother's Name," by Lucie Idlout, on our website. How would you respond if you were not recognized by your name, but only by a number given to you by the government? Discuss why you think Lucie Idlout created a song about this topic, and why her song and projects such as Project Surname are important to the identities of Inuit in Canada.

 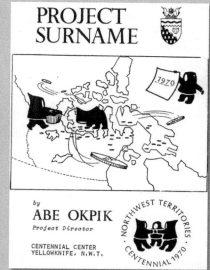

FIGURE 4.37 In 1965, Abe Okpik was the first Inuk appointed to the Northwest Territories Council. From 1968 to 1970 he toured the Northwest Territories (which then included what is now Nunavut) and northern Québec as the leader of Project Surname, interviewing Inuit and recording their preferred names.

2. Create a collage or write a poem, song, or article about an aspect of your own personal identity or the cultural identity of your family, community, or Nation. Consider representing how your identity has been formed by your own traditions and culture as well as the influences of others.

3. The medicine wheel teachings tell us that we must try to balance the physical, emotional, intellectual, and spiritual sides of our lives. Create a representation of your identity, in images or words, reflecting your physical, emotional, intellectual, and spiritual sides. Describe your emotional state, your physical attributes, your state of mind, and your spirituality.

4. Make a list of all of the television shows, movies, or video games you have seen that feature Aboriginal people. Write a critique of each example, discussing whether or not the First Nations, Métis, or Inuit characters were stereotypical or authentic. What evidence do you have for your opinions?

5. In a group, read, discuss, and develop a response to the following quotation. Consider identity by choice, identity by law, and Nations defining identity. Be prepared to present your response in your class.

In 2010, Assembly of First Nations National Chief Shawn Atleo said:
It is fair and just that Indian status will be restored to those who lost it because of inequality in the Indian Act. But the real problem is the Indian Act itself. The Government of Canada should not be able to decide who is and who is not a First Nation citizen. It is the right of any nation to identify its citizens and First Nations are no exception. We are calling on the federal government to work with us on a broader approach that goes beyond these narrow amendments and deals with the real issues of First Nations citizenship.

CHAPTER 5

Roles and Responsibilities in Family, Community, and Nation

> Will you walk with me, Grandmother?
> Will you talk with me a while?
> I'm finding life confusing
> And I'm looking for some answers
> To questions all around me
> At that school and on the street.
> You have always been here for me.
> Will you help me learn to see?...
> (Grandmother):
> Should the answer to some questions
> Not be sought within your heart?
>
> —*from* Nokum Is My Teacher *by David Bouchard*

This chapter is focused on the roles and responsibilities in families, communities, and Nations. You will learn about past and present roles—including the special roles for Elders and Wisdom Keepers, and for children. As well, you will consider challenges to Aboriginal roles and responsibilities, including the residential school system, the removal of children from their families in the Sixties Scoop, and urban life. This chapter also presents some outstanding models in addressing challenges, in healing, and in rejuvenating.

INQUIRING MINDS

Use these questions to explore the big ideas in this chapter.

1. How do the beliefs and values of First Nations, Métis, and Inuit cultures influence present-day activities?

2. How do First Nations, Métis, and Inuit families and communities define their roles and responsibilities?

3. How are First Nations, Métis, and Inuit responding to challenges to identity by healing and rejuvenating?

FIGURE 5.1 What words come to mind as you look at this photograph?

©P

FIGURE 5.2 This painting is *Little Boy* by Leland Bell. The artist was born in 1953 in Wikwemikong Unceded Indian Reserve on Manitoulin Island, Ontario. He is Anishinaabe and a member of the Loon Clan. During his youth, Leland Bell was deeply influenced by teachings, ceremonies, and art instruction at cultural arts camps. What people, ideas, and events have been strong influences in your life so far?

Roles and Responsibilities: Family, Community, and Nation

You started the unit Diverse Identities by looking in Chapter 4 at identity, realities, and perceptions. In this chapter, you will continue to explore identity by considering families, communities, and Nations. As you read, keep in mind that people and Nations are incredibly diverse; just as there is diversity in your community, you will find this diversity many times over among the many families, communities, and Nations of Aboriginal peoples in Canada. In other words, this chapter presents common themes, selected roles, and specific examples, but it cannot possibly do justice to the diversity found among First Nations, Métis, and Inuit peoples today.

Key Understandings about Identity and Groups

Before you look in depth at identity in families, communities, and Nations, here are some key points to consider:

- A common theme among First Nations, Métis, and Inuit people is concern for the group (family, community, and Nation) and a focus on relationships; the group is a vital aspect of identity. For example, miyowicehtowin means in Plains Cree "good, healthy, happy, respectful relationships." These relationships are highly valued.

- This focus on the group and on relationships sometimes contrasts sharply with the focus on the individual often found in Canadian society. However, while these two foci contrast, they cannot be separated. They are connected—as the quotation at left illustrates.

- Within Aboriginal world views, each person sees his or her path through life as a cycle of responsibilities to family, community, Nation, and the wider world. For First Nations, Métis, and Inuit people, roles for any one person are not static, and roles are all interrelated (to other people, to the land, and to animals).

- The ideas of community and Nationhood are not confined to geographical location. First Nations, Métis, and Inuit people live everywhere—on reserves and off reserves, in small towns and cities, and in large urban centres. The sense of being Anishinaabe, or Inuit, or Cree, or Dene is not necessarily tied to living in the physical community of one's ancestors. One is just as Métis, Dakota, or Onondaga whether living in Curve Lake, Winnipeg, or Oshawa. Aboriginal identity transcends geographical and spatial frontiers. The continued displacement of First Peoples from ancestral lands—among other factors—has led to **diasporas**.

The Four Hills of Life

The Four Hills of Life is an Anishinaabek teaching that describes a sacred journey through life that every person undertakes. Every stage of life—from childhood to adolescence to adulthood to old age—has its own set of responsibilities and challenges, which are represented by the Four Hills. Each of the Four Hills, or stages, can also be described as a season. During each stage, we must rise to meet our responsibilities and challenges, or using the image of the Four Hills, we must reach the peak of the hill.

1. Springtime represents birth and childhood. The first challenge is overcoming the difficulty of being born and fighting against childhood illnesses. Given that they come into the world helpless, infants must also learn to ask for help. Basically, an infant is responsible only for being someone's baby.

2. As summer comes, a person enters the stage of youth. Although there is time for fun and play, youth are responsible for learning about the world around them and preparing for their adult roles.

3. In autumn, each person begins to climb the third hill, or enter the phase of adulthood. Increasing responsibilities may include nurturing and providing for their own families, as they become parents in their turn.

4. Winter comes and snow covers the ground as each person prepares to climb the fourth hill.

FIGURE 5.3 *Comforting* (in the *Homage to Grandfather* series) by Daphne Odjig (1980). The artist was born in Wikwemikong Unceded Indian Reserve on Manitoulin Island. In what ways does this artwork illustrate the Four Hills of Life teaching?

If individuals at this stage have followed the good path and have learned many lessons throughout the previous stages, then they will fulfill the role of teacher. Because of their life experience, people at the fourth stage can serve as guides to those who are not as far along on their journey.

The circle is complete when the physical body dies. The cycle continues as new life comes into the world again.

FIGURE 5.4 Adolescence is a period of transition from childhood to adulthood. In many Nations, this transition is marked by various ceremonies. For some Anishinaabek people, coming of age is marked by a vision quest for boys and a time of seclusion when a girl has her first moon cycle (menstrual period). In the photograph, these youth are learning to drum. This photograph appears in the book *The Four Hills of Life* by Thomas Peacock and Marlene Wisuri.

Roles and Responsibilities Today: A Snapshot

You might think that the Four Hills of Life teaching and key understandings (pages 146–147) relate to the past alone. However, families, communities, and Nations remain integral to defining, nurturing, and rejuvenating Aboriginal identities. As you read through the rest of this chapter, you will find many examples in which roles and responsibilities rooted in the past continue today and offer ways for First Nations, Métis, and Inuit peoples to face challenges.

As increasing numbers of First Nations, Métis, and Inuit people live in urban areas, people are developing new ways to stay connected with their Nations and heritage. At Tungasuvvingat Inuit, Ottawa's Inuit community hosts youth gatherings, a women's healing circle, and community lunches with traditional Inuit food. The Métis Centre in Sault Ste. Marie brings together the Métis community. The poem "Urban Indian Kids" (page 149) tells about connections formed among younger and older First Nations people.

Another way that First Nations, Métis, and Inuit people—especially youth—are staying connected is through online social networking, blogs, and Aboriginal radio, television, and newspapers. Aboriginal media—such as the Aboriginal Peoples Television Network (APTN), an online Métis radio station, the newspaper *Tekawennake* from Six Nations, the *Anishinabek News*, *Windspeaker* magazine, and *Voyageur* magazine— serve to promote and maintain Aboriginal cultures, thereby strengthening Aboriginal communities and identities. Aboriginal media can also help counter negative stereotypes that are found in mainstream media about Aboriginal peoples (which you learned about in Chapter 4).

FIGURE 5.5 In many families, older children are expected to take care of younger siblings and cousins.

Core Values in Changing Times

Roles, responsibilities, and occupations of First Nations, Métis, and Inuit men, women, and children vary and have undergone change. Many of these changes have come as a result of challenges that erode family structure, but family networks and community structures are still central.

Urban Indian Kids
by Gord Bruyere

"Hey, don't play with the Sacred Fire!"
they say and then poke it,
and drop gum wrappers on it,
not knowing that they make it sacred,
these urban Indian kids.

The old man stands silently
and who can tell he is smiling,
but the light and smoke and night air
sure like having him around, just like
these urban Indian kids.

"Whose turn to tell a story?" he asks.
The corners of their mouths
pull their shoulders up and their hands
(too, which) fill the pockets of
these urban Indian kids.

Meanwhile in an equal and opposite reaction—
in keeping with the natural law—
eyes are cast down to the feet
and words cannot find
these urban Indian kids.

Rubber boots and running shoes line up
without being asked when they hear talk
about a nature walk, and the old woman
laughs at the way they say "miigwech,"
these urban Indian kids.

They sort of know what it is
and have no clue of how to make it,
but they sure can eat bannock
while making face-paint with raspberry jam,
these urban Indian kids.

And they run and scream,
and once in a while they even listen
while they tell their own story,
and so the spirits will recognize
these urban Indian kids.

THINKING IT THROUGH

1. In writing or in a diagram, summarize the Four Hills of Life teaching (page 147) and note how it illustrates the key understandings listed on page 146.

2. New technology and media can have both positive and negative effects on families. In a group, brainstorm what these effects might be for First Nations, Métis, and Inuit families.

Roles and Responsibilities in Families

First Nations, Métis, and Inuit communities vary widely. However, they share at least two core values:

- Family is considered very important.
- Children and Elders or Wisdom Keepers are highly valued.

Inuit Families

In Inuit communities, family groups often include immediate family and extended family such as grandparents, aunts, uncles, cousins, and Elders. Community members often share homes, with less focus on individual ownership and a greater focus on community life. Annie Aningmiuq, from Pangnirtung on Baffin Island and now a student at the University of Guelph, says that she is very close to her aunt who teaches her about the language, cooking, and sewing: "I'm 26 now and every time I go home, I always learn something from my aunt."

In Nunavut, Elders and youth are considered to be so important that the territorial government created a Department of Culture, Language, Elders and Youth:

> *The family is the foundation of Inuit culture, society, and economy. All our social and economic structures, customary laws, traditions, and actions have tried to recognize and affirm the strength of the family unit...*
>
> —Henoch Obed, Labrador Inuit Alcohol and Drug Abuse Program

FIGURE 5.6 One Inuit pastime for women is throat-singing, which is typically performed by two women as a form of entertainment and competition during the winter months. Cousins Cellina Kalluk (left) and Tanya Tagaq Gillis (right, whom you read about in Chapter 4) are throat-singers from Nunavut. Cellina learned throat-singing from her mother in Resolute, but Tanya learned on her own by listening to audiotapes. After moving from Cambridge Bay at age 15 in order to attend high school and then art college, Tanya was homesick, so her mother sent her audiotapes of throat-singing. Tanya now performs internationally.

©P

Métis Families

In Métis families, there can be very diverse practices and teachings. Families raise their children in ways that combine uniquely Métis, European-Canadian, and First Nations traditions. Many households are bilingual or multilingual, speaking Michif along with French and/or English. Because Michif is generally understood only within the community, the language helps unite people in their community identity.

Senator Thelma Chalifoux of the Métis Nation of Alberta recalls her experience growing up:

> *I was a product of a very strong Métis extended family that lived between the city of Calgary and the Sarcee Reserve... We each had a role. My mother's role was equal to my father's. My mother's role, my aunt's role, and my grandmother's roles were that they looked after the whole family, the children, the garden, the berry picking, the food, because the men were away working most of the time. So they had total control and [defined] roles. The man's role in the family was to make the living and bring home the money. When times were hard, everybody stuck together. When my grandmother or my aunts were out of food, everybody joined together and helped them out. We were a very, very proud extended family. There was relief in those days, but we never took it... The role of the woman...was an equal role...*

Some families and individuals continue the Métis tradition of fiddle music, performing it at family gatherings, at Métis cultural events such as Rendezvous, and to wider audiences. Sierra Noble (right) and the Métis Fiddler Quartet are examples. The Métis Fiddler Quartet is a musical group of siblings with roots in the Red River Settlement. Alyssa, Conlin, Nicholas, and Danton Delbaere-Sawchuk all have classical music training, and their influences include their older relatives and music mentors James Flett and Teddy Boy Houle from Winnipeg. Sierra Noble started playing when she was eight years old and later dedicated her first CD release, *Spirit of the Strings*, to the many musicians who had mentored her.

FIGURE 5.7 Sierra Noble, opening for Bon Jovi, performs Métis fiddle tunes. In 2005, she was the fiddler for the eight-day Aboriginal Spiritual Journey and Calling Home Ceremonies that visited battlefields and cemeteries in Belgium and France to honour the sacrifices of Aboriginal veterans.

Grandmother
by Roy A. Young Bear

if I were to see
her shape from a mile away
I'd know so quickly
that it would be her.
the purple scarf
and plastic shopping bag.
if i felt
hands on my head
i'd know that those
were her hands
warm and damp
with the smell
of roots.
if I heard a voice
coming from a rock
i'd know
and her words
would flow inside me
like the light
of someone
stirring ashes
from a sleeping fire
at night.

First Nations Families

Families, the concept of community, and the various roles within the community are incredibly diverse for First Nations peoples. In general, however, a family includes a vast web of people from grandparents to aunts and uncles, to cousins, to more distant relations. Families can also include members who are adopted (formally or informally).

> *We believe that the Creator has entrusted us with the sacred responsibility to raise our families...for we realize healthy families are the foundation of strong and healthy communities. The future of our communities lies with our children, who need to be nurtured within their families and communities.*
>
> —*Charles Morris, Nishnawbe Aski Nation and Sioux Lookout, Ontario*

Lineage ties hold great importance in many Nations. As well, some Nations have a clan system that connects all members of a clan and involves each clan in certain responsibilities within the community. Clan systems vary among the Nations that have them. In contrast to the Sandy Lake First Nation clans you read about in Chapter 2, the Oneida clans include the following and their traditional roles:

- Turtle Clan—keepers of knowledge and all to do with the environment

- Bear Clan—keepers of the medicine

- Wolf Clan—the pathfinders; those who guide others to live their lives in the way that the Creator intended

Clan systems not only indicate traditional roles in the community but also who can marry whom.

Typically, children and older members are honoured within First Nations communities—a fact that extends many families beyond a nuclear family. The community as a whole takes care of the young and old, and they are all welcome at community gatherings. As described in the Four Hills of Life teaching, older members who have lived a good life take on the role of guides to younger ones. Becky Loucks of Curve Lake First Nation in Ontario writes:

> *My Elders are the ones who look after me in all my needs. They are my lifelong friends; I can confide in them. My Elders are understanding; they have been through some of the same situations and can guide me through when the times are tough, no matter what the cost is to them.*

©P

FIGURE 5.8 Artist George Littlechild created this artwork in 1996 to honour his ancestors and the Plains Cree people. *Plains Cree Chiefs* is dedicated to the chiefs who maintained Plains Cree practices, culture, and pride in a time when Plains Cree ways were being challenged. The chiefs shown are George Littlechild's great-great grandfather, Chief Louis Bull (bottom left), and three of his great-great-great uncles—Chief Bobtail (top left), Chief Ermineskin (top right), and Chief Samson (bottom right).

THINKING IT THROUGH

1. **a)** With a partner, discuss the various roles filled by members of your family and your own specific roles.

   b) How do the roles in your family compare with those you have learned about in First Nations, Métis, and Inuit families?

2. Reread the poem "Grandmother" on page 152. List the beliefs from the Four Hills of Life teaching (page 147) and ideas about families that are expressed in the poem.

3. What questions do you have about the clan systems in various Nations? In what ways might families raise their children to take on certain roles? Do you belong to a clan or have a future role expected of you based on family and community traditions? In a group, discuss the questions, your ideas, and how they relate to or compare with your experiences.

Roles and Responsibilites in Communities

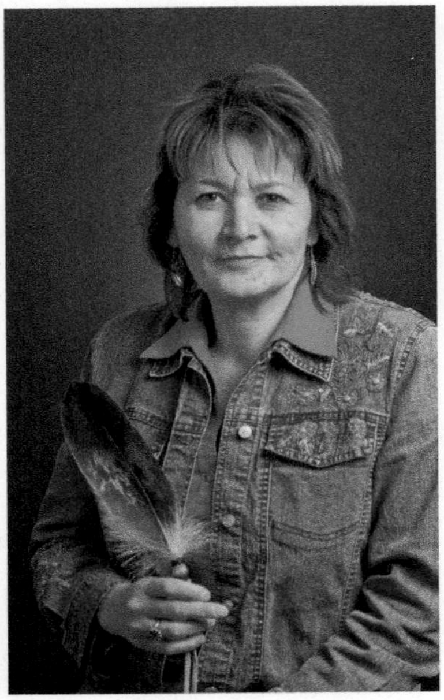

FIGURE 5.9 Diane M. Kelly of Onigaming First Nation in Ontario became the first woman Grand Chief of Treaty 3 and the first woman lawyer in Treaty 3 Nation. Diane Kelly is a Midewiwin member and pipe carrier.

This section looks at identity and some of the many, often overlapping roles in First Nations, Métis, and Inuit communities. First Nations, Métis, and Inuit women and men today take up many more and different roles in families and in communities than they did in the past. In addition, individuals may well fulfill more than one role at a time. To get an overview, take a look at the examples below and note the diversity.

- Grandmother Josephine Mandamin of the Water Walkers, community leader and activist
- Zacharias Kunuk, Inuk film director and producer, born in Igloolik, Nunavut
- Dr. Raoul J. McKay, bilingual educator and documentary film producer, of the Red River Métis community in Manitoba
- Wendy Landry, president of the Thunder Bay Métis Council, college instructor, and mother
- Dorothy Grant, Kaigani Haida fashion designer, of the West Coast
- Chief Theresa Hall of Attawapiskat First Nation in Ontario
- Edward Benton-Benai, faithkeeper, Grand Chief of the Three Fires Midewiwin Lodge, and author
- Cecil King, educator, language teacher, and translator, of the Wikwemikong Unceded Indian Reserve on Manitoulin Island
- Edith Josie, Gwich'in Elder and columnist for Old Crow in Yukon Territory
- Nathaniel Arcand, actor, Plains Cree (Nêhiyaw), from Alexander First Nation in Alberta

Recently added roles such as activist, actor, filmmaker, business person, lawyer, author, administrator, accountant, entrepreneur, scientist, and computer programmer might seem to have little to do with skills that First Nations, Métis, and Inuit peoples have used living on the land and in traditional roles with their families. The expansion of roles has many benefits, but it also has challenges. For example, if a provider who once hunted or trapped on ancestral lands can no longer do so because of pollution or being denied access to the land, the change is life-altering for both the provider and the community. However, Sheila Watt-Cloutier notes on page 155 that traditional practices and skills teach life skills that are applicable even in a greatly changed world.

WORDS MATTER

pipe carrier someone who walks a good path and has been chosen to take on the critical and laborious responsibility of caring for a specific pipe used in certain ceremonies

Community Roles

Elders and Wisdom Keepers

Called by a variety of names in different Nations, people known as Elders, Wisdom Keepers, cultural advisors, and medicine people take on many key roles. In general, we use the term Elders and Wisdom Keepers in this textbook. Elders and Wisdom Keepers include both men and women, and they are not necessarily elderly people. They are people who have learned the traditional teachings and ways of life of their communities, share them with their community, have special gifts, or have had unique life experiences. From the earliest age, children are taught to show respect to Elders and Wisdom Keepers because of their wisdom and knowledge and their readiness to share them with others. It is important to note that the role of Elders and Wisdom Keepers does not exist in isolation; being a trusted member of a community is part of the role.

In Cree communities, Elders (Kithteyayak) may have specialized knowledge—they might be spiritual advisors (who keep sacred knowledge and know protocols), healers (who know ancient medicines, and conduct sweats), or community Elders (who hold and pass forward the Nation's traditional knowledge).

In Métis communities, the term used is Elders. The Métis roles of Elder and Senator are different, although some community members may fulfill both roles. The role of Senator is an elected position. Both Senators and Elders play important roles in maintaining Métis culture.

Here is a description of the role of Elder among the Innu:

> *Elders should be role models for everyone else. Elders should be teachers to the grandchildren and all young people because of their wisdom. Elders should be advisors, law-givers, dispensers of justice. Elders should be open to everyone. Elders should be knowledgeable in all aspects of Innu culture. Elders should be teachers of the...history of Innu people [and]...recorders of history. Elders should be teachers of values important to Innu to be passed on from generation to generation...of language and oral history...of Innu medicine. We place great importance in our Elders. Their directions for us will guide our lives.*
>
> —*statement by Innu delegation from Sheshatshiu Native Canadian Centre of Toronto*

Not only does the land and the process of the hunt teach technical hunting skills, but more importantly it teaches our children character...[and] life skills such as patience. Automatically, as you're waiting for the weather to clear, the animals to show, the ice to form, the snow to fall, you are being taught how to be patient. You are also learning [courage,] determination, persistence, and [reflection]... And many Inuit who have acquired and continue to practice these traditional skills are, in large part, making it in the modern world because one way of life does not have to be at a cost of another.

—*Sheila Watt-Cloutier, Inuk leader and activist*

FIGURE 5.10 Ted Nolan is from the Ketegaunseebee Garden River First Nation, near Sault Ste. Marie in Ontario. He has played and coached in the NHL. This photograph, taken in November 2007, shows Ted Nolan as coach for the New York Islanders.

REFLECTION

In your community, who is involved in helping you develop your potential? What ideas do you have about parenting or mentoring the young? How would these ideas help develop a child's potential?

Children and Youth

In the Four Hills of Life teaching, the role of the child is relatively simple. The vital energy of children is a source of pleasure and joy for communities. However, as children grow into youth, they take on the role of learning their future roles and responsibilities—in other words, they prepare for the second hill of life. As well, they are traditionally expected to be role models for younger children.

In First Nations, Métis, and Inuit teachings, it is understood that children are born with special gifts and that the entire extended family must ensure that these gifts are cultivated. It is also the community's responsibility to create a space for an individual, so that he or she will feel a sense of belonging and purpose. Not cultivating the gifts of each person can harm the entire community because the health of the individual and that of the community are interrelated and intended to be long-lasting.

> *We believe our children are our future, the leadership of tomorrow. If you believe in that, then you have to believe also that you must equip your future with the best possible tools to lead your community and lead your nation into the twenty-first century.*
>
> —*Joe Miskokomon, former Grand Council Chief of the Anishinabek Nation*

Givers of Life, Caregivers, and Providers

Before contact with Europeans, labour in many Nations was divided along gender lines, but contributions by both women and men were recognized and equally respected. In many Nations, men would hunt, fish, and trap; women would gather berries, tend crops, prepare food, and make clothing. Roles have changed over time and expanded. Now, while women continue to be honoured as the givers of life, First Nations, Métis, and Inuit women and men take up a wider variety of roles in communities. However, with the learning of contemporary roles it is equally important that traditional men's and women's roles are remembered and understood.

Leaders

In First Nations, Métis, and Inuit communities, there are many types of leaders and leadership roles (which you will explore in Chapter 6). Leaders are not necessarily Elders and Wisdom Keepers. However, Elders and Wisdom Keepers lead by example, and the leadership in communities often seeks the guidance of Elders and Wisdom Keepers. As you read further, keep in mind that there are formal and informal leadership roles within First Nations, Métis, and Inuit communities; not every leader has a title and an official role.

Teachers and Learners

According to First Nations, Métis, and Inuit ways, everyone in a community is involved in educating children, learning is lifelong, and learning takes place through observation, listening, and guidance.

In Métis families, the Métis ways of learning are through experience and through stories. The Michif language and everything one needed to live a good life were embedded in the family and the community. Young boys and girls learned along with their parents and family members in the home and in their working lives. Experiential learning—learning from doing—is still a favoured way of learning for some Métis students.

Mi'kmaw writer Isabelle Knockwood remembers learning with the Elders and Wisdom Keepers:

The elders would sit in a circle and smoke their pipes. Some of them would be leaning on their canes listening to the stories... There was much laughter, merriment, joking, and reminiscing about the past... Sometimes they talked all night and throughout several days. Children were never allowed to interrupt or walk in front of people or in between them when they were talking. Mukk petteskuaw we were told. The underlying meaning is, "Don't walk in front of people who are talking." This custom stems back to the old belief that everyone is a spirit and a conversation between people is a spiritual experience because they are also exchanging their most valuable possession, their word. I usually sat by my mother's knee and kept very quiet because I did not want to be told to leave. I wanted to hear all the interesting stories about my ancestors. I was listening and learning... The stories we heard the elders tell referred not just to their own experiences but to those who had lived generations earlier... The stories were ancient.

FIGURE 5.11 These students in Gjoa Haven, Nunavut, are fishing after school—in August 2008. In many Nunavut schools, the school year starts in August and ends in May, so that children can go on the spring hunt with their families.

FIGURE 5.12 In Toronto, the 7th Generation Image Makers is a drop-in program with opportunities for learning and working with various art forms such as murals, regalia making, and photography. This mural is called *Reclaim the City* and was painted during a 2009 mural project.

Artists

As you read in Chapter 4, artists play a major role among First Nations, Métis, and Inuit people. Artists working in many diverse media express their individual identities and their community and National identities, inform, combat stereotypes, entertain, and much more.

Defenders

For communities to thrive, they must be secure, so communities have always needed people to defend and maintain peace. The role of defender has important cultural and spiritual significance. One of the battles a defender must continuously fight has to do with living life according to the teachings and values of the community.

It is important to note that in many First Nations, Métis, and Inuit cultures, the role of those who defend is very different from the stereotypical, mainstream perception of the "masked warrior." For example, the image that many people in Canada will remember was taken during the 78-day standoff in Kanehsatake Mohawk Territory in the summer of 1990—a young Canadian soldier and a Mohawk "warrior" (page ix). However, as Maurice Switzer noted earlier, "the majority of those 63 besieged Mohawks were not wearing masks or carrying rifles; they were unarmed women and children."

©P

In many First Nations, Métis, and Inuit languages, the words for the role of keeping a community secure have deep, multi-layered meanings that are much more complex than the English word *warrior* can convey. In Ojibwe, the word for the role is ogitchidaa, which means "community protector," not "soldier," "guerilla," or "terrorist." In Mohawk (or Kanien'kehaka) the closest word is Rotiskenraké:te. In historical documents between the British and the Iroquois allies, all men of the Nations are referred to as "warriors," which is an equivalent reference to the men who were the "defenders" of the Nation. For the Haudenosaunee today, a defender would still be those "warriors" or men of the Nations who continue to "look after the Tree of Peace" from outside danger.

Jacob (Jake) E. Thomas was a traditional Cayuga Chief and faithkeeper of the Onondaga Longhouse and professor at Trent University. He travelled extensively from his home in Six Nations to promote the Great Law of Peace. Jacob Thomas explains the literal meanings of Rotiskenraké:te (often translated as "warrior") and Raróntaron (sometimes translated as "war chief"):

> *"Rotiskenraké:te." This is what it means: Years ago the men used to make "charms" or "Medicine bags" for hunting, and they would carry this with them wherever they went. It would enable them to be a good hunter, to help them to get the animal they were looking for, because that was what they depended on...*
>
> *So this is why they call them "Rotiskenraké:te," because they carried that medicine all the time. "-ké:te" is the root word "to carry something," that something is attached to your body in some way—maybe around your neck—you carry it in some way. So that was a charm that they carried to attract the game, and so they were called "Rotiskenraké:te." But it doesn't mean he's a warrior; it means he's a young man, a hunter...*
>
> *[W]e don't use the English word "warriors" any more this day and age, because that kind of thing—warfare among the nations—ended when the Peacemaker gave us the Great Laws of Peace. So you can't have "warriors," you only have men. Young men is what it means in our language.*
>
> *The word I would use to explain or translate "Raróntaron" is "deputy." But the English word "deputy" really doesn't translate what it really means in Mohawk. When I say "Raróntaron," it means "He looks after the Tree [the Tree of Great Peace]."*

FIGURE 5.13 When Gordon Waindubence's father was dying, his father asked Gordon to conduct a pipe ceremony, but the hospital staff stopped it. Almost 20 years later, in 2010, Elder Gordon Waindubence (right, with Dr. Jack Baker, left) of Sheguindah First Nation celebrated the opening of Mshkikii-Gaming Medicine Lodge at Sudbury Regional Hospital. The circular pine-panelled lodge has a ventilated firepit where smudging or pipe ceremonies can be conducted.

Healers

First Nations, Métis, and Inuit peoples have many healing roles and typically approach health from a holistic perspective. They strive to balance mind, body, spirit, and emotions. Some healers pair traditional knowledge from their Nations with mainstream health sciences such as naturopathic medicine, nursing, midwifery, mental health, and suicide prevention. Some examples are Irnisuksiiniq—Inuit Midwifery Network in the North and De dwa da dehs nye>s Aboriginal Health Centre in Hamilton, Ontario (named for the concept of "we are taking care of each other among ourselves").

THINKING IT THROUGH

1. In your community, outside of school, who fills the role of a teacher for you? In what ways? Create a graphic organizer showing how this person's role is the same as or different from those who "teach" First Nations, Métis, and Inuit peoples.

2. Earlier in this chapter, you read about

   a) a focus on the group in First Nations, Métis, and Inuit communities in contrast to a focus on the individual

   b) a core belief of mutual aid

   In a group, find and discuss examples of (a) or (b) in this chapter, in earlier chapters, or in current news. Then summarize your findings in writing.

3. Research the protocol for approaching an Elder or Wisdom Keeper of a specific community. Share your findings in a group and explain the importance of the protocols.

Giving and Receiving Feedback

Giving and receiving feedback are essential to good communication. Writers and other artists often give and receive feedback in order to shape their work more effectively. Giving and receiving constructive, respectful feedback are important and useful skills throughout life.

Before Giving and Receiving Feedback

It is important to remember the purpose of the exercise and to approach it from a good place. Remember that

- *constructive* feedback focuses on helping improve someone's work; it builds up rather than tears down

- showing work to others can be intimidating; those giving feedback should be humble and compassionate, imagining how they would feel

- creating the work has taken time and effort, which should be respected

- giving feedback well takes time and effort, which are marks of respect

- feedback should focus on the work (not the person), the goals for the work, and how well it meets those goals—for example, whether the message is clear

- specific types of feedback might be asked for—for example, about tone

FIGURE 5.14 We all can learn from one another. How might an author such as David Bouchard (above) give and receive feedback as part of his work? How could improving your skills in giving and receiving feedback help you and others in your school life? future work? personal life? community work?

To Receive Feedback

Feedback is a two-way process of explaining goals, giving comments, asking and answering questions, clarifying, and listening attentively. The kind of feedback you ask for and receive will depend partly on the situation (with a peer, teacher, or employer) and what experience the other person brings.

To Give Feedback

- Make notes in preparation about strengths, weaknesses, and your questions.

- Start off with a comment that expresses your appreciation for the work.

- Be relevant and realistic. What is applicable? focused on the goal? feasible?

- Be encouraging, and balance your comments; don't focus only on weaknesses as you see them. Be positive and emphasize things you like.

- Ask questions, and listen to the answers—for example, about goals or focus.

- Be clear, direct, descriptive, and specific; describe your views, give reasons, and point to concrete examples. Make specific suggestions about what to do differently.

> **REFLECTION**
>
> As you receive feedback, consider whether you are listening for what is said or for what you want to hear.

> **REFLECTION**
>
> As you give feedback, consider whether you are offering your opinion or trying to impose it.

Apply Your Skills

1. For the writing you started on page 160, work with a partner to give and receive feedback. Later, reflect on the process, challenges, and outcomes.

Historical Challenges to Roles and Responsibilities

First Nations, Métis, and Inuit peoples value families and strong communities, and they maintain a sense of responsibility that extends to the well-being of their children and grandchildren and on, to future generations. However, First Nations, Métis, and Inuit families, communities, and Nations have faced enormous challenges. Historical challenges include

- the residential school system and its legacy, as well as other schooling issues

- the widespread removal of children from their families to substitute care—what is called the Sixties Scoop

- the imposition of the Indian Act, including its definition of who is "Indian," which you read about in Chapter 4

As you read about each challenge in this section, think about what it would mean to a person's sense of responsibility and about its impact on families, communities, and Nations.

> *The family in Aboriginal societies stood between the individual and the larger society, playing an interpretive or mediating role. It helped individuals understand and respond to society's expectations, and it helped Aboriginal society engage individuals in constructive ways and discipline them should they venture on a course that conflicted with prevailing social values and expectations of behaviour.*
>
> *—Royal Commission on Aboriginal Peoples, 1996*

Education and Aboriginal Roles and Responsibilities

Various systems of education in Canada have had a profound effect on the roles and responsibilities of Aboriginal peoples in their communities. First Nations, Métis, and Inuit children have attended day schools, industrial schools, residential schools, and public schools. For many, school was a place where their identity and culture were questioned, dismissed, or forcibly denied. In most cases, education was controlled by the federal government, which saw schooling as a way to prepare Aboriginal children for life in Canadian society, to prepare them for mainstream roles, and to assimilate them into Canadian society. These experiences would have a lasting impact—the residential school system, for example, affected not only those who experienced the schools directly, but also their children and grandchildren.

©P

Industrial Day Schools

As a result of the negotiations of the Numbered Treaties in the 1870s, the federal government was required to provide First Nations children with education. Industrial day schools were built close to or on reserves, enabling students to attend school during the day and go home at night.

The policy of the government focused on assimilation, and education was the government's main tool in achieving that goal. After the Indian Act made First Nations and Inuit peoples wards of the government, the Nicholas Flood Davin Report of 1879 recommended that Canada use **industrial schools** to "civilize" the First Nations, Métis, and Inuit population. Aboriginal children were trained as domestic help or labourers.

WORDS MATTER

industrial school a school that concentrates on teaching manual skills such as sewing, carpentry, or farming

Residential Schools

In contrast to the industrial day schools, residential schools were much more widespread and in operation much longer. From the mid-1800s to the 1990s, generations of First Nations, Métis, and Inuit children attended residential schools. In many cases, the schools were hundreds of kilometres away from the child's home, family, and Nation. Students were away from home for months or years at a time.

Residential schools were part of the government's plan of assimilation through education. In later chapters, you will study the residential school system in terms of justice and reconciliation. In this chapter, to look at how experiences in residential schools affected the identities of First Nations, Métis, and Inuit peoples, we must first explore the background of the schools, the experiences of survivors, and the legacy of strength and resilience among Aboriginal peoples in Canada.

FIGURE 5.15 Aboriginal girls were trained in sewing, laundry, cleaning, and cooking. Aboriginal boys learned farming, carpentry, shoemaking, and blacksmithing. These girls (in a 1955 photograph) were taught cooking and other domestic skills at a residential school in Kenora, Ontario. How might these skills have been useful to these students? Why would the schools focus on these skills rather than on more formal education?

To read more about residential
schools—including testimony from
survivors, official government statements, and church responses—visit
our website.

Policy and Implementation

Residential schools affected virtually every First Nations, Métis, and Inuit
community in Canada: in the first half of the 20th century, almost
75 percent of children between the ages of 7 and 15 attended residential
schools. In many cases, parents tried to keep their children at home or
hide them, but the RCMP could forcibly remove the children and arrest
the parents.

In 1892, the federal government made formal arrangements with
Anglican, Catholic, and the Methodist and Presbyterian (later United)
churches to run residential schools, paying them to manage day-to-day
operations.

However, the funding was inadequate, leaving schools with too few
supplies and in poor repair. Lack of proper food and clothing, along with
cold and unhygienic conditions, made disease and death common. Many
children died while at residential schools and the schools were known for a
very high rate of tuberculosis. In the 1940s and 1950s, the federal
government took full control of the residential schools.

Residential School Experiences

Each school day usually began with morning prayers. Classes were
followed by an afternoon of tasks such as farming or sewing clothing.
English or French was the language of instruction, and Aboriginal children

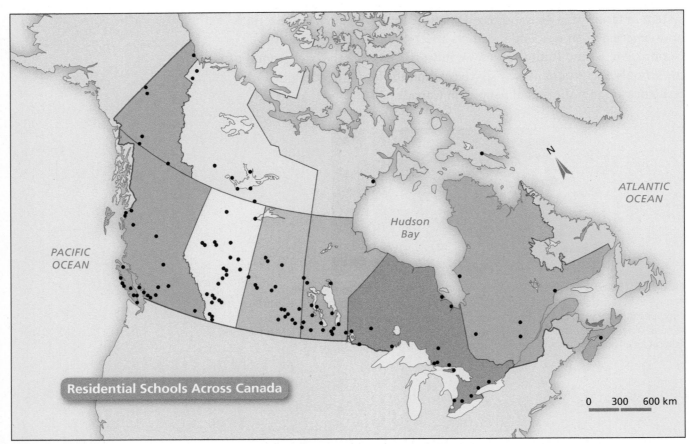

FIGURE 5.16 This map shows the locations of residential schools in Canada. Is there anything about this map that surprises you? Explain.

©P

were often prevented from speaking their own languages. Even if they did not know English or French, they were sometimes punished for speaking their first language. Cultural practices were often ignored or even banned. For most students, lessons did not reflect the beliefs and values of First Nations, Métis, and Inuit peoples.

While some individual students had positive experiences with kind, supportive teachers at the schools, and some communities had asked for schools to be built so that their children could be taught skills considered useful for success in the broader Canadian society, many children faced cultural, psychological, physical, and sexual harm. Many residential school survivors have testified about sexual, physical, and psychological abuse at the schools. Most children did not receive the emotional and cultural support they needed as they grew up.

Residential School Impact

These experiences would have an enormous impact on the identities of generations of Aboriginal peoples in Canada. In general, students were taught that their cultures—and they themselves—were not valued. At the same time, residential schools were intended to break the bonds within families, communities, and Nations. The residential school policy separated families for most of each year or for years at a time, thus disconnecting children from the support and cultures of their home communities. At home, each family, community, and Nation suffered from the absence of their children and their inability to protect them. In the residential schools, many children were forced to deny what they learned and valued at home, an experience that undermined the very core of their identity. This left

FIGURE 5.17 These photographs were taken of Thomas Moore before and after he entered the Regina Industrial Residential School in 1874. The photographs were published in 1897 to demonstrate success in "civilizing" students. Do you think the photographs show "success"? Discuss how the process of creating these images might have affected the identity of Thomas Moore.

many students with unresolved identity issues and feelings of loss, anger, guilt, and confusion. Many students grew up in a school environment of fear and violence but without the continuous love shared among parents, children, and an extended family. Residential schools contributed hugely to family breakdown, and many individuals fell into self-destructive behaviours. In many cases, residential schools did not allow children to be parented, so these children did not learn by example how to parent. The residential school policy created generations of First Nations, Métis, and Inuit people who did not learn their languages, culture, history, ways of knowing, or traditional roles and responsibilities.

> *Residential schools and the trauma that was experienced has been described as a "de-feathering process," stripping Native Peoples of their knowledge, spirituality, physical and emotional well-being, and most sadly, has led to the loss of community. Aboriginal residential school survivors may have a higher prevalence of Post Traumatic Stress Disorder (PTSD)... Possible effects include...depression;...[thoughts of] suicide;...low self-esteem;...flashbacks;...fear of authority and intimacy; domestic and [other types of] violence...*
>
> —Ashley Quinn, social worker and researcher, *in* First Peoples Child & Family Review

VOICES OF THE PEOPLES

I Lost My Talk

I lost my talk
The talk you took away.
When I was a little girl
At Shubenacadie school.

You snatched it away:
I speak like you
I think like you
I create like you
The scrambled ballad, about my world.

Two ways I talk
Both ways I say,
Your way is more powerful.

So gently I offer my hand and ask,
Let me find my talk
So I can teach you about me.

—*Rita Joe, Mi'kmaw poet*

FIGURE 5.18 Rita Joe attended the Shubenacadie Residential School until Grade 8, sometime in the 1940s. In this poem, she writes about losing her language. How would Rita Joe's loss of language affect her sense of self and her ability to communicate with other Mi'kmaq people? Do you think her loss of language affected her ability to stay connected with her cultural traditions?

©P

Healing and Reclaiming Roles and Responsibilities

The legacy of the residential school experience continues to have a long-term effect on First Nations, Métis, and Inuit peoples in Canada. Some residential school survivors—and generations following them—have reclaimed their Aboriginal roles and responsibilities by rediscovering their spiritual traditions, by becoming political activists, or by working for their communities in education, social work, the arts, and counselling.

First Nations, Métis, and Inuit peoples have spoken up about their experiences in residential schools, and have talked about the impact of the schools on their lives and in their communities. They have organized and sought justice in many ways (which you will read about in later chapters). The federal government and many churches involved in the residential schools have apologized; however, many First Nations, Métis, and Inuit people have made it clear that saying sorry is not enough: the relationship must change. The path to healing can only begin with recognition of the truth of what happened in residential schools and with acknowledgement of the strength and courage of First Nations, Métis, and Inuit people who share their stories.

To be **resilient** is to be able to recover from adversity. Resilience has been shown by Aboriginal peoples across Canada in their ability to adapt, as well as maintain their cultures and identities, despite generations of attempts to "civilize" and assimilate them. First Nations, Métis, and Inuit cultures and traditions are still very much alive and are thriving in Canada. Aboriginal peoples are proud and strong. They continue to transmit valued traditional knowledge, celebrate traditions, revive their languages, and build a stronger presence in Canadian society, especially in education and government.

Present-Day School Experiences

You will read again about education (in Chapter 9) but here we will look at Aboriginal roles and responsibilities and present-day school experiences. Think about the things you learn in school. You gain knowledge about the world around you, which helps you understand your place in the world. You learn how to express yourself, about civic duties, history, perspectives, and critical thinking. You may also figure out what you are interested in, and what you want to pursue in life.

Now imagine that you are studying the history of your culture—but it has been written by people who are not of your culture. Imagine that when your culture is brought up in class, it is depicted in a negative way, or as extinct. How would you feel about yourself? Would this education help you understand who you are?

First Nations children in Ontario have been attending public schools for a very long time, including during the time of industrial and residential schools. Most First Nations have their own elementary schools, and those that do not send their children to school nearby. First Nations children often travel by bus to these schools, much like other rural

WORDS MATTER

resilient to be able to recover from adversity or setback

Web Connect • • • • • • • • • • •

To read more about K-Net, visit our website.

students. To attend high school, students may still travel back and forth daily, or may make arrangements to live with a family in a town with a high school. Some students receive funding to help them do so. Sometimes these students, like other students, have difficulties adapting to a new place and experience homesickness. Some Aboriginal children living in urban settings have always attended public schools.

In some northern communities, programs such as the First Nations SchoolNet Program, which began in the late 1990s, provide Internet connectivity and computer hardware assistance to First Nations schools. The Keewaytinook Okimakanak (K-Net) is the regional management organization for Aboriginal Affairs and Northern Development Canada's First Nations SchoolNet program, which serves six communities: Deer Lake First Nation, Fort Severn First Nation, Keewaywin First Nation, McDowell Lake First Nation, North Spirit Lake First Nation, and Poplar Hill First Nation. K-Net also connects students and the community to teachers and other resources.

While school curricula are generally designed and written by educators and politicians who may not represent all cultures, there have been and continue to be changes in the education system, in curricula, and in the hiring of teachers. It has been acknowledged that the marginalization experienced by Aboriginal students within the curricula, textbooks, and classrooms directly affects their achievement. The textbook you are reading right now has been written by Aboriginal and non-Aboriginal educators working together to ensure more extensive, meaningful, and authentic inclusion of Aboriginal cultures in Canadian school curricula. More and more Aboriginal teachers are working in classrooms all over Ontario, and there has been greater inclusion of Aboriginal cultures in public schools across the province. Native Language Programs and cultural events are part of the regular school year. Schools host powwows, provide cultural teachings and programming, and offer other extracurricular activities that support Aboriginal identity and culture.

VOICES OF THE PEOPLES

This is my first day of school and I stand alone; I look on. Most of the kids know what to do, like they've been here before, like the teacher is a friend of the family. I am a foreigner, I stay in my seat, frozen, afraid to move, afraid to make a mistake, afraid to speak, they talk differently than I do, I don't sound the way they do, but I don't know how to sound any different, so I don't talk, don't volunteer answers to questions that teacher asks. I become invisible.

—*Marilyn Dumont, Métis author*

FIGURE 5.19 How do you think Marilyn Dumont's feeling of being different might have affected her school experiences?

©P

The Sixties Scoop

While residential schools were still active, there were additional challenges to Aboriginal identities, communities, and Nations. The first was the continued impact of the Indian Act determining who had status as an "Indian" and the result that many women lost Indian status (as you read in Chapter 4). In some cases, this meant First Nation women and their children were forced to leave their communities.

A second challenge was a policy that emerged to remove children from First Nations, Métis, and Inuit families and communities at an alarming rate. For the general population in Canada, child welfare services took children away from their homes and placed them in foster and adoption programs supposedly only as a last resort. However, removing a First Nations, Métis, or Inuk child from home, family, and community became a common practice. Because this practice was first noted in the 1960s, it became known as the Sixties Scoop, but the practice continues today.

Adoptions practised historically by First Nations and Inuit families kept children within their communities and connected to their roots. Adoptions by non-Aboriginal families often cut the children off from their roots, with no opportunity to understand their cultural identity or their traditional roles and responsibilities. Some children were raised in cities, with no connections with their homelands or Elders or Wisdom Keepers. In the Scoop, each child would suffer the impact, and communities lost great numbers of each generation.

Adoptees were separated from siblings and isolated from their culture, and sometimes subjected to substandard care. Artist George Littlechild was a foster child from infancy and lost contact with his four siblings, parents, and Nation. Over time, he became an activist, and the concept of Wahkomankanak (Plains Cree for "honouring ancestors") has inspired his art and life.

VOICES OF THE PEOPLES

It is so very strange for me to learn that, after almost 100 years since my Kokomis [grandmother] was escorted off the reservation of Golden Lake by the RCMP, me and my family members may be entitled to...status registration...

—*Lynn Gehl, April 2010 letter to the* Anishinabek News

REFLECTION

What impact would being "scooped up" from family, community, and Nation and relocated to a different and unfamiliar family, community, and culture have?

VOICES OF THE PEOPLES

Through its deliberate assault on the Aboriginal family, the residential school system created the conditions that rendered First Nations vulnerable to the next wave of intervention: child abductions sanctioned by provincial child welfare laws. Residential schools incarcerated children for ten months of the year, but at least the children stayed in an Aboriginal peer group; they always knew their First Nation of origin and who their parents were, and they knew that eventually they would be going home. In the foster and adoptive care system, Aboriginal children typically vanished without a trace, the vast majority of them placed until they were adults in non-Aboriginal homes where their cultural identity, their legal Indian status, their knowledge of their own First Nation and even their birth names were erased, often forever.

—*from* Stolen from Our Embrace *by Suzanne Fournier and Ernie Crey*

In addition to the removal of children from families and communities, another issue is the quality of alternative care that those children received. The funding for child welfare services for First Nations, Métis, and Inuit children was and continues to be lower than for non-Aboriginal populations. Lower funding means fewer resources available for the best actions to be taken for the welfare of the child.

The Scoop Continues

Although called the Sixties Scoop, the removal of First Nations, Métis, and Inuit children continues at high rates—with profound impact on individuals, families, communities, and Nations. Aboriginal children are disproportionately represented in foster care in Canada. Provincial and territorial ministries of child and family services suggest that 30 to 40 percent of children and youth placed in care from 2000 to 2002 had Aboriginal ancestry, yet Aboriginal children made up less than 5 percent of the total child population in Canada. In Manitoba, in 2000, Aboriginal children made up nearly 80 percent of children living in out-of-home care.

Aboriginal children and youth in care are frequently placed in homes apart from their own communities. This experience can contribute to a lack of connection to their heritage and cultural identities, as well as to their ancestral lands and Nations, and many feel isolated. Feelings of alienation can lead young people of any background to be drawn toward whatever might give them a sense of belonging, including gangs. Gang activity and exposure to alcohol and drugs have become an increasing concern for Aboriginal youth. A critical concern involving Aboriginal youth, however, is increasing rates of suicide, which you will consider in the next section.

FIGURE 5.20 In the 1960s, a federal government project removed three 12-year-old Inuit boys from their homes to send them south to live with non-Aboriginal families and be educated in Ottawa. Barry Greenwald's film *The Experimental Eskimos* examines the experiences of Peter Ittinuar, Zebedee Nungak, and Eric Tagoona (shown in 1964 and again in 2008), who grew into leaders in the fight for Aboriginal rights. What impact, do you think, would removing children from their Inuit culture have on their identity? What impact would it have on their relationships with their Inuit families and communities?

The Sixties Scoop

I've often asked people of western European culture if I and a bunch of other Native people came in and took your small children away and you don't know whether you are ever going to see them again, well you wouldn't stand for it. We didn't stand for it, but we were outnumbered. This had a terrible impact on our people.

—Charles W. (Charlie) Hill, Six Nations, Executive Director of the National Aboriginal Housing Association, 2007

We have never in our history had a time when more First Nations kids were in child welfare care than right now, including residential schools and the 60s scoop. If anything we are becoming more efficient at removing kids from their homes.

—Cindy Blackstock, Gitxsan First Nation, Executive Director of First Nations Child and Family Caring Society of Canada, 2007

Fortunately, I found my way back home to Mishkeegogamang... All my life I felt a huge part of me was missing...my identity...who I was and where I came from...[now] that hole inside me is becoming filled with getting to know my people and band.

—Karen Kaminawaish, born into the Mishkeegogamang Ojibway Nation, adopted and raised by a Mennonite couple in Indiana, U.S.A.

A Native child in Toronto is 10 times more likely to be apprehended and placed in the care of a Children's Aid Society. While many will return to their families, others can fall through the cracks and end up on the street as young adults.

—Kenn Richard, Executive Director, Native Child and Family Services of Toronto (NCFST)

1. Explain how the Sixties Scoop has served to (and continues to) undermine the strength of Aboriginal children, youth, families, and Nations. How does removing children from their families and communities have an impact on each child and Nation?

2. Research to learn about
   a) programs to help Aboriginal adoptees who want to reconnect with their families and communities
   b) programs to support parenting in First Nations, Métis, and Inuit families

THINKING IT THROUGH

1. Research the impact that residential schools have had on survivors and their children and grandchildren. In a short essay, comment on how residential schools have affected the passing on of traditions and language. What is the impact of trauma on the survivors and their descendants?

2. In a small group, discuss what you think would be the impact on one Nation of the three challenges described in this section—educational systems, the impact of Indian Act definitions of "status Indian," and the so-called Sixties Scoop. Make notes and summarize your discussion for the class.

Contemporary Challenges to Roles and Responsibilities

In addition to challenges you read about in the last section, First Nations, Métis, and Inuit people face more challenges to their roles and responsibilities that include

- demographic changes
- discrimination, including discrimination and violence against women and girls
- suicides
- other social pressures, such as housing shortages, unsafe water, alcohol and drug abuse, and young single-parenthood

Again, as you read, think about what each challenge might mean to a person's sense of identity and the impact on families, communities, and Nations.

Demographic Changes

First Nations, Métis, and Inuit youth make up the largest and fastest-growing segment of the Canadian population. In the future, Aboriginal youth will be a large segment of the workforce as well as the larger society. This increased presence could give First Nations, Métis, and Inuit peoples a greater voice in Canadian society. However, developing an Aboriginal identity will become more difficult for young people as Wisdom Keepers and Elders age and pass away, making it harder for youth to learn and maintain traditional roles and responsibilities. Other challenges faced by Aboriginal youth today include poverty, isolation, dysfunctional family structures, and loss of language and culture.

Another population trend is the increasing number of people living in urban centres in Canada. While populations among non-urban First Nations, Métis, and Inuit people are also increasing, the number of Aboriginal people living in cities and towns is increasing as well.

Urban Challenges

Some First Nations, Métis, and Inuit people have grown up in urban centres, while others move to urban centres from smaller communities. On average, First Nations, Métis, and Inuit youth living on reserves or in remote areas are less likely than urban youth to finish high school or go on to post-secondary education. This tendency has led many Aboriginal youth to seek opportunities for advancement and education in urban settings where there are more resources and services.

Moving to an urban setting is an incredible challenge for the young men and women who then find themselves away from their families, their friends, their communities and Nations, and everything they have known.

FIGURE 5.21 Kiel MacDonald, a Haida youth, designed this image called *Self-Pride* for the Urban Native Youth Association (UNYA), an organization formed in 1988. Why do you think he called the image *Self-Pride*?

©P

Urban life has a different pace than rural life: it is often faster, with more diverse activities and events. Youth can feel a bit lost within that diversity, and struggle to find a sense of belonging. In the face of overwhelming new experiences, some experience culture shock. They begin to feel isolated, marginalized, and unsure of how to connect to their cultural traditions. They may not know where to go for help. Imagine yourself moving from all that you've known to somewhere you've never been before, without your family or your friends. You then have to try to make new friends, and explain who you are and where you are from. What effect might this experience have on your sense of identity?

Many urban settings have cultural events, school courses, training, and language programs for First Nations, Métis, and Inuit participants. Community feasts and dances bring people together to share and spend time with one another. There are also planned events to help people feel more connected to the land, such as sweat lodge ceremonies, moon ceremonies, medicine picking expeditions, and group travel to other communities. These ways of connecting can be especially important to Aboriginal youth entering urban areas for the first time. In Vancouver, the Urban Native Youth Association (UNYA) was formed in 1988. In 2009, the association offered over 20 programs designed to empower Aboriginal youth through education, personal support, housing, and sports and recreation. UNYA also undertakes community development initiatives and advocates for positive opportunities that connect youth to community and help define roles and responsibilities. Gathering places such as friendship centres and cultural centres, such as the Native Canadian Centre of Toronto and the Ojibway and Cree Cultural Centre in Timmins, bring people together. Organizations such as the Métis Nation of Ontario develop local councils that run events for Métis people. Friendship centres host cultural events, provide teachings, act as drop-in locations, and are also a place for people to network for personal, professional, or cultural reasons.

Societal Discrimination

First Nations, Métis, and Inuit peoples have faced—and continue to face—racism in the broader Canadian society. Unfortunately, discrimination can be found in many communities throughout Canada and in many forms. However, Philo Desterres of the Québec Native Women's Association says that the battle against sexism in the Indian Act "has contributed to our understanding of the obstacles...but...has...helped to strengthen the determination of the Aboriginal women to fight discrimination wherever it is found."

FIGURE 5.22 What aspirations do you think these children have? Do girls and boys, and men and women have equal value and equal opportunities in your community?

©P

Gender Discrimination

Although great strides have been made, First Nations, Métis, and Inuit women and girls are still challenging discrimination and struggling for equality. From one of the many organizations involved in the fight against discrimination, the following example gives you a picture of the issues.

Inuit Women's Voices: Pauktuutit

In 1984, Inuit women founded Pauktuutit—the first organization to voice the concerns of Inuit women on a national level. The mission of the organization is to stand up for the equality and human rights of Inuit women in Canada. Some areas on which Pauktuutit focuses are listed below. How are they connected? What do they indicate about challenges and aspirations for girls and women?

- adequate housing
- economic development
- access to health care
- midwifery
- early childhood development
- helping residential school survivors heal

- HIV and AIDS
- justice
- sexual health
- family violence
- abuse
- working with other organizations on health, climate change, and education

Violence Against Women and Girls

Alarmingly, many studies show that First Nations, Métis, and Inuit women and girls experience more violence, both outside and within their communities, than non-Aboriginal women and girls. Here are some statistics:

- An Amnesty International study in 2004 found that First Nations, Métis, and Inuit women aged 25 to 44 were five times more likely to die of violence than other Canadian women of the same age group.

- In the last 30 years, more than 500 First Nations, Métis, and Inuit women and girls have gone missing or have been murdered.

- A Statistics Canada study in 2005 indicated that Aboriginal people were three times more likely than non-Aboriginal people to experience spousal abuse.

It is important to understand the roots of this discrimination against First Nations, Métis, and Inuit women and girls. They face the double bind of racism and gender discrimination and the legacy of colonial racism and sexism. The result is a society where First Nations, Métis, and Inuit women and girls are marginalized and endure social, cultural, economic, and political inequalities.

VOICES OF THE PEOPLES

The Grandmother Moon teaching is a reminder of the roles of women in Aboriginal communities. The Sisters In Spirit program quotes this poem:

Grandmother Moon
You know all women from birth to death
We seek your knowledge
We seek your strength
Some are STARS up there with you
Some are STARS
on Mother Earth
Grandmother, lighten our path in the dark
Creator, keep our sisters safe from harm
Maa duu? Mussi Cho Kukdookaa

Amber Tara-Lynn Redman was born in 1986. In 2005, Amber went missing from her parents' home in Standing Buffalo Dakota Nation in Saskatchewan. Her remains were found after almost three years of searching. Her mother, Gwenda Yuzicappi, says the following prayer for her:

Amber will not be forgotten...
We need...balance to help find a solution as to why our women are going missing and being murdered. Our communities need to take responsibility for the safety of our women and girls. Wrongs must be made into rights. We must honour the teachings of respect, empathy, and compassion...

FIGURE 5.23 Gwenda Yuzicappi, Amber Redman's mother, is shown here at a 2007 gathering held by the Saskatchewan Sisters In Spirit for family members of missing or murdered women.

Sisters In Spirit

The Sisters In Spirit (SIS) program of the Native Women's Association of Canada addresses the disadvantages that First Nations, Métis, and Inuit women face in Canadian society that increase the risk women will experience violence. SIS's work includes tackling poverty, expanding access to adequate housing, improving access to justice, dispelling stereotypes, and supporting child well-being. The Sisters In Spirit program conducts research, raises awareness, and influences policy.

SIS has held family gatherings for the missing or murdered First Nations, Métis, and Inuit victims and their families. These gatherings are an opportunity for people to remember their loved ones in positive ways and to join with others who have similar experiences. To raise awareness, SIS has collaborated with Amnesty International, KAIROS Canada, the National Association of Friendship Centres, and the Canadian Federation of Students to hold vigils in communities across the country to honour the lives of missing or murdered Aboriginal women, show support to the families of the victims, and raise public awareness about this crisis.

FIGURE 5.24 Sisters In Spirit uses as its logo an image of Grandmother Moon. It signifies the SIS work to address the crisis, a commitment to remember women and girls lost to violence, and a commitment to be a part of a solution. The logo was designed by late artist Dick Baker, who also designed the memorial that now stands in the Downtown Eastside of Vancouver.

Alex Jacobs comes from the Whitefish Lake First Nation and is a traditional teacher, pipe carrier, and residential school survivor. He has worked as a social worker, teaches the Ojibwe language and culture, and works with youth, men, and women needing support.

Violence Toward Women and Girls in First Nations, Métis, and Inuit Communities

From what I have witnessed and heard…most [situations involving violence] are related to the residential school and…descendants from parents that went to residential schools. The parents didn't have the proper knowledge of nurturing and educating their children and some…had relatives like aunts and uncles and even grandparents who went there, so they are suffering from that and the abuse comes from within… [T]hey take their anger out on so many other things—[anger about] the loss of culture, the loss of language, loss of…meaning of life to them, as it once was—they take it out on others… And then the alcohol and the drugs are introduced into the communities and then…men and women begin to use these substances, but it is the men that tend to be more violent towards the women…

Healing and Renewing

The first part…is regaining some of the lost ways of culture…to learn those different cultural activities. And then the next part would be to continue with the language… They have a better understanding of who they are and where they came from if they have that opportunity to [learn the cultural activities and the language]. The other part…is…youth programs…to get them back into their culture… And then the other thing is that many of them are starting to go into treatment programs that are Native-specific… I think they need to start focusing again on community so that they can bring their lives back to focus.

I really believe it's a good idea to work both ways out on the land and in town here. This way our children need to be out on the land to learn things and start feeling good about themselves because there are so many changes now…

—*Martha Rabesca, Slavey, Fort Good Hope*

Suicide

Not all Aboriginal communities have high rates of suicide. However, Statistics Canada states that the overall rates of suicide for First Nations and Inuit youth are high. Suicide rates are five to seven times higher for First Nations youth than for non-First Nations youth, and among Inuit youth the rate is 11 times the national average. Why are these rates so high? In several studies, suicide rates for First Nations and Inuit males were much higher than those for females. Studies show that communities with higher rates of suicide had several common features:

- high rates of children and youth in care
- dysfunctional family structures
- overcrowded living conditions
- unemployment or low-paying jobs
- limited education

- disconnection from the land
- loss of traditional knowledge and practices

Web Connect • • • • • • • • • • •

To learn more about River of Life, visit our website.

The factors noted on the preceding list reveal some of the many challenges faced by First Nations, Métis, and Inuit youth across the country. Many Aboriginal youth experience isolation, a lack of basic amenities, a lack of hope for the future, and a loss of connection to their culture. However, a 2007 Health Canada report showed that communities maintaining cultural and spiritual traditions had fewer instances of youth suicides. The study showed that strengthening the identities of Aboriginal youth through culturally based programs such as the Nimkee Program at the Nipowagan Healing Centre could help prevent suicides.

Suicide has a profound effect on entire communities, leading many to create suicide-prevention strategies. Millbrook Technologies, an information technology organization owned and operated by the Millbrook First Nation in Nova Scotia, has partnered with the Centre for Suicide Prevention, the Assembly of First Nations, and the Canadian Mental Health Association to create River of Life, an online program designed to train and support those who work with young people at risk. Aboriginal youth have also stepped forward to encourage discussion about suicide and to work to prevent suicide among their peers.

FIGURE 5.25 From 2003 to 2006, a group of Aboriginal youth, support staff, and volunteers walked from Nanaimo, B.C., to Ottawa to raise awareness of youth suicide in Aboriginal communities. They carried the message to young people in high schools, to friendship centres, and to officials at local, provincial, and federal government levels.

My name is Chasity Meuse and I am Mi'kmaw from Indian Brook First Nation in Shubenacadie, Nova Scotia. I first met the Aboriginal Youth Suicide Prevention Walkers in Indian Brook on March 18, 2006. They came to walk with our community to help raise awareness and to remember those who have taken their lives by their own hands. This really touched me and inspired me to want to do more, and that is why I joined the walk. I walk for my community, I walk for my family, friends, loved ones and everyone who has been affected by suicide. Every single suicide on my reserve has had an impact on my life and has made me feel strongly about helping our people. If there is one thing that I can tell someone who is contemplating suicide, it is to reach out and get some support because you are worth living on this earth. Life isn't easy and we all need to work on it and we should not feel ashamed to ask for help.

FIGURE 5.26 Chasity Meuse works to raise awareness about suicide by sharing her experiences with other teens. What can you do to help others in your community?

THINKING IT THROUGH

1. In a small group, discuss situations in which you or someone you know was discriminated against because of religion, ethnic background, or appearance.

2. Review what you have learned in this chapter and previous chapters about life in diverse First Nations, Métis, and Inuit communities and Nations. What examples do they present of family and community life, aspirations, challenges, resilience, and rejuvenation? In a brief oral presentation, share one example you noted with your class.

3. Visit or research an Aboriginal-run community or cultural organization. How does this program or centre provide Aboriginal people with a place to learn about their culture and find support from their community? What programs does the centre have that support cultural, social, and healing needs? In what ways do the programs support Aboriginal identities? Summarize your findings in a written profile.

Role Models

In First Nations, Métis, and Inuit communities throughout Canada, many people are working to address challenges and revitalize their communities. They are also furthering the understanding of all Canadians about First Nations, Métis, and Inuit values and aspirations. In the following pages, you will learn about some of the many organizations and individuals who are role models. As you read about them, think about the challenges they face and the aspirations they express.

Mary Simon

As president of the Inuit Tapiriit Kanatami, Mary Simon has had many successes. One recent way she raised awareness and led by example was in her response to the 2008 federal government apology for the residential school system. She responded first in Inuktitut, then said in English: "Mr. Prime Minister, I spoke first in my Inuit language because I wanted to illustrate to you that our language and culture are still strong."

Steve Teekins

Steve Teekins works for Na-Me-Res (Native Men's Residence) in Toronto and also teaches drumming. Na-Me-Res includes a shelter for homeless men, has outreach programs for men and youth, and offers mobile counselling services.

Dr. Evan Adams

Dr. Evan Adams of the Sliammon First Nation on the West Coast is active in many spheres. He is a family doctor, the first Aboriginal Health Physician Advisor for British Columbia, and an actor. When he visits Aboriginal communities, he talks with people about medical issues, but he also asks them to look at the big picture of planning for the health of communities and families, educational and economic opportunities, and neighbourly relations—to look with an "eagle's eye view," as he puts it.

FIGURE 5.27 Dr. Evan Adams has been acting professionally for 24 years, in medicine for 10 years, and is still learning. At home, with his family, he says his dad is still trying to teach him to be a good hunter and fisher.

FIGURE 5.28 This July 2010 meeting at the Hinton Friendship Centre Society in Hinton, Alberta, brought together the National Association of Friendship Centres Aboriginal Youth Council. Over 100 friendship centres in urban centres throughout Canada offer a range of services. How would these programs help strengthen identity, especially in urban centres? How are the members of this youth council serving as role models?

FIGURE 5.29 John Beaucage says, "Experience teaches us that the best way to build solid relationships is to listen."

John Beaucage

John Beaucage is a pipe carrier from the Bear Clan. A citizen of Wasauksing First Nation, he was raised on the Shawanaga First Nation and has extended family in Nipissing First Nation. When he was appointed as advisor to the Ontario Minister of Children and Youth Services, he brought attention to disproportionate numbers of Aboriginal children in alternative care, low funding for that care, and high suicide rates.

Frances Sanderson

A member of the Ojibwe Whitefish River First Nation and at home in the city, Frances Sanderson leads Nishnawbe Homes in Toronto. Frances Sanderson has been involved in her community in many ways, including as a member of the Toronto Police Services Aboriginal Consultative Committee, past director for Native Child and Family Services of Toronto, and past president of Native Earth Performing Arts.

Kenn Richard

Kenn Richard is a founder of Native Child and Family Services of Toronto (NCFST) and became its first executive director. NCFST provides a range of services focused on the Aboriginal children in the city—including outreach to families, day camps, youth programs, and culturally appropriate care for children needing alternative care. Kenn Richard earned his Bachelor of Social Work and Master of Social Work degrees at the University of Manitoba and now lectures graduate students at the University of Toronto. His family comes from one of the oldest Métis settlements in Manitoba, St. Frances Xavier, near Winnipeg, on the Assiniboine River.

FIGURE 5.30 Frances Sanderson is Executive Director of Nishnawbe Homes, which provides housing for homeless and under-housed Aboriginal people in Toronto.

FIGURE 5.31 This photograph from 2010 shows youth gathered for the Métis Nation of Ontario Annual General Assembly at Old Fort William in Thunder Bay. In what ways do you think they are involved in and contributing to their communities and Nation? How might you be involved in and contributing to your community?

©P

James Bartleman

James Bartleman has had a long and distinguished career as a Canadian diplomat (in Cuba, Israel, the European Union, South Africa, and Australia), defence policy advisor to the federal government, Lieutenant-Governor of Ontario, and writer. Through his many accomplishments, he never forgot his roots in Mnjikaning First Nation (now known as Rama First Nation). He continues to find innovative ways to inspire Aboriginal youth and make a difference in their lives, to fight against discrimination, and to fight the stigma attached to mental illness. For example, during his term as lieutenant-governor, he initiated a book drive that, in its first year, collected 1.2 million books for First Nations schools and native friendship centres across Ontario. The following year, he launched a twinning project between Aboriginal and non-Aboriginal schools in Ontario and Nunavut that promoted literacy and built cross-cultural bridges.

FIGURE 5.32 James Bartleman established literacy camps in over 28 communities and made sure that funding remained for them for a five-year period.

Velma Noah

In the Delaware Nation, near London, Ontario, Velma Noah is a role model, student, and teacher. She is trying to save and rejuvenate Lunaape, the language of her people. Of about 200 people in the community, only a small group of older people speak Lunaape fluently. Velma Noah is learning from older speakers so that she can teach others, including children. "I want to be a fluent speaker. That's my dream... Because if I become fluent, I can make someone else fluent."

THINKING IT THROUGH

1. Family, community, and Nation are central to the identities of First Nations, Métis, and Inuit peoples. However, Aboriginal peoples have faced challenges to their families, communities, and Nations in Canadian society. Individuals and organizations are role models in meeting these challenges. For one of the role models you have learned about, identify one challenge and one aspiration. Share your observations with a partner.

2. Earlier in the chapter, you read about resilience. Referring to people profiled in this section and/or another part of this textbook, write a short essay on resilience.

Conclusion

In this chapter, you have explored big ideas about roles and responsibilities of First Nations, Métis, and Inuit people in their in families, communities, and Nations. You have looked at historical and contemporary challenges to Aboriginal roles and responsibilities and how these challenges are being met. You have also learned about the great resilience of First Nations, Métis, and Inuit peoples, who have always adapted, and continue to adapt, to change. In learning and practising how to give and receive feedback, you will have acquired skills that will be useful all your life.

CRITICAL THINKING

In what ways are First Nations, Métis, and Inuit identities shaped by families and communities?

End-of-Chapter Activities

1. In a group, discuss what beliefs and values are reflected in the roles and aspirations for the people in this photograph? How do your aspirations compare?

FIGURE 5.33 Hallie Snake and Robby George from Aamjiwnaang First Nation are both students at St. Clair Secondary in Sarnia, Ontario. Hallie aspires to become a teacher and Robby aspires to become a police officer.

2. Reflect on the Four Hills of Life teaching and make a list showing how it is illustrated by examples in the chapter.

3. Research and create a profile of a First Nations, Métis, or Inuk person who fills one of the roles discussed in the chapter.

4. Consider how Aboriginal peoples are currently revitalizing their cultures and communities after the legacy of residential schools. Make a poster, podcast, or other creative presentation about how one individual, organization, community, or Nation is doing something to protect, promote, and teach their traditions and language.

5. Research one specific issue that has an impact on First Nations, Métis, and/or Inuit people. You could start by visiting a website for an Aboriginal women's organization or interviewing Aboriginal youth in a city. Consider the issue and how it is addressed. What are ways in which individuals or organizations address the issue? Summarize your findings in writing.

6. a) Review the poems in the chapter to see what ideas they communicate about identity.

   b) Research the work of other First Nations, Métis, and Inuit writers, especially poems concerned with identity.

   c) Present your ideas and the additional writing to your class.

©P

Unit 2 Rich Performance Tasks

Choose one or more of the following tasks:

Compare Images

1. Look again at the images on page ix, which show different perspectives on the stand-off at Kanehsatake.

a) With what you have learned to this point about identity, challenges to identity, and the skill of analyzing images (pages 130 and 131), examine the images again to compare and contrast them.

b) Summarize your findings in a written or verbal presentation.

c) Locate recent images showing First Nations, Métis, or Inuit individuals, families, or communities. Drawing from Aboriginal and mainstream sources, choose a total of two to four images to examine more closely.

d) Use the skill of analyzing images to annotate or comment on the recent images you have found. What questions do you have? What is the subject of each image? What is in the foreground? in the background? left out or cropped out? How do these recent images compare with those on page ix?

e) Research to find information about one or more of the images. Who created the image, and what is his or her perspective or relationship to the subject? How does this information add to your understanding and/or raise more questions? What values or beliefs are suggested by the image?

f) Prepare to present the two to four recent images you analyzed and your findings.

FIGURE 5.34 Look again at this photograph of Mary Two-Axe Earley (taken in August 1994, by Gordon Beck for the Montréal *Gazette*). In what different ways could it be cropped to present different understandings of the subject?

Research and Present an Artist

2. Aboriginal artists such as Jane Ash Poitras, George Littlechild, Buffy Sainte Marie, and Susan Aglukark have expressed their concern about loss of culture, traditions, language, and community values.

a) Choose one First Nations, Métis, or Inuk artist to research.

b) Find examples of the artist's work, such as reproductions of visual arts or a musician's lyrics.

c) To guide your research (through books, the Internet, or interviews), list the questions you would like to be able to answer about the artist's life, art, and motivations. You might consider questions such as these: What does the artist express about cultural, personal, or National identity? loss and challenges? accomplishments? aspirations?

d) Create a multimedia presentation (for example, a digital slide show) about the artist, the issues the artist raises through art, and key pieces of information you have found that relate to the subjects of this unit.

e) Show your presentation to another student or the teacher, and practise the skill of receiving feedback (page 161).

f) Use feedback to refine your work before presenting it to the class.

Write an Essay

3. a) Reread the teaching of the Four Hills of Life (page 147) to examine how the responsibilities of each stage in life contribute to identity for an individual and within families and communities.

b) Then consider
  – the impact on identity of one challenge explored in the unit (for example, the Sixties Scoop)
  – ways in which First Nations, Métis, and Inuit peoples are responding to the challenge, healing, and revitalizing

c) Write an essay that clearly presents the relationships among the teaching, the challenge, and various responses.

d) With a partner, use the skills of giving and receiving feedback (page 161) before finalizing your essay.

Sovereignty and Self-Determination

Ravena Williams, of the Aamjiwnaang First Nation, takes part in a protest in 2009 to protect her treaty rights.

Métis youth representatives on the Métis Nation of Ontario's Youth Council. What is the role of youth in Aboriginal governance?

Sam George (1952–2009) is shown surrounded by media after the conclusion of the Ipperwash Inquiry in 2007. His brother Dudley George was killed during the Ipperwash crisis in 1995.

Leaders such as Mary Simon, president of the Inuit Tapiriit Kanatami, are vital to re-establishing self-governance for Aboriginal peoples.

SELF-GOVERNANCE, JUSTICE, AND acknowledgement of Aboriginal rights are essential for Aboriginal peoples to regain self-determination. This unit discusses the ongoing challenges and successes of First Nations, Métis, and Inuit peoples in achieving autonomy, protecting treaty rights, and navigating the justice system.

CHAPTER 6

Governance

> Governance begins with the people and if we can engage as many people as possible in the process we continue to create a stronger and more vibrant government for our community.
>
> —*Chief Clifford Tawpisin Jr., Muskeg Lake Cree Nation*
>
> Our goal is to be treated with respect and afforded the same services that are standard for other Canadians.
>
> —*Mary Simon, president, Inuit Tapiriit Kanatami*
>
> For a people that have long yearned for a voice, the Métis Nation of Ontario occupies a position of great responsibility. This reflects the realities of a dispersed collective seeking a home within a home.
>
> —*Jennifer St. Germain, Métis Nation of Ontario*

FIGURE 6.1 Jennifer St. Germain, Métis Nation of Ontario. What are your first thoughts when you read her words, as well as those of Mary Simon and Chief Tawpisin, above? How do they reflect Aboriginal values and aspirations in regard to governance and self-determination?

Although First Nations, Métis, and Inuit peoples in Canada have unique and specific cultures, needs, hopes, and aspirations, all share the challenge of regaining self-determination through self-governance. In this chapter, you will study traditions of Aboriginal governance, how governance works today, and how First Nations, Métis, and Inuit peoples are pursuing greater power over their own lives.

INQUIRING MINDS

Use these questions to explore the big ideas in this chapter.

1. How did practices of governance evolve for First Nations, Inuit, and Métis peoples in North America?

2. How did colonialism alter governance for Aboriginal peoples?

3. Why are governance issues significant for Aboriginal peoples in Canada?

4. How do Aboriginal community leaders, political leaders, and youth view issues of governance?

©P

FIGURE 6.2 A peaceful protest by Aboriginal organizations and individuals at the G20 Summit in Toronto, 2010. What comes to mind when you view this image? What are other ways for Aboriginal peoples in Canada to go about having their voices heard?

What Is Governance?

Governance is the way in which a group—a company, non-profit organization, school, family, clan, or nation—conducts its affairs, both in its day-to-day activities and over the long term. This can involve decisions on how and when to spend money, which laws to pass, how to protect or use natural resources, and how officials are chosen or elected. Governance includes the methods, processes, structure, and authorities of the group. Governance is active. It is a system by which a group guides, manages, cares for, and safeguards its people.

What does governance mean to you and your classmates? You may be involved in decision-making structures such as a student council or helping in municipal, provincial, or federal political organizations. Perhaps you've participated in sports teams or groups such as scouts, guides, or 4H, volunteered on a committee, helped a non-profit organization, or led another group inspired to make a change.

VOICES OF THE PEOPLES

I'm 19 years old, currently attending Canadore College in the IWAP program (Indigenous Wellness and Addictions Prevention). I'm on the Nipissing First Nation's band council, in my second year, on a three-year term. And I'm enjoying every minute of it. I have served on the Recreation Committee and as a mentor in the Walking Forward program. I never really thought of myself as a leader but I kind of always ended up being a leader in different situations. I asked my mom, "Why does it happen?" and she said, "That's just who you are." I'm really outgoing and I'm really willing to listen to anybody who wants to talk to me. I believe that not being afraid to step out of my shell and meet someone new helps me as a leader. I learn from who I am leading—without the people telling me how they feel, I won't be able to do the things that I'm doing.

I feel it's really important that youth are involved in decision-making. They do have a say and most importantly they need to have an understanding of what's happening in the community. When I got on

FIGURE 6.3 Zachary Beaudette became a council member for Nipissing First Nation at the age of 18.

the council, I really didn't understand. I am still learning lots of things that go on politically. And I believe that me being on the council really helps youth in our community understand how the processes work. Youth being involved in making a decision that is for the whole community, I believe makes a stronger community.

©P

Types of Governance

Governance can involve a variety of structures and methods, and a group (organization, nation, and so on) will generally use what suits its needs. National governments around the world are diverse and are often described broadly according to types and variations on those types—for example, democracy, parliamentary democracy, republic, dictatorship, military dictatorship, monarchy, and so on. While nations might have similarities in governance, each nation develops its unique government.

What Guides Governance?

There are many factors that guide governance for nations around the world, each of them distinct and unique. These factors can include languages, histories, cultures and traditions, and social, political, and economic circumstances. The same variety of factors is true for Aboriginal peoples in Canada: diverse cultures, traditions, languages, and beliefs guide each Nation as it strives to regain **self-determination** and **self-governance**.

As you read this chapter, you will learn about Aboriginal governance, challenges to self-governance and self-determination, and current governance. While you will learn about diversity, you will also see some similarities: Aboriginal governance is shaped by connections to the land, and the understanding that land and resources are to be shared, distributing the benefits of their use in a fair manner. In Nunavut, for example, the territorial government is developing power-sharing agreements, seeking to ensure that jobs and wealth go to all residents, and providing for future generations.

REFLECTION

All citizens in Canada have the responsibility to be involved in decision-making. To what extent are you involved in governance? What ways of contributing to your nation and community would you consider?

CRITICAL THINKING

How can Aboriginal Nations and the federal, provincial, and municipal levels of government better work together to ensure that the diverse perspectives of Aboriginal peoples are effectively considered and acknowledged?

WORDS MATTER

self-determination freedom of peoples to choose their own social and political structures without outside control or pressure

self-governance political independence or autonomy

THINKING IT THROUGH

1. How do you think youth can become more involved in governance of their Nation or leadership within their community?

2. "Governance" is a term used to describe how a group manages and cares for its people. Give a real-life example of what you believe to be good governance. Discuss your answer with another student, addressing similarities and differences.

Aboriginal Governance

Consensus

While there is great diversity among First Nations, Métis, and Inuit peoples, there are several common threads, which are linked to shared values and beliefs. One of the most important aspects around which Aboriginal governance is constructed is **consensus**.

Consensus decision-making involves respecting the opinions of individuals and working together to come to an agreement that is acceptable to everyone. It does not involve parties or an official opposition, as in some governance. Consensus respects all individuals and supports the idea that everyone is responsible for helping to care for the community. The Haudenosaunee Confederacy, made up of six Nations, uses consensus as a decision-making strategy.

Leaders

There are leaders within consensus-type governments. Aboriginal leaders do not assume power. Their citizens agree to letting them speak on their behalf, a privilege that can be removed if necessary. Leaders of First Nations, Métis, and Inuit communities strive to have a rooted sense of identity, history, and culture. Additionally, leadership involves taking responsibility and leading by example. Sometimes, it means doing the best that is possible in the face of tremendous challenges—for example, a lack of funding. For the Inuit, leaders are expected not to abuse their power, and are relied on for their wisdom and survival skills. Among the Haudenosaunee, the idea of "the good mind," explained by Tom Porter below, illustrates what was expected of leaders. If they did not conduct themselves properly, they could be removed from office by the Clan Mothers—who had conditionally granted them authority.

VOICES OF THE PEOPLES

Good mind means that you're never gossiping; you're never making rumours; you're never assassinating people's character. The Clan Mothers and Chiefs and faithkeepers all are not to do that. They're supposed to be the examples for their whole clan or their whole family. They carry a good mind and they always talk about positive things. That's what their job is. That's what "good mind" means.

—*Tom Porter, Mohawk*

FIGURE 6.4 Tom Porter, Mohawk Elder and orator from Akwesasne

Consensus and the Great Law of Peace

WORDS MATTER

confederacy an organization of First Nations linked together for economic, political, or military purposes; similar to a confederation of countries, states, or provinces

The Haudenosaunee **Confederacy** presents an example of governance involving consensus. This confederacy was established when the message of Great Peace, brought by the Peacemaker, was accepted by five warring Nations. The Grand Council of 50 Chiefs representing the Mohawk, Oneida, Onondaga, Cayuga, and Seneca Nations worked to maintain a peaceful method of decision-making. The Tuscarora joined later, making it a confederacy of six Nations. The Haudenosaunee Confederacy has existed for centuries, and was retained after the creation of Six Nations of the Grand River in Upper Canada and other Mohawk and Oneida reserves in Ontario and Québec. Today, the Confederacy Council continues its work.

Maintenance of oral traditions, ceremonies, the role of Clan Mothers and the selection of Chiefs, longhouse traditions, and languages has kept the Haudenosaunee Confederacy strong. While each Nation makes its own decisions, they also work together for the benefit of all. Decisions are made through consensus, at council meetings held frequently during the year. It is not until everyone is in agreement—the Clan Mothers, the Chiefs, and the people—that decisions are final.

The Grand Council of the Haudenosaunee

The Haudenosaunee Grand Council of Chiefs, now also known as the Iroquois League Council or the Six Nations Confederacy Council, is still the centre of political and diplomatic decisions for all member Nations.

FIGURE 6.5 The Haudenosaunee Grand Council in 1898. The Council continues to provide leadership and governance for the Six Nations of the Grand River today.

The Women's Nomination Wampum

In his journey, the Peacemaker arrived at the waterfalls on the Easterly side of the river, where upon a long path, a woman lived alone. Tsikonsase (Jikonsaseh) was the woman's name. It is said the Tsikonsase was a descendant of the first woman on earth.

Tsikonsase was said to have done a lot of work in relation to the warpath, as she fed warriors who travelled from the east and also those who travelled from the west.

The Peacemaker then spoke to Tsikonsase about her business of aiding the war to continue, and told her to stop, for the Kariwiio (Good Message), Kashastensera (Power), and Skennen (Peace) were coming to the Nations. By accepting the good message brought by the Peacemaker, Tsikonsase became the first woman to accept the Kaianaraserakowa (Great Law of Peace) and would become instrumental in promoting peace amongst the Onkwehonwe.

—**Peacemaker's Journey**, *by Barbara Kanatiiosh Gray, children's author*

FIGURE 6.6 The Women's Nomination Wampum belt depicts the roles and responsibilities of the Clan Mothers of the Six Nations. Six figures, representing the Clan Mothers, are joined by a continuous line across the entire length of the belt. In the Mohawk language, the name of the belt is Ka'shastensera Kontiha:wa'ne Iotiianeh:shon (they, the Clan Mothers, have strength). This reproduction was created about 1931.

REFLECTION

What would be the benefit of having all members of a community—men, women, and youth—involved in governance? Are there any drawbacks? Explain.

The Role of Women in Aboriginal Governance

Within the Haudenosaunee Confederacy, the authority and responsibilities of the women are explained through the story of the Women's Nomination Wampum, shown above. The fact that only women could select and depose Chiefs says a great deal about the authority of the women. As well, it is acceptable for a Clan Mother to correct a Chief or council if she considers a decision to be ill-advised. Any disagreement is then resolved through consensus and a commitment to act in everyone's interest. Just as they have been for centuries, women are directly involved in governance in the Confederacy, suggesting legislation and making presentations to the councils. Clan Mothers actively participate in the political process and ensure that the Confederacy lives up to its promise of fair and just governance.

Among First Nations, Métis, and Inuit peoples, while women have always played a key role in Aboriginal governance, colonial governments disrupted this pattern by disempowering First Nations, Métis, and Inuit women (as you read in earlier chapters). This disempowerment has been countered within the last century through the work of individuals and organizations advocating for change.

Among First Nations, Métis, and Inuit peoples, women have increasingly come to the forefront as leaders in all areas and at all levels. Roles once restricted only to men are now also being filled by women.

Challenges and biases exist, but the climate is changing. Here are some examples of individual women and organizations leading the way.

- It was only in 1951 that changes to the Indian Act allowed women with Indian status to become involved in band politics (and vote). Just a few years later, in 1954, Elsie Knott became the first elected female Chief in Canada. As Chief of Curve Lake First Nation—a position she held for 16 years—she was active in improving living conditions in her community, and negotiating for new homes, paved roads, and a community centre.

- In 1955, Gwen Crane from Keeseekoose Saulteaux First Nation in Saskatchewan was elected Chief. She organized fundraisers for a hospital and promoted education in her community.

- For more than 30 years, the Native Women's Association of Canada has worked at every level of government and within communities to advocate understanding of women's issues. The organization is seen as the voice of Aboriginal women in Canada, representing them in leaders' meetings and taking an active role in the development of new legislation.

- Female First Nations Chiefs have been elected across Canada, while women such as Nellie Cournoyea, the first female premier of a Canadian territory, and Audrey Poitras, president of the Métis Nation of Alberta, have also become powerful leaders at the regional and national levels.

- Today, there are over 100 elected women Chiefs in Canada.

These trail-blazing women marked a major shift in the importance of female leadership among Aboriginal Nations, and they have inspired other Aboriginal women to follow in their footsteps. The perspectives of female leaders may affect Aboriginal governance through the development of policies that aim to improve quality of life for Aboriginal women, especially regarding developing issues such as equality, gender discrimination in Indian status, safety, and economic opportunities.

FIGURE 6.7 Elsie Knott

Web Connect

To learn more about the Native Women's Association of Canada, visit our website.

VOICES OF THE PEOPLES

The role of the woman…was an equal role… The women's role within the Elders, my grandmother's role and my aunts' roles were almost like hidden leaders… Everybody that needed advice went to my mother, went to my aunts, went to my grandmother. Even the men, when they went to the meetings and organizing, they never went before we always had a meeting and a gathering of the total family unit, the total community unit, and the women told the men what to say. It was a consensus of the total family unit.

—*Senator Thelma Chalifoux, Métis Nation of Alberta*

FIGURE 6.8 Métis Senator Thelma Chalifoux

Social Organization and Governance

Social organization helps form the framework for governance structures by outlining the roles and responsibilities of individuals and groups. For many Aboriginal peoples in Canada, family ties are very important aspects of identity (as you read in Chapter 5) and families remain the most significant form of social organization. Family ties are maintained through intermarriage, social obligations, and other connections, and individuals are tied together in a web of relationships that maintains social order.

In many First Nations, kinship does not entirely depend on heredity. For example, adoption is not uncommon and in the past provided a way of building peaceful relationships between Nations. As well, intermarriages between First Nations and French, Scottish, or English traders were generally sanctioned by both sides. These bonds aided survival and trade relations. Today, kinship ties in Métis communities are based more on community connections than on ancestry.

The social systems of some Nations involve clans, which are based on descent from a single common ancestor. Among the Haudenosaunee, clan descent is traced from a female ancestor. Different clans hold specific responsibilities in the community, depending on their skills; specific roles, such as messenger, protector, leader, or healer, are often passed down through each clan through the generations.

FIGURE 6.9 In the past, the Inuit family group was essential for survival. Today, family ties are still very strong. More Inuit now work away from home, but when a family member needs care, it is common for individuals to give up work outside the home to become caregivers.

VOICES OF THE PEOPLES

Being Métis is not so much about who you are as an individual as it is about having kin or family relationships within a Métis community. It is not so much about your individual ancestry as it is about sharing in the common heritage of the people to which you belong.

—*Paul Chartrand, Métis*

The clan system is a social order. The clan system is a justice system. The clan system is a government. The clan system is an extended family unit.

—*Leonard Nelson, Roseau River First Nation*

...women are now actively participating in insuring the empowerment of their people. Life is a daily struggle as women, as mothers, as sisters, as aunties and grandmothers. We are responsible for the children of today and those of tomorrow. It is with pure kindness and our respect for life that allows us to gladly take up this responsibility to nurture the children, to teach of what we know, from what we have learned through trial and error.

—*Nongom Ikkwe, the Indigenous Women's Collective of the South East Region, Manitoba*

©P

FIGURE 6.10 Yvon Dumont is a Métis politician from Manitoba. In 1993, he became the first Métis lieutenant-governor of Manitoba. He has been a municipal councillor and has also been involved in the Métis National Council. Throughout his career, he has maintained the importance of keeping the Métis as a distinct people and Nation, thus furthering the understanding of Métis values and beliefs. Why would his leadership be important to Métis in Manitoba and across Canada?

The Métis: The Free People

Métis Elder Maria Campbell calls the Métis the "free people." This is because values of individual freedom and independent thought are very strong in Métis culture. Within Métis governance, one of the most important guiding principles is individual **autonomy**. Métis writer and educator Dean Cunningham explains below about Métis governance from his own experience and his knowledge gained from Elders, family and extended family, and his community.

In 2002, the Métis National Council adopted a definition of Métis that outlined their identity as descendants of the historic Métis Nation. It also confirmed the Métis as a distinct Nation and as one of the Aboriginal peoples included in the 1982 Canadian Constitution Act. For many Métis, it is their identity as a distinct Nation that supports their right to self-determination.

> **WORDS MATTER**
>
> **autonomy** freedom to determine one's own actions and behaviour

> **CRITICAL THINKING**
>
> Explain what you feel is the connection between autonomy and self-determination. Why would this connection be important to the Métis today?

VOICES OF THE PEOPLES

When considering governance, the two most important guiding principles were individual autonomy and consensus-building. This is because First Nations values of individual freedom and independence of thought were very strongly adopted into Métis culture. The earliest Métis communities were governed according to respecting the independence of individuals and their voice in determining their governance through egalitarian consensus-building. Long-established rules for communities were understood and transmitted through culture, handed down through generations, so very little official governing needed to be done. The rules were understood and voluntary compliance was normal and expected. There was a reliance on common sense: the rules were practical and of obvious survival value, so non-compliance was very rare. When new rules were needed, people would gather and everyone who wanted to speak was heard.

Leaders were called upon only when needed. Those who took it upon themselves to be "bossy" were very quickly the object of ridicule and humour. A quiet humility was valued in leaders. Kinship was important, and leadership ability was expected to "run in the family," but being born into a leadership family was no guarantee of becoming a leader. Leaders emerged naturally, through observed performance and the ability to contribute. Therefore there was strong motivation to be of service to the community if one was ambitious to lead. Leaders were chosen from those with proven ability and commitment to the good of the community.

—*Métis writer Dean Cunningham*

FIGURE 6.11 The Nunavut Assembly building. Why do you think it is important for Nunavut to have a centralized government?

Nunavut

Before Nunavut came into existence as a territory on April 1, 1999, Inuit were aware that establishing a government for the vast northern region would be a challenge. Made up of only 28 communities spread across 2 million square kilometres, Nunavut is now a unique example of traditional forms of governance at work, including consensus decision-making. Nunavut also shows self-determination in action.

In 1993, the Nunavut Land Claims Agreement gave Inuit, who have inhabited the North for thousands of years, title to their land, and established their right to manage wildlife and natural resources. It also led to the creation of a new territorial government.

Nunavut has no political parties at the territorial level, and residents can vote for anyone who is running for office. When making decisions, the government uses consensus. The Nunavut legislative assembly resolves differences through discussion and cooperation. The government still requires a majority decision before passing laws, but it uses consensus to get there.

Achieving consensus means that members of the assembly speak and listen respectfully until a decision is reached. Although compromise is often necessary, the goal is agreement, rather than imposing one position over the other.

Leaders are also chosen by consensus. The premier of Nunavut is directly elected by the members of the assembly through consensus. Eva Aariak became the second premier of Nunavut under this system in 2008.

CRITICAL THINKING

How does the Nunavut Land Claims Agreement enable Inuit of Nunavut to exercise self-determination?

THINKING IT THROUGH

1. Based on what you have learned so far, work in a group to make point-form notes about examples of Aboriginal governance, the beliefs and values they reflect, similarities and differences described so far, and your questions.

2. What issues do you think First Nations, Métis, and Inuit communities address in their decision making? For example, what do band councils address during their meetings? In a group, research Aboriginal media sources to start a list of issues.

©P

Building Your Skills

Consensus Decision-Making

You and your family need to agree on what movie to see tonight. What should you do? Take a vote? Have one person decide for all? What if one person disagrees and feels very strongly about his or her decision? Should one opinion be worth less simply because the individual is outnumbered? Consensus decision-making sees the opinions of everyone as being equal. This process for decision-making is about finding common ground and seeking solutions that are acceptable to everyone. It is a process in which there are no winners and no losers; all members are guaranteed to be taken seriously by the others, no matter whether they are in the minority or the majority.

How Does Consensus Work?

The process of consensus decision-making may not be the same for all groups, but it can involve the following:

- **A common goal:** All members of the group share a common goal; everyone agrees to what should be discussed. When consensus might seem difficult to achieve, the group returns to the common goal as a reminder.

- **Commitment:** All members of the group are committed to reaching consensus. This commitment requires patience and placing the goal of the group first.

- **Sufficient time:** It can take time for consensus decisions to be made.

- **Understanding:** All members of the group understand the consensus process. They agree ahead of time on processes and guidelines.

- **Defined roles:** A leader can help the group move through the process. Others may be in charge of keeping notes or making sure the discussion meets the agreed-upon goal.

- **Active listening:** All members of the group are prepared to actively listen to the opinions of others.

Apply Your Skills

1. Brainstorm how you could use consensus decision-making in a class situation. For example, could you use consensus in a group project to ensure that all voices and opinions are heard? How important is it for a group to make decisions that all members are comfortable with? Under what circumstances might it be better to have one person make the decisions?

2. Compare consensus decision-making with a system that uses unilateral decision-making and with a system that uses vote-taking and majority rule. How do you think these three strategies differ? When would each one be most useful? Why?

The Impact of Colonialism

Colonialism is a relationship between two peoples, in which one group takes over the lands of another and imposes on those people its own traditions. **Sovereignty** is a vital issue in colonialism, because colonists typically wish to transfer their own governments and laws into the territory that is new to them despite the forms of governance that may already be in place. In North America, this has meant attempts to dismantle Aboriginal governance and impose a new system, one based on the customs and practices of, for the most part, the English and French.

When French and English explorers and traders arrived in what is now Canada, First Nations peoples met with them on a Nation-to-Nation basis. Peace and trade alliances were formed, and the First Nations became allies to the English and French. After the English gained control in 1763, after

COMMUNITY CLOSE-UP

Akwesasne and the Jay Treaty

The Jay Treaty was signed by Great Britain and the United States in 1794 and decided the location of the border between the U.S. and Canada (then a territory of Great Britain). The treaty came into effect in 1796, lasted until 1803, but continues to affect trade in the area. Article III of the Jay Treaty declared the right of U.S. and Canadian citizens to trade and travel between the U.S. and Canada. Because the Jay Treaty was not a treaty signed with First Nations people, it does not specifically give border-crossing rights to First Nations. However, according to the Aboriginal Rights and Research Office of the Mohawk Council of Akwesasne, the Jay Treaty confirms a range of rights—including unimpeded travel, trade, and commerce—that had been practised since time immemorial.

Akwesasne is located on both sides of the border between Canada and the United States. In the 1950s, a Mohawk man named Louis Francis was charged duty on a washing machine he bought on the American side of the border. The people of Akwesasne took the case to the Supreme Court of Canada, but the court ruled that the Jay Treaty could not be enforced because the Canadian government had not legislated the treaty's benefits to First

Nations peoples. After the Francis case, the charging of duty was sometimes enforced, but sometimes not. Goods brought over the border were often seized. The Mohawks challenged these seizures, and decisions were often reversed.

In 1988, Akwesasne Grand Chief Michael Kanentakeron Mitchell, accompanied by Assembly of First Nations National Chief Georges Erasmus, Chiefs from other First Nations, and approximately 400 Akwesasne community members, walked across the International Bridge from the United States to Canada, carrying gifts for the Mohawks at Tyendinaga Mohawk Territory near Belleville, Ontario. Grand Chief Mitchell was charged under the Customs Act and brought before the Federal Court of Canada. He argued that the traditional activities of trade and transportation of goods are pre-contact Aboriginal rights. The court ruled against the Mohawks' use of the Jay Treaty in their argument but did agree that the Mohawks had pre-existing border-crossing rights. These rights included the right to bring goods into Canada for personal and community use, and for non-commercial trade with other First Nations, without having to pay duty.

©P

the American War of Independence, and then again after the War of 1812, the value of First Nations as allies in times of war seemed to diminish. When the colonial powers arranged treaties between each other, those treaties did not involve their former First Nations allies. As well, promises made to First Nations by the British in earlier treaties were ignored.

The Sale of Rupert's Land

In 1869, the Canadian government purchased Rupert's Land from the Hudson's Bay Company, giving that government control over a vast stretch of land in the north and west. This transfer was completed without consultation with those living in the area, including settlers, First Nations, and Métis. In the decades that followed, the Canadian government sought to increase settlement by building a railroad and encouraging settlers to come from Europe. The North-West Mounted Police was formed and sent into the area. To secure peaceful settlement, the government also negotiated treaties with the First Nations, which you will learn more about in Chapter 7.

The Indian Act

The Indian Act, which was created in 1876, was designed to control every aspect of the lives of First Nations peoples. The Indian Act created **bands** and established reserve lands. As you read in Chapter 4, the Act separated Aboriginal peoples and communities, and many First Nations people were not registered, becoming "non-status Indians" with none of the rights granted under the Act.

The introduction of the Indian Act, its application, and its enforcement caused many challenges for First Nations peoples. Not only did the Act seek to change governance structures, but it also would outlaw spiritual ceremonies, radically change the position of First Nations women within society, and make attendance at residential schools mandatory.

VOICES OF THE PEOPLES

The Indian Act is a cradle-to-grave set of rules, regulations and directives. From the time of birth, when an Indian child must be registered in one of seventeen categories defining who is an "Indian," until the time of death, when the Minister of Indian Affairs acts as executor of the deceased person's estate, our lives are ruled by the Act and the overwhelming bureaucracy that administers it.

—*Ovide Mercredi, former National Chief of the Assembly of First Nations*

FIGURE 6.12 Young Métis paddlers on the Assiniboine River in Manitoba fly the Métis flag, which first came into use in the early 1800s. The infinity symbol found on the flag shows the coming together of two cultures, as well as the enduring nature of the Métis as a people and a Nation. Its use shows that the Métis of the West considered themselves a Nation well before the sale of Rupert's Land. Could the sale of a large area of land happen today without the consent of the people who live there? Explain why or why not.

The Imposition of the Band Council System

When the federal government established the reserve system, it imposed a system of bands and band councils on Nations at the same time as Canada determined citizenship rules and funding. In some Nations, the historical and the imposed systems of governance were able to co-exist. However, in other cases, the historical systems of governance were pushed aside.

Under the imposed band system, each band would elect one Chief and as many as 12 council members every two years. However, the federal government retained the right to overturn any election result, and any resolution made by a band council had to be approved by Indian and Northern Affairs Canada (now known as Aboriginal Affairs and Northern Development Canada).

Imposition of the band council system would in some cases create open conflict between the federal government and the councils and Chiefs already in place. For example, the sovereignty of the Haudenosaunee Confederacy remained intact until 1924, when Prime Minister William Lyon Mackenzie King ordered the replacement of the Haudenosaunee Confederacy Council with a band council elected under the Indian Act. Members of the RCMP entered the Ohsweken Council House with a decree dissolving the traditional Confederacy Council and government, and seized historic documents and wampum belts. Elections authorized by the federal government were held two weeks later. Out of a population of 4500, only 26 citizens voted. The Confederacy Council retained the support of most of the Onkwehonweh, but had no official power and no funding. However, the Council remained intact and is still active today. Members are still chosen in accordance with the Great Law—the Chiefs, Clan Mothers, and faithkeepers still hold positions of leadership and influence.

CRITICAL THINKING

Why do you think the Indian Act sought to impose one governance system for all?

CRITICAL THINKING

Although the Indian Act is well over 100 years old, and has been revised twice, it still affects First Nations today. What are some possible alternatives to the Act? How can it reflect the modern needs of First Nations peoples? Consider your answer again after reading the following sections.

Changes to the Indian Act

As you have read, the Indian Act was revised in 1951 and 1985. Among the many changes made, Bill C-31 (enacted in 1985) brought changes to the Indian Act that affected control over band membership, and First Nations could finally use their own rules to determine membership if they chose to do so. However, as Chapter 4 describes, First Nations did not regain ultimate authority in determining membership. Now, some leaders are calling for First Nations peoples not to talk of "band membership" but of "First Nation membership" and "citizenship;" these changes are related to the call for self-determination, which we will look at again later in this chapter.

Barriere Lake, Québec

In 1991, the Algonquins of Barriere Lake, a community three hours north of Ottawa, signed an agreement with the governments of Canada and Québec to create a sustainable development, conservation, and resource co-management process. This agreement would allow the community to share in management and revenue from logging in their territory. However, many residents feel that since then the federal government has tried to evade its obligation to the agreement by interfering with the governance in the community.

In March 2008, the federal government rejected the status of Customary Chief Benjamin Nottaway and his council, invoking the Indian Act and running an election that would set in place a Chief and council not selected in accordance with the community's customs. (Section 74 of the Indian Act states that the Minister of Indian Affairs can impose an electoral system on a First Nation, even though it may have customary leadership selection processes already in place.) The conflict has divided the community and disrupted logging activities, leaving many people without work for long periods of time.

QUESTION

1. With a partner, investigate possible solutions to the governance issues in Barriere Lake.

Ahousaht First Nation

Ahousaht First Nation in British Columbia uses a hereditary system to determine who becomes Chief. When someone is born into this position, the family and community will prepare the person for this responsibility from the time of the child's birth. Part of the preparation includes learning and living by ancient teachings in order to speak honourably for the House of Glakishpiitl and in order to look after the community and territories. Important teachings to help guide the Chief in decisions and actions include the teachings of Hish-ook-ish Tsa'walk (everything and everyone is connected), Ya-akstalth (loving and caring for one another), Hahopstalth (teaching wisdom), Hopiitsalth (be helpful and caring to each other), and Ap-haystalth (always be kind and friendly). In 1999, Shawn Atleo became Chief of the House of Glakishpiitl and his people gave him the name A-in-chut (meaning "everyone depends on you").

FIGURE 6.13 Chief Shawn A-in-chut Atleo also became National Chief of the Assembly of First Nations in 2009.

QUESTION

1. What values and beliefs can you see reflected in the description of the Ahousaht First Nation hereditary system?

The White Paper

In 1969, Pierre Elliott Trudeau and his Liberal government issued what they called *The Statement of the Government of Canada on Indian Policy*. Also known as the White Paper, it proposed to abolish the Indian Act. The White Paper outlined the Indian Act as dated and oppressive, and something that kept First Nations and Inuit peoples apart from other Canadians in ways that did not allow them to prosper. The government stated that without the Indian Act, First Nations and Inuit peoples would have the full benefits and services that many Canadians took for granted. Without reserves, First Nations people would join the larger Canadian community, and it would be easier for them to take part in education and training, to find jobs, and to prosper economically. This document was part of Trudeau's vision of a "Just Society," one in which all peoples in Canada would have equal benefits and opportunities.

However, the price of implementing the White Paper would be the end of treaty agreements, treaty rights, and the unique status of First Nations and Inuit peoples. The reactions of many First Nations peoples to the White Paper were negative. Many saw the White Paper as a means of terminating or assimilating Aboriginal peoples, not helping them. The government would later withdraw the White Paper. Read the main points of the White Paper and the possible consequences in the chart below.

FIGURE 6.14 George Manuel (of the Shuswap First Nation) was National Chief of the National Indian Brotherhood (NIB) from 1970 to 1976. The NIB, which later became the Assembly of First Nations, played a key role in the fight against the White Paper. This role gave the NIB vital experience in dealing with the federal government and unified First Nations across the country.

CRITICAL THINKING

What idea of a "just society" did Trudeau have? How did he see ending treaties as being fair to everyone? What might have happened if the White Paper had been enacted? Discuss your opinions in a group.

	Main Points of the White Paper	Consequences
1	Legal Structure: Legislative and constitutional bases of discrimination must be removed.	The Indian Act would be abolished.
2	Indian Cultural Heritage: There must be positive recognition by everyone of the unique contribution of Indian culture to Canadian society.	Instead of trying to assimilate Aboriginal peoples, the importance of Aboriginal peoples would be acknowledged.
3	Programs and Services: Services must come through the same channels and from the same government agencies for all Canadians.	Services would come to Aboriginal peoples through provincial and territorial governments, instead of through Indian and Northern Affairs Canada, a federal department.
4	Enriched Services: Those who are furthest behind must be helped most.	Aboriginal peoples would be helped not because of treaty obligations, but for humanitarian reasons.
5	Claims and Treaties: Lawful obligations must be recognized.	While the document acknowledged the importance of historical treaties, once they were settled, First Nations peoples would be discharged from all treaties.
6	Indian Lands: Control of Indian lands should be transferred to the Indian people.	First Nations peoples would be given complete ownership of the lands, and could sell the land as they wished in the future.

FIGURE 6.15 What was the White Paper trying to accomplish? Why do you think so many First Nations leaders lobbied against it?

©P

The Red Paper

The White Paper was met with fierce opposition from First Nations, who had never been properly consulted on the issue. Also, many First Nations people were upset that the government proposed to terminate treaty agreements. Rather than passively accepting these proposed changes, First Nations leaders spoke out strongly, particularly through the Red Paper, which was created by the Indian Association of Alberta, led by Harold Cardinal.

Harold Cardinal, a Cree writer, activist, and leader, galvanized the political actions of First Nations peoples during the 1970s. His bestselling 1969 book, *The Unjust Society,* was a personal, direct, and very critical response to the White Paper. Opposition provoked by the book along with the 1973 Calder case, which affirmed Aboriginal rights in the courts, is credited with influencing the Trudeau government to abandon the proposed policies of the White Paper.

After the White Paper, First Nations continued to assert their right to be involved in national decision-making. In 1980, when faced with upcoming changes to the Canadian Constitution, and the potential effects of those changes on Aboriginal rights, First Nations activists organized a peaceful protest called the Constitution Express. Led by Chief George Manuel, the Express was made up of two trains that travelled from Vancouver to Ottawa, collecting 1000 passengers along the way. After protests took place in Ottawa, a smaller contingent of representatives went on to the United Nations in New York and then to five countries in Europe, where Aboriginal leaders gave speeches and brought international attention to this cause.

CRITICAL THINKING

One of the key points of the Red Paper was that the Indian Act should be reviewed, not repealed. Do you think most First Nations peoples would agree with that statement today? Do some research to find out various perspectives on the Indian Act and what First Nations peoples consider to be important to keep and important to change in the Act. Why do you think Trudeau changed his mind?

FIGURE 6.16 Harold Cardinal (1945–2005) was a Cree activist and writer. He was also a lawyer and a political leader, and received a Lifetime Achievement Award from the National Aboriginal Achievement Foundation in 2001. What were the impacts of his actions? Discuss the importance of individual contributions to local, regional, and national politics.

VOICES OF THE PEOPLES

I have always said to our
people: We are a great Nation,
a great people and greatness
is not measured by how much
money you have, how much
land you have. Greatness is
measured by how much
you're willing to give and
share, and we've shared this
country.

—*Elijah Harper, Cree politician*

The Constitution Act

The Canadian Constitution was **patriated** in 1982 by the government
of Pierre Trudeau. This patriation gave the Canadian government the legal
right to implement legislation and increased its independence from the
British Crown. For many Canadians, this was a welcome move,
representing a new phase in Canadian history. Among Aboriginal peoples,
however, there was less enthusiasm.

The concern of First Nations peoples was relatively simple: the treaties
had been made with the Crown. Would the Canadian government still
honour the treaties? Many leaders, including Noel Starblanket, Fred Plain,
and John Tootoosis, lobbied hard for the inclusion and protection of
treaties within the Canadian Constitution. Treaties were eventually
included in Section 35, but actual treaty rights were not listed or defined.
This has resulted in Canadian courts having to define what treaty rights
exist on a case-by-case basis.

The government introduced amendments to the Constitution with
both the Meech Lake and Charlottetown Accords. The Meech Lake Accord
of 1987 recognized Québec as a distinct society. First Nations leaders
argued that the Accord ignored Aboriginal peoples as founding nations.
A Cree member of the Manitoba legislature, Elijah Harper, was
instrumental in preventing the ratification of the Meech Lake Accord.
Harper stalled the decision in the Manitoba parliament and refused to
consent to a vote. Because the accord could be passed only by unanimous
consent of the provinces, this refusal led directly to its defeat.

The federal government addressed the country's constitutional
problems again in 1992. The government, the Assembly of First Nations,
the Native Council of Canada, the Inuit Tapirisat of Canada, and the Métis
National Council met in Charlottetown, Prince Edward Island, and agreed
to a new accord. This accord addressed the unique issues of Québec, and
also recognized Aboriginal rights to self-governance. Although the accord
had won favour with politicians, it was rejected by Canadians voting in a
referendum.

FIGURE 6.17 In 1990, Elijah Harper
(above) opposed the Meech Lake
Accord because Aboriginal peoples
had not been consulted about it,
even though it would directly affect
their lives.

THINKING IT THROUGH

1. What was the effect of the Indian Act on Aboriginal governance? Are the
   effects still apparent today? Explain.

2. Do some additional research on Harold Cardinal and his work after the
   Red Paper. What were his contributions? How did he further the
   understanding of Aboriginal perspectives among all Canadians?

3. Why did Elijah Harper choose to block the Meech Lake Accord?
   Prepare a one-page summary of your findings.

4. Read Section 35 of the Constitution Act of 1982. Why do you think
   this section was an important inclusion? What were the reactions of
   Aboriginal peoples to the addition at the time?

Current Governance

Recall that governance is a system of managing a group's day-to-day and long-term affairs. Every community in Canada has some form of governance. For First Nations, Métis, and Inuit peoples, governance must also work within laws and regulations that can affect Aboriginal peoples in different ways.

First Nations peoples continue to seek ways to invoke their own methods of governance, despite the imposed rules and regulations of the Indian Act. Many Métis people follow customs endorsed by their Métis community, such as rules about harvesting and membership. Inuit governments and organizations continue to govern within Inuit beliefs and values in the face of social, political, and environmental challenges, including global warming.

At the same time that Aboriginal systems of governance work within their own Nations and communities, there are also First Nations, Métis, and Inuit organizations that work to provide their own voice in federal, provincial, and territorial politics. These organizations work with different levels of political government to advocate for Aboriginal peoples, organize services, provide cultural support, organize treaty and land rights cases, and work toward regaining self-governance. These organizations employ and are led by Aboriginal people. In general, their power lies in support from Aboriginal communities and in their ability to voice Aboriginal perspectives across Canada and internationally.

Some of the many examples of current Aboriginal governance are described in the section following. As you read, think about which examples of governance are found in your local area and how you could learn more about them.

Urban Governance Issues

Urban Aboriginal communities tend to have diverse populations, including First Nations, non-status Indians, Métis, and Inuit. An urban population also tends to be mobile, with members moving around within the community or back and forth between reserves, small communities, and larger urban areas. Providing governance for urban Aboriginal communities is a challenging undertaking. Who should be responsible for delivering services—federal, provincial, or municipal governments? How should Aboriginal organizations be involved? Should First Nations individuals living off-reserve be able to participate in band elections?

For many Aboriginal people living in an urban environment, the focus of their community is the friendship centre, where they can find a sense of community and can gain access to needed services such as job training, education, cultural support, and recreational activities. While friendship centres do not necessarily shape governance policies, a sense of community may begin there.

CRITICAL THINKING

Should friendship centres be involved in politics? Or are the purposes of friendship centres contrary to political agendas? Explain your views.

FIGURE 6.18 This 2009 photograph shows ITK leader Mary Simon (left) and Leona Aglukkaq (right), minister of health in the federal government, after signing a task group agreement aimed at improving Inuit health.

Inuit Tapiriit Kanatami

As you read in Chapter 4, the Inuit Tapiriit Kanatami (ITK) is the national voice for Inuit. The Inuit Tapiriit Kanatami was founded in 1971 as the Inuit Tapirisat of Canada. Organizations such as ITK and Makivik Kuapuriisat (Makivik Corporation) (page 210) work with political governments at various levels.

Governance on First Nations Reserves

Today, some First Nations still determine their own approach to selecting leaders. The Ahousaht First Nation (page 201) is one example. In addition to hereditary leaders, the Ahousaht First Nation has an elected band council and Chief. In general, the Hereditary Chief and council are responsible for the land and resources, while the elected Chief and council run the administration of the band.

For most First Nations, band council elections are held every two years. One Chief and up to 12 band council members are elected, and through this council Aboriginal Affairs and Northern Development Canada (AANDC) grants money for housing, health care, education, and services such as road maintenance. Some Nations have their own police services, but many do not (as you will read in Chapter 8). For example, the Ontario Police Services Act does not mandate policing in First Nations communities, so the resources for funding are not assured.

Ideally, democratic government serves the best interests of voting citizens. This is often difficult on reserves, because ultimately AANDC controls budgets and grant applications, not the elected council members or Chief. Some reserves may be located in areas rich with natural resources, but many are isolated and have little economic development. As a result unemployment is high and welfare needs are great. The band council has a limited budget to work with and no tax base to expand its budget, making it dependent on federal government policies.

The issues that a band council addresses on a regular basis vary from Nation to Nation, just as they do in municipal governments across Canada. However, Dave Mowat (page 207) provides an example by describing his key concerns as band councillor: economic development for revenues over the long term, resolution of their Williams Treaty claim, housing development, establishing by-laws and the capacity to enforce them, the environment, ecology, employment, boundaries and surveys, source water protection, financial capacity, maintaining strong health services, and policy development.

Changes in membership and leadership rules have had impact in First Nations across Canada. As you read in Chapter 4, one significant concern when Bill C-31 was introduced was that reserve resources were stretched thin and some leaders questioned whether reserves could provide for additional residents. Kahnawake First Nation, in Québec, is one example of a reserve concerned about housing.

©P

In 2007, a federal court ruling determined that First Nations citizens who live off-reserve may run for band council election. The change came about when the residency requirement (in the Indian Act) for band council members was challenged on the basis of the Charter of Rights and Freedoms. Gull Bay First Nation Chief Wilfred King asserted that someone living off-reserve can be just as effective in representing those living in the community.

VOICES OF THE PEOPLES

Dave Mowat is a band councillor for Alderville First Nation. We asked him about his personal views on his work as a band councillor.

I sought election for band councillor because I saw that there was a need for new viewpoints. I felt a need to implement positive change. My one objective was to help create wealth for the community, but equally important for me was history. I am a historian, and I ran for election so that our history could get a better reading and understanding, and our traditions could find a stronger footing in the community. Another important reason in running for office was to help reinforce the work that has been done on the environmental and ecological file at Alderville. This is the key to everything, because this is the underpinning of our cultural and natural heritage.

I am not in the office from 8:30 to 4:30, 35 hours a week, but in fact could spend more time than that on issues, projects, research, community visits, and inspections. As a councillor I have to be ready to commit as much time as required. Often we get called out for individual matters that may involve someone wishing to discuss an issue. I attend as many community events as possible. I write a bulletin called the Quarterly Update and send it out by email. I visit people's homes, and attend council meetings. I keep up with what is happening regionally and nationally. I also visit schools and institutions to share our community's history.

What I have learned is that a band councillor, or anyone for that matter, can never foresee everything that will occur in a community, big or

FIGURE 6.19 Dave Mowat

small. We often react to situations, and policy becomes an evolving aspect of what we do to meet changes. I do not get frustrated that much—I get passionate and concerned, but I do not allow frustration to cloud my decision-making ability.

Sometimes it is simply about having a good mind in council, and creating a new way of thinking about certain aspects of the organization that do not necessarily need money, but rather a new way of using the resources they already have. Often the funding that flows to First Nations is discretionary and at the mercy of Parliament. I might be dealing with socio-economic breakdown and may always experience that not enough money in the world can heal my community! And that is why it is critical that students of First Nations issues take one community at a time because numerous First Nations communities have their own unique issues to contend with.

The Assembly of First Nations

The Assembly of First Nations (AFN) is an organization that represents First Nations across Canada. Before 1968, organizations that tried to unite First Nations and Métis peoples in single broad organizations soon realized that all of these members did not necessarily have common needs and battles. So, in 1968, the National Indian Brotherhood (NIB) was founded to represent First Nations peoples. The NIB became the Assembly of First Nations in 1982. Over the years, the NIB and then AFN have undergone many transitions.

The AFN has grown to represent the interests of over 630 First Nations throughout Canada to provincial and federal governments. Finding a common voice for a huge diversity of communities and Nations can be challenging, yet a united voice has great impact. NIB/AFN leaders including Walter Dieter, George Manuel, Noel Starblanket, David Ahenakew, Georges Erasmus, Ovide Mercredi, Matthew Coon Come, Phil Fontaine, and Shawn A-in-chut Atleo have achieved many successes in the fight for justice for First Nations peoples.

Through the years, the NIB and then the AFN have worked to overcome many challenges including distance, financing, cultural and linguistic differences, and the diverse histories of different Nations. Many Nations had very different relationships with the federal and provincial governments. Despite these challenges, the AFN proved to be a useful vehicle for First Nations peoples to defend their rights on a national scale. The organization played a key role in shaping several important issues, such as control of First Nations education.

The AFN has several mandates:

- to create and promote policy about First Nations concerns
- to create strong and peaceful relations among Nations
- to build understanding by raising awareness of First Nations cultures and concerns

FIGURE 6.20 Shawn A-in-chut Atleo became National Chief of the AFN in 2009. What is the importance of having national advocacy organizations for Aboriginal peoples in Canada?

Métis National Council and the Métis Nation of Ontario

The Métis National Council (MNC) was founded to represent Métis citizens and Métis interests. The Métis National Council is made up of the Métis Nation of Ontario, Manitoba Métis Federation, Métis Nation— Saskatchewan, Métis Nation of Alberta, and the Métis Nation of British Columbia. MNC leaders have included Clément Chartier and Tony Belcourt.

The Métis Nation of Ontario (MNO) is the collective expression of Métis self-governance in Ontario. The president of the MNO is the chief spokesperson for the Métis Nation in Ontario. The president oversees the day-to-day management of the MNO and is accountable to the Provisional Council and the Annual General Assembly. The Provisional Council is made up of nine elected representatives, one for each region in Ontario. This council includes the MNO Executive and leaders of the Women's Secretariat and the Youth Council. The Provisional Council carries out priorities set by citizens of the MNO through consensus at gatherings such as the Annual General Assembly. Within each region, Community Councils authorize local programming and services. These councils host meetings, annual rendezvous, and other community celebrations.

Senators play an important role throughout the MNO. Senators are elected to Community Councils and are responsible for maintaining and transmitting Métis culture, traditions, and history. Four Senators sit on the Provisional Council.

The MNO also plays a key role in regulating the constitutional harvesting rights of Métis. Each region appoints a Captain of the Hunt who has full authority over Métis hunts, gathers detailed information on harvests, and liaises between harvesters and MNO leadership.

FIGURE 6.21 The MNO Youth Council consists of nine regional councillors and one province-wide representative who acts as president. This council's purpose is to work within the MNO to address issues facing Métis youth.

CRITICAL THINKING

Earlier you read about the Métis concern for individual freedom and consensus. In what ways do the Métis governance systems today reflect those values? How do they reflect the values of inclusivity and Nation-building?

VOICES OF THE PEOPLES

The MNO is effectively the political voice of Métis within Ontario. I function as a proud member of its public service. As Director of Education and Training, I have been fortunate to oversee a program that creates measurable benefits for Métis across Ontario. This is a position that I have not always fully appreciated, as the days can be long and sometimes it seems as though the work is never done. We have many layers of accountability to our government partners, and more importantly to the people themselves. This is a critical part of maintaining a responsive, efficient, and effective government. The rewards are endless and the work monumentally important to the Métis of Ontario.

—*Jennifer St. Germain, Director of Education and Training, Métis Nation of Ontario*

FIGURE 6.22 Jennifer St. Germain

Makivik Kuapuriisat

Makivik Kuapuriisat (Makivik Corporation) was formed in 1975 as part of the James Bay Agreement. The agreement involved the transfer of $90 million to Inuit of the region and the creation of several institutions: Kativik Regional Government, Kativik School Board, and the Nunavik Regional Board of Health and Social Services. These institutions are open to all residents of Nunavik (the northern third of the province of Québec). Makivik Kuapuriisat was established to protect the rights and interests of Inuit within the James Bay Agreement. It also represents Inuit in negotiations with provincial and federal levels of government. Members of the Executive Committee and the Board of Directors are elected into those positions.

Makivik Kuapuriisat owns and operates (either in whole or jointly) two airlines, a shipping company, a shrimp-harvesting firm, a clothing manufacturing company, and a construction company. Makivik Kuapuriisat employs Inuit across northern Québec.

VOICES OF THE PEOPLES

Since its creation, Makivik has been very active in pursuing recognition of Inuit rights. The challenges still exist. Our region lacks the necessary employment possibilities and economic independence that will ensure that our youth will have a financially secure future. This is, in my opinion, the most challenging and crucial of Makivik's responsibilities. As a younger leader, I thank our past Inuit leaders, as well as the people behind the scenes at Makivik, for the work they have done in the spirit of improving Nunavik living conditions and in providing a contemporary way for Inuit to adapt to the modern world.

—*Pita Aatami, president of Makivik Kuapuriisat*

FIGURE 6.23 Pita Aatami

THINKING IT THROUGH

1. Research one First Nation that uses a traditional form of governance, such as Hereditary Chiefs. Explain the differences between their governance traditions and other forms of electoral governance.

2. Look at the governance of a national Aboriginal organization such as the Native Women's Association of Canada, the Pauktuutit Inuit Women's Association, the Assembly of First Nations, the Métis National Council, or the Inuit Tapiriit Kanatami. How are leaders chosen? What different roles do the representatives play? How are decisions made?

What Does Aboriginal Self-Governance Look Like?

The government of Canada and Aboriginal peoples living within Canada have difficult questions to answer when it comes to Aboriginal self-governance. Would political autonomy and independence look the same for everyone? Would it be different for those living in cities than for those living on reserves? Would it mean the end of the Indian Act? What would happen to Crown lands and the natural resources found within them? How would laws be altered?

Despite the challenges, Aboriginal leaders are currently exploring ways to regain self-governance. Their goal is to give their people more freedom and independence to establish a better quality of life for themselves, their communities, and their Nations. There are some big issues that require careful consideration by Aboriginal peoples. Some Aboriginal peoples have already taken part in negotiations with the federal government, such as the Westbank First Nation in British Columbia and Inuit of Nunavut. In 2010, the Canadian government announced that it would adopt the United Nations Declaration on the Rights of Indigenous Peoples, which recognizes the basic right of indigenous peoples to self-governance. This decision will affect negotiations for self-governance in the future.

FIGURE 6.24 Pamela Palmater, a Mi'kmaw lawyer and professor, was announced as the chair of the newly launched Centre in Indigenous Governance at Ryerson University. The centre will provide leadership seminars and will support research on governance issues. How might a program such as this be important to the development of Aboriginal governance in Canada?

Sovereignty and Self-Governance

> *The Creator has given us the right to govern ourselves and the right to self-determination.*
>
> *The rights and responsibilities given to us by the Creator cannot be altered or taken away by any other Nation.*
>
> —*from the Declaration of First Nations, Assembly of First Nations*

The right to self-governance for Aboriginal peoples derives from sovereignty, or the independent power of Nations, which Aboriginal peoples hold because of their continuous occupation of the land. To date, Aboriginal self-government agreements negotiated with Canada have stipulated that certain Canadian laws and human rights statutes will remain in force for First Nations and Inuit citizens. Agreements already in place have involved the creation of public governments such as in Nunavut, which serve all residents of an area regardless of the residents' ethnic background. Other agreements create new forms of government, similar to those in provinces or cities. Whatever form self-governance takes, it is clear that it will provide opportunities for spiritual, cultural, economic, and political renewal.

VOICES OF THE PEOPLES

...self-government based upon the inherent right to be self-determining must hear the weaker voices as well as the stronger voices. Self-government must be built upon the foundation of all Aboriginal people...[and] must provide for those people in need. Self-government must be built upon fairness and equality.

—*Dorothy McKay, Big Trout Lake, Ontario*

The Iroquois Nationals

The Iroquois Nationals is the lacrosse team of the Six Nations of the Iroquois Confederacy, also known as the Haudenosaunee Confederacy. The Iroquois Confederacy includes the Seneca, Mohawk, Oneida, Onondaga, Tuscarora, and Cayuga peoples. Their traditional territories straddle the international border between Canada and the United States. The team, which was admitted to the International Lacrosse Federation as a full-member nation in 1990, represents the Confederacy in international lacrosse competitions. The Iroquois Nationals is the only First Nations team sanctioned by an international sporting body to compete internationally.

In 2010, members of the Iroquois Nationals, who travel using passports issued by the Haudenosaunee Confederacy, were planning to compete in the World Lacrosse Championships in Manchester, England. However, they were prevented from playing because of a passport dispute with the United States and the United Kingdom. The U.K. refused to grant the team visas, and the U.S. said the players would not be able to re-enter the United States unless team members presented a Canadian or U.S. passport. The players refused, stating that the Haudenosaunee Confederacy pre-dated both the U.S. and Canada, and that the Haudenosaunee have a right to self-determination as a sovereign nation. In this sense, using a Canadian or U.S. passport was a strike against their identity; they are neither Canadian nor American, but are Haudenosaunee.

The American government stated that the issue wasn't one of sovereignty, but security. Iroquois Confederacy passports lack the identification chips required for international travel after September 11, 2001, and some information in the documents is handwritten. However, the U.S. reconsidered its decision after American Secretary of State Hillary Rodham Clinton issued a one-time waiver that cleared the team for travel due to the "unique circumstances" of the trip. At the time of the tournament, the Iroquois Nationals were ranked fourth in the world. The team had raised more than $300 000 to make the trip. Rodham Clinton offered to vouch for the U.S.-born members of the team. The U.K. would not reconsider its decision, however, and the Iroquois Nationals returned home. Germany took the team's place in the elite Blue Division of tournament play.

FIGURE 6.25 Percy Abrams, Iroquois Nationals executive director, shows his Haudenosaunee passport. How do other nations officially recognize a person's citizenship?

1. How does the experience of the Iroquois Nationals add to your understanding of the Jay Treaty and its implications (page 198)?

2. How does the perspective of the athletes playing for the Iroquois Nationals reflect the values, beliefs, and aspirations of First Nations peoples regarding sovereignty?

A Model for Self-Governance

Web Connect • • • • • • • • • • • •
To learn more about the Harvard Project, visit our website.

Communities working toward self-governance in Canada can be found from coast to coast. Each must face its own challenges and create a unique method of attaining autonomy and self-determination through its people, its institutions, and its resources. First Nations, Métis, and Inuit leaders have spoken out to influence public opinion, and lawyers have successfully used the court system to establish rights for Aboriginal peoples, especially in regard to sovereignty, education, resources, and health care. However, re-establishing rights is not the same as reclaiming self-governance, and circumstances are different for every community.

An established model could help guide the journey to self-governance. In the United States, the Harvard Project on American Indian Economic Development set out to explore the connection between economic success and Aboriginal sovereignty, self-governance, and self-determination. Although this research was conducted in the United States, the findings have generated much interest in Canada. Overall, the Harvard Project studies indicate that successful self-governance involves these factors:

- Sovereignty: The freedom of a group to make its own decisions.

- Institutions: Stable and independent institutions, such as systems of justice.

- Culturally appropriate governance: Successful governance reflects the unique culture of the community.

- Leaders: Leaders with knowledge and experience are able to draw the community together and inspire growth and change.

- Strategic thinking: Long-term planning—not just reactions to problems.

Questions of self-governance necessarily raise questions of

- what defines a *government*

- what is or can be the relationship of self-governing Aboriginal Nations with Canada

One description of *government* is that a government has key characteristics including an inherent right to govern, provision of services and programs to its citizens, representative political leadership by its citizens, a revenue source (such as taxation) to pay for services and programs, the ability to make laws and enforce them, and cooperation with other levels of government.

Based on the above definition, in what ways are specific Aboriginal governance systems governments? This question leads to the issue of the relationship with Canada. As you read in Chapter 5, many Aboriginal leaders are calling for a fundamental change in the relationship with Canada. The relationship with Canada is a subject you will continue to explore in this chapter and the rest of the unit.

REFLECTION

Which factor do you feel is the most important for Aboriginal self-governance? What is your understanding of the term *government*? Explain your views.

VOICES OF THE PEOPLES

I look across the country and I see well-educated and experienced people who want to be part of building the future for their Nations. But they need hardcore skills— they need knowledge of financial management, resource management, legal issues and more. We want to open up avenues for them to take an active role and be a force for positive change.

—Satsan (Herb George), president of the National Centre for First Nations Governance

---

Perspectives on Self-Governance and Self-Determination

What will Aboriginal self-governance look like? What will it involve? For First Nations, Métis, and Inuit peoples, self-governance and self-determination must reflect and grow from their diverse cultures and communities. Here are some perspectives.

> We want nothing less than capable governments with true decision-making power over the matters that affect our lives. Continued tinkering with sections of the Indian Act will not get us there. It is like painting a house when the foundation is crumbling. We need to build a new structure from the foundation up and to move away from trying to implement a policy direction set in the late 1800s.
>
> —Regional Chief Angus Toulouse, Sagamok Anishnawbek First Nation

> April 19th, 2010, we took a giant step forward on the road to reconciliation as the declaration of 2010 as the "Year of the Métis" by the Ontario Legislature was announced... We are finally taking our rightful place as a distinct Aboriginal people in Ontario and Canada, and...the rich Métis history in Ontario will begin to be told and cherished!
>
> —President Gary Lipinski, Métis Nation of Ontario

> The other alternative [to the traditional court system] that we have is to devise within our self-government model a way to resolve disputes that fits with our traditional teachings. An Aboriginal court system that is acceptable to all parties of an inter- or intra-tribal dispute could be developed and used to resolve disputes that previously had to go before non-Native courts. It is incumbent upon us as leaders to pursue this concept. We have seen time and time again the difficulties that we have with systems that are not our own.
>
> —John Beaucage, former Grand Council Chief, Anishinabek Nation

The ultimate show of sovereignty is taking responsibility to make your own decisions. At the same time you also have to take responsibility for the consequences. I think it is going to have to be the women that take that message forward. We have the role of keeping the communities together, keeping our communities healthy, and at the same time overseeing the leadership.

—Grand Chief Angie Barnes, Mohawks of Akwesasne

It's believing in your people and keeping them on board. Include your people in the visioning process for your Nation. If you have your community working as a team, it makes success a lot easier to achieve.

—Chief Terrance Paul, Membertou Mi'kmaq Nation

This will allow us, Canada and the Métis Nation, to develop a relationship together rather than using the courts to define the relationship. Frankly, this is in the best interest of the Government of Canada, the Métis Nation, and all Canadians. It is in the tradition of Canadian values.

—Audrey Poitras, vice president of the Métis Nation of Canada and president of the Métis Nation of Alberta (MNA), after the signing of the Métis Nation Framework Agreement

A notable challenge has been to incorporate Inuit Qaujimajatuqangit, or IQ, within government. IQ refers to a way of viewing the world and the values associated with positive living. It encompasses Inuit knowledge, philosophy, language and culture. Our government has committed to making IQ a component in the development of policies, as well as having it included in the day-to-day operations of our government, wherever possible. This has certainly broadened the thinking within our public service and has tapped into a new sense of creativity in providing public programs and services.

—Paul Okalik, Inuk, first premier of Nunavut

CRITICAL THINKING

What do these perspectives tell you about Aboriginal peoples' main concerns regarding governance? How do these perspectives relate to the questions raised on page 213? In a small group, discuss what you see as the main concerns, and how these concerns may be resolved.

The First Nations Self-Governance Process

The process of achieving self-governance is different for each Nation. However, negotiations generally begin with opening talks with the federal government. The next step is to agree on the main areas to be discussed, such as laws, control over land and resources, or education. After negotiations, an Agreement-in-Principle is written and signed. This agreement will guide the more detailed Final Agreement.

Once the Final Agreement is signed, it must be approved by members of the Nation and the federal government. At that point, the agreement becomes law.

COMMUNITY CLOSE-UP

Membertou, Nova Scotia

One of five Mi'kmaq communities in Cape Breton, Membertou is an urban First Nations community, with a population of over 1050 people. Membertou has undergone successful economic development since 1995, when leaders embarked on a determined mission to eliminate the band's financial deficit and create new opportunities in business and land management. This mission resulted in partnerships with the oil and gas industries, and in engineering, consultation, and business management. Inspired by this success, in 2009 the Mi'kmaq of this community moved toward self-governance by seeking to develop their own legislation to define citizenship, land use, and leadership succession. In essence, this would move the community out from under legislation such as the Indian Act.

For the people of Membertou, the desire for self-governance comes from frustration over status, the need to have greater control over their lands in order to further their economic development, and a feeling of pride, independence, and confidence in the community.

Moving beyond the Indian Act is a goal that's been near and dear to us for a long time. It's part of our desire to be self-sufficient and to manage our own affairs independently of the federal government.

—**Dan Christmas, Senior Advisor to Chief and Council of Membertou**

FIGURE 6.26 The Membertou Business Centre opened in 2010. It houses the Membertou Entrepreneur Centre, which provides entrepreneur training and business support to the community. Why did this community focus on business development as a means to gain self-determination?

Westbank First Nation

The Westbank First Nation is near the city of Kelowna, British Columbia. Rapid development in the region and internal conflicts over leadership led to problems within the band's administration. In 1986, the Hall Inquiry was established to look into the conflicts, and the Inquiry recommended that the band pursue self-governance in order to improve its administration.

The Westbank First Nation Self-Government Act became law in 2005. The agreement gives the Westbank First Nation control over land management, resources, language, and culture. It also sets out rules for financial accountability; an advisory council deals with any concerns raised by other residents of the region. Over 100 businesses operate within Westbank territory, and they too can raise concerns over laws or regulations that affect them directly. As with all self-governance agreements, Canadian laws, the Charter of Rights, and the Human Rights Act still remain in force.

FIGURE 6.27 Martin Bayer, a citizen of Aundeck Omni Kaning First Nation, is the chief negotiator for the Anishinabek Nation.

The Anishinabek Nation

The Anishinabek Nation is a confederation of seven tribal Nations in 40 communities, which together account for one third of the population of First Nations people in Ontario. Its corporate arm, the Union of Ontario Indians, began negotiations for control over its education system in 1998. An Agreement-in-Principle was signed in 2002. While the process has involved the federal government and the Union, the provincial government has also been consulted to ensure interaction between the Ontario education system and that of the First Nations.

A separate agreement that recognizes Anishinabek governance over citizenship, culture, and language is also underway. An Agreement-in-Principle on governance was signed in 2007. If the Final Agreement is passed, it will partially remove the Anishinabek Nation from the Indian Act. This new government will be modelled on the Anishinabek clan system. Members hope that restoring their governance structure will revitalize their communities and provide a firm foundation for their new administration.

> *..our governments must have legitimacy and the trust of our people. This means that the governing institutions we build need to match the customs and unique cultures of our people, and the rules about how things are done need to be stable, fair, and transparent. With more effective governing institutions, we can create a more rich environment for attracting investment to our communities and in the result, help to improve the quality of life for our people. This is what self-government is about to us.*
>
> **—Martin Bayer, chief negotiator for the Anishinabek Nation**

Leaders of Today

More and more First Nations, Inuit, and Métis leaders are stepping into the spotlight to work and speak for the benefit of their peoples. Some are federal or provincial Members of Parliament, such as Leona Aglukkaq, Frank Calder, or Paul DeVillers. Others are Hereditary Chiefs, elected band leaders, or community activists. With the development of new forms of self-governance, leadership of all kinds will be increasingly important in First Nations, Inuit, and Métis communities in the future. According to Brenda Etienne, Senior Negotiator, Mohawk Council of Kanehsatake, traditional decision-making values and structures play an important role in rebuilding Aboriginal Nations:

> *Our journey toward rebuilding our nations requires an intricate balance in our approach... We must first ensure that traditional concepts are reflected in the leadership and governance structures. We must then have all the capabilities needed to work and live successfully in a global environment.*

In their diversity, the leaders express the belief that societies derive their strength from all of their members: people of all ages and genders.

> *As women we...are the keepers of our culture and we are the teachers of our children. I would just like to say that for our men that we don't want to walk behind you. We want to walk beside you. We want to heal with you and we want to help you make those decisions that are needing to be made for the future of our people and that we walk together.*
>
> —Lillian Sanderson, La Ronge Native Women's Council, Saskatchewan

VOICES OF THE PEOPLES

A former assistant professor in Aboriginal Studies and the School of Social Work at the University of Toronto, Cynthia Wesley-Esquimaux is also an active community leader, researcher, land-rights coordinator, and political advocate. In 2010, she became the Liberal candidate in the riding of York-Simcoe (Ontario).

We've moved from land-based economies to cash-based, from models of communal child care to single families. We can either guide these transitions ourselves, or let them happen to us. We have to decide what traditions we want to maintain, and make sure we build them into our communities' social, economic, and governance plans for the future.

FIGURE 6.28 Cynthia Wesley-Esquimaux, Ph.D., lives on the Chippewas of Georgina Island First Nation.

The Role of Youth

Across Canada, First Nations, Métis, and Inuit youth are taking on leadership roles in their communities. Some may take part in elected governance by becoming band councillors. Others may contribute to youth councils in organizations such as the Assembly of First Nations or the Métis Nation of Ontario. Youth also take an active role in leading and encouraging their peers by becoming role models.

Lead Your Way is part of the National Aboriginal Role Model program. Every year, youth aged 13 to 30 are asked to nominate one of their peers as an Aboriginal role model. Twelve are chosen based on their achievements in life and their leadership skills. The program is designed to promote healthy lifestyles and self-esteem, create positive role models, and inspire leadership.

Web Connect • • • • • • • • • • •

To learn more about Lead Your Way, visit our website.

FIGURE 6.29 The Green Teens of Aamjiwnaang is an organization bringing young people together to share knowledge and views about environmental issues in their communities. The Green Teens, who are aged 12 to 29, are aware of their environment and the problems caused by pollution. As part of this group, they are able to tell their own stories.

VOICES OF THE PEOPLES

Youth represent 50 percent of the Inuit population, so we have an important role to play, not only at community events...but also in our families and communities.

—Jennifer Watkins, President of the National Inuit Youth Council

VOICES OF THE PEOPLES

I feel that it's important that the next generation really step into leadership from a place of remembrance and thorough understanding of their history, their culture, their traditions, their language... [I]t is going to be up to them to ensure that the nation-to-nation relationship is honoured, the treaties are honoured. So we're really looking to this next generation to step forward in a good way and to build upon the continuum of restoration of First Peoples to their rightful place in Canada.

—Jan Beaver, Alderville First Nation

©P

Tiffany Harrington, the Métis Youth representative from the Oshawa Métis Council, gave a speech during the 2008 Riel Day celebrations that expresses the connection of the past, present, and future community. Here is an excerpt from her speech in which she movingly asked the young people in the audience to listen to the Elders and to live up to Riel's legacy.

It is not an unachievable ideal to try and be the best that we can be; if anything, we [Métis] are living proof that anything is possible, that justice and equality are attainable. That is what Riel set out to teach us, that each and every person is in fact a leader and that only together can we achieve greatness...

THINKING IT THROUGH

1. Explain your views on self-governance and self-determination. What is the relationship between the two?

2. Do you think regaining self-governance would change the relationship between Aboriginal peoples and the government of Canada and between Aboriginal peoples and other Canadians? Explain.

3. Choose one of the leaders presented on pages 214 and 215. Explain what you feel to be this person's main message. How does this message relate to self-governance and self-determination for Aboriginal peoples?

4. Find more information on the Lead Your Way National Aboriginal Role Model program. Read the profiles of the current role models and their contributions to their communities. Create a plan to have one of the role models visit your school or community, and work with your class to write a list of questions you would ask this person.

CRITICAL THINKING

What are the challenges for First Nations, Métis, and Inuit peoples in their quest for self-governance and self-determination today?

Conclusion

The journey to regain self-governance and self-determination is only beginning for many First Nations, Métis, and Inuit Nations in Canada. For many, the basis of renewed self-governance is found in governance that existed within Aboriginal Nations before colonialism and the Indian Act. The rewards of self-governance—revitalized cultures, economic viability, and the ability to control daily life—are vital to the futures of these Nations. However, there is no one answer to the question of self-governance for these diverse peoples. Each Nation or community must make its own journey, using the wisdom, experience, and enthusiasm of all community members to achieve that goal.

End-of-Chapter Activities

1. This painting, called *New Chiefs on the Land,* is by Salish artist Lawrence Paul Yuxweluptun.

   a) In your own words, explain what you see in this image. How are the leaders portrayed? What might their appearance imply?

   b) Research this artist and look at more of his paintings. Read about the artist. Choose two other pieces of his art and describe each one, making sure to discuss what you feel each work is saying. What might the artist be communicating through his work?

FIGURE 6.30 *New Chiefs on the Land* (2006) by Lawrence Paul Yuxweluptun

2. What does Tom Porter mean by the good mind (page 190)? Research the Great Law of Peace by finding an authentic and reliable source. As you read or listen (if an Elder is your source), consider the following.

   a) What are the expectations placed on leaders?

   b) What qualities must leaders demonstrate?

   c) What happens when a leader does not meet his or her obligations?

   d) How do leaders work with consensus-type governance?

3. Investigate examples of governance in your school. You could choose a student council or another group that oversees the organization and day-to-day activities of your school.

   a) How is the group organized? How does it make decisions, and who enforces those decisions? Does it work by consensus? Does it have the authority to make its own decisions?

   b) Are there recommendations you would make to improve the governance structure of the group? Explain.

4. Research a leader who is well-respected by the community and who appears to be making positive changes and creating well-being within his or her community or Nation. Create a profile of this leader answering these questions: How is the leader advocating for the good of his or her people? What does this advocacy mean in terms of people, land, cultures, families, community, beliefs, and values? How is he or she demonstrating good leadership?

5. Investigate the social and political challenges presently facing a First Nations, Métis, or Inuit community or Nation. Discuss what is going well in that community or Nation, as well as what could be changed to ensure good governance. Create a short presentation about one aspect of the governance of that Nation or community. Include examples of how the challenges faced by the people are being addressed.

6. This chapter has explored some effects of the Indian Act along with proposed and implemented changes to the Canadian Constitution. Describe how these changes have brought attention to issues of sovereignty, self-governance, and self-determination for Aboriginal peoples.

CHAPTER 7

Treaties and Self-Determination

Aboriginal peoples are the first peoples in what is now Canada. Existing Aboriginal and treaty rights are enshrined in our Constitution. I think it is important that we have a public education system in which every student has an opportunity to learn about Aboriginal peoples, their histories, perspectives, and current concerns. It is imperative that the phrase "we are all treaty people" resonate with all Ontarians. In the longer term, this will help to improve relations between Aboriginal and non-Aboriginal peoples.

—Justice Sidney B. Linden, in the Final Report of the Ipperwash Inquiry

FIGURE 7.1 Algonquin Elder William Commanda is Keeper of three wampum belts. What is the significance of his role as a Keeper of the wampum belts? What might this role mean to future treaty negotiations?

What does the phrase "we are all treaty people" mean to you? What are the implications of treaty agreements between governments and Aboriginal peoples in Canada? This chapter will examine treaties and how the beliefs and values of First Nations, Métis, and Inuit peoples shape their negotiations of treaties. You will gain an understanding of the challenges surrounding treaties and land rights, possible future directions, and modern agreements.

INQUIRING MINDS

Use these questions to explore the big ideas in this chapter.

1. What is the history of treaty-making in Canada?

2. How do Aboriginal beliefs and values guide the negotiations of treaties and land rights?

3. Why are land and land use at the centre of treaty negotiations?

4. What are the relationships between Aboriginal peoples and provincial and federal governments in Canada regarding land and treaty issues?

©P

FIGURE 7.2 Justice Sidney Linden is greeted by Sam George, brother of Dudley George, after the closing ceremonies for the Ipperwash Inquiry in August 2006. The inquiry into the events surrounding the Ipperwash crisis investigated not only the death of Dudley George, but the history behind the issues at Ipperwash. The report made 98 recommendations designed to improve relations with Aboriginal peoples in Ontario, as you will learn on page 231.

We Are All Treaty People

WORDS MATTER

treaty a formal agreement between two or more nations in reference to peace, alliance, commerce, territory, or other relations

VOICES OF THE PEOPLES

What we speak of and do now will last as long as the sun shines and the river runs, we are looking forward to our children's children...

—*Mistawasis, Cree Chief, speaking at Treaty 6 proceedings, 1876*

CRITICAL THINKING

Discuss what you think is the meaning behind the phrase "as long as the sun shines and the river runs." Why is this phrase part of all treaty agreements in Canada?

Treaties are agreements that provide for peaceful relationships between two nations. They can provide for peace in times of war, for trade, and for the sharing of resources. Each party in a treaty has equal status; each party has duties and obligations to the other.

To the First Nations, Métis, and Inuit peoples of Canada, treaties are more than just agreements on written documents. They are living things, meant to last "as long as the sun shines and the river runs." They are based on values and principles that centre on peaceful relationships and living together on the land. Records of treaties are kept by Aboriginal peoples within wampum belts or by oral tradition. The Creator was considered to be a witness to the treaties, making the treaties sacred agreements.

Today, treaties are recognized as lasting agreements that can be enforced by law. Since 1982, treaties have been protected in Canada by the Canadian Constitution, which affirms "existing Aboriginal treaty rights." Treaties are also supported by international law.

What does the phrase "we are all treaty people" mean? Treaties are not only agreements between Aboriginal peoples and the federal government, or between Aboriginal peoples of the past and historical colonial powers such as England or France. Treaties exist, are renewed, created, and supported today. They continue to be beneficial for all members of the nations within the agreements. This means that all Canadians are members of treaty agreements. All Canadians are treaty people.

FIGURE 7.3 Noel Knockwood, sergeant-at-arms for the Nova Scotia Legislature, conducts a sweetgrass ceremony during Mi'kmaq Treaty Day celebrations. Treaty Day is held every year to mark the beginning of Mi'kmaq History Month and the anniversary of the Friendship Treaties. The day also reaffirms the historic presence of the Mi'kmaq in Nova Scotia. The Mi'kmaq and the government still exchange gifts to mark the anniversary. Why are these celebrations meaningful today?

Treaty-Making: Aboriginal Values and Beliefs

First Nations, Métis, and Inuit peoples regard treaties as an essential part of peoples living together, creating connections with each other, and sharing resources fairly and responsibly.

For the French and English explorers, traders, and settlers who came to what is now North America, treaties with Aboriginal peoples were also a way to ensure peace, encourage trade, and share resources such as land, wildlife, and water. However, differences between the world views of Aboriginal peoples and the newcomers, especially in regard to land, would eventually affect the interpretations of treaties between Aboriginal peoples and the English, French, and Canadian governments.

First Nations, Métis, and Inuit peoples do not see the land as something that can be "owned" by an individual. The land is a gift from the Creator, and should not be bought or sold, but cared for. Aboriginal peoples view themselves as spiritual guardians of the land.

From the perspectives of the English, French, and Canadian governments, treaties were agreements in which Aboriginal peoples surrendered the land in exchange for payments and other promises. In most cases, the government interpreted this exchange to mean that First Nations peoples had given up ownership of the land—that although a Nation may live on what it considers its territory, that land is actually owned by the Crown.

The Spirit and Intent of Treaties

Many First Nations used a pipe during a treaty-making process. The pipe was used to make a promise not only between Nations, but also with other elements of creation. The pipe made a treaty agreement a sacred oath—one that would be kept for all time.

In addition to being a sacred bond, First Nations considered a treaty to be a living document that bound individuals on both sides, like a marriage. In Mi'kmaq society, the treaties were recited every year at a formal gathering. That way, every Mi'kmaw was aware of his or her responsibilities toward the Nation's allies. As well, treaty terms could not be put aside or renegotiated just because one side wanted to do so.

Colonial and, later, Canadian governments, however, tended to view treaties with other Nations as a way of advancing trade or legitimizing their claim to new territories.

VOICES OF THE PEOPLES

Treaty, or innaihtsiini, is when two powerful nations come together into a peace agreement, both parties coming forward in a peaceful, reconciliatory approach by exercising a sacred oath through the symbolic way of peace, which is smoking a sacred pipe and also through the exchange of gifts to sanction the agreement which can never be broken.

—Louise Crop Eared Wolf, Blood Elder

CRITICAL THINKING

Before reading the rest of this chapter, discuss with a partner why you think Aboriginal peoples signed treaties between Nations and with the British, French, and Canadian governments. Make notes about your discussion and return to them at the end of the chapter. Has your opinion changed? Explain.

An exchange during negotiations for Treaty 6, 1876, as recorded by Alexander Morris and his assistants.

You will remember the promises which I have already made; I said you would get seed; you need not concern yourselves so much about what your grandchildren are going to eat; your children will be taught, and then they will be as well able to take care of themselves as the whites around them.

—*Alexander Morris (lieutenant-governor of Manitoba and the Northwest Territories)*

It is well known that if we had plenty to live on from our gardens we would not still insist on getting more provision, but it is in case of any extremity...we are as yet in the dark; this is not a trivial matter for us. We were glad to hear what the Governor was saying to us and we understood it, but we are not understood, we do not mean to ask for food for every day but only when we commence and in case of famine or calamity.

—*Mistawasis (Cree Chief)*

1. Read the quotation by Alexander Morris. Do you think he is concerned about future generations? What presumptions does he make about Aboriginal peoples and their needs? Support your answers with evidence from the quotation.

2. Read the quotation by Mistawasis. Do you think he is concerned with future generations of his people? What evidence from this quotation backs up your viewpoint?

Ways of Knowing

The Hiawatha Belt

Wampum, or quohog shell beads, were used by some First Nations, including the Haudenosaunee and the Mi'kmaq, to record significant agreements. The images and patterns woven using different-coloured beads kept the memory of the agreement alive. The unity of the Five Nations under the Great Law of Peace is recorded in a visual record of the founding of the Haudenosaunee Confederacy. The white pine at the centre of the Hiawatha Wampum Belt represents the Tree of Peace, to which all Nations in the Confederacy connect. It also symbolizes the Onondaga Nation, which was charged with keeping the Confederacy alive. The squares are the Nations, representing the Seneca, Cayuga, Oneida, and Mohawk. This reproduction Hiawatha belt was created in 2006 by Ken Maracle, Cayuga.

FIGURE 7.4 Why was it important to have a visual record of a treaty as well as an oral history of the agreement?

©P

Treaties, Sovereignty, and Self-Determination

Indigenous peoples have the right to self-determination. By virtue of that right they freely determine their political status and freely pursue their economic, social and cultural development.

—Article 3 in the United Nations Declaration of the Rights of Indigenous Peoples

Self-determination is the right of First Nations, Métis, and Inuit peoples to control and manage the issues and matters that directly affect them. For Aboriginal peoples, all Aboriginal rights and responsibilities stem from their identities as the original occupants of the land. For most First Nations in Canada, their rights are acknowledged in treaties, which are nation-to-nation agreements. For the Inuit, self-determination and control of land and resources have been gained, to some extent, with the creation of Nunavut and other agreements with the Canadian government. Métis peoples currently have land claims before the Supreme Court of Canada, and their right to hunt and fish has been acknowledged by some provincial courts.

First Nations, Métis, and Inuit peoples do not seek approval from the Canadian government for their right to self-determination, but rather want their existing rights acknowledged by the government and all Canadians. The basis of the right to self-determination for Aboriginal peoples lies within treaties, which are themselves protected within the Canadian Constitution.

Self-determination also starts with individuals deciding to take personal action to make their communities and Nations better, regardless of what their governments are doing.

VOICES OF THE PEOPLES

When Indigenous Peoples talk about the land and the making of treaty, we are talking about our life and the life of future generations. Land is central to that process. We have a relationship with our Creator based on a legal system designed to protect and honour the land.

—*Sharon H. Venne, Plains Cree*

Web Connect • • • • • • • • • • • • •

To read the Declaration of the Rights of Indigenous Peoples, visit our website.

VOICES OF THE PEOPLES

A leader within the Poplar River First Nation in the boreal region of Manitoba, Sophia Rabliauskas has worked with her people for eight years to secure the protection of two million acres of undisturbed forest land. Under the direction of Elders, Sophia Rabliauskas and her team created a plan to sustainably manage Poplar River's forests by respecting traditional knowledge, using environmental analysis, and developing economic opportunities. In 2004, Sophia Rabliauskas helped secure five years of "interim protected status" for Poplar River territory, which prohibited logging, hydro, gas, and mining development.

Creator gave us the responsibility to care for the land, the land that sustains our life. Our Elders have always believed that how we treat our land today will affect the health of the planet and the lives of many generations to come. It is critical now more than ever, that we fulfill that responsibility that was passed down to us from our ancestors.

FIGURE 7.5 Discuss Sophia Rabliauskas's vision of responsibility for the land. How is this connected to her approach toward negotiations for the protection of the land?

Nation to Nation

Treaties were used between First Nations well before the arrival of English and French explorers, missionaries, and traders. Nations within the Great Law of Peace, for example, joined in a confederacy but remained separate, sovereign Nations. In making treaties with England (later, Great Britain) and France, First Nations would still consider themselves to be sovereign, equal Nations.

Early treaties between First Nations and the English and French involved peacemaking (the Mi'kmaq Concordat in 1640, or the Great Peace of Montréal in 1701, for example) or trade agreements. Great Britain's Royal Proclamation of 1763 identified First Nations as "Nations" and set aside lands for their exclusive use. The Royal Proclamation is still considered to be the basis for all treaties between the British Crown and First Nations since then.

After the War of 1812, First Nations peoples were no longer needed as allies, and the Crown began to concentrate on obtaining land for settlement. To do this, it used treaties. These treaties established a pattern for the future: payments of cash and other goods in exchange for use of the land, with smaller areas reserved for the exclusive use of First Nations. First Nations saw the treaties as agreements to share their territory with the newcomers. To the Crown, the goal was to ensure land for settlers and development.

Issues surrounding land—who controls resources, where people live, and what ownership of land really means—remain of vital interest to all Canadians. For Aboriginal peoples, treaties support their sovereign right to their lands, to the resources within those lands, and to the right of self-determination.

FIGURE 7.6 A poster for the 2010 celebration of Membertou 400, the 400th anniversary of the signing of the Mi'kmaq Concordat. This historic signing showed the commitment of Mi'kmaq leaders to ensuring a peaceful future for their people.

THINKING IT THROUGH

1. In one paragraph, explain the differences between the way Aboriginal peoples viewed treaties and the way colonial and Canadian governments viewed treaties. In a second paragraph, speculate on how these outlooks have affected modern treaty negotiations and/or conflicts.

2. With a partner, discuss why the Royal Proclamation of 1763 remains an important document in modern treaty negotiations.

3. Reread the United Nations quotation about self-determination on page 227. In a small group, discuss the connections between self-determination and the sovereignty of Indigenous peoples. Groups can share the connections they discover with the class.

©P

Honouring Treaty Rights

As you read in Chapter 6, First Nations, Métis, and Inuit peoples in Canada have been making advances in achieving self-determination and greater control over lands and resources. In many cases, Aboriginal peoples have sought to regain **jurisdiction** over their ancestral territories, management of resources, justice, and education.

The Land

The Numbered Treaties were created in western Canada after the vast area known as Rupert's Land was transferred from the control of the Hudson's Bay Company to the government of the Dominion of Canada in 1869. However, increased settlement of the West would not be possible if the government could not first negotiate agreements with the First Nations who held title to the land.

From the perspective of the government, these treaties were agreements in which First Nations **ceded** their rights and title to their lands in exchange for a small area of land set aside for them as a reserve, annual payments, protection, and the right to continue to hunt, trap, and fish. First Nations peoples affected by the near-extinction of the bison were eager to receive assistance, and it was hard for them to refuse negotiations. However, many Nations still contend that their lands were never surrendered.

WORDS MATTER

jurisdiction formal recognition of a people's right to make decisions, administer control, and enforce laws

cede to yield or formally surrender

VOICES OF THE PEOPLES

The treaty was essential for the survival of the Tsuu T'ina. People did not understand the treaty—they only understood that they needed to enter the treaty to survive.

—*Louise Big Plume, Tsuu T'ina Elder*

Web Connect • • • • • • • • • • • •

To learn more about the Numbered Treaties, visit our website.

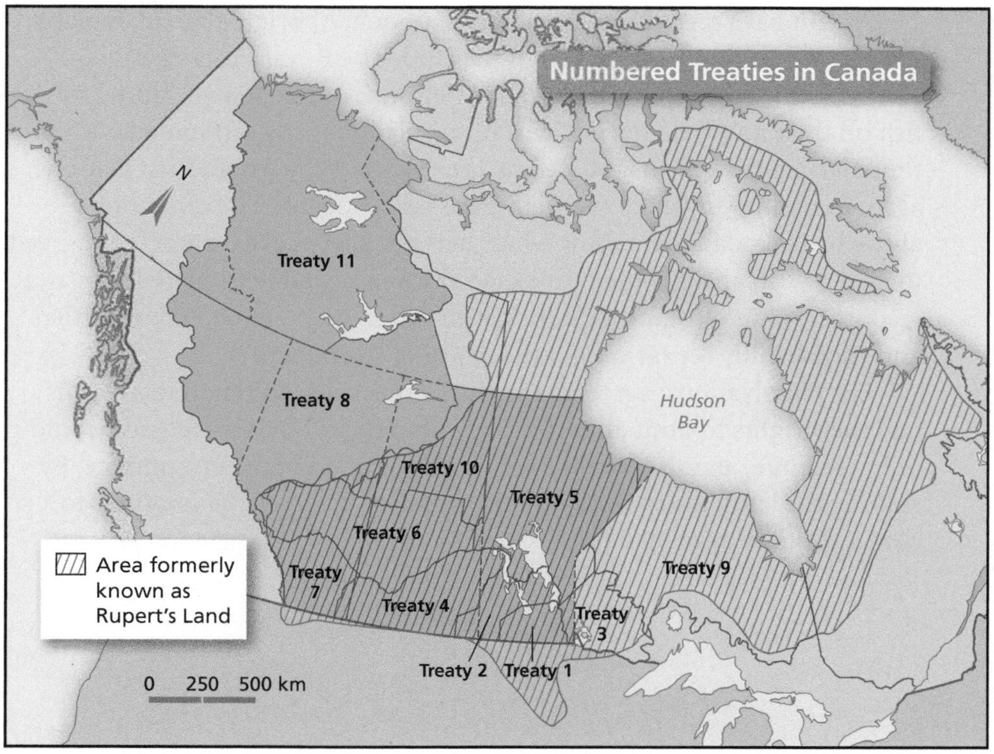

Numbered Treaties in Canada

Treaty 11
Treaty 8
Treaty 10
Treaty 6
Treaty 5
Treaty 7
Treaty 4
Treaty 3
Treaty 9
Treaty 2
Treaty 1

Hudson Bay

▧ Area formerly known as Rupert's Land

0   250   500 km

FIGURE 7.7 The Numbered Treaties involved lands that are now within Ontario, Saskatchewan, Manitoba, Alberta, British Columbia, the Northwest Territories, Nunavut, and Yukon Territory. What did each side hope to achieve in negotiating a treaty?

It is said there were discussions on the treaty amongst the commissioners, the heads of police, and the Natives. However, the government people had a pre-written document containing only their concept of what the treaty entails. They told the Indian chiefs, "This is our terms of the treaty and this is what will be in the treaty agreement." But in those days there was nobody at all from the Native's side to translate or understand exactly the legal jargon in the treaty document. Nonetheless, the Indian chiefs had an indication of why they were there—to make a peace treaty.

—*Bill Mclean, Nakoda Elder*

They did not know they were being asked to give up their land. What they thought was that the government was only saying that they would plough the land to grow something, nothing more. They didn't know that they were giving up their land.

—*Lazurus Wesley, Nakoda Elder*

FIGURE 7.8 A commemorative treaty medal. Silver medals were meant to offer a lasting visual reminder to all participants of their treaty commitments. Look closely at the images on the medal. What do you think they represent?

Our songs, our spirits, and our identities are written on this land, and the future of our peoples is tied to it. It is not a possession or a commodity for us. It is the heart of our nations. In our traditional spirituality it is our mother.

—*Grand Chief Anthony Mercredi, Assembly of First Nations*

Web Connect • • • • • • • • • • •

To read the Report of the Ipperwash Inquiry, visit our website.

As you have seen throughout this textbook, Aboriginal peoples place great value on their connection to the land. The Royal Proclamation of 1763 acknowledged the right of First Nations peoples to live, hunt, and fish on their ancestral territories. It also ruled that any settlement within those lands was to be negotiated by the Crown. Why would First Nations agree to treaties in which their land was surrendered? The quotations above by Nakoda Elders show what their people believed when they agreed to Treaty 7. In an agreement of peace, it was acceptable to share lands and resources. They also understood that the land was to be shared by settlers and used mainly for farming ("the depth of the plough").

For First Nations, agreeing to treaties was a way to retain their lands and their rights to hunt and fish. They understood that settlement would only continue, and that settlers would be coming in greater numbers. By sharing the land, they would not lose it entirely, and the generations to come would be provided for.

Ipperwash and the Kettle and Stony Point First Nation

After the War of 1812, the British wanted more land for settlement along the southern shores of Lake Huron. The Huron Tract Treaty with the Anishinaabe was agreed to in 1827. The treaty covered over 288 136 hectares (2 million acres) of land; the Anishinaabe were compensated with the equivalent of about $10 per person each year. Less than one percent of that area was set aside for the Anishinaabe in four separate reserves—Sarnia, Stoney Point, Kettle Point, and Walpole Island. Over time, the Sarnia Reserve was under pressure from the growing city of Sarnia, and both Kettle Point and Stoney Point were pressured for valuable shoreline. In 1928, the men of the Stoney Point reserve agreed to the sale of 152.6 hectares (377 acres) of their land, including shoreline. They received $87.50 per hectare ($35 per acre). In 1932, a portion of that land was used to create Ipperwash Provincial Park.

In 1942, during World War II, the Canadian Department of National Defence (DND) wanted land for a training camp, and chose what remained of the Stoney Point reserve land. Government agents at the time decided to move the residents of Stoney Point to Kettle Point, making administration easier, clearing the way for the military camp, and creating what would afterward be known as the Kettle and Stony Point First Nation.

On April 1, 1942, male Stoney Point residents who were over 18 voted on this proposal; 58 of 72 votes were against. The people did not want to leave their ancestral lands, especially because of the presence of burial grounds. Many residents were worried that the gravesites would not be respected. Despite the vote results, as well as many letters and petitions of protest, the land of Stoney Point was expropriated under the War Measures Act. The Stoney Point people were paid $37.50 per hectare ($15 per acre). Still, they believed that when the war was over, their land would be returned; the DND at

first indicated it would return the land, but that offer was then withdrawn. Attempts to regain the land in 1946, 1948, and in the 1960s, which included legal action, failed. Even though the federal government agreed in 1972 that the Stoney Point people had a "legitimate grievance," the land was not returned.

In 1993, unarmed women, men, and children from Stoney Point began to move back into the military camp. Remaining military personnel left the camp in 1995. In September 1995, First Nations men and women began an occupation of Ipperwash Provincial Park to bring attention to the long struggle to regain the land taken from them. A confrontation between unarmed Stoney Pointers and armed Ontario Provincial Police took place. Dudley George was shot and killed by OPP Sergeant Kenneth Deane.

Almost 10 years later, after prolonged efforts by Dudley George's brother, Sam George, and others, the Ontario government called an inquiry. This inquiry, which you will read more about in Chapter 8, was meant to look into the events of September 1995 as well as investigate the history of the issue and recommend changes for the future. Justice Sidney Linden led the inquiry, which lasted two years and involved 139 witnesses, including former Ontario Premier Mike Harris. In May 2007, the Ipperwash Inquiry report was released. It made 98 recommendations, including better police training and more public education about Aboriginal treaty issues. In 2010, the Ontario government introduced legislation meant to deregulate Ipperwash Park as a step toward restoring the lands. In 2010, archaeologists discovered human remains in the park that were over 1000 years old.

QUESTION

1. Why would knowledge about Aboriginal issues help the public understand what had happened at Ipperwash? Why do you think this recommendation was included in the final report?

Harvesting Rights

Hunting, fishing, trapping, or any other activity Aboriginal peoples maintain for their survival is protected under the treaties. This promise was sometimes made orally, and in other cases, such as in the Numbered Treaties or in the Robinson Treaties in Ontario, was part of the written agreement. Today, these rights tend to be determined on a case-by-case basis, as you saw in Chapter 3 in the cases of Métis hunter Steve Powley and Mi'kmaw fisher Donald Marshall Jr. In both of these instances, the right to hunt or fish was upheld by the courts, but only after the people involved were charged with hunting and fishing outside of regulations. Each province has its own rules and regulations regarding the management of wildlife and fisheries, and these were originally formed without consideration of Aboriginal rights.

First Nations, Métis, and Inuit peoples also see harvesting rights not only as a treaty right, but as part of their responsibility to care for the land. As harvesters, they are responsible for making sure that the needs of future generations will still be met. In this view, the knowledge of Aboriginal peoples is a part of managing natural resources, and some Nations, such as the Moricetown Band in British Columbia, below, work with the provinces to manage resources. These issues are now becoming part of modern land claims and other agreements, as Aboriginal peoples seek to co-manage their lands.

FIGURE 7.9 A Wet'suwet'en fisher from the Moricetown Band uses a dipnet to catch salmon at Moricetown Falls, British Columbia. The Wet'suwet'en have always fished for salmon in the river using weirs, nets, and baskets. To help manage salmon stocks, the office of the Wet'suwet'en Nation works closely with the B.C. Department of Fisheries and Oceans to monitor fish numbers. This work helps to maintain fish stocks for generations to come.

©P

Issues of Justice

By signing treaties, Aboriginal peoples did not surrender their cultures or governance systems. These systems include specific laws and customs, including ways of resolving disputes that are in accordance with community values. As new agreements are forged, connections to the land are recognized, and jurisdiction is restored, Aboriginal peoples are beginning to achieve self-determination.

Acknowledging Community and Restorative Justice

For Aboriginal peoples, **restorative justice** is based on the values of community well-being and balance. The goal of restorative justice is not to punish the offender, but to restore harmony in the community. Restorative justice practices, previously very much a part of Aboriginal cultures, are increasingly being used in Aboriginal communities in Canada, as you will study further in Chapter 8. They appear at the regional and community level. In Nunavut, for example, the territory's criminal justice system includes restorative justice programs. They include the use of healing circles and community-based committees following Inuit principles of justice. These programs show the integration of self-governance, connection to values, and self-determination.

WORDS MATTER

restorative justice an approach to justice in which offenders are encouraged to take responsibility for their actions and to help restore harmony to the community through mediation, compensation, or other actions

CRITICAL THINKING

Why would community-based justice programs and committees be effective for First Nations, Métis, and Inuit peoples?

THINKING IT THROUGH

1. Explain the connections among treaties, access to the land, and Aboriginal rights.

2. Based on your knowledge of Aboriginal world views, discuss why Aboriginal peoples would be determined to retain their lands and provide for future generations.

3. The federal Department of Justice in Canada has implemented an Aboriginal Justice Strategy, in which Aboriginal peoples will be assisted in taking greater control of justice in their communities. How does this strategy reflect a return to self-determination for Aboriginal peoples?

4. Doing additional research as necessary, discuss the history behind the changes to the reserve lands of the Kettle and Stony Point First Nation. Why did changes occur? What were the effects on the people? What lessons can be learned for the future?

1923	Williams Treaties signed
1975	James Bay and Northern Quebec Agreement signed
1987–1997	*Delgamuukw* v. *B.C.*
1990	Oka crisis
1991	Indian Claims Commission created
2000	Nisga'a Final Agreement signed
2008	Specific Claims Tribunal formed

FIGURE 7.10 Billy Diamond was elected Chief of Waskaganish First Nation when he was 21 years old. Within a few years he had been elected Grand Chief of the Crees of Northern Québec, and led the fight against the James Bay hydroelectric project. Chief Diamond died September 30, 2010, at the age of 61.

CRITICAL THINKING

What would be the impact of restricting legal advice?

Modern Treaty Claims and Agreements

Today, the rights of Aboriginal peoples to control their territories are more often being recognized by Canadian courts. However, resolution of treaty rights still poses challenges for First Nations, Métis, and Inuit peoples in Canada. Most Canadians still have difficulty appreciating and understanding treaty rights. Another barrier to settling treaty disputes originated within the Indian Act, in which First Nations were prevented from hiring lawyers to represent their interests. This rule did not change until 1951.

Land Rights and Land Use

First Nations have entered into negotiations with various levels of government over land rights and use since the 1700s. However, it was not until 1973 that the Canadian government established policies for dealing with land claims. After several legal decisions that established Aboriginal rights to land not covered by treaties, the government chose to negotiate.

The Office of Native Claims (ONC) first opened in 1974. The Office, part of the Department of Indian and Northern Affairs, was intended to deal with both specific and comprehensive claims brought forward by First Nations. Specific claims concern issues arising from treaties, while comprehensive claims cover claims by First Nations, Métis, or Inuit peoples who did not sign treaties. Until 1974, many claims went unresolved, were rejected, or stalled in the system.

The James Bay and Northern Quebec Agreement

In 1971, the Québec government announced the construction of a massive hydroelectric project in the James Bay region of northern Québec. The ten thousand Cree and Inuit who lived, hunted, trapped, and fished in the region were not consulted about the development, even though they stood to lose their livelihoods and their way of life. The Cree and Inuit quickly sought and were granted a court ruling to stop the project until their rights were recognized. Although the Québec Superior Court later overturned the ruling, the government recognized the need to negotiate.

In 1975, the James Bay and Northern Québec Agreement was signed. The Crown acknowledged Cree and Inuit ownership of 14 000 square kilometres of land and their exclusive hunting, fishing, and trapping rights over a further 150 000 square kilometres. Financial compensation was to be provided, and the Cree and Inuit gained more control over health, education, and justice in their communities. As the first modern treaty between Aboriginal peoples and the Canadian government, the James Bay and Northern Quebec Agreement became the model for many modern treaties that followed.

The Response to Oka: The Indian Claims Commission

The 1990 Oka Crisis was a land dispute between the Mohawk Nation and the town of Oka, Québec. The Mohawk Council of Kanehsatake had filed a land claim for the territory under dispute, but its claim had been rejected in 1986. The crisis, which made international news when Mohawk people clashed with police, made it clear that the government needed to deal with land claims in a more effective way.

The Indian Claims Commission (ICC) was created in 1991 to resolve claims outside of the courts and to review claims the government had previously rejected. The ICC operated until 2009, but it could only make recommendations, while the government retained the power to veto any proposals.

The Specific Claims Tribunal

In an effort to ensure fairness and effectiveness, the Specific Claims Tribunal Act was passed in 2008. The tribunal is the first independent organization with the power to make binding decisions on land claims. However, the tribunal does not have the power to award land.

First Nations claimants may submit to the tribunal if

- they have been informed by the government of a decision not to negotiate

- three years have passed without a decision or resolution on a claim

The Specific Claims Tribunal was created through a collaborative effort by the Assembly of First Nations and the federal government. National Chief Phil Fontaine called it a positive response to the efforts First Nations peoples have made for decades in terms of land rights.

This table shows land claims in Canada, by province, as of late 2010. What patterns do you see?

Province or Territory	Claims in Progress	Concluded Claims	Active Litigation
Alberta	49	80	8
British Columbia	265	298	10
Manitoba	30	66	1
New Brunswick	5	25	0
Nova Scotia	9	22	0
Northwest Territories	2	9	0
Ontario	98	133	51
Prince Edward Island	1	1	0
Québec	68	64	1
Saskatchewan	43	108	5
Yukon Territory	3	22	0
Newfoundland and Labrador	NA	NA	NA

Web Connect • • • • • • • • • • •

To learn more about the Specific Claims Tribunal, visit our website.

CRITICAL THINKING

What are the key differences between the Indian Claims Commission (ICC) and the Specific Claims Tribunal? How might these differences have affected the negotiation or resolution of modern claims?

VOICES OF THE PEOPLES

British Columbia is unceded indigenous territory. Unlike the rest of Canada, we have not entered into nor have we signed treaties, and therefore we still enjoy unextinguished Aboriginal title to all the land and resources of British Columbia.

—Stewart Phillip, president of the Union of British Columbia Indian Chiefs

The Nisga'a Final Agreement

The Nisga'a Final Agreement took 130 years to resolve. It transferred 2019 square kilometres in the Nass Valley from the Crown to the Nisga'a, recognized their right to self-government, and provided a one-time payment of $196.1 million. The agreement was the first modern treaty in British Columbia. Its final passage into Canadian law, on May 11, 2000, made news around the world.

FIGURE 7.11 In 1998, a group of Nisga'a drummers and dancers arrived at the British Columbia legislature to witness the introduction of Bill 51, legislation that would officially recognize the Nisga'a as a self-governing Nation.

©P

1870	British Columbia government denies Aboriginal title to any lands in B.C., claiming the Royal Proclamation does not apply.
1880s	Crown surveyors are sent to Nisga'a territory to divide the land for settlement. They are turned away by Nisga'a Chief Israel Sgat'iin.
1887	Nisga'a and Tsimshian Chiefs travel by water to Victoria to ask the premier to recognize their right to their ancestral lands. They are not permitted to enter the Legislature.
1890	Nisga'a land committee is formed.
1913	Nisga'a petition the British Privy Council in London to resolve their land issues.
1967	The Nisga'a begin legal proceedings against the province in what eventually becomes known as the Calder case.
1973	The Supreme Court recognizes the existence of Aboriginal title at the time of the Royal Proclamation.
1976	The Canadian government opens negotiations with the Nisga'a Tribal Council. B.C. joins the negotiations months later.
1996	An Agreement-in-Principle is signed.
1998	The Final Agreement is reached.
1999	After months of debate, the B.C. government ratifies the agreement.
2000	On April 13, the Nisga'a Final Agreement becomes law. The agreement takes effect on May 11.

FIGURE 7.12 Nisga'a Chief Israel Sgat'iin, photographed in the 1890s

Web Connect • • • • • • • • • • • •

To read more about the Nisga'a Final Agreement, visit our website.

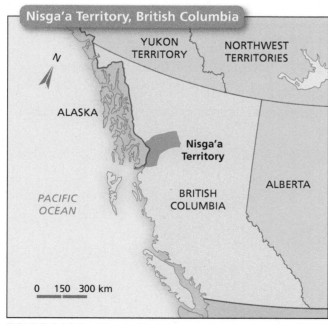

FIGURE 7.13 The Nisga'a Final Agreement recognizes over 2000 square kilometres near the northwest coast of B.C. as Nisga'a territory.

FIGURE 7.14 Dr. Frank Calder served in the B.C. legislature for 26 years. In 1967, he initiated a lawsuit against the Canadian government, arguing that Aboriginal title to Nisga'a land had never been extinguished. The Calder case paved the way for negotiations that led to the Nisga'a Final Agreement.

Never before has a Canadian court been given the opportunity to hear Indian witnesses describe within their own structure the history and nature of their societies. The challenge for this court is to hear this evidence, in all its complexity, in all its elaboration, as the articulation of a way of looking at the world which pre-dates the Canadian Constitution by many thousands of years.

—statement of the Gitxsan and Wet'suwet'en Chiefs and Elders

CRITICAL THINKING

Will the ability to share stories and discuss issues from Aboriginal perspectives help the process of negotiating treaty agreements? Explain.

Oral Tradition and the Courts

First Nations, Métis, and Inuit peoples have systems that ensure the passing on of knowledge and history through oral tradition. In 1997, the resolution of *Delgamuukw v. British Columbia* created a precedent on the use of oral tradition as evidence. The initial land title action was launched in 1987 by 35 Gitxsan and 13 Wet'suwet'en Hereditary Chiefs claiming jurisdiction over their hereditary territories—58 000 square kilometres of northwestern British Columbia.

At the initial trial, Chiefs and Elders spoke of their peoples' occupation of their territories, and the rights that they had never renounced. This account was supported by their oral histories, which are preserved by repeated performances during which anyone who disagrees with what is being recited can raise objections. This system ensures legitimacy.

In 1991, Judge Allan McEachern dismissed the claim, adding that Aboriginal rights exist only at the pleasure of the Crown. This ruling extinguished the land rights of the Gitxsan and the Wet'suwet'en peoples.

The B.C. Supreme Court overturned the ruling, stating that governments must confer with the Gitxsan and the Wet'suwet'en peoples before carrying out activities on their traditional territories. The case also went to the Supreme Court of Canada, which in 1997 ruled that provinces could not extinguish Aboriginal land rights.

Because oral histories are used to establish historical occupation of a territory, the court also ruled that Judge McEachern had not given oral history proper weight during the original trial. *Delgamuukw v. British Columbia* was a landmark case, asserting that in future cases dealing with Aboriginal peoples, oral histories must be given the same consideration as written evidence.

THINKING IT THROUGH

1. In what ways is the James Bay and Northern Quebec Agreement a model for modern treaties?

2. Discuss the importance of the Delgamuukw decision on the use of oral histories as evidence.

©P

Developing Historical Perspective

People who live in different times develop different perspectives on events or issues. Realizing that perspectives can vary plays an important part in understanding history. As you study people and events from the past, you will also develop your own perspective on what happened. Here are some tips to help you develop a historical perspective.

Identifying Your Perspective

Before you can recognize other perspectives, you have to realize that your perspective comes from the time and culture in which you live, as well as understanding brought about by your own knowledge and experiences. Not everyone necessarily shares your perspective. When you consider an issue, ask yourself the following questions:

- What do I think about the issue and the best way to resolve it?

- What are my reasons for holding these views?

- How have my circumstances, culture, or time period influenced my positions?

Identifying Other Perspectives

People from different cultures and time periods develop different perspectives, and those perspectives often change over time, sometimes quite radically. When you consider an issue, ask yourself the following questions:

- What other perspectives (apart from my own) could there be on this issue? (These perspectives may reflect the present or other historical periods.)

- Who shares these perspectives?

- How have circumstances, culture, or time period influenced those involved?

Apply Your Skills

1. Choose two quotations you have read so far in this chapter. For each of the quotations, identify specific examples of the speaker's perspectives on land, self-determination, or the needs of future generations.

2. Are the perspectives of the speakers (from Question 1) the same or different? What social, cultural, emotional, and intellectual factors helped create the perspectives demonstrated in the quotations you chose?

Inuit Agreements

Because of their remote location, the pressures of population and settlement did not affect Inuit as much as they did the First Nations and Métis. As a result, Inuit continued to live a lifestyle of hunting, trapping, and fishing on their traditional territories well into the 20th century, and there were no treaties in place between them and the government.

Toward Self-Determination

When change did come, it came rapidly. Within one or two generations, most Inuit were living in communities set up by the federal government. Health care, education, and social services could be delivered more efficiently in these settlements, but it was a difficult change. Inuit were soon seeking control of their lives and welfare through agreements involving self-government. The pressures of resource development in the North soon brought a sense of urgency to the process.

In the 1970s, Inuit began to lobby for recognition of their right to self-government with the formation of groups such as the Inuit Tapirisat of Canada (later, the Inuit Tapiriit Kanatami, or ITK) and the Committee for Original Peoples' Entitlement.

Nunavik

The James Bay and Northern Québec Agreement was the first treaty involving Inuit. While the agreement recognized that the Inuit of Nunavik, in northern Québec, had a right to hunt, fish, and trap across a broad area, it did not include any provision for self-government. Negotiations to establish self-government in Nunavik were reopened in 1994, and an Agreement-in-Principle was signed in 2007.

Inuvialuit

Originally, Inuit of the western Arctic, or Inuvialuit, planned to pursue a self-government claim along with Inuit of the eastern Arctic. However, threats to their territory from oil and gas development in the Beaufort Sea during the 1970s prompted Inuit of the western Arctic to withdraw from that process and pursue their own claim. The Inuvialuit Final Agreement was the first comprehensive land rights agreement in the Northwest Territories, covering more than 200 000 square kilometres around the Mackenzie Delta. A little less than half of that area is owned by Inuit; they have hunting and fishing rights on the rest. In addition, they own the subsurface mineral rights on about 13 000 square kilometres and have received transfer payments of $152 million from the federal government over 14 years.

VOICES OF THE PEOPLES

For our elders, it was also difficult to understand the need to "claim" our own homeland. Land "ownership" was a new concept for our people.

—*John Amagoalik, Inuk*

Web Connect • • • • • • • • • • • •

To read more about Inuit agreements, visit our website.

Nunavut

Negotiations with the Inuit Tapirisat of Canada (ITC) over Inuit land in the eastern Arctic followed a different route. Instead of negotiating an exclusive area for Inuit, the ITC chose to pursue a public form of government that would represent all the inhabitants of the eastern Arctic—including the 15 percent of the population that is not Inuit. This negotiation represented an entirely new approach—one that led, in April 1999, to the creation of Nunavut. The 1.9 million square kilometres that make up Nunavut represents one fifth of Canada. It is the largest Aboriginal land rights settlement in Canada.

Nunatsiavut

The last Inuit group to settle with the Canadian government was the Inuit of Labrador. Negotiations with the federal and provincial governments began in 1977, but did not conclude until 2004, with the passing of the Labrador Inuit Land Claims Agreement Act. Inuit self-government in the region took effect in December 2005, giving Inuit in the region greater control over education, justice, health care, and economic and environmental initiatives. Nunatsiavut consists of 72 520 square kilometres of land and another 48 690 square kilometres of sea. Inuit own 15 800 square kilometres of this area. They will also receive 25 percent of provincial royalties from any future mining, oil and gas, or quarry developments on Inuit land, and 5 percent from development on co-managed land.

Ongoing negotiations over self-government in Nunavik are expected to be ratified in 2011. With the resolution of this land claim, all Inuit in Canada will be covered by modern treaties or agreements.

FIGURE 7.15 The Nunatsiavut Land Claims Agreement also covers offshore rights. These rights give Inuit co-management powers over fishing licences and stock quotas.

THINKING IT THROUGH

1. Why did Inuit open negotiations for land and self-government agreements?

2. What circumstances might have given Inuit both advantages and disadvantages in treaty negotiations compared to the First Nations of the Numbered Treaties?

3. Do you think Inuit agreements might have an effect on future negotiations for land and self-government rights in southern Canada? Explain.

Métis Agreements

1850	Robinson Treaties include some Métis
1870	Manitoba Act
1932	Métis Association of Alberta formed
1938	Métis Population Betterment Act, Alberta
1990	Métis Settlements Act, Alberta
2004	Métis Nation of Ontario negotiates harvesting rights with province of Ontario
2004	Interim Métis Harvesting Agreement signed in Alberta
2005	Canada–Métis Framework Agreement
2007	Interim Métis Harvesting Agreement cancelled by Alberta government
2008	Métis of Ontario sign Framework Agreement with province of Ontario

During the treaty negotiations between First Nations and the Crown in the 19th and early 20th centuries, the Métis occupied a unique position between the two sides. At that time, there was no recognition of the Métis as a separate Nation with Aboriginal rights. Métis served as translators, ambassadors, and witnesses during negotiations, but rarely attained any rights of their own unless they chose to be identified with a First Nation.

However, the Métis were not excluded from all agreements. In the Robinson Treaties, individual Métis were given land rights. Another example was the "Half-Breed Adhesion to Treaty 3" in 1875. Under the terms of the Adhesion to Treaty 3, two reserves were set aside for the Métis community near Fort Frances in northwestern Ontario. In addition, the treaty granted yearly payments. However, the Department of Indian Affairs did not ratify the agreement, and the Métis had to fight for their payments. Eventually, the community became part of the Little Eagle Band, now the Couchiching First Nation.

The Manitoba Act and Scrip

Following the Red River Resistance, discussions between Manitoba Métis and the government resulted in the Manitoba Act of 1870. The Act marked the founding of the province and, under Section 31, set out clear rights for the Métis people. It recognized land that was already farmed by the Métis as their own, and set aside 567 000 hectares of land for their children.

However, rather than providing direct transfer of land title or inclusion in a formal treaty, the government introduced a new system that required Métis to register their claim and—if they qualified—receive scrip. Scrip was a certificate that entitled Métis individuals to claim either land or payment. It was a one-time grant that many Métis did not pursue for various reasons. For instance, it took a long time for scrip to be issued. Frustrated by the slow process, large numbers of Métis left Manitoba for the western provinces. Some Métis abandoned their claims altogether while others chose to sell their scrip to land speculators, often receiving far less than its actual value.

In spite of the difficulties and inequities associated with the scrip system, the government continued to issue the certificates to Métis in the Northwest Territories and Saskatchewan until 1923.

The Alberta Métis

In 1932, Métis living in Alberta organized to form the Métis Association of Alberta, later called the Métis Nation of Alberta (MNA). Six years later, in 1938, the Ewing Commission, a collaborative effort between the Métis and the federal government, passed the Métis Population Betterment Act. This

Act set aside 12 sections of land for Métis settlements, although by 1960, four of these settlements had rescinded their rights. In 1990, the Métis Settlements Act provided for land title and self-governance over the eight remaining settlements.

In 2004, the Alberta government signed an Interim Métis Harvesting Agreement with the Métis Nation of Alberta, allowing Métis harvesters to hunt, fish, and trap for food in Alberta under the province's conservation and safety rules. In 2007, this agreement was cancelled by a new provincial government. Alberta Métis rejected this cancellation, and conducted several community hunts for food in October 2010. Two hunters were arrested.

Negotiations with the Federal Government

Métis across Canada recognized the need to negotiate with the federal government as a unified Nation. The Métis National Council, formed in 1983, represents the interests of Métis nationwide, while provincial groups in Alberta, British Columbia, Saskatchewan, Manitoba, and Ontario oversee Métis concerns in those areas. The signing of the Canada–Métis Framework Agreement in 2005 marked a significant turning point in the acceptance of Métis as a separate Aboriginal Nation.

Ontario Métis Today

The Métis Nation of Ontario (MNO), with representative councils across the province, has developed a strong presence and voice. In 2004, the MNO negotiated harvesting rights in the province and, in 2008, created its own Framework Agreement for negotiations with the Ontario government.

As testament to the strides that Métis people have made in establishing their identity within Ontario, the Ontario legislature marked 2010 as the Year of the Métis, in recognition of the Nation's contribution to the province in the past and in the future.

VOICES OF THE PEOPLES

What did the Government do? It laid hands on the land of the Métis as if it were its own. By this one act it showed its plan to defraud them of their future.

—*Louis Riel, Métis leader*

Web Connect • • • • • • • • • • • •

To learn more about the Métis Nation of Ontario, visit our website.

THINKING IT THROUGH

1. Providing examples, explain some of the problems and limitations of the scrip system.

2. How have Métis organizations such as the Métis National Council and the Métis Nation of Ontario contributed to progress in asserting their members' rights?

Future Directions

Aboriginal peoples in Canada have made great strides regarding land rights and self-determination rights, but there is still much work to be done. Although the recognition of Aboriginal rights by the Crown is very important, the time and work involved in achieving those acknowledgements are significant. Still, this work protects the interests of future generations.

Resource Sharing

First Nations, Métis, and Inuit communities and peoples continue to assert their rights to consultation and fair resource sharing. This action honours treaty agreements, and works within amendments to previous legislation and court decisions recognizing land rights and the right to self-determination. For First Nations, Métis, and Inuit peoples, these partnerships and consultations will assist in protecting future generations.

In Ontario, the Mining Amendment Act of 2009 requires consultation with First Nations before and during any mining activities, and recognizes existing Aboriginal land and treaty rights. However, the Far North Act of 2010 seems to step away from consultation with Aboriginal peoples in the province of Ontario.

The Far North Act

In 2009, the Ontario Ministry of Resources proposed the Far North Act. The Act set out plans for over 450 000 square kilometres of public land in Northern Ontario that would recognize environmental, social, and economic interests, create conservation lands, allow for sustainable economic development, and bring First Nations into land-use planning.

The position of the provincial government is to establish legislation for an area that represents about 42 percent of Ontario's land mass. First Nations peoples represent over 90 percent of this area's population. The provincial government has stated that the Far North Act would apply only to public lands, but not to First Nations reserves.

VOICES OF THE PEOPLES

As we have stated time and again, NAN First Nations and Tribal Councils will continue to oppose this legislation on our homelands. We will continue to uphold our Aboriginal and Treaty rights and jurisdiction over our land.

—*Deputy Grand Chief Mike Metatawabin, Nishnawbe Aski Nation, speaking about the Far North Act*

> *Ontario is undertaking an ambitious approach to protection that will both conserve the vast Far North Boreal forest, wetlands, tundra and peatlands and contribute to an environmentally sustainable economic future and greater prosperity for the area's First Nations people.*
>
> *The Far North is valuable to all people of Ontario. Protecting the Far North preserves greenspace, helps mitigate climate change and safeguards our natural biodiversity.*
>
> —*Statement from the Ontario Ministry of Natural Resources*

On September 23, 2010, the Far North Act was passed in the provincial legislature. However, some First Nations communities will not recognize the Act. Nishnawbe Aski Nation (NAN) represents 49 First Nations communities in Northern Ontario. They believe the legislation infringes upon their lands and treaty rights, and that it is an attempt to legislate traditional lands without first dealing with land claims. First Nations communities also protest that the legislation was passed without any consultation with First Nations or municipal leaders in the surrounding areas.

Youth Taking Action

Aboriginal youth are also working on treaty issues and land rights across the country. Youth groups and other organizations are making their voices heard, and youth participate in conferences and other public forums to educate others on Aboriginal issues. Some youth have spoken to political leaders, and some have taken on leadership roles in their communities; others have taken part in protest marches or spoken out through social media on the Internet. Others use creative projects, such as online magazines, music, or art, to spread their message. It is not surprising that many Aboriginal youth are at the forefront of taking action on behalf of their communities and honouring their ancestors in the process.

REFLECTION

Express your position on the Far North Act by drafting a letter to your MPP that either supports the provincial government or supports NAN.

FIGURE 7.16 Ravena Williams, of the Aamjiwnaang First Nation, takes part in a protest in 2009 to protect her treaty rights.

VOICES OF THE PEOPLES

In September 2010, Robert Animikii Horton wrote an article about his vision for recognition of treaties in Canada. Below is an excerpt from his article.

I have a dream that one day on the banks of the traditional territories along Northwest Angle and within the neighbourhoods of Gatineau with the shining view of Ottawa, our coming generations of First Nation people and those of European descent will scarcely recall the time when sacred agreements of partnership and brotherhood faltered before the true meaning of such obligations of the Promise and the Price were once again realized, accepted, and lived out by example.

FIGURE 7.17 Robert Animikii Horton is an activist from the Rainy River First Nation. In 2008, Robert Horton was named a National Aboriginal Role Model.

CRITICAL THINKING

Using what you have learned in this chapter and other parts of this textbook, discuss the link between land rights, treaty rights, and self-determination for Aboriginal peoples.

THINKING IT THROUGH

1. Why is Ontario's Far North Act not recognized by the Nishnawbe Aski Nation?

2. Review two recent news articles about a current land-rights proceeding in Canada—one from an Aboriginal source, and the other from a mainstream media source. Establish the points of view being presented. Can you identify any bias in the articles? Using examples, explain where and how bias appears. Then write a reflection on the differing views provided.

3. Find an example of how Aboriginal youth are learning leadership skills and using their voices on the Internet to promote the interests of their Nations and communities. Why do they think it is important for their voices to be heard?

Conclusion

For First Nations, Métis, and Inuit peoples, treaties are regarded as genuine and sacred promises between peoples and governments. Aboriginal peoples have a long-standing tradition of negotiating agreements, and therefore bargained in good faith, expecting in return that promises made to them would be respected. When negotiating treaties with the colonial and Canadian governments, the First Nations believed they were sharing their land for the protection and support of their people. The agreements were signed not for themselves, but for the children of future generations.

There are many complex and difficult challenges that First Nations, Métis, and Inuit peoples face regarding treaties and land rights. Long struggles to regain lost lands, as in the Ipperwash case; lack of recognition; and a need for increased knowledge of the issues still remain. Yet significant gains have been made. Respect for human rights and acknowledgement of multiple perspectives, including historical ones, are steadily growing.

End-of-Chapter Activities

1. Examine this image and read the caption. In a paragraph, discuss the message you think the cartoonist is trying to give his audience, using examples from the image and text to support your statements. Why do you think the cartoonist created this image? Whom do you think he is addressing?

"... and the Great White Mother shall honor this treaty for as long as the river runs, the mountain stands, and the buffalo roams ... or as under subsection Q (para. 2) until a duly elected politician chooses to ram through patriation of the BNA Act, see section H, subsection 16 (paras. 6 through 81)."

FIGURE 7.18 This Canadian political cartoon was published in 1980. The caption reads: "...and the Great White Mother shall honor this treaty for as long as the river runs, the mountain stands, and the buffalo roams...or as under subsection Q (para. 2) until a duly elected politician chooses to ram through patriation of the BNA Act, see section H, subsection 16 (paras. 6 through 81)."

2. What are Aboriginal beliefs and values regarding "ownership" of the land? How do these beliefs work within treaties in place in Canada today? How do you think they will affect future land negotiations? Be prepared to present your findings and opinions orally.

3. Research an ongoing treaty or land-rights case in Canada. In your written analysis, include the following:

   a) the historic basis of the case
   b) the specific issues of the case
   c) the position of the federal and/or provincial government
   d) a way in which you think the case could be settled fairly

4. Read an article or view a documentary on the Vancouver 2010 Olympic and Paralympic Winter Games. In a few paragraphs, identify the historical perspectives to explain why there was controversy surrounding the games among First Nations people.

5. In a small group, discuss the challenges that First Nations, Métis, and Inuit peoples face concerning land rights and self-government. Provide examples to support your group's answers.

6. Reread the quotation from Justice Sidney Linden on page 222. Has your understanding of Justice Linden's words changed after completing this chapter? Explain in a few sentences.

CHAPTER 8

Justice

> The imposition of foreign laws as supreme is totally unjust. The notion that English Common Law and French Civil Law supersede First Nations Law was and is based on racist and colonial attitudes. To imagine inviting a person into your home and having that person dictate to you that your authority and your laws are of no value and that theirs are supreme is totally racist and borders on insanity.
>
> —*Carl Roberts, former Chief of the Roseau River First Nation*

This chapter explores questions related to justice—what justice is, what injustices are and why they have taken place, how to address them, and how to pursue justice. You will learn about First Nations, Métis, and Inuit peoples' practices of justice and the challenges that Aboriginal peoples face in the justice system of Canada. Finally, you will look at the pursuit of justice and new initiatives in justice. Throughout the chapter, you will also build the skills of giving support, crediting sources, and quoting effectively.

FIGURE 8.1 Adam Beach is an award-winning actor from Dog Creek First Nation and Winnipeg. He has spoken out about the challenges he faced as a youth. His anti-gang public service announcement recalls how he redirected himself toward acting.

INQUIRING MINDS

Use these questions to explore the big ideas in this chapter.

1. What are the past and current values and beliefs of Aboriginal peoples regarding justice and conflict resolution?

2. What injustices of the past have affected Aboriginal and Canadian relationships, and how have they been (or can they be) addressed?

3. How are Aboriginal peoples revitalizing their communities with traditional justice beliefs, values, and practices and new initiatives?

FIGURE 8.2 When you think of *justice*, what images come to mind? On television and in newspapers, most images related to justice show courtrooms, jail cells, police officers, and arrests. In contrast, the image above shows a healing circle held in April 2008 after the death of three children. What questions do you have about justice?

What Is Justice?

Before you begin to learn about justice and injustice, you need to consider your understandings of these words. What associations, experiences, and knowledge do you have related to these words? How would you define *justice* and *injustice*, and why? How do your understandings and beliefs compare with those of others?

Defining Justice

The age-old questions of what is right, what is wrong, and what is fair are at the very heart of the question "What is justice?" Maybe you associate *justice* and *laws* with questions about the legal age for driving, or about custody or rental agreements, or maybe even about police, lawyers, and courts. *Justice* encompasses all of these aspects and more. On the next pages, some brief accounts of people, places, and events will help you think about what *justice* means.

FIGURE 8.3 This diagram shows some notes from thinking about *justice*. What do you have questions about? What do you agree and disagree with? What changes would you make to this diagram?

©P

G'psgolox Mortuary Pole

Mis'kusa is a Haisla village in the Kitlope Valley of British Columbia. After a smallpox epidemic decimated the village population, Chief G'psgolox grieved for his children and all the members of his Nation. The nine-metre mortuary pole he commissioned in 1872 tells the sacred story of the community's rebirth.

FIGURE 8.4 The G'psgolox pole was returned to the Haisla Nation on June 21, 2006 —National Aboriginal Day.

In 1929, an Indian agent cut down the pole and, under questionable circumstances, sold it to the Swedish National Museum of Ethnography in Stockholm. When the Haisla people returned home from a fishing trip, they found that their pole had been cut at the base and taken. The pole's location remained a mystery to the Haisla people for 60 years, but the pole and Chief G'psgolox lived on in the Nation's stories.

When the pole was finally located, the Haisla people began negotiations with the Swedish government. Swedish officials believed that their government had bought the pole and therefore owned it. However, the Swedish government eventually agreed to **repatriate** the pole on two conditions:

- the community house the pole in a building that would preserve it

- the Haisla carve a replica of the pole for the Swedish museum

The Haisla carved a replica pole for the Museum of Ethnography, but finding a place with museum-like conditions to house the original proved problematic. First, the community did not have a suitable building nor the money available to build one. Second, the idea of preserving the pole itself conflicts with the belief that the pole is animate, like any other organism that experiences the life cycle, and is meant to stay outside so that it returns to Mother Earth. Eventually, it was agreed that the pole could return to British Columbia to a temporary home until a cultural centre could be built. In the meantime, the Haisla raised a second replica of the pole at the original site.

Chester Cunningham

In the 1960s, Chester Cunningham started working at a Native friendship centre and spent part of the time with clients who were dealing with the Canadian justice system. He was shocked to learn that Aboriginal people would often plead guilty to charges they did not understand or of which they were innocent. Some were convicted without ever having appeared before a judge. After consulting with several judges, Chester Cunningham created the Native Courtworker Services, which became Native Counselling Services of Alberta. Its services have grown to include support, education, and halfway houses.

WORDS MATTER

repatriate to return a person, cultural object, or piece of art back to its home, place of origin, or rightful owner

Web Connect • • • • • • • • • • •

To learn more about the repatriation of the G'psgolox pole, visit our website.

FIGURE 8.5 Chester Cunningham grew up in a Métis family in Slave Lake, Alberta. To fund the court service at first, he mortgaged his home. Chester Cunningham has been honoured in many ways, including with an honorary degree in law and the Order of Canada.

Stella Bignell: Neil Stonechild's Mother

Later in this chapter, you will read about how Cree teenager Neil Stonechild was found frozen to death in a field in Saskatoon in 1990. Neil's friend had last seen him, bloodied and handcuffed, in the back seat of a police cruiser. Neil's mother, Stella Bignell, relentlessly sought justice for her son. Don Worme, a lawyer from Kawacatoose First Nation who represented her at the inquiry into Neil's death, recalls:

> I take a lot of comfort in knowing that there are mothers out there who love their children and who will do anything for them in order to achieve the kind of justice that she achieved for her son.

FIGURE 8.6 It took until 2004 for a full inquiry into Neil Stonechild's death to be held and the findings to be released. At the 2004 release, Stella Bignell wipes away tears while speaking about her son.

The Residential School System: Seeking Justice

On June 11, 2008, Prime Minister Stephen Harper delivered a formal apology on behalf of the government of Canada for the residential school system. The apology said, in part, the following:

> To the approximately 80 000 living former students, and all family members and communities, the Government of Canada now recognizes that it was wrong to forcibly remove children from their homes and we apologize for having done this. We now recognize that it was wrong to separate children from rich and vibrant cultures and traditions[,] that it created a void in many lives and communities, and we apologize for having done this. We now recognize that, in separating children from their families, we undermined the ability of many to adequately parent their own children and sowed the seeds for generations to follow, and we apologize for having done this. We now recognize that, far too often, these institutions gave rise to abuse or neglect and were inadequately controlled, and we apologize for failing to protect you. Not only did you suffer these abuses as children, but as you became parents, you were powerless to protect your own children from suffering the same experience, and for this we are sorry.

Frank Brown and the Bella Bella Rediscovery

Frank Brown of the Heiltsuk First Nation in British Columbia appeared in court to face charges of robbery that included a serious beating. It was 1979 and Frank was 14. His family suggested to the court that Frank face traditional restorative justice rather than go to juvenile detention. In this historic case, it was decided that Frank Brown would be banished to a remote island off the coast of central B.C. and live there for eight months. Frank Brown credits the experience with helping him turn his life around. He has since developed the Bella Bella Rediscovery program and participated in a documentary about his experience—*Voyage of Rediscovery*.

VOICES OF THE PEOPLES

With the support of the Assembly of First Nations and Inuit organizations, former residential school students took the federal government and the churches to court. Their cases led to the Indian Residential Schools Settlement Agreement, the largest class-action settlement in Canadian history. The agreement sought to begin repairing the harm caused by residential schools. Aside from providing compensation to former students, the agreement called for the establishment of the Truth and Reconciliation Commission of Canada [which] has a mandate to learn the truth about what happened in the residential schools and to inform all Canadians about what happened in the schools.

—*from the Truth and Reconciliation Commission of Canada website*

©P

Peace, Harmony, and Justice

From the preceding examples, you can see that *justice* has many aspects and it relates to many subjects raised in other chapters of this textbook. For example, not only criminal court cases but also legal and policing systems, actions on Aboriginal lands, and international disputes raise questions about what is right, fair, and just. As the report of the Royal Commission on Aboriginal Peoples concluded in 1996:

> *Canada is a test case for a grand notion—the notion that dissimilar peoples can share lands, resources, power and dreams while respecting and sustaining their differences. The story of Canada is the story of many such peoples, trying and failing and trying again, to live together in peace and harmony.*
>
> ***But there cannot be peace or harmony unless there is justice.*** *It was to help restore justice to the relationship between Aboriginal and non-Aboriginal people in Canada, and to propose practical solutions to stubborn problems, that the Royal Commission on Aboriginal Peoples was established…*
>
> *We held 178 days of public hearings, visited 96 communities, consulted dozens of experts, commissioned scores of research studies, reviewed numerous past inquiries and reports. Our central conclusion can be summarized simply: The main policy direction, pursued for more than 150 years, first by colonial then by Canadian governments, has been wrong.*
>
> *Successive governments have tried—sometimes intentionally, sometimes in ignorance—to absorb Aboriginal people into Canadian society, thus eliminating them as distinct peoples. Policies pursued over the decades have undermined—and almost erased—Aboriginal cultures and identities.*
>
> *This is assimilation. It is a denial of the principles of peace, harmony and justice for which this country stands—and it has failed.*

This chapter will focus primarily on justice, injustices, and the pursuit of justice in the legal system, especially the court system. However, you will find many connections to subjects explored in other chapters, including land rights, self-determination, governance, and education.

VOICES OF THE PEOPLES

After the June 2008 apology from the federal government for the residential school system, Phil Fontaine, National Chief of the Assembly of First Nations at the time and a residential school survivor, said:

The common road of hope will bring us to reconciliation more than any words, laws, or legal claims ever could. We still have to struggle, but now we are in this together. I reach out to all Canadians today in this spirit of reconciliation.

THINKING IT THROUGH

1. Based on your thoughts and discussions related to pages 250 to 253, write a short definition of the word *justice* and write any questions that the word raises for you.

2. The example of the G'psgolox pole is not unique and raises many issues. Research the subject of Aboriginal cultural artifacts or remains in museums in order to summarize some legal, ethical, and cultural issues.

3. Identify the purposes of the Truth and Reconciliation Commission. What is a possible definition of *reconciliation*?

©P

Community Values and Law

Aboriginal Perspectives on Justice

The concept of community is highly valued by First Nations, Métis, and Inuit peoples. This emphasis on the value of community informs Aboriginal perspectives on laws and justice. While the methods of establishing justice are as diverse as the Nations themselves, there are some shared views. As you read about Aboriginal perspectives on justice and specific examples, you will see both common threads and differences.

Before the arrival of Europeans in North America, Inuit and First Nations peoples were self-governing societies. Each culture had its own justice system, consisting of practices based on the society's values.

One key understanding was that, if someone committed a wrong, that person had committed a wrong against the community. The community, therefore, needed to be healed and restored.

Another understanding was that the whole truth cannot be known—there is no one absolute truth. Anishinaabe writer Basil Johnston says:

FIGURE 8.7 Ovide Mercredi, from Grand Rapids in Manitoba, was National Chief of the Assembly of First Nations (AFN) from 1991 to 1997. In this 2000 photograph, Ovide Mercredi speaks in Ottawa about a lobster-fishing dispute in Burnt Church, New Brunswick.

The highest compliment or tribute they could pay a speaker was to say of him or her "w'daeb-wae," taken to mean "he/she is right, correct, accurate, truthful." It is an expression approximating the word for "truth" in the English language, except that it means one casts one's knowledge as far as one has perceived it and as accurately as one can describe it, given one's command of language. Beyond this one cannot go. According to this understanding, there can be no such thing as absolute truth.

Web Connect

To learn about the dispute in Burnt Church, visit our website.

Judge Murray Sinclair, the first Aboriginal judge in Manitoba, notes that the legal concept of innocence and guilt is not granted the same importance by Aboriginal cultures as it is in the Canadian criminal justice system. In Aboriginal communities, guilt is usually secondary to the primary concern: "something is wrong and it has to be fixed." Because the main objective is the restoration of harmony rather than the imposition of punishment, the accused is more likely to admit wrongdoing. Judge Sinclair suggests that perhaps this explains why so many Aboriginal people plead guilty when in court.

©P

Aboriginal Values of Right and Wrong

Certain values are shared in Aboriginal communities that create the sense of right and wrong. These values are as follows:

- desire for community harmony
- a focus on preserving relationships
- respect for life in all forms
- teaching through example
- sharing and generosity for all
- respect for freedom
- avoidance of confrontation and adversarial positions

Things that are considered wrong would, for example, disrupt harmony, present a poor example, and/or negatively affect relationships. Conflict, in moderation, is seen as part of life; however, not taking responsibility for one's actions, words, and behaviours can escalate conflict. When someone has committed a wrong, that person has a personal responsibility for his or her behaviour, but there is also shared collective responsibility for restoring balance and harmony to the community.

REFLECTION

How do the values of a culture help create a system of laws? Why might implementing laws be difficult when there are many differing values?

VOICES OF THE PEOPLES

Nunavut has many accounts of justice. Here are two excerpts from Uqalurait: An Oral History of Nunavut, *compiled by John Bennett and Susan Rowley:*

They would all talk about what was wrong and what was expected. Everyone had a chance to express his or her side of the story [aniaslutik]. Once this was over, they were able to restore harmony and strengthen their mutual bonds and family kinship ties. Everyone felt better afterwards.

—**Hubert Amarualik, Amitturmiut**

Peace, order, and stability were essential. To survive, people needed to share and cooperate, and this meant getting along well with each other. Elders discouraged behaviour that caused uncertainty—gossiping, lying, stealing, laziness, and unpredictable behaviour. When such an offence did occur, they tried to make sure that it was not repeated.

One person in the community had this function to perform. He would gather the people together,

FIGURE 8.8 Community feasts are a large part of many celebrations. Inuit feasts can be opportunities to deal with community trouble-makers.

say for a feast, and this would be the time to deal with the problem-makers as well. He would begin to say their wrongdoings to their faces in public. It was an embarrassing affair with sometimes the person being brought to tears as others would join in the criticizing. This was considered better than hiding behind people's backs and it brought everyone together to deal with the problem.

—**James Muckpah, Tununuirmuiut**

Traditional Laws

What do the understandings of right and wrong mean for laws and how they are enforced? All traditional Aboriginal laws value balance and harmony, and sharing and generosity to maintain good relationships.

For the Anishinaabe, aggressive behaviour was not permitted, and when it was necessary, it was closely monitored and minimized so that misfortune would not come upon the entire community. Among western Cree Nations hunting for bison, the rules of the hunt included maintaining order (primarily not rushing ahead and frightening the herd) and sharing.

VOICES OF THE PEOPLES

What a people value, their laws, and how they educate their children to uphold values are all related. These excerpts from the book The Four Hills of Life *look at the second "hill" in Anishinaabe (Ojibwe) communities—youth.*

On many evenings, young people would receive advice from the village announcer... Always a respected elder, the announcer would walk through the community, letting people know the next day's activities and important news. He would tell young people to obey and respect their parents and to heed their advice. Sometimes he would describe examples of improper behavior among certain young people without mentioning their names...

[Adults] modeled accepted behaviors... Kindness was stressed above all else.

Behaviors like fighting, stealing, lying, and bragging were uncommon in Ojibwe communities of the past. Adults, observing such behavior would "snap their eyes" at the young person or pretend he or she was invisible to them, often causing the child to stop the behavior immediately and weep bitterly...

All adults in the village were concerned about the responsible behavior of every child. In all of

FIGURE 8.9 This photograph from 1909 shows an Anishinaabe woman and children in Fort Churchill, Manitoba.

daily life, in storytelling and songs and in spiritual ceremonies, the values of minobimaadiziwin (the Good Path) were stressed: honor the Creator, honor elders, honor women, honor the elder brothers (plants and animals), be peaceful, keep promises, be kind, be courageous, and be moderate.

©P

Resolving Conflicts, Addressing Harm

When conflicts take place or wrongs are committed, Nations have various ways of dealing with them. Some of these methods include mediation and compensation. Primarily for First Nations and Inuit communities, disputes are resolved through mediation: the wrongdoer is confronted directly and brought to understand how his or her actions have negatively affected others. The focus is on healing the community instead of punishing the person. In some Nations, Elders and Wisdom Keepers have been responsible for mediation.

VOICES OF THE PEOPLES

The Métis Nation became a dominant force on the plains during the late 1700s and way into the 1800s. They were a highly organized body of people. They enacted laws, rules, and regulations around the buffalo hunt which later became the "Laws of the Prairie" and the beginning of law enforcement in the area and subsequently adopted by the North West Mounted Police. These buffalo hunting expeditions were carefully organized and became the foundation of Métis government.

The hunt involved organizing hundreds of men, women, children, Red River carts, and horses for the westward journeys extending hundreds of kilometres to where the buffalo grazed. A leader of the hunt was selected, scouts were chosen, and rules were arranged before the expedition ever set forth. On the return trip, tons of processed buffalo meat and hides had to be transported.

The buffalo hunts provided the Métis with an impressive organizational structure and by 1820 the hunts were a permanent feature of life for all individuals on or near the Red River and other Métis communities. There were usually two organized hunts each year: one in the spring and one in the autumn. The buffalo hunts of this time were carried out through almost militaristic precision and the combined force of a Métis hunt was larger than any other force of its time.

After the first day of travel through the dust raised by 1240 carts and 1630 Métis, camp was made and the first organizational meeting for the hunt would be held and a President was selected. A number of

FIGURE 8.10 Making and trading pemmican was an important economic activity for Métis. This photograph, taken around 1925 in English River, Ontario, shows drying moose meat. Moose meat can be used to make pemmican.

captains were nominated by the President and the people jointly. The captains then proceeded to appoint their own policemen, the number assigned to each not exceeding ten. Their duty was to see that the Laws of the Hunt were strictly carried out. Guides were responsible for the camp flag that remained raised until it was time to settle for the night. At the end of the day the captains took charge. At night the carts were placed in the form of a circle with the horses and cattle inside the ring. It was the duty of the captains and their policemen to see that this was rightly done.

—*Jason Madden, Métis Nation of Ontario*

©P

FIGURE 8.11 The painting *The Healing Circle* (2005) is by Métis artist Dennis Weber. How does the painting indicate that the circle has healing power? How does the image of the circle relate to the community?

REFLECTION

How might banishment be used today? What factors would need to be considered for it to be effective?

Conflict Resolution and Mediation

Historically, some Nations had a very structured approach to conflict resolution. The Dene Nation had a three-tiered system. For a conflict between two individuals, the first attempt was for the individuals to resolve it themselves. If unsuccessful, the individuals would approach an Elder or Wisdom Keeper to mediate. If that also failed, then the community would become involved and state its disapproval, which was often enough pressure to get the offender to make amends. In Métis communities, the role of mediator was initially a responsibility of the women; the goal was to regain harmony, balance, and understanding within the community.

Compensation

Compensating the community or individual has been a way to give back to the community, restore relationships, or replace what was lost or taken away. One traditional system of compensation is called xsiisxw (compensation/cleansing). This Gitxsan system involves giving in compensation wealth, territory (temporarily or forever), names, or crests.

Social Pressure or Banishment

Social pressure is another way to bring about justice in communities. With adults who had committed a wrong, one way to apply pressure was to involve the victim and the family of the offender. If that approach was unsuccessful, the community would collectively show its disapproval through shunning, avoiding, and teasing until amends were made.

The most extreme form of justice was to banish the offender from the community for a period of time. However, exile or banishment would be a last resort, because every member was considered vital to the community. According to James Youngblood Henderson, director of the Saskatoon-based Native Law Centre of Canada, banishment relates to the importance of community and the concept of consent: a person who behaves in a way that is destructive or disruptive is not consenting to be part of the community and its values. So that person must leave until he or she is ready and willing to respect those values.

Restorative Justice and Community Healing

The main goal for the justice traditions of many Aboriginal communities is not to focus on the particular act of wrongdoing, but to restore social harmony. Approaches such as restorative justice and healing/sentencing circles today are rooted in these values. This subject is explored again later in this chapter.

People involved in sentencing circles and restorative justice circles include the offender, the person against whom the wrong was committed, others affected by the event, and other community members. Each person within the circle is regarded as an equal. Each has an opportunity to speak about how the wrong affected him or her and how he or she thinks the relationships can be restored and compensated.

In restorative justice, including healing/sentencing circles, the community, with the input of the offender, decides on a way of repairing

©P

Restoring Harmony

Lawyer Don Worme, a member of the Indigenous Bar Association, contrasts the "retributive and punishing" understanding of justice in the mainstream Canadian justice system with the sense of justice in Aboriginal communities. He describes the Aboriginal understanding as follows:

[The] traditional concept of justice is restorative in the sense that traditionally, [in] First Nations communities, you [were] obliged to understand and obey the norms of your society, and if you didn't, then it was the obligation of those around you to remind you and to bring you back into the fold. And where, of course, that couldn't be achieved— and obviously there are those instances where people, for whatever reason, simply cannot or will not observe the social construct—then there were ways and means to deal with those as well. But the idea was to bring people back into the circle of the community, to restore the community, to restore the harmony, and to restore the relationships between those that have been harmed and those that have offended.

the harm that has been caused. By being allowed to give input on the method of restitution, offenders can say whether they are capable of doing what is being asked of them.

Restorative justice focuses on

- rebuilding relationships

- encouraging offenders to understand the consequences of their actions

- helping those who have been wronged to be heard and to heal

- giving others an opportunity to express how the actions had an impact on them

- honouring what the offender is able to do to make amends

THINKING IT THROUGH

1. What are some Aboriginal ways of achieving justice? Do you think these methods would be successful in an Aboriginal community? a non-Aboriginal community? Why or why not?

2. With a small group, discuss how the examples of the G'psgolox mortuary pole (page 251) and Frank Brown (page 252) reflect ideas and practices of Aboriginal justice.

3. How does the following quotation relate to the painting on page 258 and to the ideas and practices of Aboriginal justice described in pages 254 to 259? Dave Chief (Oglala Lakota) says: "The Circle has healing power. In the Circle, we are all equal. When in the Circle, no one is in front of you. No one is behind you. No one is above you. No one is below you. The Sacred Circle is designed to create unity. The Hoop of Life is also a circle. On this hoop there is a place for every species, every race, every tree and every plant. It is this completeness of Life that must be respected in order to bring about health on this planet."

Issues in the Justice System

The Canadian criminal justice system has failed the Aboriginal peoples of Canada—First Nations, Inuit and Métis people—on-reserve and off-reserve, urban and rural—in all territorial and governmental jurisdictions. The principal reason for this crushing failure is the fundamentally different world views of Aboriginal and non-Aboriginal people with respect to such elemental issues as the substantive content of justice and the process of achieving justice.

—*Royal Commission on Aboriginal Peoples*

VOICES OF THE PEOPLES

My dad was the first person from our community to get a university degree. He did this even though the government took away his rights as an Indian for doing so. I knew that it wasn't fair that my father and his entire family should lose their rights as Indians just because he decided to go to university. So about that time, I really began to question and challenge those things that were happening.

—*Jan Beaver, Anishinaabe educator, Alderville First Nation*

WORDS MATTER

justice system the network of roles, processes, and organizations of policing, courts, and correctional services—including, for example, police, lawyers, judges, hearings, courts, and prisons

Web Connect • • • • • • • • • • •

To learn more about key studies and sources regarding the justice system, visit our website.

Historical Wrongs

Imagine if you were forbidden by law from going to a neighbouring community without permission, holding a ceremony or dance of your culture, or getting together with two friends. This first activity was banned under an 1884 amendment to the Indian Act when an uprising was feared. The second was prohibited by a law that infamously banned potlatches. And in 1886, it was forbidden to incite, induce, or stir up "three or more Indians, non-treaty Indians, or half-breeds apparently acting in concert…to breach the peace."

Imagine if you were not allowed to hire a lawyer to make a claim, and if any lawyer you tried to hire would be fined or jailed. And imagine that, if you tried to become a lawyer yourself, you would lose your status. This was the case for status Indians under the Indian Act and the Gradual Enfranchisement Act culminating in the 1920s.

In other ways, First Nations, Métis, and Inuit peoples have seen the law, courts, and policing used against them. Parents who tried to keep their children home from residential schools could be threatened with prison, and then the RCMP could forcibly remove the children. At the same time, police have sometimes failed to intervene: in 1889, a principal at Rupert's Land Industrial School in Selkirk, Manitoba, was accused of physical and sexual abuse of girls. After confessing, the principal was simply reprimanded. Such injustices were part of the residential school experiences that you have learned about in earlier chapters.

The Justice System

While the Gradual Enfranchisement Act and other similar laws are no longer in effect, there are many issues and failures in the **justice system** for First Nations, Métis, and Inuit peoples today.

To think about the justice system and issues with it, first think about the definition of *justice* earlier in this chapter. Justice includes many formal roles and processes involved in how laws are administered in Canada today. Together, the roles and processes of policing, courts, and correctional services form the justice system.

©P

The arrest, trial, and execution of Louis Riel has been hotly debated in Canada since 1885. The controversy is often over legal technicalities and often divides people along political lines. Following his hanging, Louis Riel was called a traitor, martyr, rebel, hero, and even one of the Fathers of Confederation. How can one man and a court decision hold so many contradictions?

At the conclusion of the Battle of Batoche, Riel was arrested on May 12, 1885, in Batoche, Saskatchewan. At the request of Sir John A. Macdonald, Riel was accused of high treason and tried in Regina from July 28 to August 1. The jury, in many ways not "a jury of his peers" but composed of English and Scottish settlers, found Riel guilty. The jury recommended mercy in sentencing, but Riel was sentenced to death by Judge Hugh Richardson. Juror Edwin Brooks later said that although Riel was tried for high treason, he was hanged for the 1870 execution of Thomas Scott (an Irish-born Protestant Anglophone from Ontario who opposed the Métis in the Red River Resistance).

The trial is seen by many as one of the great legal injustices for Aboriginal peoples. Riel provided a voice for the Métis struggle for a place in Canada against a government that did not uphold treaty rights and obligations. The Métis wanted to be included in the decision-making process over the sale of Rupert's Land from the Hudson's Bay Company to the Canadian government. The Métis wanted to keep their farms, pasture lands, and communities intact.

After Riel's conviction, he was denied retrial and appeals to the Privy Council of England. Prime Minister Macdonald upheld the sentence despite overwhelming criticism from the Métis, the Francophone community, and Québec. Riel was executed on November 16, 1885.

—*Chris Paci, Chris McLeod, and Jason Madden, Métis Nation of Ontario*

FIGURE 8.12 This statue in Winnipeg commemorates Louis Riel. In 1992, Parliament passed a resolution identifying Louis Riel as the founder of Manitoba.

Overrepresentation and Discrimination

Several studies have examined the relationship between the contemporary Canadian justice system and First Nations, Métis, and Inuit peoples. These studies include the Royal Commission on Aboriginal Peoples (which released its findings in 1996), the Ipperwash Inquiry (in Ontario, released in 2007), the Commission on First Nations and Métis Peoples and Justice Reform (in Saskatchewan, released in 2004), the Aboriginal Justice Inquiry (in Manitoba, released in 1991), and studies from Statistics Canada. These studies have reached many of the same conclusions: Aboriginal peoples are overrepresented in the Canadian justice system, and this fact is largely the result of **systemic discrimination**.

In Aboriginal Peoples and the Criminal Justice System, *a report written as a submission to the Ipperwash Inquiry (which released its findings in 2007 and which you will read about later in this chapter), Jonathan Rudin reported as follows:*

Overrepresentation

Aboriginal overrepresentation in the criminal justice system is one of the clearest markers of what the Supreme Court of Canada has referred to as "a crisis in the Canadian justice system." Aboriginal overrepresentation is often thought of as a problem in western Canada but, in fact, Ontario ranks third in terms of overrepresentation across the country. Aboriginal youth are overrepresented in Ontario correctional facilities at a much higher rate than Aboriginal adults…

In order to address this problem, it is first necessary to understand what the major causes of the problem are. The three explanations that have been advanced as significant causal factors are: 1) culture clash, 2) socio-economic, and 3) colonialism. While all three explanations have their strengths, [this] paper agrees with the Royal Commission on Aboriginal Peoples and other commissions and reports that it is the experience of colonialism that best explains the persistence of Aboriginal overrepresentation.

Policing

Over- and under-policing, although more difficult to demonstrate statistically, are equally serious [as overrepresentation]. Over-policing refers to the practice of police targeting people of particular ethnic or racial backgrounds or people who live in particular neighbourhoods…

At the same time, Aboriginal people are also under-policed. [They are] overrepresented in the criminal justice system…as victims as well [and] requests for assistance are often ignored or downplayed.

—**"Aboriginal Peoples and the Criminal Justice System," by Jonathan Rudin**

Issues in Policing

Policing and court processes have historically been fuelled by prejudice, discrimination, and lack of knowledge of First Nations, Métis, and Inuit peoples. Studies have found that police frequently use **racial profiling**—in other words, make assumptions about Aboriginal people being more likely to commit crimes and thus warranting greater scrutiny. In cities with significant Aboriginal populations, police tend to patrol Aboriginal neighbourhoods more often than non-Aboriginal neighbourhoods. As well, police arrest Aboriginal people at a higher rate for minor offences, but under-police for serious crimes such as assaults committed against Aboriginal people.

According to Jonathan Rudin's report (quoted above), and findings from Statistics Canada, Aboriginal people in Canada are more likely than non-Aboriginal people to be victims of crime, to be witnesses to crime, and to be put under police surveillance.

An Aboriginal person is more likely to be charged with an offence than a non-Aboriginal person who is suspected of committing the same offence. Also, an Aboriginal person is more likely than a non-Aboriginal person to be arrested for committing petty crimes, and is more likely to be charged with multiple offences.

Web Connect • • • • • • • • •

To learn more about statistics related to justice, visit our website.

©P

As you read in Chapter 5, First Nations, Métis, and Inuit women and girls are more likely than non-Aboriginal women and girls to be subject to violence. As well, Aboriginal people are at three times higher risk than non-Aboriginal people of being victims of assault, sexual assault, robbery, and other violent crimes. And finally, justice for Aboriginal victims of crimes, especially violent crimes, does not receive as much attention as justice for non-Aboriginal victims. One example is the case of Helen Betty Osborne, from Norway House Cree Nation. She was brutally murdered in The Pas, Manitoba, in 1971. Although her killers' identities were known for years, the case was not tried in court until 1987. The case of serial killer Robert Pickton (in which Pickton, a pig farmer, preyed on women from Vancouver's Downtown Eastside, many of them Aboriginal women) and the investigation into women missing on the Highway of Tears (from Prince George to Prince Rupert, B.C.) are other examples.

The Case of J.J. Harper

One case that tragically illustrates the issue of over-policing is the case of J.J. Harper. In the early hours of March 9, 1988, John Joseph (J.J.) Harper, executive director of the Island Lake Tribal Council, was walking along Logan Avenue in Winnipeg when he was stopped by Constable Robert Cross. The officer stopped J.J. Harper about a car theft even though a suspect was already in custody. Harper was nearly twice the age and considerably larger than the suspect, but they were both Aboriginal people. J.J. Harper protested, and a struggle began. J.J. Harper was shot and killed. The police board of inquiry ruled the shooting accidental, but public outcry demanded further investigation. The Aboriginal Justice Inquiry was appointed to examine how Aboriginal peoples in Manitoba were being treated by the justice system and to conduct specific investigations into the death of J.J. Harper and the murder of Helen Betty Osborne.

Web Connect • • • • • • • • • • •

To learn more about cases involving violence against Aboriginal women and girls and the people and organizations addressing the issue, visit our website.

FIGURE 8.13 The Helen Betty Osborne memorial stands at Clearwater Lake, Manitoba. The memorial foundation named for Helen Betty Osborne remembers her aspirations of becoming a teacher by awarding scholarships to Aboriginal students in Manitoba.

FIGURE 8.14 Neil Stonechild

The Case of Neil Stonechild

Other legal cases that have raised policing issues include the deaths of Dudley George (see Ipperwash, below) and Neil Stonechild. When Neil Stonechild (whom you read about earlier) was found dead in Saskatoon after night temperatures fell below −28°C, there were accusations that the Saskatoon police had taken him on what is known as a "starlight tour." This unsanctioned practice involves picking up marginalized individuals in police cruisers and taking them to the outskirts of towns where they are beaten and abandoned on the side of the road.

Jason Roy said that he had last seen his friend Neil Stonechild in the back seat of a police cruiser.

The initial investigation resulted in Saskatoon police determining there was no foul play involved. However, in 2000, the Royal Canadian Mounted Police investigated Neil Stonechild's death again while also investigating the deaths of two other First Nations individuals thought to have been in police custody.

Then in 2003, the provincial government of Saskatchewan began a formal inquiry into his death. The inquiry concluded in 2004 that Neil Stonechild had been picked up by the police shortly before his death on the outskirts of the city. However, because of inadequacies in the initial police investigation, there was not enough information to determine the circumstances surrounding his death.

Two officers connected by the inquiry to Neil Stonechild's death were fired in 2004 and lost an appeal in 2006.

The questions the case raised were not only about the treatment of Neil Stonechild but also about subsequent police investigations.

COMMUNITY CLOSE-UP

Ipperwash and Dudley George

In Chapter 7, you read about the land, burial grounds, and extended struggle of the people of Stoney Point Reserve. A small portion of the reserve land (shown in the map opposite) was sold under pressure in 1928 and later used to create Ipperwash Provincial Park. In 1942, the federal government expropriated land for a military camp.

In May 1993, First Nations people peacefully entered the military camp and occupied the rifle ranges in order to reclaim the land and restart negotiations for its return. Some of the occupiers, such as Clifford George (quoted on page 265), had been born at Stoney Point. Others, such as Clifford's younger cousin Anthony O'Brien ("Dudley") George were born after the Stoney Point homes had been moved or bulldozed to make way for the military

camp. The occupation extended through 1993, 1994, and 1995. On July 29, 1995, the occupiers took control of the military camp, and the military left.

On September 4, when the provincial park closed for the season, First Nations people entered Ipperwash Provincial Park to reclaim the land and burial grounds.

In September 1995, a confrontation occurred at the park between the Ontario Provincial Police and the First Nations people. Dudley George was shot by the police and died. He was 38 years old.

—Summer 2010 newsletter Dibaajimowin

The events that immediately preceded Dudley George's death are described in detail in the Ipperwash Inquiry report, which you will read about again later in this chapter.

©P

Clifford George participated in the occupation of the military camp and Ipperwash Provincial Park (shown in the map below). As well, in July 1993, Clifford George and two other Stoney Pointers set up a toll booth to charge visitors to the Ipperwash beach; they were arrested, jailed for three days, and released on bail. What would lead a man in his 70s to take part in occupations, risk criminal charges and jail, and ultimately risk his life?

Clifford George and two brothers volunteered to serve in the Second World War and were written about in the Goderich newspapers as heroes. When Clifford George returned to Canada, he no longer had a home in Stoney Point, lost his Indian status, and was given a $400 deposit for a house in nearby Forest—not the $2200 that First Nations veterans were getting through Indian Affairs and not the $5500 resettlement payment expected for non-Aboriginal veterans. Clifford George said of his wartime experience that he and his brothers all become proud Canadians and proud soldiers while overseas, but when he returned:

> I came home to nothing. I'll never forget the feeling I had when I first went there [to Stoney Point] and couldn't find my mother's grave. They had removed the headstones and there were bullet holes and trenches dug… That would never happen to white people.

—*quoted in* **One Dead Indian,** *by Peter Edwards*

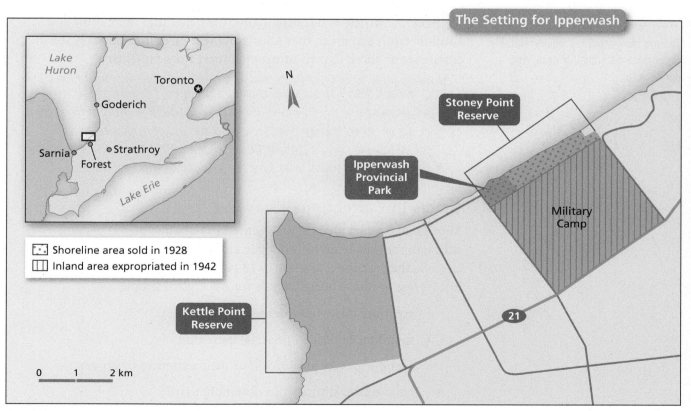

FIGURE 8.15 Ipperwash Beach, Stoney Point, and Kettle Point are all on the Lake Huron shoreline.

FIGURE 8.16 Mi'kmaw teenager Donald Marshall Jr. and his friend Sandy Seale were walking through a park in Sydney, Nova Scotia, and asked two older men for money. One of the men was drunk and had a history of violence with knives. Donald and Sandy were both injured, and Sandy died the next day. Donald was charged with the 1971 murder and found guilty. In 1983, Donald Marshall Jr. was finally acquitted. The resulting Royal Commission determined that the justice system had failed him at all stages and that this failure was due, at least partly, to racism. (The photo above shows him at a 1983 news conference.)

Web Connect • • • • • • • • • • • • • •

To learn more about the inquiry related to the Donald Marshall Jr. case, visit our website.

Issues in the Courts

Preparing for court and in the courtroom, First Nations, Métis, and Inuit people may face discrimination, and they often misunderstand the system. As well, they are under-represented as workers within the system (as police, lawyers, or judges).

One significant issue is language. In the courts, either English or French is spoken. Interpreters provided to defendants and witnesses have limited legal knowledge and are not typically well trained for their task. As for jurors, they must speak English or French; in communities where most members speak their Aboriginal language, this restriction can prevent a fair trial by a jury of one's peers.

Because of language barriers and cultural values (including the belief that it is dishonest to plead "not guilty" if one is guilty), Aboriginal offenders plead guilty more often than non-Aboriginal offenders and thus receive prison sentences more frequently.

And for witnesses and defendants, the belief that there is no one absolute truth can mean that Aboriginal witnesses may be easily led in cross-examination. Crown Attorney Rupert Ross explains:

> *If we ask "Isn't it possible that X happened?" [Aboriginal witnesses] are much more likely than non-Aboriginal witnesses to agree, even if they have just said the exact opposite to the other lawyer. What [might be regarded as] "uncertainty" lessens their credibility and destroys the impact of their evidence.*

Issues in Correctional Services

Aboriginal peoples are overrepresented in Canada's prison system: although they make up only 4.4 percent of the adult population in Canada, they account for close to 18 percent of people in detention. In contrast to non-Aboriginal people, Aboriginal people

- are more likely to be denied bail

- spend more time in pre-trial detention

- spend a greater proportion of their sentences in prison

- have greater difficulty in obtaining parole

- have more difficulty accessing Elders and Wisdom Keepers as spiritual advisors than inmates wanting to access priests, chaplains, and other spiritual advisors

Land and Justice Issues

As noted earlier in this chapter, some issues of justice relate to Aboriginal lands and resources. Some examples from this and previous chapters are the High Arctic relocations, the ongoing struggles of Grassy Narrows First Nation in Ontario, and the sale of Rupert's Land.

While there are many more land and resource disputes outstanding, the example of the forced relocations of Inuit to the High Arctic provides one illustration of injustice, the lengthy pursuit of justice, and some signs of resolution. The following is part of the apology from the federal government, given in 2010.

Web Connect • • • • • • • • • •

To learn more about the High Arctic relocations, visit our website.

> *Over half a century has gone by since the relocation of Inuit from this community to the High Arctic. I am here on behalf of the Prime Minister, the Government of Canada, and all Canadians to offer an apology for these events.*
>
> *Today's ceremony is an important step towards healing and reconciliation. Please accept the apology I am about to offer on behalf of all Canadians. I hope that it will form the basis of a strengthened relationship with the Government of Canada.*
>
> *On behalf of the Government of Canada and all Canadians, we would like to offer a full and sincere apology to Inuit for the relocation of families from Inukjuak and Pond Inlet to Grise Fiord and Resolute Bay during the 1950s.*
>
> *We would like to express our deepest sorrow for the extreme hardship and suffering caused by the relocation. The families were separated from their home communities and extended families by more than a thousand kilometres. They were not provided with adequate shelter and supplies. They were not properly informed of how far away and how different from Inukjuak their new homes would be, and they were not aware that they would be separated into two communities once they arrived in the High Arctic...*

THINKING IT THROUGH

1. What do you think is meant by *systemic discrimination*? Look at pages 260 to 267 to create a list of examples from various aspects of the justice system.

2. For one legal case mentioned in this section (for example, the case related to the death of Neil Stonechild), gather information from the chapter and from additional sources. Then create a summary of the case and begin to develop an opinion about it. For example, how was the Aboriginal person involved treated at each stage in the justice system? How was he or she served by the justice system? Was the outcome fair and just or not?

Giving Support, Crediting Sources, and Quoting

How do people effectively present their opinions and perspectives to get others to understand their views and consider them seriously? How do lawyers make their arguments in a court of law? How do history textbooks or newspapers present an argument? When writing an essay, how do you support your opinion with reasoned arguments?

When you are communicating your ideas, opinions, and perspectives, you have three responsibilities:

- **Provide support.** It is not enough simply to say, for example, "I think that justice was achieved in this case." You need to explain why you think so. You need to provide support for your opinion by using examples, research, case studies, and quotations from a range of credible sources.

- **Acknowledge sources; don't plagiarize.** If you are using someone else's words, ideas, or theory, or information from studies, books, newspapers, or other materials such as a website, you *must* give credit to your sources by citing them in some way (footnote, endnote, bibliography, etc.). Giving credit also means not copying another person's work and passing it off as your own (plagiarizing); this is against the law. Also, citing sources makes your work more credible.

- **Use quotations effectively.** When you are using quotations, it is important
  – to check that the quotation is relevant to your topic and
  – to cite the source
  Also, make sure that you do not take a quotation out of context.

FIGURE 8.17 Lawyer Delia Opekokew (from the Canoe Lake First Nation) attended two residential schools, and York University in Toronto. She was called to the bar in both Ontario and Saskatchewan. Delia Opekokew has been involved in cases concerning treaty rights, land rights, the shooting of Dudley George, and many other pivotal cases.

Apply Your Skills

1. For the legal case you gathered information about (on page 267), review your summary and write down your preliminary opinion.

2. Examine the information you have about the case to see what supports your opinion. Do you have support from a range of sources? What additional information do you need to strengthen your argument?

3. To your classmates, briefly state your opinion, present your support (including at least one quotation), and acknowledge your sources.

Pursuing Justice

First Nations, Métis, and Inuit peoples are pursuing justice in a variety of ways:

- through royal commissions and public inquiries
- through increased roles and better relationships in the justice system
- through new initiatives
- through using the justice system with court challenges

FIGURE 8.18 Clifford George testified at the Ipperwash Inquiry and attended most sessions until his death in 2005.

Commissions and Inquiries

Canada has a long tradition of commissions and public inquiries. These investigations have a range of mandates and can be national, provincial, or territorial in scope. They might focus on investigating past events, focus on policy recommendations for the future, or combine the two. Reports from the Royal Commission on Aboriginal Peoples, the Aboriginal Justice Inquiry of Manitoba, and other such inquiries continue to ask the question "What is justice?" and to help promote justice. As you read the rest of this chapter, you will not only learn about different findings and recommendations from these commissions and inquiries, but also see many positive actions that have resulted.

New Roles, Initiatives, and Practices

Akitsiraq Law School

Paul Okalik was Nunavut's first premier and the first Inuk lawyer in Canadian history. Now, a new program has been developed to educate more lawyers in Nunavut and the Canadian Arctic. The Akitsiraq Law School offers a Bachelor of Laws degree in Iqaluit in partnership with the Faculty of Law at the University of Victoria, Nunavut Arctic College, and the Akitsiraq Law School Society. Its course electives include Inuit traditional law, environmental law, and Inuit Qaujimajatuqangit.

Indigenous Bar Association

Delia Opekokew and Don Worme are among many lawyers who are members of the Indigenous Bar Association. The existence of this association and the achievements of its members provide a strong contrast to the laws of the past that kept Aboriginal people from becoming lawyers, or even from hiring lawyers.

VOICES OF THE PEOPLES

The objectives of the Indigenous Bar Association include the following:

1. To recognize and respect the spiritual basis of our Indigenous laws, customs and traditions.

2. To promote the advancement of legal and social justice for Indigenous peoples in Canada.

3. To promote the reform of policies and laws affecting Indigenous peoples in Canada.

4. To foster public awareness within the legal community, the Indigenous community and the general public in respect of legal and social issues of concern to Indigenous peoples in Canada.

—from the Indigenous Bar Association website

FIGURE 8.19 Prevention and intervention programs are part of revitalizing communities to make them healthy for all members. Outings such as this school field trip are positive steps.

Aboriginal Justice Strategy

Some recent strategies to improve the justice system in Canada for First Nations, Métis, and Inuit peoples are part of the federal Department of Justice's Aboriginal Justice Strategy (AJS), which was renewed in 2007. AJS is a way for Aboriginal communities to have more direct, increased involvement in administering justice for their communities. The goal is to promote alternatives to the mainstream justice system in order to respond effectively to the needs and values of communities while reducing the rates of victimization, crime, and incarceration of Aboriginal people.

Some of the community-based justice programs established by AJS include developing pre-sentencing options, community sentencing circles, Aboriginal justices of the peace, family and civil mediation, and additional community services for victims and for the reintegration of offenders. You will read about many of these programs and initiatives in later pages.

Some communities that have developed alternative, community-based justice programs are

- Métis Settlements General Council Justice Program in Alberta: The council supports eight communities in creating youth and adult diversion programs, alternative measures, and justice committees. The program has a strong emphasis on mediation, family conferences, conflict resolution, and developing communication skills. Elders and other community members are heavily involved in the program.

- Thunder Bay Indian Friendship Centre diversion program: The friendship centre runs a program for youth aged 16 to 17 and adults. The offender is expected to take responsibility for his or her behaviour, be accountable, and actively try to rectify the wrong. Part of the healing and wellness plan involves a circle that includes the accused, the victim, and support for each.

- Aboriginal Legal Services of Toronto Community Council Project: In this program, the Community Council (a panel of four volunteers) and the offender take part in a hearing to discuss the offence, harm, and the offender's responsibility. The resulting council agreement might include counselling, treatment, apologies, restitution, and other restorative options.

Prevention and Intervention

Many communities and organizations are developing programs that focus on preventing harm or intervening to reduce harm. Public awareness messages, such as one by Adam Beach (page 248), the Kanawayhitowin program, the Kizhaay Anishinaabe Niin (I Am a Kind Man) program, and the advice and support of Elders, Wisdom Keepers, role models, and Aboriginal social workers (such as Alex Jacobs) are all working toward prevention and harm reduction. Kanawayhitowin is a program that addresses violence against Aboriginal women. The Kizhaay Anishinaabe Niin (I Am a Kind Man) program focuses youth on the Seven Grandfather Teachings to address violence against Aboriginal women.

VOICES OF THE PEOPLES

Alex Jacobs (in Chapters 1 and 5) talks about the importance of role models, healing in communities, and prevention. He says to youth:

You need to look at who your friends are. Are they the kind of people that you want to model yourself after. Are they...leading you in the right direction? Or are they the ones that are in and out of being incarcerated or always getting in fights or known to be untrustworthy. If they are...then you need to back away from them.

Saskatchewan's Justice Reform Commission

In November 2001, the Commission on First Nations and Métis Peoples and Justice Reform was set up. This excerpt from "Saskatchewan's justice reform commission" from CBC News Online, July 2, 2004, summarizes details:

> There had been allegations of police misconduct—claims police were dropping off aboriginal men on the outskirts of Saskatoon in the dead of winter, leaving them to find their own way home.
>
> Darrell Night said that's exactly what happened to him on Feb. 4, 2000. He identified Dan Hatchen and Ken Munson as the officers who kicked him out of a police cruiser near the Queen Elizabeth power station—the same spot where two aboriginal men were found frozen to death in the previous week.
>
> On Sept. 20, 2001, Hatchen and Munson were convicted of unlawful confinement. They were sentenced to eight months in jail. The former police officers would serve about half of that before being released.
>
> Set up by former justice and Aboriginal Affairs minister Chris Axworthy, the goal of the commission was to "identify efficient, effective and financially responsible reforms to the justice system." The commission's mandate was to recommend how to improve the province's justice system in a way that reflected "the strengths and values of aboriginal people," ultimately leading to safer communities... The commission looked at everything from police forces to jails, including why such a large number of aboriginal people are behind bars. It was chaired by Wilton Littlechild, an Alberta lawyer, former MP and vice-president of the Indigenous Parliament of the Americas. Other commission members included former Saskatoon Tribal Council chief Joe Quewezance, Prince Albert lawyer Hugh Harradence, Saskatchewan's deputy children's advocate Glenda Cooney, and Métis corrections official Irene Fraser.

The commission was far-ranging, looking at

- the number of Aboriginal people in Saskatchewan jails
- the proportion of young people in jail
- how to investigate complaints against police
- how to keep young Aboriginal offenders out of jail and divert them to culturally appropriate programs or services
- community and parents' roles
- including more Aboriginal people working in the court system
- sentencing alternatives

The CBC report continues:

> On June 21, 2004, the commission released its final report—complete with 122 recommendations... It cites racism among the province's police services as a major reason why aboriginal people misunderstand and mistrust the justice system. The report suggests the way to eliminate racism in policing is through better screening, beefed-up training programs for officers who exhibit racist attitudes, and a more proactive strategy to recruit First Nations and Métis officers.

Web Connect • ·············

To learn more about the findings and recommendations of the Ipperwash Inquiry, and progress in applying them, visit our website.

Pursuing Justice in Policing

Various communities, organizations, commissions, and inquiries (including the Saskatchewan Commission and Ipperwash Inquiry) have worked toward and/or recommended improvements to policing. Such positive efforts can lead to policing that is more preventative and holistic than reactive.

After Dudley George's death in 1995, two significant ways in which justice was pursued was through a police investigation and through the Ipperwash Inquiry (right). Since that time, positive steps have been taken in policing, which you will read about below.

In July 1996, following an investigation into Dudley George's death, the OPP Special Investigations Unit (SIU) recommended that the officer who shot Dudley George (Sergeant Kenneth Deane) be charged with criminal negligence causing death. In April 1997, he was found guilty and later sentenced to two years less a day (to be served in the community). In January 2002, Kenneth Deane was asked to submit his resignation and did so in September 2002.

Peter Edwards, a *Toronto Star* reporter who started covering the events at Ipperwash on September 7, 1995, clarifies the implications of a "guilty" verdict for the charge of criminal negligence causing death:

> *It wasn't enough for the judge to determine that Dudley George had been unarmed. The judge had to conclude, that beyond a reasonable doubt, he was confident that Deane had* knowingly *shot an unarmed man. All it would take for Deane to walk free was for the judge to conclude that Deane had a mistaken but honest split-second* belief *that Dudley George had been armed.*

Subsequent positive developments in policing for Aboriginal peoples have included

- increased Aboriginal policing

- training of police in cultural, historical, and legal issues

- efforts to improve police–Aboriginal community relationships

- planning for effectively addressing conflicts and crises involving Aboriginal people—for example, related to land and treaty issues

The Ontario Provincial Police, for example, made Aboriginal awareness training a requirement for all new officers and specialty unit members. As well, officers have participated in programs to reach and engage youth, such as Walking the Path and Niigan Mosewak. In one summer program called North of 50 Cops and Kids, youth from Pikangikum First Nation and officers (as their camp counsellors) share two-week camp experiences.

Community policing practices have resulted in better relationships, partnerships between the police and community to maintain law and order, respect for community values and beliefs, and a greater understanding between police and Aboriginal communities in both rural and urban centres.

FIGURE 8.20 Among those giving testimony was Mike Harris. The CBC later reported on the Inquiry: "The government of former Ontario premier Mike Harris, Ottawa, and the OPP all bear responsibility for events that led to the 1995 death of Dudley George, the head of the Ipperwash inquiry said... Commissioner Sidney Linden found Harris did not order provincial police into Ipperwash Provincial Park to remove unarmed aboriginal protesters, but he could have 'urged patience, rather than speed' at resolving the dispute."

©P

The Ipperwash Inquiry

Sam George led the call for a public inquiry into his brother's death (as explored in greater depth on page 280). The public inquiry announced in 2003 was led by Justice Sidney B. Linden.

The inquiry was far-reaching in its considerations and called for testimony from a vast number of people: occupiers and officers; expert witnesses on Aboriginal burials, media, and riot police; the former premier and other public officials. Kenneth Deane had died in a car accident prior to the inquiry, but his court evidence was examined.

On May 31, 2007, Justice Sidney Linden's statement about the inquiry report included this:

> *Questions about the death of Mr. Dudley George were raised almost immediately. How could an apparently peaceful occupation and protest turn violent? What was the urgency in taking action? What was the role of the provincial and of the federal government? Was racism or cultural insensitivity a factor?... It is impossible to attribute Mr. George's death to a single person, factor, decision, or institution. On the contrary, it was the combination of these that made a violent result more likely, particularly when they all came together in the space of a few short days and hours in the context of a highly charged confrontation. Individuals and institutions need to be held accountable for the consequences of their decisions and actions, whether those consequences were intended or not...*
>
> —**Commissioner's Statement, Public Release of Report,**
> **May 31, 2007**

Here are some findings from the inquiry:

- There was a general lack of understanding of First Nations cultures and history.

- Cultural insensitivity and racism played a significant role on many levels and among key players.

- Outcomes of those attitudes were, for example, that the occupiers were treated as trespassers to be removed, and statements about burial grounds were forgotten or disregarded.

- The First Nations occupiers were frustrated in their experiences with both the federal and provincial governments.

- Opportunities were missed: to use skilled negotiators to find peaceful resolutions, to involve First Nations police officers, for officers to communicate better with occupiers.

- Police preparations did not include a well-developed communication plan and communication was poor within the local force.

- The decision to use the Crowd Management Unit and Tactics and Rescue Unit was made based on unverified and inaccurate information.

- The police officers involved did not understand or anticipate how an Aboriginal protest and occupation would differ in its response to police tactics as compared with, for example, fans at a soccer game.

- The media, with some exceptions, lacked sufficient context and depended on too few sources to report well on the issues.

The report made 98 recommendations, including improvements in policing and police training, a public apology to one occupier for use of excessive force, the return of Stoney Point lands, the creation of a Treaty Commission of Ontario, provincial-federal cooperation to address issues underlying disputes, and increased public education about Aboriginal peoples and issues.

Progress has been made and the Ipperwash Inquiry Priorities and Action Committee (IIPAC) continues to work on implementing the recommendations. As you read this chapter, you will see some of these and other positive initiatives.

The Toronto Police Services headquarters marked National Aboriginal Day with a celebration mainly focused on children and youth. Why? Court officer Darryl Morrison (who is Anishinaabe) says it is a great opportunity for people to learn about the Aboriginal community in Toronto. In the Aboriginal Peacekeeping Unit, Darryl Morrison works with Constable Kim Turner, who also has an Anishinaabe background. The Aboriginal Peacekeeping Unit was founded by Bob Crawford—an officer who retired after a long, distinguished career, and died in 2004. Kim Turner describes what the unit does:

I provide the liaison between the various police divisions, and the Native community who live in those divisions...because they are scattered... We do a lot of outreach from this office. We have such a vast area to cover.

This unit was established to meet the need of the aboriginal people in Toronto. We know, historically, that the relationship between the police and the aboriginal people has not been good.

That goes way back to the residential schools, and the RCMP taking the children out of their homes at the order of the government—with police, in general, having to carry the can for that abuse.

So, the unit was desperately needed, and Bob Crawford made it happen. He convinced me...to be proud of where I came from. And to instill that pride in your children, just as he instilled it in his.

—**Aboriginal Policing, Mark Bonokoski, Sun Media, Dec. 15, 2008**

Speaking at the Aboriginal Day event, Kim Turner says she wants these children to celebrate their culture and be proud of who they are. They should not be afraid of coming to a police station. Rather, it should be seen as a place where officers will listen to them and have fun with them.

Kim Turner hopes for a future where her job nurturing the relationship between the Aboriginal community and Police Service is no longer needed:

I would like to say that I could work myself out of a job one day. It would be great if there's an understanding between all the cultures so we don't need this kind of thing.

—**Toronto Police Services: National Aboriginal Day marked at HQ**

FIGURE 8.21 Constable Kim Turner (in uniform) and Toronto Police Services Board Chair Alok Mukherjee (on her left) are shown with guests on National Aboriginal Day at Toronto Police Headquarters. How might such events at police headquarters help improve relationships and contribute to the pursuit of justice?

©P

Justices of the Peace, Court Workers, and Legal Clinics

Some new, positive initiatives are Aboriginal justices of the peace and more Aboriginal court workers and legal clinics. Court workers and clinics ensure that legal counsel is available, explain the court process to defendants, write pre-sentencing reports, and translate communications into Aboriginal languages. Aboriginal Legal Services of Toronto (ALST) has court workers, victim support services, and community council/diversion services, as well as the ALST Community Council program that you read about earlier.

Gladue Courts

Aboriginal Legal Services of Toronto and other legal clinics often assist in what are called Gladue Courts or Aboriginal Persons Courts. Gladue Courts and the reports that are written by Aboriginal court workers take into account the life circumstances of an Aboriginal offender and give recommendations to be considered in sentencing. These courts result from the 1999 Supreme Court of Canada decision in *Regina v. Gladue* and section 718.2(e) of the Criminal Code of Canada:

> *A court that imposes a sentence shall also take into consideration the following principle[:] "all available sanctions other than imprisonment that are reasonable in the circumstances should be considered for all offenders, with particular attention to the circumstances of aboriginal offenders."*

Web Connect • • • • • • • • • • • •

To learn more about Gladue Courts, visit our website.

VOICES OF THE PEOPLES

In Moving Toward Native Justice, *Jean-Paul Restoule (Anishinaabe and French-Canadian, from the Dokis First Nation) says:*

Sentencing circles are not perfect. However, they are, for Native people, an improvement over the Canadian court system in many ways. They attempt to heal the offender rather than merely punish him. They give Native offenders a sense of self-esteem. They restore the relationships and health of the community. They save money by reducing rates of recidivism, by reducing both the number and length of prison sentences, and by reducing the amount of time spent in court hearing cases... One can see the benefit this system would have in dealing with young offenders and offenders with drug and alcohol abuse problems. The hurdles that currently face the sentencing circle are awareness and education...

The sentencing circle is not an infallible method for all legal cases. Aboriginal people themselves executed very severe punishments for the very worst offences. It is likely that murder charges and similarly heinous crimes would be tried in Canadian courts without the option of a sentencing circle. But having the choice of the sentencing circle for Aboriginal people is increasing as more communities educate themselves about the process.

—**Moving Toward Native Justice,** *by Jean-Paul Restoule*

Restorative Justice and Healing/Sentencing Circles

Restorative approaches and the healing/sentencing circles you read about earlier in the chapter are increasingly an option. One outstanding example of restorative justice and the use of healing/sentencing circles is Hollow Water First Nation. Hollow Water First Nation is an Anishinaabe community of about 600 people located east of Lake Winnipeg, 200 kilometres north of Winnipeg.

In Hollow Water, the community has developed the Community Holistic Circle Healing Program (CHCHP) that reclaims many of the Nation's traditional practices, including the healing circle. The CHCHP is designed to help prevent, intervene in, and heal the intergenerational effects of sexual abuse and domestic violence. The program delivers community sentencing, healing circles, and alternative measures to prison sentences. Counselling is made available to those involved and their extended families, and the CHCHP offers support groups, oversight of court-ordered assessments, and traditional healing therapy.

Hollow Water First Nation's approach started in 1985 and has been seen as both a milestone and a model in Aboriginal communities renewing justice for themselves. The Nation and its program have been much discussed and studied—noting, for example, a rigorous 13-step approach for dealing with abusers, a low recidivism rate, community-wide benefits, and lower financial costs than with conventional justice approaches.

FIGURE 8.22 In this photograph, Garry Raven of Hollow Water First Nation is harvesting cattail root. How can maintaining or reclaiming practices (such as using healing circles or harvesting traditional plants) help revitalize communities?

Compensation

Earlier in this chapter, you read about compensation used as a traditional justice method. In some communities now, compensation is being used as one of many approaches in restorative justice. In Ontario, the Mnjikaning First Nation (now known as Rama First Nation) has a community healing and restorative justice program called Biidaaban (future present past). After two community employees with gambling addictions stole $100 000 from the community, the sentencing circle was attended by the offenders, 75 community members, lawyers, court clerks, and a judge. Those who stole the money apologized for their wrongdoing. They were sentenced to pay back all the money and to house arrest, probation, and community service for three years, and treatment.

Another example is from Akwesasne Mohawk Nation and involved some adolescent boys. They vandalized properties in the community and were brought before the council. They admitted what they had done and were asked why. When the youth explained that they had nothing else to do that night and were bored, they were asked what they could do to help. Over the course of the discussion, the youth developed a plan to rebuild properties and do other work for those harmed.

Healing Lodges

In 1994, Correctional Service of Canada introduced a new option for Aboriginal offenders serving a federal sentence: healing lodges. Healing lodges offer a physical space and programming that reflects the needs and cultures of First Nations, Métis, and Inuit peoples by offering teachings, ceremonies, contact with Elders, Wisdom Keepers, and children, and interaction with nature. One healing lodge is Waseskun Healing Center in Québec, and more are being developed across the country. The approach is holistic and involves community relationships to prepare for release.

The concept of healing lodges was initially proposed by an Aboriginal women's group and was reinforced by the 1990 Task Force on Federally Sentenced Women. The results have been promising, with reductions in repeat offenders. In 1995, the Okimaw Ohci Healing Lodge was opened in Maple Creek, Saskatchewan. In 1997, Pê Sâkâstêw (New Beginnings) Centre opened in Alberta on the Samson Cree First Nation. Elsewhere, existing facilities have been converted to incorporate healing lodges and sweat lodges in prisons.

In Brampton, Ontario, a youth centre was built in 2009 with programming and space for Aboriginal young offenders to access counselling, spirituality, and connections to their identities from community members. And in 2009, Fort Frances, Ontario, established the first secure custody facility for Aboriginal youth—the Ge-Da-Gi Binez (Spotted Eagle) Youth Centre.

Victim, Witness, and Community Support

Communities have been developing many ways to help those who have been harmed. The Victim Witness Liaison service for Nishnawbe Aski Nation is one example. In Ottawa, the Tungasuvvingat Inuit Centre has the Mamisarvik Healing Centre for victims of crime.

As well, programs such as the Native Community Worker program at St. Clair College are training students in traditional healing methods. This and other programs prepare students to provide culturally sensitive counselling, mental health services, and social services.

Other justice programs are focusing on children and families. One example is the Talking Together program for Nishnawbe Aski Nation. The program focuses on dispute resolution based on the traditional circle, and the program aims to restore harmony. The Talking Together program and similar approaches can be an alternative to the mainstream court process, which has often resulted in Aboriginal children being removed from their communities.

REFLECTION

How might programs at healing lodges help return individuals and communities to harmony?

CRITICAL THINKING

In the mainstream justice system, the Victim Offender Reconciliation Program (VORP) has its roots in the Mennonite community in Kitchener, Ontario, and has been used in parts of Canada and the United States. VORP aims to help bring victim and offender together in a safe way so that the offender can take responsibility for his or her actions and try to make things right. In what ways might VORP compare with other approaches in this chapter?

Aboriginal Children: Schools and Care

Schools

Related to the residential school system, some milestones in the pursuit of justice have been the apologies from churches that operated the schools, the 2008 apology from the federal government, and the creation of the Truth and Reconciliation Commission.

While the residential schools operated, church-run day schools were also operating in Canada. In Manitoba, these "Indian day schools" are the subject of a recent class-action suit by former students. Ray Mason of Spirit Wind (a Winnipeg-based organization) says:

> *Many Canadians don't realize that the current [settlement] only dealt with our people who went to the residential schools, as defined by the government of Canada. Today we are seeking justice and compensation for Indian day school survivors who suffered the same. The abuses were the same if not worse...*
>
> —"Indian day school survivors launch $15B lawsuit," CBC News online, July 31, 2009

Foster Care and Adoption of Aboriginal Children

As you read in Chapter 5, First Nations, Métis, and Inuit children in Canada have been taken from their homes, families, and communities and placed in non-Aboriginal homes in great numbers as part of the Sixties Scoop. In their book *Stolen from Our Embrace*, Ernie Crey and Suzanne Fournier make some key connections that include the following:

> *In many cases, children were taken from parents whose only crime was poverty—and being aboriginal... In rural areas, often the only difference between the parents whose children were stolen away and those who took in foster children for a little extra cash was the colour of their skin...*
>
> *There is still no far-reaching federal statute in Canada comparable to the U.S. Indian Child Welfare Act, which stipulates the inalienable right of an Indian child to grow up within his or her tribe. The act...has ensured that almost 85 percent of all American Indian children are reared in Indian homes...*
>
> *All across Canada, homeless shelters, courtrooms, youth detention centres, and prisons are full of aboriginal people who grew up in non-native substitute care.*

In 2007, the historic Canadian human rights case on First Nations child welfare was filed against the federal government on behalf of children in care. This landmark case has brought attention to the ongoing funding discrepancies, systemic discrimination, and assimilation practices of the federal and provincial governments where Aboriginal children are concerned.

FIGURE 8.23 By growing up together, in their community, these children will know their culture.

Web Connect

To learn more about the Canadian human rights case on First Nations child welfare, visit our website.

Court Challenges

Oral Tradition in the Courts

In Chapter 7, you read about the Delgamuukw case. Not only was it a victory for land rights, but the original case and the Supreme Court ruling also represented a huge contrast. Whereas the judge in the original case dismissed the lives of the Gitxsan and Wet'suwet'en peoples before contact as "nasty, brutish, and short" given that they had "no written language, no horses or wheeled vehicles…," the Supreme Court ruling established as precedent that future cases dealing with First Nations must give the same weight to oral tradition and written evidence.

Traditional Hunting and Fishing Rights

One of the key legal issues for First Nations, Métis, and Inuit peoples is maintaining their hunting and fishing rights. There have been several legal battles and some violent confrontations in different parts of Canada over these rights—including the Powley and the Marshall cases and the Burnt Church First Nation stand.

In the 1990 Sparrow case, Ronald Edward Sparrow of the Musqueam First Nation in British Columbia was fishing with a net longer than was allowed by the licence to the band under the Fisheries Act. Key points in this pivotal case were the difference between treaty rights and inherent rights to fish, priority to Aboriginal rights, and limits to rights.

Another case involved Will Goodon, a Métis hunter who shot a ringneck duck in October 2004 and was charged by provincial authorities with hunting without a licence. Goodon argued that he needed only his Manitoba Métis Federation harvester card. However, provincial officials disagreed. The court heard evidence about the traditional hunting lands of Will Goodon's ancestors. In 2009, the case was decided in Will Goodon's favour—confirming his Métis hunting rights.

Education

Beyond the courts and the wider justice system, many commissions, inquiries, and experts highlight the critical need for educating all people in Canada about Aboriginal peoples, history, treaty rights, values, and aspirations. Keith Lickers is an award-winning educator, former Education Officer with the Ontario Ministry of Education for over 30 years, and Seneca from Six Nations of Grand River. This book has long been a part of his vision for educating all students.

Think back to the statements in Call to Consciousness, Chapter 7, and this chapter about the importance of education. How would you summarize these statements?

VOICES OF THE PEOPLES

In 2010, Grand Chief Stan Beardy of the Nishnawbe Aski Nation said:

The 1995 shooting death of Dudley George at Ipperwash Provincial Park has a direct impact on Nishnawbe Aski Nation territory. There is urgency for land claims and land-related issues within our territory to be resolved to prevent an incident such as this happening again. In order for beneficial working relationships to exist between all levels of government and First Nations, there must be a political will and a sincere effort in implementing our Treaty rights…

—Dibaajimowin (Ipperwash Inquiry Priorities and Action Committee newsletter), Summer 2010

VOICES OF THE PEOPLES

Keith Lickers says the following:

Since all Canadians share a common destiny, the issues that today concern the Aboriginal peoples of Canada are important to all Canadians. All students, Aboriginal and non-Aboriginal alike, need an opportunity to become aware of these concerns and to develop informed opinions so that, as the mature citizens of the future, they can make intelligent decisions.

Finding Truth

In a 2010 interview, lawyer Don Worme explains the Anishinaabe word "debwewin" (which is often translated as "truth") and what Sam George (Dudley George's brother who led the call for a public inquiry) meant by debwewin:

He wanted the facts—not just the facts [in terms of] what happened, but he wanted the context because it was necessary for him to understand the facts only once you understand the context. And the context…wasn't just Officer Kenneth Deane pointing his Heckler & Koch MP5 and shooting…three times and killing [Sam's brother]. But it was, how did the police arrive at that point…50 riot police officers in full riot gear… their shields coming down on a group of 25 unarmed men, women, and children… How did the police get there? Who gave them…the orders to be there? Where did those orders come from? Why were those orders given? Why were…the Indians there in the first place? What were they upset about? Why did they want their land back? Why were they upset that there [was] a horseshoe game over top of their grave sites?

The Debwewin Citations award is presented by the Anishinabek Nation. The award was first presented in 2002 to Toronto Star *journalist Peter Edwards for his reporting on the events that led to the 1995 death of Dudley George. According to the Anishinabek Nation and regarding the award:*

…for journalists, "truth" should mean more than accuracy; it also implies fairness, balance and context. Rationale for the Debwewin Citations: Due to the deficiencies of mainstream education curricula, most Canadians have been exposed to inaccurate and incomplete portrayals of aboriginal culture, tradition, and contemporary issues. As a result, mainstream media reporting is the primary public education source for information about Native issues, often with disastrous results.

Sam George said:

My tradition is we learn by our mistakes and if you're honest with yourself, it only helps you be a better person.

In a research paper for the Ipperwash Inquiry about media, Professor John Miller of Ryerson University had many criticisms of the news coverage, including the following:

Reporters relied heavily on interviews with "official" sources—police, outside First Nation leaders and politicians—in the aftermath of the shooting. Very little ongoing news coverage was told from the perspective of those occupying the park.

Julie Carl was one of three journalists interviewed for Professor Miller's report about how media coverage could have been improved. She strived for balance and was surprised how her writing for the London Free Press *was seen as biased. She said she realized from interviews and from listening to call-in radio shows how deep racism was in Canada.*

Peter Edwards wrote in the Toronto Star *on December 29, 2004:*

Mr. Justice Sidney Linden hopes the inquiry he is chairing into [Dudley] George's death will help to heal the wounds inflicted on the community that night—as well as fulfill its mandate of making recommendations to avoid similarly violent situations. "I'd like to see the inquiry be a constructive force in the healing process," Linden said in an interview [in December 2004]… The inquiry has been under way since July, long enough for Linden to see how raw wounds remain in the local native communities of Kettle and Stoney Point, despite the passage of almost a decade. Linden is hopeful he can leave things better than when he arrived. "Most of the experience that I've had in the law has been constructive and positive," Linden continued. "That's my nature. I'd like to make a positive contribution that the community can use for healing."

1. In a group, discuss what the perspectives above mean for individuals, for people in the justice system, for students, and for the media.

FIGURE 8.24 Sam George is shown above, surrounded by media during the Ipperwash Inquiry. He was later honoured with the Order of Ontario, and the Ontario Ministry of Aboriginal Affairs library is named for him. He died in 2009 from cancer. Sam's wife, Veronica, told reporter Peter Edwards that Sam George followed the Seven Grandfather teachings traditionally taught to children: love, respect, truth, honesty, bravery, wisdom, and humility. Peter Edwards says, "I think he eventually won out and turned people around because he embodied those values."

FIGURE 8.25 The family of Dudley George (above left) included Sam, eight other siblings, their parents, and many grandchildren.

THINKING IT THROUGH

1. What are some examples of contemporary justice issues that affect Aboriginal peoples? What are some of the initiatives and practices that Aboriginal peoples are using in their pursuits of justice?

2. Describe some of the achievements of Aboriginal peoples in the justice system.

3. For one subject (such as non-Aboriginal substitute care for First Nations, Métis, and Inuit children), research the issue to develop an opinion piece using the skills of giving support, crediting sources, and quoting effectively.

FIGURE 8.26 Peter Edwards covered the events at Ipperwash from September 1995. His book *One Dead Indian* was adapted to become a film. In what ways do the media and inquiries have the potential to contribute to the pursuit of justice?

Conclusion

After considering how to define justice and injustices, you have learned about traditional justice among First Nations, Métis, and Inuit peoples, injustices in Canadian history and recently, and the pursuit of justice. Throughout this chapter, you have also developed the skills of giving support, crediting sources, and quoting effectively.

CRITICAL THINKING

How has your understanding of the terms *justice* and *injustice* changed? What does the opening quotation by Carl Roberts on page 248 now mean to you in its implications?

End-of-Chapter Activities

1. Consider the examples of Adam Beach (Figure 8.1 on page 248) and Alex Jacobs (Voices of the Peoples on page 270). What other examples in this chapter or an earlier chapter can you find that would divert someone from the justice system, prevent crime, and/or contribute to healthy communities? Share your examples and ideas in a group.

FIGURE 8.27 Kathleen Lickers is Seneca from the Six Nations of the Grand River. She has been the legal counsel for the Indian Claims Commission and now lectures and runs a law practice in Six Nations. During the Ipperwash Inquiry, Kathleen Lickers served as co-counsel for the Chiefs of Ontario.

2. In a group or with a partner, research the subject of a recent banishment: the reasons, the results, and perspectives on it. Also consider your own perspective on banishment as a method to achieve justice. Present a summary of your findings and opinions to the class.

3. a) Choose one aspect of the Ipperwash Inquiry to examine, for example, the burial grounds, the use of the tactical units, or media bias. Use the inquiry report and submissions to the inquiry for your research.

   b) Using the skills of giving support, crediting sources, and quoting effectively, report on that subject to your class.

4. Research the legacy of the events at Ipperwash. For example, what is one recommendation that has been acted upon, and what are the results?

5. What challenges are there in how issues relevant to First Nations, Métis, and Inuit people are presented in mainstream media? Examine examples in the current news to see if they support the statement that the media lacks sufficient context and depends on too few sources to report well on the issues. Discuss your findings in a group and come to conclusions to present to the class.

6. One way to think about justice is through looking at historic cases or key decisions, such as in the example of Donald Marshall Jr.'s wrongful conviction, Ipperwash, or the High Arctic relocations. For one key example, review what you know, research to learn more, and note how the example adds to your understanding of the chapter subject. Note especially what lessons were learned from the case or decision and what positive actions were (or could be) taken. Share your results in a display combining writing and visuals or in an oral presentation.

Unit 3 Rich Performance Tasks

Choose one or more of the following tasks:

Analyze a Treaty Document

1. Consider where you live and whose traditional territory it is. Research this information by using reliable maps of the First Nations in that area or the website of an Aboriginal or governmental organization. Next, research the territory's history. Are you living in unceded territory, or has a treaty been signed? If a treaty has been signed for the area, find it and read it. What relationships are established, how is the land to be used, and who must be consulted prior to development? Research when the treaty was written and signed and by whom. Consider how that historical perspective might differ from contemporary interpretations of the treaty. Are there any outstanding issues in this treaty process? Has the treaty been honoured? Have there been court cases regarding this treaty? Have media, protests, or other forms of social activism been used to see the treaty honoured?

If you live in an area of unceded land of a First Nation or near a Métis Settlement, research whether a negotiation process has begun. How long has the process been going on? If an Agreement-in-Principle has been reached, what concepts does it outline?

Keep track of your sources. After your research, write a five-paragraph summary of the land claims and treaties in your area. Include a bibliography of the sources you quote. Refer to Building Your Skills (page 268) to assist you.

Make a Presentation

2. Research the topic of First Nations, Métis, and Inuit self-governance. Read sections of the United Nations Declaration on the Rights of Indigenous Peoples that relate to governance. Also read what Aboriginal organizations, such as First Nations band councils or Inuit regions (for example, in a negotiated settlement), have said about self-governance.

Consider aspects of governance such as political decision-making, fiscal responsibility, health and education, and land use. How does having decision-making control affect a Nation's ability to ensure its well-being?

Find examples of Aboriginal Nations that have taken back the control of their Nation. Consider historical perspectives that affect the current approaches of these governments. Present your findings in a panel discussion or presentation.

Work in a Group

3. Form a group with three or more students. Choose one current justice topic, for example, the court system and First Nations, Métis, and Inuit peoples.

Use consensus decision-making to decide how you will break up the topic into subtopics for research. Agree on how to present the research (for example, a skit).

Consider historical perspectives that might have an influence on contemporary issues. Consider possible sources, such as interviewing Elders and Wisdom Keepers or Aboriginal people who work in the field of justice. You could also use books and reliable websites. After working together, present your findings to the class.

UNIT 4 Resilience, Renewal, and Rejuvenation

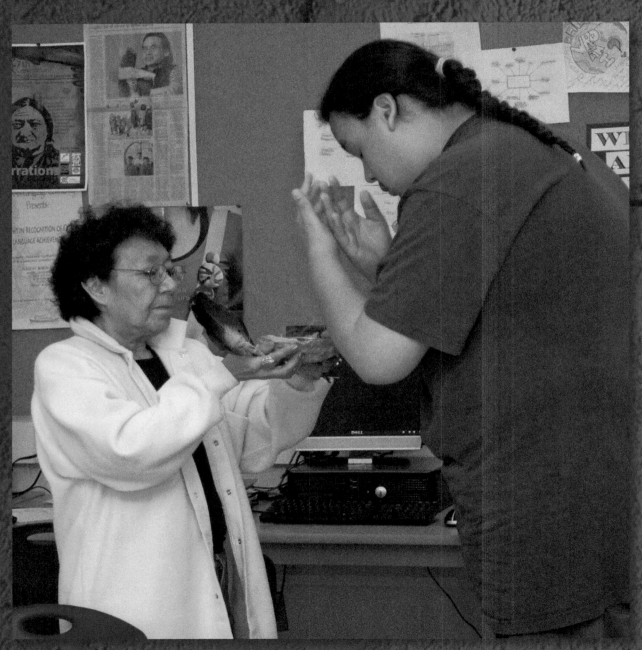

Whether on the land or in a big city, Elders and Wisdom Keepers are vital to maintaining languages and cultural knowledge. Students at the Native Learning Centre in Toronto learn Aboriginal history and culture, and the Ojibwe language. Respected Elder Jacqui Lavalley (left) is an honoured visitor to the Centre.

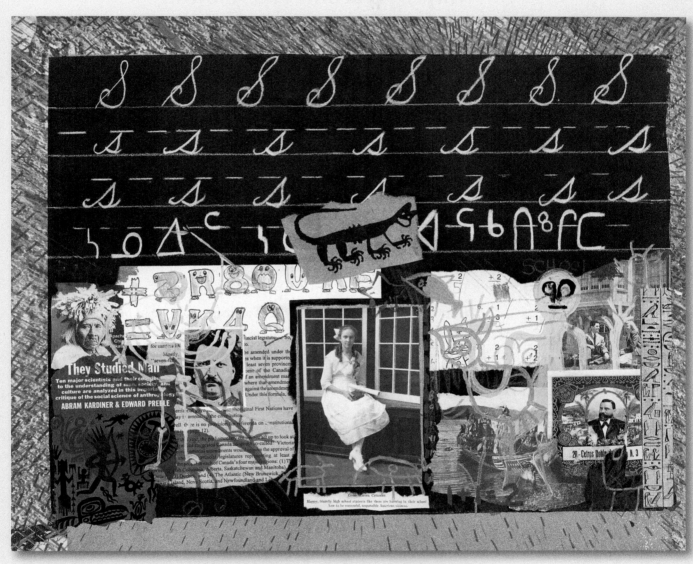

FIGURE 9.2 Artist Jane Ash Poitras (whose work also appears in Chapter 2) contributed this collage entitled *School Blackboard* (1992) to a group exhibition called *Rethinking History*. How has the artist rethought history? What new story does she present?

Challenges and Aspirations

REFLECTION

What has your experience of school been like so far? How does it compare with the experiences that others you know have had? What would you like your experience of education to be throughout your life?

When you think of your aspirations—the hopes, dreams, and goals that you have for your education and lifelong learning—they often build on your past. The same is true for every student in Canada. To take a look at education—for First Nations, Métis, and Inuit peoples—we will need to look again at the past.

Ways of Learning and Knowing

First Nations, Métis, and Inuit peoples had been educated in their homes, in their families and communities, and on the land for centuries. What children learned would depend on their Nation, roles, and environments. For example, boys and girls of all Nations would learn to set rabbit snares; a Haudenosaunee girl would learn how to make pinch pots as a step toward making her own pottery, and an Inuk boy from Hiukitak River would learn what foods caribou eat, where caribou could be found, and how to hunt them. Learning came through observation and experience. Knowledge and wisdom were also gained through oral traditions and through Elders and Wisdom Keepers. Learning was woven into daily life. It was holistic, intergenerational, and lifelong, not something that took place in a formal classroom. For individuals and for whole communities, since time immemorial, this was what education meant to Aboriginal peoples.

Individual and Community Resources

Knowledge has long been viewed as a group resource in most First Nations, Métis, and Inuit communities. Knowledge is shared in order to maintain balance and harmony within each person and within the community, and to contribute to the overall well-being of the community. The purpose of learning is to encourage the growth of each person within the community so that community well-being—physical, mental, spiritual, social, economic, and environmental—is guaranteed.

FIGURE 9.3 Traditional education is not just a thing of the past. This photograph from 2008 shows youth learning alongside Elders and Wisdom Keepers as part of a Canoe Brigade in Waskaganish Cree Nation.

Education Changes

With the arrival of European explorers, traders, missionaries, and settlers came new ideas about education. Aboriginal peoples saw education as a right and as a way for their children to gain the knowledge and skills needed to survive in a changing world. The actions of the federal government suggest that the federal government saw education as a means to assimilate Aboriginal peoples. This government perspective led to the establishment of industrial schools, the residential school system, and Indian day schools (which First Nations and Métis students attended), and to experiences such as those described in *The Experimental Eskimos* (Chapter 5).

FIGURE 9.4 This photograph of the Indian Residential School in Lebret in the Qu'Appelle Valley was taken around 1885. Parents had to camp outside the gates of this residential school in order to visit their children.

The Legacy of the Residential School System

Think back to what you learned about the residential school system in earlier chapters. Although some former students say they learned valuable skills at residential school, it is now generally agreed that the residential school system was an attempt to forcibly assimilate First Nations, Métis, and Inuit children into the dominant culture, and that, for the most part, it had a devastating impact on individuals, communities, and ancestral cultures.

Action	Effect
By forbidding students to speak their first languages…	the schools contributed to endangering or extinguishing many Aboriginal languages.
By banning the practice of Aboriginal spiritualities…	the schools denied students access to Aboriginal world views.
By claiming that Western European culture was better than First Nations, Métis, and Inuit cultures…	the schools ensured that students felt devalued and became ashamed of themselves and their cultures.
By separating children from their parents…	the schools contributed to a breakdown in First Nations, Métis, and Inuit families that continues today. The neglect and abuse of students in residential schools left emotional, physical, psychological, and spiritual damage that has been passed down through generations.
By disconnecting children from their communities and homelands…	the schools disrupted the passing of cultural knowledge from one generation to another.
By delivering substandard education…	the schools denied many First Nations, Métis, and Inuit people life skills.
By abusing authority…	the schools contributed to survivors' fear and mistrust of both schools and authority figures. Many survivors do not trust anyone in authority, including the police, because of the role government authorities played in removing children from their homes and forcing them into residential school.

Education Recently and Today

Even before many residential schools closed down in the 1970s and the last federally run residential school (Gordon Residential School in Saskatchewan) closed in 1996, First Nations, Métis, and Inuit peoples began working toward gaining control of education and renewing education for all their children. For example, in 1972, the National Indian Brotherhood issued a key policy paper called "Indian Control of Indian Education." This was a time when cultural survival schools were started.

Cultural Survival Schools

In the late 1970s, several cultural survival schools sprang up in communities across Canada. Today, many of these schools are flourishing. One example is Kahnawake Survival School in Québec, which serves over 250 students. Another is Ben Calf Robe—St. Clare Catholic Elementary and Junior High School in Edmonton, which is home to about 160 First Nations and Métis students. The students begin each day with a smudging ceremony and study Cree as a second language. In addition to the usual physical activities, powwow dancing and jigging are taught in gym class. Music options include drumming, flute, and fiddling. In Toronto, Wandering Spirit Survival School became First Nations School of Toronto.

Education Today

Some people might think that all Canadian students have about the same educational experiences and opportunities, but this is far from the case. In reality, there is a glaring gap between the quality of education for Aboriginal and for non-Aboriginal students; First Nations, Métis, and Inuit students have higher dropout rates, lower literacy rates, and less success within the education system.

Access, Opportunity, and Funding

According to Canada's Constitution Act, 1867 and Constitution Act, 1982, education is a provincial responsibility, and yet the federal government is to make laws for "Indians and lands reserved for Indians." While this appears to be a contradiction, the Constitution Act, 1982 and 11 treaties between the federal government and various First Nations leave no doubt that the federal government has primary responsibility for First Nations education. What this means for First Nations ("status Indian" and "non-status Indian"), Métis, and Inuit students is a wide range of experiences and funding arrangements.

Nunavut (which has a primarily Inuit population) determines its own education policy and has embedded the Inuit Qaujimajatuqangit (IQ) guiding principles in its Education Act. In other areas of Canada, schools on reserves have often been federal schools (operated by Aboriginal Affairs and Northern Development Canada—AANDC), but increasingly First Nations band councils are running their own schools under agreements with AANDC. In Ontario, Six Nations and Tyendinaga reserves still have federal schools. On-reserve schooling in Ontario often goes up only to Grade 8, so about

©P

In 2008, 13-year-old Shannen Koostachin was one of many Mushkegowuk (Cree) protesting about conditions at her school in Attawapiskat, an isolated fly-in community on James Bay:

I don't want others to go to school in portables that leak, [with] windows that don't open, washroom doors that don't close, and ceilings that are cracked. This is not an atmosphere for learning… All students in Canada deserve a learning environment that they are proud to attend, that gives them hope… We want the same hope as every other Canadian student.

Why was she protesting about her school? The Attawapiskat Education Authority, funded by the federal government, closed the elementary school in 2000 due to health problems reported after a 1979 diesel spill. When the education authority closed the school, the federal government provided portables and agreed to plan for a new school. However, the plan was cancelled. In 2009, Indian and Northern Affairs Canada announced that the community had been awarded funding for school design and construction.

half of First Nations high-school students in Ontario attend provincial public schools. Typically, when First Nations elementary or high-school students attend provincial public schools, AANDC (or the First Nation's Education Authority) makes tuition agreements with the province. However, as you will learn in the coming pages, there can be significant funding differences among students under these arrangements.

In the Classroom and Community

Beyond the experience of industrial schools and residential schools, First Nations, Métis, and Inuit students

- have often experienced stereotyping and racism

- have not seen themselves reflected in what they were learning

- have not seen their values reflected in the classroom or school life

Additionally, families and communities have felt excluded from school decisions, unwelcome, or unnoticed. To some, the legacy of the residential school system and other assimilation policies has not been addressed.

In summarizing the 1996 report of the Royal Commission on Aboriginal Peoples, Mi'kmaw scholar Dr. Marie Battiste noted that

FIGURE 9.5 These students at the Native Learning Centre in Toronto have opportunities to take part in ceremonies and meet with Elders and Wisdom Keepers.

The current curriculum in Canada projects European knowledge as universal, normative, and ideal. It marginalizes or excludes Aboriginal cultures, voices, and ways of knowing… Modern educational theory and practice have, in large part, destroyed or distorted the ways of life, histories, identities, cultures, and languages of Aboriginal peoples.

What has schooling been like beyond residential schools and reserve schools? Sto:lo author Ernie Crey and Métis leader France Picotte give their recollections.

I attended a public school where I was made aware daily of the gap between my family's standard of living and that of my non-Indian classmates. The town of Hope [British Columbia] was a working-class white community of loggers and miners mixed in with a few civil servants, social workers and police officers. At school I concentrated on surviving with some of my dignity intact; actually learning anything was secondary. At first I was bright and eager to learn, but my initial openness was not reciprocated by either the teachers or the other students. My relationship with teachers was combative. They expected me to do poorly academically. I received little encouragement or help... I learned not to expect smiles from teachers. I'd stick my hand up to answer a question, but I knew I wouldn't be called on.

Teachers frequently showed their resentment at having me in the room by not including me in the lessons or in the social interaction between children in the classroom. I could expect to be treated curtly and summarily, without warmth or respect... There were exceptions. I recall a teacher at Coquihalla Elementary School, a young man who seemed to make no distinction between me and the other children. [He] went out of his way to encourage me. He'd draw my attention to Aboriginal role models in the fields of entertainment and athletics... He made me feel that I, too, could be a high achiever. My improved self-esteem was reflected in the high marks I got in [his] class.

—**Ernie Crey, writer and fisheries advisor to the Sto:lo Nation in British Columbia**

When I look back at the history of schooling in Timmins the early teachers were mostly young women who taught English and French students together in a one-room school. The *Soeurs Assumption* came when they segregated the schools into public and separate Catholic systems. Métis students were largely traumatized by the schools, even though they were not residential schools. ...For the most part...Métis in Ontario attended either publicly or church-run schools. As part of the general student body, Métis students often faced discrimination and racism from teachers, school administrators, and other students. Michif was treated as a poor version of French and often there was a conflict between how Métis students saw themselves and how they were ignored or misrepresented in school textbooks.

Children were often ridiculed publicly by the teacher because of the Michif language. There was little consideration for Métis families... Because of a lack of sensitivity and ignorance on the part of teachers and schools, Métis students, up until recently, could expect a much lower level of education and most did not graduate... This is the historical basis upon which today Métis seek to reconcile; to forgive but never forget... Generations later, the scars of this era for Métis students is still not being fully addressed and our governments are fighting to ensure this history is not forgotten, in order to not repeat this past, and to heal from a dark period in our history. While the issues surrounding residential school abuses are beginning to be addressed for First Nations, Métis students continue to fight for recognition and reconciliation. Moreover, the issue of day schools for all Aboriginal children has not yet been addressed.

—**France Picotte, chair of the Provisional Council of the Métis Nation of Ontario**

©P

FIGURE 9.6 An event that shows the increasing pride of Métis in Ontario is Rendezvous, pictured here. Celebrating and sharing Métis heritage is one way of expressing pride and recalling heritage. What are other ways in which Métis people might "forgive but never forget"—especially in connection with education?

Aspirations

From their bitter experience of educational policies designed to assimilate or isolate, First Nations, Métis, and Inuit peoples know how powerful education is. Education shapes how people think, transmits cultural values as well as facts, teaches communication and social skills, shows people where their creativity lies, and can shape the ways in which people will contribute to society.

First Nations, Métis, and Inuit peoples want the same authority other Canadians have through school boards and parent councils—the chance to have a say in what their children will become. As you read the perspectives in the coming pages, think about and list what goals First Nations, Métis, and Inuit leaders, organizations (such as education authorities), and communities have been setting.

The "New Buffalo" and "New Whale"

Among Aboriginal leaders, many talk about the key role that education will play in the future of First Nations, Métis, and Inuit peoples. For example, Blair Stonechild is a member of the Muscowpetung First Nation in Saskatchewan, a residential school survivor, and a professor of Indigenous Studies. In his book *The New Buffalo*, he explains why education—specifically, post-secondary education—is the "new buffalo." Just as the buffalo was the sustaining force for Stonechild's people, Stonechild sees education as the means to ensure survival, renewal, and sustainability.

Shawn A-in-chut Atleo uses a similar metaphor. The National Chief of the Assembly of First Nations (AFN), Chief Atleo says that education is the "new whale." Chief Atleo is hereditary Chief of Ahousaht First Nation, a Nation on Vancouver Island that traditionally depended on food from the ocean. He also has a master's degree in education.

> **VOICES OF THE PEOPLES**
>
> Let us put our minds together and see what we can do for our children.
>
> —*Tatanka-Iyotanka (Chief Sitting Bull)*

> **CRITICAL THINKING**
>
> A successful whale hunt not only provides food and other goods essential for survival, but also strengthens the community by contributing to its overall health and well-being. Why do you think education plays an important role in strengthening Aboriginal communities?

Chief Atleo believes that Aboriginal communities will once again become healthy, economically sustainable, and balanced. He sees education as the key for social and economic health, creating vital links to other priorities such as governance and sustainable economic development.

Soon after his election as the National Chief of AFN, Chief Atleo wrote an article in February 2010 in the *Globe and Mail* entitled "Education is the key to Aboriginal (and Canadian) potential." In it, he put investment in First Nations youth at the centre of an agenda—with benefits for First Nations youth, First Nations communities, and Canada as a whole:

FIGURE 9.7 Shawn Atleo was elected as the Assembly of First Nations National Chief in July 2009.

First Nations youth are the youngest and fastest-growing segment of our population. Their share of the labour force will triple over the next 20 years. First Nations youth who complete high school are twice as likely to be employed, and those who get university degrees triple their earning potential. Increasing their graduation rates to match those of other Canadians would inject an additional $71-billion into Canada's economy over the next 10 years. This would help eliminate the employment gap, adding another $160-billion to the economy over a 10-year period. Investing in First Nations is a long-term, sustainable stimulus plan for Canada's economy.

…[Yet] First Nations children receive $2000 less per year than non-Aboriginal students. Schools lack libraries, computers, even heat and drinking water. Some of our communities lack permanent schools. Simple fairness dictates that we address this intolerable inequity.

Chief Atleo believes that education is a means to retain and maintain the strength of Aboriginal languages, history, teachings, and values while increasing understanding with the rest of Canada. For him, education is an opportunity to overcome the damaging and destructive effects of the residential school system, and a way to empower youth and ensure future opportunities, prosperity, and success. Chief Atleo says:

I still feel there is lots of work to do [in] the area of education through the entire system, from the funding supports to curriculum development to leaders in the education system accepting responsibility… While we didn't create the Indian Act or the residential-school legacy, I suggest that all of us share responsibility for doing something about it. I would ask the leaders in the field of education to really step up.

Looking at post-secondary education in particular, Blair Stonechild says that the role of post-secondary education can be seen as moving from a form of assimilation and cultural suppression to a means of empowerment, self-determination, and self-government.

Yet there are challenges to overcome. How should post-secondary education for First Nations, Métis, and Inuit students be funded? The Indian Act, the Constitution Act, and other historical legal documents do not make that clear. And ironically (from today's perspective), up until 1951, a First Nations person who graduated from university could face immediate enfranchisement—being declared a Canadian citizen and being stripped of legal status as "Indian."

Access to post-secondary education is often controversial, but it is critical to First Nations, Métis, and Inuit peoples and the future of Canadian society. Treaty 7 Elders and Tribal Council, among others, have argued that access to education at all levels is a treaty right. In contrast, the federal government has viewed its responsibilities as legislated for the elementary and secondary levels, but provides some funding for post-secondary education to registered status Indian students and Inuit students. These significant differences in opinion and funding gaps are why First Nations, Métis, and Inuit peoples want control over their own higher education institutions.

FIGURE 9.8 What aspirations might these students at Lakehead University in Thunder Bay have? What are your aspirations?

VOICES OF THE PEOPLES

In Iqaluit in 2007, at a workshop called Redefining Success in Inuit Learning, participants focused on

- education as a lifelong process
- using the eight Inuit Qaujimajatuqangit (IQ) guiding principles and 38 IQ values and beliefs as the foundation for redefining success

Participants also said:

- *Inuit must design any model of Inuit education themselves in order for this process to be truly representative.*
- *Elders should be present since they must be involved when language and culture are being discussed.*
- *Only at physical death do we stop learning.*
- *Education is not preparation for life—education is life itself.*
- *…any model from Inuit should be formed using Inuktitut terms first rather than English terms.*

FIGURE 9.9 Other ideas mentioned in the workshop were "'the climate is the boss' and 'All of our knowledge is held inside of us… It's in our DNA.'" What do you understand from these statements?

©P

VOICES OF THE PEOPLES

Annie Aningmiuq is an Inuk student studying environmental governance at the University of Guelph. Annie completed high school in Pangnirtung, Nunavut, studied at Nunavut Sivuniksavut (a transitional college program in Ottawa) for two years, and...volunteered with Canada World Youth before...Guelph.

My community is 1400 people and probably, when I went to high school, 90 percent of the population was Inuit... I remember being in elementary school and looking around...it was all the Inuit women being teachers, so it was always a very comfortable feeling. And then...junior high, more Southern teachers and then high school, completely Southern teachers... We [were] learning about farms and the prairies...when probably 80 percent of the people [who were] learning it haven't been anywhere near that kind of stuff.

Just graduating from high school was a big accomplishment in my family. [Nunavut Sivuniksavut] was another huge thing for my entire family.

With World Youth, I went to India for three months and that's completely different from my community... I value...my travelling experiences, like performing in Germany for 200 people and...going to South Africa and learning about different cultures, counting trees in New Zealand... I never really knew what to expect... So...first

year was really hard for me. ... I didn't know anybody in Guelph...

Every year, I go to Guelph and I can say that I'm the only Inuit in all of Guelph... It gets a little bit lonely in terms of not being able to speak my language or having that connection... I'm completely fluent in writing and speaking Inuktitut except when I go home after that eight months. I have to watch how I'm pronouncing words or make sure that I'm saying my sentences right.

[With] Aboriginal students...the common theme when we're talking about what's troubling us in school is always funding... Things that I worry about in school are funding and money and how and where am I going to get the money for this $200 book that I need.

And I always go back to thinking what about our Elders who don't have that degree...they're just as smart as that person that has that doctorate or something. Because they have all this history in them and all these stories and they know, for example, how to catch fish with very limited resources.

In terms of university and getting my degrees, I have two possible life goals... I want to be a teacher...but also I really want to work for the Department of Fisheries and Oceans... Once you're more educated...you can help your people fight for that right, whatever it might be.

THINKING IT THROUGH

1. How could the education system in Canada create more opportunities for First Nations, Métis, and Inuit students?

2. Why do you think education is such an important issue for Aboriginal peoples?

3. To what extent do you believe that educational change should be guided by economic forces? What other factors are important in developing education, both in general and with special relevance to the diversity of First Nations, Métis, and Inuit peoples in Canada?

©P

Building Your Skills

Analyzing Issues

"What's your opinion?"

"What do you think about this?"

"Where do you stand on this issue?"

Every day you are asked to give your response to ideas and issues. Sometimes you respond by giving information; other times you simply state your opinion. Use this Building Your Skills feature to practise analyzing an issue and formulating a response.

Suppose your class is discussing the subject of how much time young people should spend online. You might come up with a statement that expresses one way of looking at the issue, such as "Young people spend too much time online. They are isolating themselves instead of participating in their communities." Or "By sharing information online, young people are creating communities and becoming globally connected." You can brainstorm this issue and use an issue chart to record the responses. On the chart, note comments that agree with the issue statement under "Yes"; those that disagree, under "No"; and those that are undecided, mixed, or questioning, under "Maybe So."

FIGURE 9.10 What difference might living in an urban community versus a remote rural community make to your computer use?

Issue Statement: "Young people spend too much time online."		
Yes	**Maybe So**	**No**
Yes—spending hours online isolates people.	Creating a virtual community is good, but it's not the same as a real community.	No—by going online, young people are creating communities and becoming globally connected.

Apply Your Skills

1. Now decide on an issue that you've read about related to this chapter and express the issue as a statement. For example, "Issue Statement: It is possible for Canada to address the historic injustices of the residential school system."

2. In a group or as a class, brainstorm about the issue and record the different responses in the appropriate sections of the issue chart.

3. Read over the responses in each section of the chart. As a class, discuss which section contains the strongest arguments so far. Then discuss how someone could conduct research to find support from several sources of information.

Program Innovations

REFLECTION

As you read about innovations in the following section, think about how these programs address the needs of the Nations that have developed them. Also consider how your own educational experiences compare to the programs featured.

As you read in the previous section, First Nations, Métis, and Inuit peoples want a meaningful and relevant education for their children—education that will strengthen and sustain their cultural and linguistic identities and prepare them for their lives as they determine them. They also believe that when First Nations, Métis, and Inuit perspectives are included in Canadian education in meaningful ways, all students benefit. This inclusion allows all students in Canada to develop an understanding of and respect for the cultures, history, and accomplishments of Aboriginal peoples. This approach will better prepare all students to participate in forming a more inclusive society.

Schools and specific programs across Canada are taking up the challenge of improving, changing, and renewing education for First Nations, Métis, and Inuit students.

FIGURE 9.11 Haa'uukmin Tribal Park, north of Tofino on Vancouver Island. Tla-o-qui-aht students learn about their traditional territory and enjoy a zipline ride. Programs that reflect pride and that link school, community, and the land have proven successful.

Characteristics Leading to Success

What are the characteristics of those schools that serve First Nations, Métis, and Inuit students well? In *Sharing Our Success: Ten Case Studies of Aboriginal Success*, the study authors looked at a range of schools in British Columbia, Alberta, Saskatchewan, Manitoba, and Yukon Territory. They found these common characteristics of successful schools:

- a safe and welcoming environment for students and families
- respect for Aboriginal cultures and traditions to make learning relevant
- high expectations
- a focus on academic learning and long-term success
- a wide range of programs and supports for learning
- strong leadership and governance

Additionally, the schools have developed trust within their communities, have high numbers of Aboriginal teachers, and have strong relationships with community Elders, Wisdom Keepers, and language teachers.

Some innovations in education that illustrate strong connections to the community are schools linked with Native friendship centres and organizations such as Seven Generations Educational Initiative. N'Swakamok Native Alternative Secondary School (which you will read about later in this chapter) is one school located in a friendship centre. Another example is the Alternative School in the United Native Friendship Centre in Fort Frances, Ontario. Seven Generations Educational Institute (which you will also read about later in this chapter) is based in the Rainy Lake Tribal Area.

Elders and Aboriginal Languages

The many ways that schools and communities are working to renew education for First Nations, Métis, and Inuit students include Aboriginal language classes and involving Elders and Wisdom Keepers in school programs. In the pages to come, you will read about Aboriginal language classes and how Aboriginal languages are being rejuvenated. Elders and Wisdom Keepers share oral traditions with students, teach traditional skills, train to teach ancestral languages, and participate in developing what is taught and how.

COMMUNITY CLOSE-UP

Akwesasne: Incorporating World View

In 1988, the Mohawk community of Akwesasne created a project to incorporate the Mohawk world view into the community's mathematics and science curriculum. Mohawk health and science professionals, Elders and Wisdom Keepers, parents, and non-Aboriginal advisors created the curriculum for Grades 7 to 9. As a result, students focus on global connections and incorporate the belief that everything in the world is interrelated. They also study science and mathematics concepts from non-Aboriginal sources.

Examples of Mohawk-centred lessons include the following:

- Animal study includes the animal-based Haudenosaunee clan system used in Mohawk society, as well as cells, cell functions, and the common scientific classification system for animals.

- In addition to the common scientific classification system for plants, plant study focuses on how plants contribute to Mother Earth, people, and animals; the medicinal uses of plants; and the cultural significance of the crops known as Our Sustainers (corn, beans, and squash).

- Mathematics includes Mohawk number systems and practical applications of the numbers to agriculture and forestry.

FIGURE 9.12 Jake Swamp was a respected teacher, author, Mohawk Chief, Wolf Clan diplomat, and family man, who died in 2010. He was known for his great knowledge of the Mohawk language and Haudenosaunee cultural heritage, his teaching skills, and humour. He was a founder of the Akwesasne Freedom School in 1979, helped develop a curriculum based on Haudenosaunee values, and established the Tree of Peace Society in 1984 to promote the teachings of the Peacemaker.

CRITICAL THINKING

Do you think that land-based programs are important? Why? Why not?

Experiential and Land-Based Education

Other innovations include hands-on or experiential learning, outdoor education, and traditional education on the land. Some programs teach school-aged youth canoeing, trapping, and winter survival skills. In other cases, such a school system has a land-based or place-based focus.

Students in the Cree Nation of Chisasibi, east of James Bay, get hands-on experience making snowshoes, moccasins, and sleds in their school. In the Ermineskin First Nation, in Alberta, Miyo Wahkohtowin Education Authority runs the Kindergarten, elementary, and high schools; at Ermineskin's Ehpewapahk Alternate Secondary School, students have Cree cultural education, hands-on work-skills training, and other flexible programming to meet students' needs. Students can pursue special projects to explore their talents, and the school has also created an outdoor education program to promote land-based learning.

FIGURE 9.13 This photograph shows J.R. Abel canoeing in the shallows of the Yellowknife River. Canoe skills are among many traditional life skills that school-age youth can learn as part of the Take a Kid Trapping program in the Northwest Territories. Building birchbark canoes, hunting, trapping, fishing, and outdoor survival are other skills in the program. How do programs such as this strengthen Aboriginal identity, develop relationships with Elders and Wisdom Keepers, and create connections to the land?

Self-Directed and Reciprocal Education

Aboriginal communities are also creating school programs that reflect traditional ideas on how learning should be self-directed and reciprocal. One example is the Aronhiatekha School, which is located in the Kanehsatake Mohawk Territory near Oka, Québec. At the school, students are grouped in classes of 10 to 15 students, and each student has two years to master the skills and concepts in a "cycle" (rather than one year for one grade). The school emphasizes students working in small groups to help each other learn. The school has high academic standards and also promotes respect as a central value, including respect for the self, for others, for the community, and for Mother Earth.

Attawapiskat First Nation runs the Vezina Secondary Online School through which students use the Internet to complete individualized, self-directed learning programs rather than having to leave Attawapiskat to attend high school. In northwestern Ontario, the Keewaytinook Internet High School (KiHS) connects classrooms in remote communities so that students can get their secondary education while living at home with family and community support.

Holistic Education

Many First Nations, Métis, and Inuit people have attended schools where their world views were not considered, leading some to have unsuccessful school experiences. To address this issue, First Nations, Métis, and Inuit organizations and institutions are designing programs that integrate their own world views, including the belief that everything is connected. Holistic programs look at the whole student and his or her connections with home, family, and community life.

CRITICAL THINKING

Holistic education involves individuals' diverse ways of understanding the world around them using their minds, bodies, relationships, spirits, and creativity. Specific examples might include hands-on plant studies rooted in Mohawk beliefs (page 291), involving Elders and other community members in school programs (page 303), or relating a lesson on human physiology and the heart to the understanding of the drum beat as the heart beat of the Earth. As you read this chapter, note examples of holistic education.

FIGURE 9.14 Waapihtiiwewan School, located in Oujé-Bougoumou in Québec, was designed by Métis/Blackfoot architect Douglas Cardinal. The school was designed to promote interconnectedness between humans and nature, using skylights and large windows. The students there are taught in Cree until Grade 3. In Grade 4, they choose English or French as the language of instruction.

In this feature, four schools illustrate holistic approaches. All four are found in urban areas. Because an increasing number of First Nations, Métis, and Inuit people now live in urban centres—and some students must move from their home communities just to attend high school—holistic education also takes that into account.

As you read about these schools, think about their similarities and differences. How do they compare with your own school? In what ways might First Nations, Métis, and Inuit people maintain their cultural identities in cities and towns?

N'Swakamok Native Alternative Secondary School

In Sudbury, N'Swakamok Native Alternative Secondary School serves the Anishinaabe students living in mid-Northern Ontario. The school is located in the N'Swakamok Native Friendship Centre and works with the local school board and the Ministry of Education to offer an individualized approach to learning, culturally appropriate support, and flexible start dates.

Many N'Swakamok students are Anishinaabe, living in Sudbury and originally from First Nations on Manitoulin Island. The school understands that the students might face challenges such as boarding with families they do not know well, having no family support close by, being single parents without daycare, or having no financial support. Although the program is fluid and aims to meet students' needs, N'Swakamok also has high expectations of its students.

FIGURE 9.15 At N'Swakamok, students participate in relationship-building, student-led projects (such as a newsletter featuring student writing), and health-related activities to develop intellectual, physical, emotional, and spiritual health. In the photograph above, the students learn how to make quill boxes as part of their Ojibwe language class.

Native Learning Centre

The Native Learning Centre (NLC) is a classroom where First Nations, Métis, and Inuit students in Toronto can each work toward a high-school diploma. The program has a flexible curriculum, a non-competitive environment, and instruction in Aboriginal history, the Ojibwe language, and Aboriginal cultures. Native Child and Family Services offers counselling, instruction in life skills, housing support, employment assistance, and legal services.

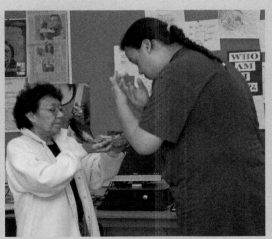

FIGURE 9.16 Students at NLC have the opportunity to participate in traditional ceremonies.

©P

Children of the Earth High School

A large Aboriginal population—including people who have been negatively affected by colonialism, marginalization, and the residential school system—lives in the North End neighbourhood of Winnipeg. The North End has numerous characteristics of large urban inner-city populations that have been socio-economically repressed, but it has developed positive approaches to heal and overcome challenges. The Children of the Earth High School is one example.

The school teaches the heritage languages of Cree and Ojibwe, teaches ancestral knowledge, and incorporates Aboriginal values and perspectives into the Manitoba curriculum. Students participate in monthly pipe ceremonies, and are invited to sweat lodges, naming ceremonies, and various traditional teaching ceremonies.

The school's curriculum is flexible and centred on the needs of students and the community—for example, programs address future careers of students as well as the shortage of Aboriginal people in various professional sectors. An entrepreneurship program (developed in partnership with the Martin Aboriginal Initiative, founded by former prime minister Paul Martin and his family) involves students in developing and running their own businesses. A medical careers internship has students intern directly with health professionals in patient care and operating rooms.

FIGURE 9.17 Sharing circles, language conferences, and family gatherings are all part of life at Children of the Earth High School. The school plans seasonal feasts, men's and women's retreats, and student–parent trips to gather traditional medicines.

Scott Collegiate

Scott Collegiate was started in the North Central neighbourhood of Regina. Although many people in the area face poverty and cultural dislocation, the school is trying to make a difference in students' lives.

Scott Collegiate is a community school for Grades 9 to 12. The school's vision is to nurture academic growth and promote self-development, healthy lifestyles, and cultural understanding.

The school year has been divided into quarters so that students can start school at flexible times; if students want to take extra credits each year, they can; a student who needs time to deal with an issue at home can do so without losing the whole school year. During the year, Kokum's Club (Grandmother's Club) involves students interacting with Elders in both formal and informal counselling sessions over tea.

FIGURE 9.18 Even as Scott Collegiate was planning for a move to a new building, students were participating in developing ideas for features the school would include. These students are in an entrepreneurship class.

The school also offers project-based learning. Students explore concepts and develop skills in long-term projects that they plan and carry out (for example, entrepreneurship and business design, photojournalism, hip hop, dinner theatre). Many projects aim to revitalize the community. The entrepreneurship program is part of the Martin Aboriginal Initiative.

Cultural Education

The programs you have read about so far all focus on culturally appropriate education. Rather than presenting European knowledge as the norm and ideal, these programs include and honour their Aboriginal cultures. Because First Nations, Métis, and Inuit Nations are diverse, so are the programs.

Cultural Programs

Here are more examples of culturally appropriate education programs:

- In the Kingsclear First Nation in New Brunswick, the Wulastukw Elementary School aims to help students develop positive attitudes toward the Malecite culture and toward themselves. The school has a Peer Helper Club that encourages conflict resolution, responsibility, and cooperation and communication skills.

- At the Acwsalcta School in Bella Coola, students from Kindergarten to Grade 12 study the British Columbia curriculum along with Nuxalk language, history, and the art of carving. The school intends to improve academic standards and access to technology, and create a timetable that allows students to move easily from one level to another. The school organizes events such as exchange trips to other First Nations and arts festivals highlighting the Nuxalk culture.

Teacher Training

There is a shortage of First Nations, Métis, and Inuit teachers. New teacher-training programs are addressing this need. A new program in Nunavut was designed with input from Inuit Elders and reflects a blend of Inuit and non-Inuit ways. It combines

- teaching in both the Inuit language and English

- written work in the Inuit language and/or English

- part-time distance learning

- classes in Rankin Inlet and Iqaluit

- in-person sessions with instructors twice yearly

The program allows students to complete their degrees without leaving Nunavut. The result is that more Nunavut schools will be staffed and run by Inuit, making a difference in how Inuit youth are educated, and enabling Inuit to reclaim control over their education.

FIGURE 9.19 Masters of Education Leadership graduates Peesee Pitsiulak-Stephens and Elisapee Elizabeth Nurrahaq Karetak stand with Dr. Fiona Walton of the University of Prince Edward Island (UPEI). The degree program was developed by the Nunavut Department of Education, UPEI, Nunavut Arctic College, and St. Francis Xavier University in Nova Scotia.

Remote and Distance Education

First Nations, Métis, and Inuit students enrolled in northern and remote areas of Canada face many challenges. Some students must cope with long daily bus rides or move hundreds of kilometres away from home simply to attend high school. Distance learning is one response to these challenges; some First Nations schools in northwestern Ontario offer secondary school courses through distance education linked to the high school in Sioux Lookout. However, while distances to attend high school can be a challenge, the distances are usually much greater for post-secondary education. An increasing number of programs are being offered remotely or online, connecting students virtually while allowing them to stay at home.

CRITICAL THINKING

Nunavut has become an early adopter of many technologies for teaching and learning in remote communities and among Internet-linked classrooms. What ways could you imagine new technologies supporting aspirations for education in the North?

Post-Secondary Education

Some challenges that First Nations, Métis, and Inuit students encounter in post-secondary institutions are shared by other students—geographic distance and lack of access to financial and other resources. However, the difference is that the barriers faced by First Nations, Métis, and Inuit students are the result of colonization, including oppression, marginalization, and forced assimilation.

Many post-secondary institutions are addressing these barriers. Two responses are on-site mentoring and access to technology (such as computers, the Internet). The University of Manitoba in Winnipeg offers a transition-year program. First Nations House at the University of Toronto offers support and referrals to First Nations, Métis, and Inuit students; the House also educates the wider university community. The University of British Columbia (UBC) established the First Nations House of Learning in 1987 for First Nations, Métis, and Inuit students. At UBC, the First Nations House uses the "Four Rs" (respect, relevance, reciprocity, and responsibility) to strengthen relationships, provide relevant curriculum, and respect First Nations, Métis, and Inuit beliefs, values, and aspirations.

FIGURE 9.20 Trent University in Peterborough has many programs available in the department of Indigenous Studies. Twice weekly through the school year, Elder Vern Douglas (standing, Cultural Advisor in the Department of Indigenous Studies) and the department host an "open tipi" at which Elder Vern Douglas might give a teaching or students lead a discussion. Sandra Lamouche and Lowell Yellowhorn (students in masters programs) participate.

Post-secondary programs that specifically address Aboriginal cultural identities can be found at Trent University and in the recent creation of the Research Chair of Métis Studies at the University of Ottawa.

First Nations communities have also developed their own post-secondary institutions—for example, First Nations Technical Institute on Tyendinaga Mohawk Territory (in Ontario), Six Nations Polytechnic in Ontario, Yellowquill College in Manitoba, and others.

Unique Teacher-Training Programs

There are a number of university programs across Canada preparing teachers to work with First Nations, Métis, and Inuit students. In addition to the Nunavut program described earlier, here are some examples:

- Toronto's York University offers the Indigenous Teacher Education Program (in Barrie) to prepare students to teach First Nations, Métis, and Inuit content to both Aboriginal and non-Aboriginal students in rural or urban environments.

- Queen's University has an On-Campus Aboriginal Teacher Education program as well as a Community-Based Teacher Education distance program with three main sites to serve Ontario—Seven Generations Education Institute (in Fort Frances), Kenjgewin Teg Educational Institute (on Manitoulin Island), and Six Nations Polytechnic (at Grand River). The programs specifically address the shortage of teachers at First Nations schools.

- Many Elders and Wisdom Keepers have trained to be Aboriginal language teachers in programs at such universities as Lakehead University in Thunder Bay.

THINKING IT THROUGH

1. Use Building Your Skills: Analyzing Issues (page 297) to develop an issue statement about Aboriginal students' access to education and to respond to this issue.

2. How are First Nations, Métis, and Inuit peoples using technology in education and for cultural revitalization? Examine the examples in this chapter and research to find one additional example to present to your class in a media release.

3. Research one college, university, or Aboriginal-run post-secondary education program that addresses the specific needs of Aboriginal students. Consider programs that are structured around First Nations, Métis, or Inuit values and beliefs.

©P

Rejuvenating Languages

Renewing education also means rejuvenating First Nations, Métis, and Inuit languages. Aboriginal peoples in what is now Canada spoke a wide variety of distinct languages before colonization, with each language reflecting the world views, beliefs, experiences, and environments of the speakers. However, some of these languages have become extinct, and others are in danger of dying.

In considering First Nations, Métis, and Inuit languages today, we will look at why they matter, why they are at risk, what their status is today, and what is being done to rejuvenate them.

Why Do Aboriginal Languages Matter?

A culture's shared language provides those using the language with a sense of belonging, identity, and continuity with their past. Language also provides a framework that, in part, guides one's values, behaviours, and attitudes, since it is an expression of that culture. For First Nations, Métis, and Inuit cultures, the deep spiritual connection to one's environment and one's responsibilities to family and the natural world are expressed in their distinct languages.

Similar to how Francophones were not allowed to use their language (under the 1912 Ontario Regulation 17 on French Schools), Aboriginal languages were banned in most residential schools. (The Ontario government's Regulation 17 was issued in 1912, amended in 1913, and repealed in 1927; it severely limited the use of the French language by students in schools.) Years later, the 1996 Royal Commission on Aboriginal Peoples recognized the importance of Aboriginal languages:

The threat of their languages disappearing means that Aboriginal people's distinctive world view, the wisdom of their ancestors and their ways of being human could vanish as well. Language protection requires maintaining or increasing the number of fluent speakers [and] using the language as a medium of communication in everyday life—especially in the family.

FIGURE 9.21 Amos Key Jr. is the Director of First Nations Languages at the Woodland Cultural Centre at Six Nations/Brantford, Ontario. He says that students who learn their own Aboriginal languages "learn about their own traditions and customs...their First Nations emotional, moral, artistic, civil, and social intelligences and their own spirituality and faith, all of which are the hallmarks of First Nations civilizations in this country." He says the languages were taken away but we too have a human and civil right and moral compass in this country to become bilingual. The Immersion/Bilingual Private School Board he helped establish is called Gaweni:yo, in the Cayuga language meaning "the Beautiful Words," and has grades from Kindergarten to Grade 12.

CRITICAL THINKING

Why might a child be prevented from using his or her original language in school? Why do you think this was the case for the French language? What would be the impact for you if you could not speak, hear, or read your original language all day?

VOICES OF THE PEOPLES

Our language is a gift from the Creator that we carry for our children; our language carries the knowledge of this land; our language carries our knowledge of who we are; our language carries our future.

—*Blue Quills First Nations College*

©P

Web Connect • • • • • • • • • • •

To learn more about Aboriginal languages, visit our website.

FIGURE 9.22 This student is learning Cree.

CRITICAL THINKING

Note that there are variations in how languages and their dialects are described. For example, the territory of Nunavut considers Inuinnaqtun a separate language and it is spoken by Inuvialuit. It is one of Nunavut's four official languages, along with Inuktitut, French, and English. Michif can be distinguished as western or eastern Michif.

Why Are Aboriginal Languages at Risk?

Many factors have contributed to the severe decline of once-thriving First Nations, Métis, and Inuit languages, the first of which is colonization.

Some languages became extinct in a relatively short time after contact when entire cultures were decimated as a result of disease, warfare, and/or genocide. The Beothuk language is one example.

As assimilation strategies and policies in Canada began to take shape, languages were targeted—for example, in the residential school system.

There are many other factors that contribute to declines:

- English and French dominate mainstream culture, media, school systems, and workplaces. Their widespread use and influence limit the use and influence of Aboriginal languages.

- More Aboriginal people are living in urban areas where it is more difficult to learn, use, and pass on their original languages.

- Often, a family bringing together two languages will speak mainly (or only) the dominant mainstream language at home.

- Parents and grandparents forbidden to speak their languages at residential schools are unable to pass on these languages.

- Older family members have sometimes decided not to teach children their ancestral language for fear that their children will not succeed in mainstream society.

- Native language programs are often under-funded in schools and there are often systemic obstacles to establishing such programs.

Aboriginal Languages Today

According to Statistics Canada, in 2001, approximately 235 000 people spoke Aboriginal languages in Canada, or about 24 percent of those who identified themselves as Aboriginal people. However, many First Nations, Métis, and Inuit organizations believe that this figure underestimates the actual number. Regardless of the exact number, the variety among First Nations, Métis, and Inuit languages—and their resilience in the face of adversity—are amazing.

Today, there are over 50 Aboriginal languages in use, and they are often divided into family groups of languages. The page opposite shows a summary overview from a 2010 description by scholars at the University of Calgary.

Language Family	Example Languages	Number Fluent in Canada	Notes
Algonquian	Cree	117 000	The most widely spoken Aboriginal languages in Canada are Cree and Ojibwe. Cree dialects are Plains, Swampy, Woods, Moose, At(t)ikamek(w), Montagnais, and Naskapi Innu. Ojibwe dialects are Odawa, Saulteau(x), Ojibwa/Chippewa, Algonquin, and Severn/Oji-Cree.
	Ojibwe/Anishinaabemowin	47 000	
	Mi'kmaq	8000	
	Blackfoot	3000	
	Malecite–Passamaquoddy	750	
Eskimo–Aleut	Inuktitut	34 000	Inuktitut dialects are used from the northwestern part of the Northwest Territories (Inuvialuit) to northern Labrador. About two thirds of Inuit people speak Inuktitut.
Athabaskan	Dene Suline/Chipewyan	15 000	There are 16 distinct Athabaskan languages within Canada alone—from the Yukon and British Columbia, east to Manitoba. While Dene is spoken by many people, fewer than 5 speak Hän and only 2 speak Tagish.
	Slave(y), including Hare	3850	
	Dogrib	1900	
	Tsúut'ína/Sarcee	40	
Siouan	Yankton & Santee/Dakota	400	In Canada, the Siouan languages are Yankton, which is spoken primarily in northern Saskatchewan; Santee, in southern Manitoba; Stoney, in Alberta; Assiniboine, in southeastern Saskatchewan; and Teton, in southern Saskatchewan. Teton/Lak(h)ota is spoken by about 6000 people in the U.S. and 25 in Canada.
	Stoney/Nakoda	1500	
	Assiniboine/Nakota	34	
Salish	Secwepemctsín/Shuswap	250	There are 10 Salish family languages, all centred in British Columbia. The total number of speakers for the language family is less than 2400.
	Okanagan/Nsilxcín	250	
	Squamish/Sḵwx̱wú7mesh	10	
Tsimshianic	Nass-Gitxsan	1400	Tsimshinaic languages are spoken in northwestern British Columbia. Nass-Gitxsan includes Gitxsan and Nisg̱a'a speakers.
	Tsimshian	431	
Iroquoian	Mohawk	< 2000	Mohawk is spoken by about equal numbers in Canada and the U.S. The Iroquoian languages are Mohawk, Oneida, Cayuga, Onondaga, Seneca, and Tuscarora.
	Oneida	150	
	Cayuga	50	
Wakashan	Nuu-chah-nulth/Nootka	100	Five Wakashan languages are spoken on Vancouver Island and on the British Columbia mainland coast.
	Kwakw'ala/Kwakiutl	150	
	X̱aad Kil/Haida	35	Some languages do not fall into language families, but are called isolates. One isolate is X̱aad Kil, spoken in Haida Gwaii (the Queen Charlotte Islands). Another isolate is Ktunaxa, which is spoken in the Rockies in southeastern British Columbia.
	Ktunaxa/Kutenai–Kinbasket	26	
	Michif	1000	Michif is described as a contact language. There are different variations of Michif spoken by Métis people in Ontario, northern Canada, and the Canadian Prairies (and extending to Montana and North Dakota).

Chart adapted from "Aboriginal languages of Canada" by Eung-Do Cook & Darin Flynn in *Contemporary linguistic analysis: An introduction,* 6th ed.

Language Rejuvenation Efforts

Web Connect • • • • • • • • • • • •

To hear the national anthem sung in Cree, visit our website.

Although there are signs that many Aboriginal languages are at risk of dying out in the near future, this information has also sparked many efforts to save languages and keep them alive and vibrant.

Language Rejuvenation Through Policy

The 1996 Royal Commission on Aboriginal Peoples put forth recommendations that could help First Nations, Métis, and Inuit languages endure.

Since 1996, many individuals and organizations have followed up on the Royal Commission's recommendations regarding language.

One such project is First Voices, which you will read about shortly. Others include the celebration of National Aboriginal Languages Day, March 31. Others are focused in communities—such as the Mohawk language program for adults being run by Tsi Tyonnheht Onkwawenna Language Circle in the Tyendinaga Mohawk Territory.

Another initiative (through the Michif Language Project and the Gabriel Dumont Institute) arises from the fact that, in 1991, only one percent of people who identified themselves as Métis could speak Michif, and many of these speakers were elderly and lived in remote areas. In 2000, the Métis National Council initiated a Michif revival strategy. The project identifies and links Michif speakers.

VOICES OF THE PEOPLES

Tomson Highway is a renowned writer, playwright, and musician from the Brochet Reserve in Manitoba. He explains that his creative writing comes to him in Cree:

That's the world I come from. My parents didn't speak English. ...My older brothers and sisters didn't. I come from a part of the world that's so isolated that English has only arrived with the last generation. You write about what you know best, which in my case, is my community. So my characters all speak Cree in my head, and the biggest challenge is the simultaneous translation.

FIGURE 9.23 Tomson Highway describes English as an intellectual language, French as an emotional language, and Cree as a visceral language: "When you speak Cree, you laugh all the time." In 2008, he immersed himself in Spanish, to learn yet another language.

©P

Language Rejuvenation in Schools

Earlier in this chapter, you read about Cree, Ojibwe, and Nuxalk language classes. There are an increasing number of Aboriginal language programs for students. For English-speaking Aboriginal students in Ontario schools, Aboriginal languages have the same status as French; Aboriginal students can study Aboriginal languages instead of French.

Language immersion programs have now been established in many Canadian communities. The Mohawk community of Kahnawake in Québec introduced the first Indigenous language immersion programs in the 1970s.

Many on-reserve schools (such as Quinte Mohawk School) also teach the community's original language throughout all grades. As well, some public school boards are now offering Aboriginal language courses. As a result, in Tyendinaga Territory, Mohawk classes are provided in both the on-reserve elementary school and the off-reserve high school.

One teacher leading in language education is Muriel Sawyer. Muriel Sawyer is a tireless teacher and vice-principal at Nbisiing Secondary School in North Bay. She teaches Ojibwe language and culture and is a language keeper for the Nipissing dialect of Ojibwe. She has been honoured with the Anishinabek Nation Lifetime Achievement Award and the Prime Minister's Award for Teaching Excellence.

FIGURE 9.24 Muriel Sawyer (at far right) is teaching by storytelling in Ojibwe while making bannock.

VOICES OF THE PEOPLES

Isadore Toulouse is a member of the Wikwemikong First Nation and a leading Ontario educator. He teaches at Sutton High School and his classes include students from the Chippewas of Georgina Island First Nation on Lake Simcoe. He says:

We as Anishinaabe are the most influential people to provide educational development for our future generations. We can accomplish this through spirituality and communicating in our language.

—Isadore Toulouse, Report of the Royal Commission on Aboriginal Peoples, 1996

FIGURE 9.25 Isadore Toulouse earned a degree at Trent University, has taught in both Toronto District and York Region District School Boards, studied and now teaches in the Native Languages Instructor Program at Lakehead University, and has travelled to study Indigenous languages in New Zealand, Australia, and Hawaii.

Many communities promote using their original languages beyond classrooms—in families, workplaces, and beyond. In general,

- Older members (often the only fluent speakers) are vital to youth programs.

- Having more speakers and a higher proportion of speakers ensures a greater language retention rate.

- Geography typically influences language retention rates. The more isolated a community is from dominantly English- or French-speaking towns and cities, the more vibrant a language is.

One example is the Arctic, in which there are many isolated communities where European settlement was slower to come and very few people come to settle in general. The Arctic has high language retention rates.

In Wemotaci, Manawan, and Opitciwan, in Québec, over 90 percent of people speak Atikamekw. The communities work hard to maintain Atikamekw and keep it relevant. Rather than borrow from French or English, Atikamekw speakers have developed words for new needs:

English Term	Atikamekw Term	Literal Translation of Atikamekw Term
automobile	ickote otapan	an object that travels over earth
computer	kinokepitcikan	a machine with a huge memory
Internet	pa mikicikwe pitcikan	apparatus that allows one to communicate through time and space

COMMUNITY CLOSE-UP

Mashteuiatsh

The Innu-Montagnais community of Mashteuiatsh (in Québec) has developed many creative ways to encourage and support the use of its original language, Innu. Language courses are offered for community members in the schools. More specifically, the Amishk elementary school offers an Innu language immersion program for preschoolers and Grade 1 students. Language courses are offered to all grades as schooling continues. As a result of these courses, many Innu language resources, such as dictionaries and CDs, are now being produced.

FIGURE 9.26 All of the street names in Mashteuiatsh and most building names are in Innu.

©P

Language Rejuvenation Through Media and Technology

Recently, television, radio, newspapers, magazines, and the Internet have also taken up language rejuvenation and cultural revitalization. For example, the Aboriginal Peoples Television Network (APTN) has programming in Aboriginal languages, French, and English. APTN provides Aboriginal language speakers with content in their own languages and helps Canadians learn about diverse Aboriginal cultures.

Many Nations across Canada have their own local radio stations, many of which offer some programming in Aboriginal languages. The same is true of community newspapers. The *Anishinabek News* regularly publishes articles about the resurgence of Anishinaabemowin—the language—and lessons from such respected teachers as Shirley Williams from Curve Lake First Nation.

Many First Nations, Métis, and Inuit people and communities are also making use of computer and Internet technology to support, share, and maintain ancestral languages. Some websites are in traditional languages, syllabic keys are now available for languages such as Inuktitut and Cree, and online audio dictionaries are being created. The Mi'gmaq-Mi'kmaq online talking dictionary includes over 6000 words pronounced by three different speakers. First Voices is another example: this interactive website offers a variety of tools and services to support First Nations, Métis, and Inuit people who are committed to archiving and teaching languages.

FIGURE 9.27 In January 2010, for the first time ever, Inuit commentators (Annie Ford and Charlie Panigoniak) did live TV coverage of a hockey game. Mary Simon of the Inuit Tapiriit Kanatami applauded the Inuit language coverage of the Ottawa Senators/Montréal Canadiens game as another milestone in the use of Inuktitut.

Web Connect • • • • • • • • • • • • •

To learn more about First Voices, visit our website.

THINKING IT THROUGH

1. Refer to the quotation from Blue Quills First Nations College on page 307. Explain in your own words why preserving First Nations, Métis, and Inuit languages matters.

2. Research a current example of how a First Nations, Métis, or Inuk person or community is using an Aboriginal language. In a group, share examples.

3. Research a current example of a person or organization promoting the retention of one or more Aboriginal languages through media, teaching, or other activities.

CRITICAL THINKING

Think about examples you have read about or know yourself that illustrate these two core beliefs from Norway House Cree Nation. How do you view education in your life? in your family? in your community?

CRITICAL THINKING

The Seven Generations Educational Institute has many programs including language camps and day and evening high-school credit courses. It offers a choice of locations, as well as guidance and support services to students and families. How do such programs relate to the Seven Generations teaching?

Lifelong Learning and Community Renewal

Some people think of "education" and "learning" as meaning "school," and school ending with graduation from high school or a post-secondary program. However, education and learning can better be defined as a lifelong process—beginning in infancy and continuing well into old age.

First Nations, Métis, and Inuit peoples view education broadly—as lifelong and intergenerational. They also value education highly. In the study noted at left, in interviews with over 2500 First Nations, Métis, and Inuit people who live in cities, most considered education a top priority.

Another example is Norway House Cree Nation in Manitoba, which runs several educational programs for community members of all ages and abilities. The Norway House Education, Training, and Culture Division has six core beliefs including learning is a lifelong process and everyone has skills and expertise to share.

Community Renewal

Earlier in this chapter, you read about education as the "new buffalo" and the "new whale"—education as a sustaining community resource. The context of community is very important to note: education is not only for the individual but also for the community, both present and future.

According to many traditional beliefs, the purpose of lifelong learning is to maintain, strengthen, and sustain the interconnectedness of relationships to the land, the community, and future generations. Learning is very social, and it nurtures relationships in the family and the community. Learning about ancestral languages, cultures, and histories benefits both individuals and their communities. As well, each new generation has a responsibility to future generations.

For many First Nations, Métis, and Inuit peoples, lifelong learning in Canada today means taking in both Aboriginal and non-Aboriginal knowledge and experiences. First Nations, Métis, and Inuit peoples want their children to receive education that will enable them to live in Canada today with its diverse cultural heritages as responsible, active, and informed participants. But they still want to ensure that children and youth learn the traditional knowledge they need to develop strong personal and cultural identities and to succeed in their own societies.

One example of Aboriginal initiatives for renewing education is Seven Generations Educational Institute. In 1985, 10 First Nations of the Rainy Lake Tribal Area (Big Grassy, Big Island, Couchiching, Lac La Croix, Naicatchewenin, Nicickousemenecaning, Ojibways of the Onigaming, Rainy River, Seine River, and Mitaanjigaming First Nations) created the Rainy Lake Ojibway Education Authority. In 1999, the education authority changed its name to Seven Generations Educational Institute. The institute provides educational instruction at secondary, post-secondary, and vocational levels while supporting cultural values and language.

Culture-Based Learning

For First Nations, Métis, and Inuit peoples, education can take place in many settings—at home, in a classroom, on the land, and in the community. Each way of learning is valid. What links these different ways and makes them a powerful force for growth and change is their focus on cultural content and a culturally appropriate framework for transmitting knowledge. However, one significant factor is access to learning opportunities.

Access

Although education is highly valued, access is not equitable. For example, the 2010 Environics study of First Nations, Métis, and Inuit people living in Canadian cities reported that money was the top barrier for 36 percent of those planning to attend a university or college, and for 45 percent already attending.

However, leaders are working toward more equitable access and greater opportunities that address both personal and community aspirations. Schools such as Children of the Earth School are addressing shortages in particular careers. Teaching programs are training more educators. A Queen's University program was created exclusively for First Nations, Métis, and Inuit people interested in becoming teachers. It allows those without a post-secondary degree to enter the program; by equating "life knowledge" with "book/credential knowledge," the program allows qualified candidates who have faced barriers in accessing higher education to share their knowledge and become teachers.

VOICES OF THE PEOPLES

Education is essential for all Métis and for the Métis Nation...the way to move our people economically forward as [well as] providing the building blocks for a good life, on all levels, spiritually, physically, and economically.

We have started to work with the Ministry of Education, with school boards, schools, teachers, to make sure that they are teaching accurate and culturally relevant education that builds both essential skills and will assist Métis to live a good life.

[We] are also working with the Ministry of Training, Colleges and Universities, as well as with individual colleges and universities throughout the province. ...This work isn't just to build a productive Métis workforce; it is to improve the knowledge of all Ontarians.

—*France Picotte, chair of the Provisional Council of the Métis Nation of Ontario*

FIGURE 9.28 Outdoor and survival education programs teach cultural knowledge and are opportunities to strengthen youth–Elder relationships, use ancestral languages, and increase both community and individual pride. Three examples are Haa'uukmin Tribal Park, Waskaganish Cree Nation, and the Spring Camp for senior students at Jonah Amitnaaq Secondary School (above). During the Spring Camp near Nuvu'tuaq (The Point), just outside Baker Lake, Nunavut, the students gather around to hear stories from Elders.

In "Our Language, Our Selves," Alexina Kublu (a teacher of Inuktitut) and Mick Mallon write:

For an Inuk like Kublu, language and culture are inextricably entwined in the perception of who she is, to herself and to others. In the eyes of older people in the community, she is a child who has tapped into the mysterious powers of the qallunaat (white people), but who still depends on her Elders for so many answers about daily life in the past.

To her colleagues at the college where Kublu works, she is, we hope, an equal, with a professional competence extending beyond her particular role as instructor of interpretation and translation. To her students, she is a role model, one who has attained a balance between two worlds.

Trent University has a range of programs that strengthen education for First Nations, Métis, and Inuit students, including foundation programs, an Indigenous Studies Program for Aboriginal and non-Aboriginal students, and an Indigenous Studies Ph.D. program (started in 1999 and mentioned earlier in this chapter).

Lifelong Learning and Role Models

As individuals, many First Nations, Métis, and Inuit people are leading by example and mentoring others. A language teacher can be both a lifelong learner and a role model while helping to maintain an ancestral language. How does each individual described on these pages and throughout this chapter demonstrate lifelong learning and also serve as a role model?

Collette Bourgonje

In her hometown of Saskatoon, Collette Bourgonje is a teacher, an outstanding athlete, and a role model. As a teacher, she promotes active living by taking students of all abilities skiing. As an athlete, since 1988, she has been winning medals in the Paralympic Games in wheelchair athletics and more recently in sit-skiing. Prior to a car accident in 1980, Collette Bourgonje had been a cross-country runner at the national level. At the 2010 Paralympics in Vancouver and Whistler, she won silver and bronze medals and was awarded the prestigious Whang Youn Dai Adversity Award, which is given to only one male and one female athlete in each Paralympic Games. Winners exemplify the values of the Games—determination, inspiration, courage, and equality.

FIGURE 9.29 Like her ancestor, Métis leader Gabriel Dumont, teacher and athlete Collette Bourgonje inspires those she meets. This photograph shows Collette Bourgonje winning at the 2010 Winter Paralympics.

©P

Eileen Antone

Eileen M. Antone, also named Ka li wi suks (she who gathers information), is a member of the Oneida of the Thames First Nation and is very active in both her community and the University of Toronto. She is an associate professor at the Ontario Institute for Studies in Education at the university and director of the university's Aboriginal Studies Program.

Eileen is a member of the Wahahi:o Iroquois Drumming and Singing Group, and she is a member of the Taam Kaadinakiijik Elders' Council at the Native Canadian Centre of Toronto. She has been a board member for organizations such as Native Child and Family Services.

Dr. Antone works to ensure Aboriginal perspectives are heard, and she works to learn about and preserve Aboriginal knowledge and traditional ways of being. She believes that Aboriginal education must include Aboriginal identity, culture, and language. Thus, education will promote a sense of purpose that will lead to achievement.

Larry Loyie

Larry Loyie was born in Slave Lake, a small town in northern Alberta, and lived a traditional Cree life as a child. His grandparents taught him how to survive in the bush and how to respect the plants and animals the family depended upon. However, at age nine, Larry was forced to attend residential school at St. Bernard Mission, in Grouard, Alberta. He left school at age 13, joined the Canadian Armed Forces at age 20, and spent many years working in fishing and logging.

After visiting a public library and finding very few books written by First Nations writers, Larry Loyie decided to write some himself. At the age of 55, he went back to school to learn English grammar and typing. Since then, he has written books, interviewed for radio documentaries, and co-edited an anthology. His books attempt to preserve Cree culture and counter inaccuracies he has found in other books.

CRITICAL THINKING

North of the Arctic Circle, the community of Clyde River, Nunavut, is home to a new cultural school called Piqqusilirivvik ("a place that has those things important to us"), which is modelled on a "folk school" in Greenland. In Clyde River and with two satellite communities, Piqqusilirivvik is designed to focus on teaching land-based skills and preserving Inuit cultural knowledge. Elders experienced in land-based skills will teach students, who will then return to their home communities throughout Nunavut to share their knowledge. In what ways do role models educate?

FIGURE 9.30 Larry Loyie's books include *Goodbye Buffalo Bay* (which he holds above—about his teen years), *As Long as the Rivers Flow*, *The Moon Speaks Cree*, *When the Spirits Dance*, and *The Gathering Tree*.

©P

Young Aspirations and Voices of Elders

*As a student at Scott Collegiate in Regina, **Rebecca Pratt** participated in a Martin Aboriginal Initiative that brought members of the local Chamber of Commerce to the school.*

I like anything business related… I think it's really good to give you…a taste of what business is all about… I think every school should have an entrepreneurship program… I would actually like to own my own business. I want to get into a kind of partnership with bead making, and still go to University and take Fine Arts.

Karihwakeron Tim Thompson *(former president of First Nations Technical Institute) answers the question "Why should we define success?" with the following:*

because we should, because we can, because someone else will if we don't.

Jordin Tootoo*, an NHL player, says:*

It's always good to be different. Being the first [Inuk] player to play in the National Hockey League was a goal of mine. And I don't think any kid should be shy of being different from anyone else. It sets the tone for a lot of different things.

James Bartleman *says:*

After more than three decades in the Foreign Service I became an expert in at least a dozen specialties. The real lesson was that there was so much to learn from the people around me.

France Picotte *is fluent in Michif, English, and French. She was the Timmins Métis Community Council president, then Métis Nation of Ontario vice-chair, before becoming the MNO chair. However, she notes that her position with MNO has little to do with her professional background; she trained as a medical laboratory technician:*

It was a learning experience. It was a time when I thought to myself: I have to do what I need to do, what I want to do and what needs to be done… [Success lies in] having confidence in who you are, confidence in your ability and not being stopped at not knowing something. You have to ask, you have to know and you have to move forward.

Tracy Boese *was a Métis student considering her future. She applied for a Métis Nation of Ontario bursary and has since finished her program:*

All I wanted to do was get a higher education. I pondered for years on what my options were and what I actually was interested in. One day I looked at what I enjoyed most, the outdoors, and decided to find a program that would get me closer to nature. I had a knack for science and a connection with the natural world. The Environmental Technician program at Niagara College seemed to be the perfect fit… It is never too late to start on the path of your dreams; there is always something out there that will make sure your path is clear before you start on your new journey.

1. Create a list of five to ten issues raised in the above quotations. Choose one to discuss with a partner, research independently, and then discuss your findings with your partner.

Jennifer Podemski was born and raised in Toronto, and has an Israeli-born father and a Saulteaux mother. She is an award-winning actress in film, television, and theatre, and co-founder of Big Soul Productions. She now runs Redcloud Studios.

Jennifer is committed to strengthening Aboriginal visibility in the film and television industry, behind the scenes and in front of the camera. Redcloud Studios is breaking down barriers and paving the way for the future generation of media makers.

As a child, Jennifer says that she often denied her Aboriginal ancestry because she was the only Aboriginal kid in school. Her family struggled with alcoholism, and this problem became a source of shame for her, so she did her best to blend in. Her experience ultimately became the fuel to change things for Aboriginal youth.

Jennifer Podemski hopes that her work with youth will help them overcome the barriers they face in developing both skills and identity.

Nothing I do seems worth it if I can't use what I know and pass it on to youth. That's what inspired me to live my dream: learning from people who I related to and who inspired me. I have had so many wonderful teachers, and I believe it is my job to give back.

FIGURE 9.31 Jennifer Podemski is best known for roles in Bruce McDonald's film *Dance Me Outside*, CBC's *The Rez*, and *Riverdale*. She won Best Actress awards at the Dreamspeakers Aboriginal Film Festival and the American Indian Film Festival. Big Soul Productions has produced award-winning film and television programs including *The Seventh Generation* and *Moccasin Flats*. Growing up, she trained extensively in drama and dance.

THINKING IT THROUGH

1. Describe and explain the goals and functions of outdoor schools and other community-based education programs for Aboriginal students.

2. Identify, research, and create a detailed profile of a First Nations, Métis, or Inuk person who could serve as a role model to youth.

Conclusion

In this chapter, you learned how First Nations, Métis, and Inuit peoples are making changes to education and about the challenges they have faced. You have learned about efforts to reclaim education and renew it for First Nations, Métis, and Inuit peoples in order to fulfil their aspirations. Activities in this chapter have helped you to analyze issues, research role models and educational opportunities, and more.

CRITICAL THINKING

In what ways are education and lifetime learning the "new buffalo" or "new whale" for First Nations, Métis, and Inuit peoples?

1. If your school were to include ancestral knowledge and traditional ways of life of First Nations, Métis, and Inuit peoples in its curriculum, what would that curriculum look like? In a small group, create a plan for your school that includes First Nations, Métis, and Inuit peoples in meaningful ways. Using words and images, create a poster or a three-panel display that showcases and explains your plan.

FIGURE 9.32 What experiences have you had with learning languages? Describe some of your goals, challenges, and accomplishments.

2. With a partner, research post-secondary institutions to find three specific examples of programs or institutions that interest you. Evaluate each for how inclusive and welcoming to First Nations, Métis, and Inuit students it seems to you. Create a list of criteria and evaluate each program or institution against your list. Present your findings aloud or summarize them in writing.

3. Choose one issue raised in this chapter. Using the model for analyzing issues in Building Your Skills, first state the issue clearly and then create a list of comments that relate to the issue. Ask for input from other students to see if their perspectives bring additional considerations. Then write an opinion piece on the issue that clearly demonstrates your final opinion on the topic. Build your argument using the comment list and provide the reasons for your opinion.

4. Consider your future goals and aspirations. What would you really like to do in your life? How do you picture your life in five or ten years? What relationships will you have? What career path will you follow? Will you be an employee, a self-employed business owner, or will you have some other role in life? Create an art piece, poem, or short story that demonstrates your aspirations. Consider what your gifts are in life and how you can move toward meeting your goals.

5. On page 295, access to post-secondary education is described as critical to First Nations, Métis, and Inuit people but also to the future of Canadian society. How can education benefit individuals, communities, Nations, and Canadian society as a whole? Discuss your ideas in a group and develop at least one example (real or hypothetical) that illustrates your ideas. Present your group's ideas and example(s) to your class.

Unit 4 Rich Performance Tasks

Choose one or more of the following tasks:

Present a Profile

1. Research one First Nations, Métis, or Inuk person to present in a profile.

   a) Identify and research (through the Internet, books, magazines, or personal interviews) one First Nations, Métis, or Inuk person connected to the big ideas of education, lifelong learning, and language in this unit.

   b) In your research, consider this person's educational experiences, lifelong learning, challenges, achievements, contributions, and aspirations. How is this person a role model? How does he or she contribute to the rejuvenation of his or her community? What advice does this person offer to the youth of today?

   c) Create a detailed profile that presents your information to your classmates in text and visuals.

Propose a Program

2. Consider Aboriginal-specific programming in order to present one idea in a letter or presentation.

   a) Find out (through Ministry of Education documents or school board information) what options could be offered to Aboriginal students in urban settings.

   b) Find examples of programs in urban schools that are created for Aboriginal students—for example, urban Aboriginal alternative programs, Aboriginal resource rooms in schools, teaching lodges in schools, Native Studies programs in schools, Aboriginal language courses, or culture camps.

   c) Consider the benefits of these programs, their goals, and how effective they are for urban Aboriginal youth.

   d) Brainstorm a list of ideas for programs that you could imagine being created.

   e) Choose one idea that you believe addresses the physical, emotion, intellectual, and spiritual needs of Aboriginal youth.

   f) In a letter or taped presentation directed to a decision-maker in education (such as the director of education in a school board or the Ministry of Education), propose, outline, and support your program idea.

FIGURE 9.33 Alex Jacobs (seen here with former Assembly of First Nations National Chief Phil Fontaine) is both a lifelong learner and role model.

Write an Essay on Funding

3. Research the issue of funding equity for federally funded First Nations schools in order to write an essay on the topic.

   a) Gather information from sources such as the Assembly of First Nations, the Chiefs of Ontario, and the federal government of Canada.

   b) Once you have a basic understanding of the information, write an issue statement using the model in Building Your Skills: Analyzing Issues (on page 297).

   c) Research further to gather facts and opinions related to the issue and write them on an issue chart, using the model on page 297. Consider the various viewpoints in the information you find. What shared understandings and differences of opinion do you see?

   d) Based on your research, develop a thesis statement for an essay that clearly states *your* opinion on the issue.

   e) Create an outline for a five-paragraph essay on this issue in which you state and defend your position.

   f) Write a draft of your essay, and either submit it to your teacher or show it to a partner for feedback.

   g) Based on feedback, create a final draft of your essay.

CALL TO ACTION

Think about the journey you have taken throughout this course, what you have learned, and how you feel about what you have learned. How has it changed you and your understanding of the beliefs, values, and aspirations of First Nations, Métis, and Inuit peoples?

Increasing your knowledge and understanding is a big step. Your understanding has an impact not only on you but also on others, and it can change how you live your life. You can, for example, pass your understanding on to others and help develop a common long-term vision that is respectful of the perspectives and experiences of First Nations, Métis, and Inuit peoples in Canada.

Based on your understanding, how can you move toward a shared vision and take action? As students, as citizens, and as future leaders, you can take action. For example, you might start by participating in events that raise awareness, in letter-writing campaigns, or in a book drive. What can you do to help bring about one local concrete change?

What are your visions of the future? What are your aspirations? What do you hope for—for yourself and for society? Plains Cree lawyer Don Worme outlines his aspirations and gives a call to action.

For youth—whether they are First Nations, Métis, Inuit, green, purple, I don't care— my aspirations for them are to be contributing and productive and happy members of a society, a society that is accommodating, a society that is compassionate, and a society that is, above all, fair and just. We don't have that right now. Let's acknowledge it. But that's an aspiration. That's what I would hope for all peoples.

If you see something wrong, then do something about it or say something, and if you can do more than simply saying something, then you must do it. That's an obligation.

As you finish reading this book, ask yourself and your classmates:

- What part or role do you see yourself playing in moving toward reconciliation and building more just, more equitable relationships between Aboriginal peoples and Canadian society as a whole?

- How can you speak out and take positive action?

Aaron Paquette (whose heritage is Cree, Cherokee, and Norwegian) has called this painting *Transformation*. What does this artwork and its title suggest to you?

appropriate to take or make use of an object, idea, or specific knowledge that is not yours, without authority or right (pronounced differently as a verb)

aspiration a desire to achieve something; aspirations determine what we believe is possible for us and our community to do in the future

assimilate to absorb one group of people into another by causing them to adopt the customs, beliefs, culture, and attitudes of the majority group

attitude the way a person views something or tends to behave toward it; based on beliefs

autonomy freedom to determine one's own actions and behaviour

band the legal and administrative unit of governance for a First Nation, as defined by the federal government. The functioning of a band is controlled by the Indian Act.

belief what a person accepts as true or real, usually with an emotional or spiritual sense of certainty

bias a prejudice or predisposition to view something in a certain way

blood quantum a way to describe the degree of ancestry for an individual of a specific racial or ethnic group; based on the ancestry of parents

caricature a picture or description that comically exaggerates the peculiarities or defects of persons or things

cede to yield or formally surrender

colonialism a relationship between two peoples in which one takes over the other's land and imposes traditions

commodity an article of trade or commerce

community a group of people organized around common values and linked together by common histories, social and political interests, and/or geography

confederacy an organization of First Nations linked together for economic, political, or military purposes; similar to a confederation of countries, states, or provinces

consensus the process and the outcome of reaching an agreement through respectful discussion toward a shared goal.

creation stories accounts or series of accounts that tell about the beginnings of time, the structure of the earth and the universe, and the establishment of the social order

culture the way of life for a people that includes their values,

beliefs, knowledge, symbols, traditions, and history and is transmitted from generation to generation

eco-cultural tourism responsible and sustainable travel to natural areas and places of cultural interest

ecological concerns pollution, displacement of species, soil erosion, loss of natural habitats caused by industrial growth and development

diaspora the dispersion of a people; from the Greek word for "scatter"

Elder a person who has gained significant wisdom and understanding of Aboriginal history, traditional teachings, ceremonies, and healing practices. Elders are recognized by their communities, who have acknowledged their wisdom and granted them permission to pass on knowledges and give guidance.

faithkeeper a person responsible for learning ceremonies, songs, and stories from their community. A faithkeeper maintains these teachings by ensuring that all aspects of ceremonies are followed according to protocol. Faithkeepers are expected to continue learning and to share what they learn.

geocultural zone an area of land that has common characteristics in the physical environment that makes it distinct from other environments

governance a system of managing a group's day-to-day and long-term affairs

Indigenous traditional knowledge the long-standing, local, unique understanding that guides the inhabitants' relationships with their environment and with all beings

industrial school a school that concentrates on teaching manual skills such as sewing, carpentry, or farming

industrialization the increased development of industry such as large-scale manufacturing, forestry, or mining

interconnectedness having mutual relationships among members of a group. These include spiritual, emotional, physical, and intellectual connections, as well as relationships with the natural world and the concept of reciprocity.

Inuk the singular form of Inuit. *Inuit* means "the people."

jurisdiction formal recognition of a peoples' right to make decisions, administer control, and enforce laws

justice system the network of roles, processes, and organizations of policing, courts, and correctional services—including, for example, police, lawyers, judges, hearings, courts, and prisons

kinship family relationships

market economy a system in which businesses and consumers decide what they will produce and purchase; individuals acquire wealth based on their entrepreneurial spirit

matrilineal based on kinship with the mother; the female line in a family tree

Mi'kmaw the singular form of Mi'kmaq. The Mi'kmaq are a First Nations people in what is now Nova Scotia, New Brunswick, Prince Edward Island, the Gaspé region of Québec, and New England. The name *Mi'kmaq* is preferred over the English term *Micmac*.

mixed economy an economy in which income derives from a variety of sources, including private enterprise, government assistance or subsidies, and activities such as hunting and fishing (which provide food and other materials)

nationalism the belief that a people who share a common language, history, and culture constitute an independent nation

oral tradition a way of remembering the past through stories and spoken explanation, rather than in writing; objects to aid memory can also be used

patriate the process of returning back to the home country; in this case indicating the return of control over the Constitution to Canada

patrilineal based on kinship with the father; the male line in a family tree

perspective a way of making sense of an issue or topic; perspective also reflects one's beliefs, values, attitudes, and world view

pipe carrier someone who walks a good path and has been chosen to take on the critical and laborious responsibility of caring for a specific pipe used in certain ceremonies

point of view a personal or collective expression of opinion on a particular issue or topic; reflects one's beliefs, values, attitudes, and world view

protocol established rules for respectful behaviour

racial profiling the controversial practice of using a person's race as a key factor in identifying how and when to enforce laws and investigate alleged crimes

repatriate to return a person, cultural object, or piece of art back to its home, place of origin, or rightful owner

resilient to be able to recover from adversity or setback

restorative justice an approach to justice in which offenders are encouraged to take responsibility for their actions and to help restore harmony to the community through mediation, compensation, or other actions

sacred regarded with reverence; entitled to veneration or respect by virtue of a connection to divinity or divine things

scrip a piece of paper used to certify possession of land; could be exchanged for money

self-determination freedom of peoples to choose their own social and political structures without outside control or pressure

self-governance political independence or autonomy

self-identification the traits, groups, or people that you consider your own

Senators persons elected by their Métis communities as leaders and advisors

skew to distort or depict something in order to make it conform to a specific concept, attitude, or planned result

sovereignty a nation or state's supreme power within its borders

spiritual relating to the sacred essence of the soul or spirit. *Spiritual* is often contrasted with *worldly*, which relates to the things we see in the world.

stereotype a generalization about a group of people

stewardship an ethic of responsibly caring for lands, resources, or knowledge with the goal of long-term sustainability

subsistence economy a system in which enough food is grown, hunted, or gathered to provide for the basic needs of the people

supply and demand the relationship between the production and consumption of goods and services

sustainable development a practice in which resources are taken for human use in a way that preserves those resources for the future

systemic discrimination through policies or practices, having the impact of making an unjust distinction among individuals on the basis of race, gender, age, or other factors. The policies and practices of institutions and systems can appear to be neutral on the surface but have a discriminatory impact.

talking circle a tool used by many Nations to share and solve problems

©P

temporal related to the physical world of matter, time, and space

Three Fires Midewiwin Lodge a specific set of spiritual beliefs and practices followed by certain peoples, such as the Anishinaabe; while there is no direct English translation for Midewiwin, it is sometimes translated as "the way of the heart"

traditional teacher a person who carries the traditional teachings and ceremonies of his or her community and Nation

treaty a formal agreement between two or more nations in reference to peace, alliance, commerce, territory, or other relations

value a principle or standard that a person or a group accepts; our values guide us in thinking about what is right, what is important, what is meaningful. Values may include things such as morals, ethics, justice, and fair play.

world view a collection of beliefs, values, and assumptions held by an individual or a group about life, people, and the universe, and the interrelationships among them

Note: The Pronunciation Guide includes selected words from the text. The Guide may not be accurate for everyone. There will be regional differences based on local dialects.

Aboriginal Word	Pronunciation	Aboriginal Word	Pronunciation
aakde'win	ack-DAY-win	illamareit	ee-la-ma-reet
Akwesasne	ah-kwa-SAWS-nee	illageit	ee-la-geet
Anishinaabe	u-NEESH-in-ah-bee	indinawemaaganidog	uhn-din-uh-way-mah-gun-i-dog
Anishinaabemowin	u-NEESH-in-ah-bee-moo-win	Innu-Montagnais	IN-noo-moan-tahn-YAY
Atikamekw	Ah-dik-AH-meck	Inuinaqtun	IN-oo-ee-nak-tun
avatitinnik kamatsiarniq	A-va-tit-ti-ni ka-mat-si-ak-nik	Inuit Nunaat / Inuit Nunangat	IN-oo-it NOO-nat / IN-oo-it NUN-an-gat
Beothuk	bay-AH-tick	Inuit Tapiriit Kanatami	IN-oo-it ta-PEER-it ka-NA-tami
dbadendizwin	dbah-den-DIZ-win	Inuktitut	In-NOOK-tee-toot
debwewin	day-BWAY-win	Inuvialuit	In-NEW-vee-ah-loo-EET
Dëne Su,łiné	DEH-nay su-LEE-nay	Iqaluit	I-KA-loo-eet
Eeyou Itschee	EE-you I-schee	Kahnawake	gaah-naa-WAA-gay
Ganohonyohk	gaa-NO-hon-nyohk	Kaianeraserakowa	gaa-yaa-nay-raa-sey-raa-go-waa
Gichi Gumme	Gi-chi-GUM-mee	Kanehsatake	gaa-ness-aa-DAA-gay
Git'xsan	GIT-san	Kashastensera	gaa-saas-DUN-seh-ra
gwekwaadziwin	gway-kwah-dzee-win	keezhik	KEE-zhick
Gwich'in	GWUCH-en	Kinomagewapkong	kin-oo-mah-gay-wop-gong-g
Haida Gwaii	HY-dah-g-WHY	Kithteyayak	kith-tay-YA-yuck
Haudenosaunee	Ho-dee-no-SHOW-nee	Kokomis	Koo-gum-iss
Heiltsuk	HEL-sic	kokum	Koo-gum
Hoya:neh	ho-YAA-nay	Kwakwaka'wakw	Kwa-KWA-ka-wak

©P

Aboriginal Word	Pronunciation	Aboriginal Word	Pronunciation
Lutselk'e	LOOT-sel-kay	Nuxalk	NOO-hawk
makushan	muck-oo-SHAN	Onkwehonwe	On-gway-HON-way
Malecite	MAL-uh-seet	Otipaymsuwuk	oo-tip-bay-MISS-uh-wuck
Mi'kmaq / Mi'kmaw	MEEG-maw	Potawatomi	Pot-a-WOT-omi
Michif	mi-CHIFF	qallunaat	ha-loo-NAHT
miigwech / miigwetch	MEEG-wech	Saulteaux	SO-toe
minobimaadiziwin	Mino-bi-MAA-diz-i-win	Secwepemc	Shi-HUEP-muh / She-KWE-pem
mitayuke oyasin	me-ta-KOO-yay O-yah-seen	shkodawabuk	shkoo-DOW-ah-buck
miyo-wicehtowin	mi-YOH-wee-TSAY-too-win	Sto:lo	STAH-lo
mnaadendiwin	mu-nah-DEN-doo-win	Tabaldak	dah-BAL-duck
Mnjikaning	Mu-JIG-a-nee	Tapiriit Kanatami	ta-pi-REET ka-NA-tam-mi
msit No'kmaq	MM-sit no-GO-mah	Teme-Augama-Anishnaabe	Te-meh-Au-GAM-ah-Ah-nish-NA-bay
Musqueam	MUSS-quee-um	Tłı .cho.	TLEE-choh
'Namgis	NOM-gees	Tsimshian	Sim-SHE-an
n'dalgommek	un-DAL-go-meck	Tsúut'ína	tsoot-IN-na
nbwaakaawin	un-bwa-KA-win	Tyendinaga	Tie-en-daa-NAU-gaa
Nishnawbe Aski	Nish-NAW-bee ASS-kee	w'daeb-wae	odah-BWAY
Note terre	Not tehr	wahkomankanak	wa-ko-mah-gun-uck
Nuliajuk	noo-lee-AH-juk	Wendake	Wen-DAK-eh
Nunatsiavut	Noo-natsi-A-vut	wiigwaasabakoon	wee-gwah-suh-buh-GOON
Nunavik	NOO-na-vik	wiingashk	WEEN-gushk
Nunavut	NOO-na-vut	zaagidiwin	Za-gi-di-WIN

©P

©P

©P

CREDITS

The publisher would like to thank the following people and institutions for permission to use their © copyright materials. Every reasonable effort has been made to find copyright holders of the material in this text. The publisher would be pleased to know of any errors or omissions.

Photo Credits

t/c/b/l/r: top/centre/bottom/left/right
bg/i: background/inset

Cover: © Alison Nick/iStockphoto. Call to Consciousness viii Courtesy of Cynthia Wesley-Esquimaux; ixbg Courtesy of Canadore College, bl The Canadian Press/Shaney Komulainen, br *Kanehsatake: 270 Years of Resistance* © 1993 National Film Board of Canada; xt Courtesy of Jennifer Henry, b Tara Mae Hillyer. Courtesy of MorningStar River/www.morningstarriver.com; xiit Courtesy of David Bouchard, b The Canadian Press/Sean Kilpatrick; xiiit Courtesy of Jan Beaver, b Courtesy of the Métis Nation of Ontario; xiv Courtesy of Barbara Filion; xv Courtesy of the National Aboriginal Achievement Foundation naaf.ca. Unit 1 2 The Canadian Press/Winnipeg Free Press/Ken Gigliotti; 3t-b © ArcticPhoto/Alamy, Mark Bonokoski, Sun Media, Courtesy of Métis Nation of Ontario. Chapter 1 4 Mark Bonokoski, Sun Media; 5 *Tranquility* by William Anthony Monague, Beausoleil First Nation of Christian Island, Ontario, Canada; 8 Dick Hemingway; 11 Lawrence Migdale/Photo Researchers/First Light; 12 © Ginevre Marlow/Alamy/Getstock.com; 14 © Aaron Paquette; 15t With permission of the Royal Ontario Museum © ROM/ROM2005_5891_1, b © Nadya Kwandibens; 16t © Canadian Museum of Civilization/D2004-24781 (Artifact VI-Z-196, bag), b Photography: Feheley Fine Arts. Reproduced with the permission of Dorset Fine Arts; 17 Courtesy of the Debajehmujig Theatre Group; 18t Courtesy of the Métis Nation of Ontario, b Courtesy of the Miywasin Society of Aboriginal Services (Medicine Hat); 19 © Christi Belcourt; 20 © B&C Alexander/ArcticPhoto; 21t Courtesy of Shannon Kyles, b Bill Brooks/Masterfile; 22 Sun Media; 23 Courtesy of Amy Sayers, Shingwauk Education Trust; 24 Collection of Indian And Northern Affairs Canada. Photographer: Lawrence Cook. Used with permission of Zoey Wood-Salomon; 25 Len Gillis, Sun Media; 26 The Canadian Press/Winnipeg Free Press-Joe Bryksa; 29 Courtesy of Janice Longboat; 32 © Sylvain Grandadam/Age Fotostock/Maxx Images; 33t Courtesy of Christian Pilon/www.voyageurextraordinaire.ca, b Élise Racicot; 35 © 2004 Moses Amik Beaver. Chapter 2 36 © Robert McGouey/Alamy/Getstock.com; 37 Bearclaw Gallery, Edmonton. Used with permission of Maxine Noel; 38 Paul Nopper; 39 © Alyce Taylor; 40 Tara Mae Hillyer. Courtesy of MorningStar River/www.morningstarriver.com; 41t Courtesy of Iroquois Indian Museum in Howes, Cave, NY, b The Canadian Press/Winnipeg Free Press/Ken Gigliotti; 43 Darlene Maracle; 44 Cape May County Herald; 47 © Kinta-Way (Sharon Hitchcock) Photo courtesy of Great Spirited Productions; 48 Gordon Wiltsie/National Geographic Stock; 49t Janna MacKay, b Stan Navratil/All Canada Photos; 50t Courtesy of Métis Nation of Ontario, b The Canadian Press/Larry MacDougal; 51 Deni Bown © Dorling Kindersley; 52t Bill Curtsinger/National Geographic Stock, b Arthur Renwick. Courtesy of Eden Robinson; 53 Courtesy of Jan Beaver; 54 Courtesy of In-SHUCK-ch Nation; 56 Cat Criger; 57 © Christi Belcourt; 59t Based on Library and Archives Canada/C-016133, cl-r Pearson Canada, Plate 48 from *The Concise Historical Atlas of Canada*, University of Toronto Press, 1998. Reprinted and adapted with permission of the publisher, bl-r Plate 52 from The Concise Historical Atlas of Canada University of Toronto Press, 1998. Reprinted and adapted with permission of the publisher, *The Free People – Li gens libres*, by Diane P. Payment, Calgary: University of Calgary Press, 2009, page 222. Used with permission of the publisher; 62 Courtesy of Métis Nation of Ontario; 63 Courtesy of Douglas Cardinal Architect Inc.; 64 © Taffi Rosen; 65t Daniel Wiedemann/Dreamstime.com/Getstock.com, b Jane Ash Poitras. *Buffalo Seed*, 2004, mixed media and oil on canvas, 243.8 x 152.4 cm. Image courtesy of the Thunder Bay Art Gallery. Photography: Dean Goodwin, XL. © Jane Ash Poitras; 66 © Rick Beaver, www.rickbeaver.com; 68 © Shaughn Clements/Alamy/ Getstock.com; 69 Courtesy of Biidaajiwun Inc. www.motherearthwaterwalk.com; 70 The Canadian Press/Chris Windeyer; 72 Scott Stephens. © Kevin Lee Burton, Urban Shaman: Contemporary Aboriginal Art; 73 Scott Paradis/Timmins Daily Express/Sun Media. Chapter 3 74 Tim Swanky/University of Northern British Columbia; 75 © Hemis/Alamy; 76 © James Smedley/Alamy/Getstock.com; 79 Gerry Cariou; 80 Courtesy, National Museum of the American Indian, Smithsonian Institution (6/4020). Photo by Ernest Amoroso; 81t Library and Archives Canada/C-073635, b Courtesy of Métis Nation of Ontario; 82 © Hemis/Alamy; 83 Courtesy of Karliin Aariak and Diane Giroux/Nunavut Arctic College; 86 Courtesy Iroquois Cranberry Growers; 88 Union of B.C. Indian Chiefs/Photo 030211-025; 90 Glenbow Archives/NA-250-15; 91 Courtesy of Northern Transportation Company Limited (NTCL); 92 The Canadian Press/Fred Chartrand; 93 W.E. Garrett/National Geographic Stock; 94 Courtesy of Xeni Gwet'in First Nation; 95 Courtesy of the Whitefeather Forest Management Corporation; 96 Todd Korol/Reuters/Landov; 97l The Canadian Press/Andrew Vaughan, r The Canadian Press/Tom Hanson; 100 Courtesy of the Business Development Bank of Canada; 101 Courtesy of Mariette Lafreniere-Gaudet. Used with permission of Marcel Labelle; 102t John Farrington, Air Creebec Destinations magazine, b Courtesy of Dawn Madahbee; 103t Kirsten Murphy Photography, b © ArcticPhoto/Alamy; 104tl Edited by Samuel W. Corrigan and Lawrence J. Barkwell, *The struggle for recognition: Canadian justice and the Métis nation*, 1991. © Pemmican Publications, bl Manitoba Métis Federation Michif Language Program, *La Lawng: Michif Peekishkwewin: the heritage language of the Canadian Métis*, 2004. © Pemmican Publications. These works are protected by copyright and the making of these copies was with the permission of Access Copyright. Any alteration of its content or further copying in any form whatsoever is strictly prohibited unless otherwise permitted by law, bl The Canadian Press/Hamilton Spectator-John Rennison, br Steve Carty for Digging Roots www.diggingrootsmusic.com; 106 © Adrienne Fox-Keesic. Unit 2 108 Courtesy of the Métis Nation of Ontario; 109t-b Artists: Jonathan Cruz, Patrick Thompson and Celina Kalluk/www.nuschool.ca, Singular Photography/Courtesy of Grand Council Treaty #3. Chapter 4 110 © John Branch; 111 © Caroline Gomersall; 113 © Alamy/Getstock.com; 115 Courtesy of Indian and Northern Affairs Canada; 116 Hulton Archive/Getty Images; 118 The Canadian Press/Brunswick Telegraph-Journal/Noel Chenier; 119t Gordon Beck, The Gazette (Montreal) © 1994, b Courtesy of Meghan McGill; 120t Artists: Jonathan Cruz, Patrick Thompson and Celina Kalluk/ www.nuschool.ca, b The Canadian Press/Jonathan Hayward; 121 Photos by pottlebee; 123 © Wayne Shiels/Lone Pine Photo, b; 124 Photo of Alootook Ipellie courtesy of Annick Press; used with permission; 125t Courtesy of Reddnation, www.reddnation.com, r The Canadian Press/Robert Dall; 126t Courtesy of Douglas Cardinal Architect Inc., b Courtesy of Rick Beaver; 127 Toronto Star/ GetStock.com; 128 Photo: Cylla von Tiedemann. Used with permission of Red Sky Performance. www.redskyperformance.com, 129 Courtoisie de L' écho d'un peuple : spectacle *L'esprit du lys et du trille*

Mike Needham. Courtesy of Dr. Fiona Walton, UPEI; **305** John Horton Photography. Courtesy of the Department of Indigenous Studies/Trent University; **307** Used with permission of Elma Miller; **308** Michel Tournay; **310** Courtesy of Lakehead University. Used with permission of Tomson Highway; **311t** Ian Crysler Photographer, **b** Courtesy of Isadore Toulouse; **312** Courtesy of Roger Kenner; **313** Kirsten Murphy Photography; **315** Craig Vincent; **316** Ezra Shaw/Getty Images; **317** Courtesy of Larry Loyie and Constance Brissenden. www.firstnationswriter.com; **319** Courtesy of Jennifer Podemski; **320** Rene Johnston/GetStock.com; **321** The Canadian Press/Colin Perkel. **Call to Action 323** © Aaron Paquette.

Literary Credits

Call to Consciousness viii Cynthia Wesley; **viii–ix** Maurice Switzer; **x** Jennifer Henry; Eddy Robinson; **xii** Don Worme; David Bouchard; Mary Simon; **xiii** Jan Beaver; Larry Hill; **xiv** Barbara Filion; Don Worme; **Chapter 1 4** Dr Cecil King; **9** Dr Marie Battiste; First Peoples' Heritage, Language and Culture Council; Burt McKay; **12** Darren Préfontaine and Lawrence Barkwell; **13** Kappianaqtut: Strange Creatures and Fantastic Beings from Inuit Myths and Legends, Volume 1: The Mother of the Sea Beasts & The Giants of the North, Published in Canada by Inhabit Media Inc. (www.inhabitmedia.com), © 2007 by Neil Christopher, pages 36–37; Reprinted with permission by Key Porter Books Ltd. Copyright © 1996 by Arthur J. Ray is available in stores across Canada; Métis Nation of Ontario; **14** Excerpt from "Follow the Trickroutes" by Gerald Vizenor from Survival This Way: Interviews with American Indian Poets by Joseph Bruchac © 1987 The Arizona Board of Regents. Reprinted by permission of the University of Arizona Press; Aaron Paquette; **15** "Concrete Indians" www.redworks.ca; **17** National Aboriginal Achievement Foundation; **19** www.christibelcourt.com; **20** Northern Voices: Inuit Writings in English; Penny Petrone ed., page 27, © University of Toronto Press 1992, Reprinted with permission of the publisher; Senator Roland St Germain; **21** Nick Martin Winnipeg Free Press print edition April 24, 2010; **22** Canadian Journal of Native Education, "Thoughts on an Indigenous Research Methodology", by Evelyn Steinhauer, Vol 26, no. 2, 2002, 69–81, University of Alberta, reprinted with permission; **23** Edward Benton Banai. The Mishomis Book: The Voice of the Ojibway with permission of Indian Country Communications Inc.; **24** Native American Stories Told by Joseph Bruchac. Fulcrum Publishing (www.fulcrumbooks.com), 1991; **25** Paul Nadjiwan; **27** Jessica Yee, Shameless Magazine; **28** Mary Lou Smoke; **29** Janice Kehehti:io Longboat; Michelle Corneau; **30** Laura Stevens, Ontario Birchbark-AMMSA; **34** Métis Nation of Ontario; **Chapter 2 36** © 1990 by Steve Wall and Harvey Arden from the book Wisdomkeepers: Meetings with Native American Spiritual Elders. Reprinted with permission from Beyond Words Publishing, Hillsboro OR.; **38** Excerpt from Honour Earth Mother by Basil Johnston and published by Kegedonce Press – www.kegedonce.com; Joseph Boyden; **39** Pauline Decontie; **40** Eddy Robinson; **41** Iroquois Indian Museum, Howes Cave, NY; Métis Nation of Ontario; **42** "On the Trail of the First Inhabitants, or Objects, Stories and Rituals: A Dialogue with the Living World." Student Handout, pages 21–22. McCord Museum. http://www.mccord-museum.qc.ca/pdf/eduweb/autochtone.eleve. En.doc; **43** Courtesy of George Beaver; Tim Thompson; **44** "On the Trail of the First Inhabitants, or Objects, Stories and Rituals: A Dialogue withthe Living World." Student Handout, pages 22–23. McCord Museum. http://www.mccord-museum.qc.ca/pdf/eduweb/

autochtone.eleve. En.doc; **45** by Tantanga Mani (Walking Buffalo), Stoney, 1958, quoted in Words of Power: Voices from Indian America, edited by Norbert J. Hill, Jr., (Golden, Colorado: Fulcrum Publishing, 1994); Melissa (Missy) Elliott Ojistari:yo; **46** adapted from Statistics Canada, 2006 Census of Population; **47** www.itk.ca; Alex McKay, University of Toronto; **52** from "Go Fish" by Eden Robinson, in Spirit magazine, Spring 2007; **53** Jan Beaver; **56, 57, 58** Christi Belcourt; **60** Excerpt from "Stolen from Our Embrace", by Suzanne Fournier & Ernie Crey, published 1997 by Douglas & McIntyre Ltd (now Douglas & McIntyre: an imprint of D&M Publishers Inc). Reprinted with permission from the publisher; Ricard Hardisty Papers from AG Archibald to W.J. Christie, January 11 1872 file M-477-140 page 4 & 5 http://www.glenbow.org/collections/search/findingAids/archhtm/ hardisty.cfm; **65** courtesy of the Artist Jane Ash Poitras, RCA; **66** Lee Maracle; **67** "Doorways to a Younger World" by Philip Paul, Little Hunger, Nightwood Editions, 2008, www.nightwoodeditions.com used with permission; Report of the Royal Commission on Aboriginal Peoples. Volume 2: Restructuring the relationship, P. 449, 1996. Reproduced with the permission of the Minister of Public Works and Government Services, 2010, and Courtesy of the Privy Council Office; **68** from "Native women and supporters walking around the Great Lakes," Media Release April 2006; **69** Sherrole Benton; **70** Jessica Simpson, Spirit Magazine; **71** Jim St Arnold; Ipperwash Inquiry Report, © Queen's Printer for Ontario, 2007. Reproduced with permission; used with permission of Roseway Publishing an imprint of Fernwood Publishing Co. Ltd; **72** Kevin Lee Burton; **Chapter 3 74** Chief Marilyn BaptisteTsilhqot'in (Chilcotin) Nation **85** France Picotte; **89** Sheila Watt-Cloutier; **90** Lawrence Barkwell Métis Legacy (Volume II): Michif Culture, Heritage, and Folkways. Saskatoon: Gabriel Dumont Institute and Pemmican Publications, 2006. Page 214; **92** Lubicon Lake Nation; **94** Chief Marilyn Baptiste Tsilhqot'in (Chilcotin) Nation; **100** Chief James Norman; **101** Marcelle Labelle; **Chapter 4 110** Bathroom Book of Canadian "Quotes," Humourous, Witty, Ridiculous & Inspiring, Wojna, Lisa. Blue Bike Books Ltd., Canada, 2005; **114** Report of the Royal Commission on Aboriginal Peoples. Volume 4: Perspectives and Realities, P. 201, 1996. Reproduced with the permission of the Minister of Public Works and Government Services, 2010, and Courtesy of the Privy Council Office,; Constitution Act 1982; **115** Assembly of First Nations "A Declaration of First Nations"; **116** from The Best of Chief Dan George by Chief Dan George and Helmut Himschall, courtesy of Hancockhouse.com; **117** Marilyn Kane and Sylvia Maracle"Our World", Canadian Woman Studies; **119** Canadian Press; Meghan McGill; **121** Ann Meekitjuk Hanson; **122** Métis Nation; **123** Métis Nation of Ontario; **124** from Metis oral history, Anonymous, Qu'Appelle Valley 1885; Nunatsiaq News, January 26, 1996 Ipellie's Shadow: The Shy Man Comes Out of the Shadows; **127** Ian Ross; Blake Debassige; **128** Brent Wesley/Wawatay News; **132** Royal Commission on Aboriginal Peoples. Vol 4 – Perspectives and Realities p. 1 Reproduced with the permission of the Minister of Public Works and Government Services Canada, 2010; **134** Maureen Googoo; **136** "Indian enough" from my heart is a stray bullet, wiith permission of the author; **141** Jessica Yee, Executive Director, Native Youth Sexual Health Network; **143** National Chief Shawn A-in-Chut Atleo, AFN; **Chapter 5 144** from "Nokum is My Teacher" David Bouchard, © 2006 Red Deer Press, Fitzhenry & Whiteside Ltd; **146** Chief Jean-Charles Piétan and Sylvie Basile; **149** Gordon Bruyere; **150** Royal Commission on Aboriginal Peoples, 1996 © Government of Canada. Reproduced with the permission of the Minister of Public Works and Government Services Canada (2010).

Source: Library and Archives Canada/Report of the Royal Commission on Aboriginal Peoples/Amicus No. 15088153 p. 1; **151** Dr Thelma Chalifoux; **152** Printed with permission by Author Ray Young Bear; In Honour of our Elders Becky Loucks; Royal Commission on Aboriginal Peoples, 1996 © Government of Canada. Reproduced with the permission of the Minister of Public Works and Government Services Canada (2010). Source: Library and Archives Canada/Report of the Royal Commission on Aboriginal Peoples/Amicus No. 15088153 p. 1; **155** Sheila Watt-Cloutier; Canadian Journal of Native Studies; **156** Grand Chief Joe Miskokomon; **157** Isabelle Knockwood Out of Depths pp. 14–15 used with permission of Roseway Publishing an imprint of Fernwood Publishing Co. Ltd; **159** The Constitution of the Confederacy by the Peacemaker, 1897 Revised by Chief Jacob E. Thomas, www.jakethomaslearningcentre.ca; Métis Voyageur, Métis Nation of Ontario; **162** Royal Commission on Aboriginal Peoples, 1996 © Government of Canada. Reproduced with the permission of the Minister of Public Works and Government Services Canada (2010). Source: Library and Archives Canada/Report of the Royal Commission on Aboriginal Peoples/Amicus No. 15088153. p. 1.3; Royal Commission on Aboriginal Peoples, 1996 © Government of Canada. Reproduced with the permission of the Minister of Public Works and Government Services Canada (2010). Source: Library and Archives Canada/Report of the Royal Commission on Aboriginal Peoples/Amicus No. 15088153 p. 1; **166** Ashley Quinn; Breton Books Ltd.; **167** Isabelle Knockwood Out of the Depths p. 159 used with permission of Roseway Publishing an imprint of Fernwood Publishing Co. Ltd; France Picotte; **168** Excerpt from "Memoirs of a Really Good Brown Girl" by Marilyn Dumont, Brick Books, 1998; **169** Courtesy Anishinabek News; Excerpt from "Stolen from Our Embrace", by Suzanne Fournier & Ernie Crey, published 1997 by Douglas & McIntyre Ltd (now Douglas & McIntyre: an imprint of D&M Publishers Inc). Reprinted with permission from the publisher; **173** Courtesy Anishinabek News; **174** Native Women's Association of Canada website http://www.nwac.ca/ programs/sis-history; **175** Native Women's Association of Canada. 2009. Voices of our Sisters In Spirit: A research and policy report to families and communities. 2nd ed. Ottawa: Native Women's Association of Canada. http://www.nwac.ca/sites/default/files/ imce/NWAC_Voices %20of%20Our%20Sisters%20In%20Spirit_2nd%20Edition_March%20 2009.pdf; **176** Alex Jacobs; In the Words of Elders, P. Kulchyski, D. McCaskill and D. Newhouse, pp. 374–375 © 1999 UTP, Reprinted with permission of the publisher; **178** Chasity Meuse; **179** Mary Simon President Inuit Tapiriit Kanatami; **180** John Beaucage; **181** Velma Noah; **Chapter 6 186** Chief Clifford Tawpisin; Mary Simon President Inuit Tapiriit Kanatami; Jennifer St Germain; **188** Zachary Beaudette; **190** Leonard George Chief Tsleil-Waututh Nation 1989–2001; Tom Porter and Lesley Forrester leslelyforrester@xplornet.com; **192** Peacemaker's Journey, Kanatiiosh Gray; **193** Senator Thelma Chalifoux; **194** Paul Chartrand; Report of the Royal Commission on Aboriginal Peoples. Volume 2: Restructuring the Relationship, P. 128, 1996. Reproduced with the permission of the Minister of Public Works and Government Services, 2010, and Courtesy of the Privy Council Office; Joyce Eileen Courchene Nongom Ikkwe, the Indigenous Women's Collective of the South East Region, Manitoba; **199** Ovide Mercredi, former Grand Chief of the Assembly of First Nations, Mercredi & Turpel IN THE RAPIDS Viking Press, 1993, p. 81; **204** Elijah Harper; **206** Preamble to Haida Nation Constitution; **207** Dave Mowat; **208** Josh Gottfriedson; National Chief Shawn

A-in-Chut Atleo, from "It's Our Time: a vision for our future", AFN Annual General Assembly 2010 http://www.afn.ca/article.asp?id=3 page 10; **209** Jennifer St Germain; **210** Pita Aatami; **211** Assembly of First Nations "A Declaration of First Nations"; Report of the Royal Commission on Aboriginal Peoples. Volume 4: Perspectives and Realities, pp. 74–75, 1996. Reproduced with the permission of the Minister of Public Works and Government Services, 2010, and Courtesy of the Privy Council Office; **213** Satsan (Herb George) President of the National Centre for First Nations Governance; **214** Regional Chief Angus Toulouse; Métis Nation of Ontario; John Beaucage; **215** Grand Chief Angie Barnes; Chief Terrance Paul; Audrey Poitras President Métis Nation of Alberta; Paul Okalik; **216** Dan Christmas; **217** Martin Bayer; **218** Brenda Etienne; Lillian Sanderson; Cynthia-Wesley Esquimaux, Nexen Chair in Aboriginal Leadership; **219** Jennifer Watkins; Jan Beaver; **220** Métis Voyageur, Métis Nation of Ontario; **Chapter 7 222** © Queen's Printer for Ontario, 2007. Reproduced with permission; **224** Belfords, Clarke & Co. Toronto March 1880 p. 213; **225** The True Spirit and Original Intent of Treaty 7, Treaty 7 Elders and Tribal Council, with Walter Hildebrandt, Sarah Carter, and Dorothy First RiderMcGill-Queen's University Press, 1996, McGill University; **226** Belfords, Clarke & Co. Toronto March 1880 p. 213; **227** United Nations Declaration of the Rights of Indigenous Peoples Article 3; The University of Alberta Press and the Canadian Review of Comparative Literature/Revue Canadienne de Littérature Comparée; **227** Sophia Rabliauskas, Spokesperson/Community Coordinator for Pimachiowin Aki World Heritage Project; **228** 1763 Royal Proclamation; **229, 230** The True Spirit and Original Intent of Treaty 7, Treaty 7 Elders and Tribal Council, with Walter Hildebrandt, Sarah Carter, and Dorothy First Rider McGill-Queen's University Press, 1996, McGill University; Report of the Royal Commission on Aboriginal Peoples. Volume 2: Restructuring the Relationship, P. 465, 1996. Reproduced with the permission of the Minister of Public Works and Government Services, 2010, and Courtesy of the Privy Council Office; **231** Grand Council Chief John Beaucage; **235** Grand Chief Stewart Phillip, President, Union of BC Indian Chiefs; **236** Dr Joseph Gosnell, Former President of Nisga'a Lisims Government; Nisga'a Petition 1913; Nisga'a Chief David Mackay, 1888; **238** Colonialism on Trial: Indigenous Land Rights and the Gitksan and Wet'suwet'en Sovereignty Case, Don Monet and Ardythe Wilson (1992); **240** John Amagoalik Qikiqtani Inuit Association; **241** William Barbour, president of the Labrador Inuit Association; **243** Testament of Louis Riel 1885; **244** Deputy Grand Chief Mike Metatawabin; © Queen's Printer for Ontario, 2009. Reproduced with permission; **245** Robert Animikii Horton, "Bebaamweyaazh" Rainy River First Nations, Marten Clan; **246** Grand Council Chief Patrick Madahbee; **Chapter 8 248** Winnipeg: Aboriginal Justice Implementation Commission, November 1999, Permission to reproduce this text is provided by the Queen's Printer for Manitoba. The Queen's Printer does not warrant the accuracy or currency of the reproduction of this information; **252** Don Worme; The Truth and Reconciliation Commission of Canada, http://www.trc.ca/websites/ trcinstitution/ index.php?p=4; Statement of Apology, June 11, 2008 http://www.ainc-inac.gc.ca/ai/rqpi/apo/index-eng.asp Reproduced with the permission of the Minister of Public Works and Government Services, 2010, and Courtesy of the Privy Council Office; **253** Phil Fontaine; People to People, Nation to Nation: Highlights from the Report of the Royal Commission on Aboriginal Peoples, 1996. pp. ix–x. Reproduced with the permission of the Minister of Public Works and Government

©P

Services, 2010, and Courtesy of the Privy Council Office; **254** Ovide Mercredi; "From Dancing with a Ghost by Rupert Ross. Forward copyright © Basil H. Johnston, 1992, 2006. Reprinted by permission of Penguin Group (Canada), a Division of Pearson Canada Inc."; **255** Uqalurait: An Oral History of Nunavut, compiled and edited by John Bennett and Susan Rowley, p. 99 McGill-Queens University Press 2004; **256** Four Hills of Life, Minnesota Historical Society; **257** Jason Madden, Métis Nation of Ontario; **259** Don Worme; 365 Days of Walking the Red Road: The Native American path to leading a spiritual life every day, (Avon, Massachusetts: Adams Media Corporation, 2003), p. 50; **260** Commission on Aboriginal Peoples. Bridging the Cultural Divide: A Report on Aboriginal People and Criminal Justice in Canada. 1996, p. 309. Reproduced with the permission of the Minister of Public Works and Government Services, 2010, and Courtesy of the Privy Council Office; Jan Beaver; **261** Chris Paci, Chris McLeod, and Jason Madden, Métis Nation of Ontario; **262** Jonathan Rudin; **264** Dibaajiomowin Summer 2010 newsletter; **265** From One Dead Indian: The Premier, The Police and The Ipperwash Crisis by Peter Edwards © 2003. Published by McClelland & Stewart Ltd. Used with permission from the author and the publisher; **266** "From Returning to the Teachings by Rupert Ross. Copyright © University of Saskatchewan, 1992, 2006. Reprinted by permission of Penguin Group (Canada), a Division of Pearson Canada Inc."; **267** Source: Duncan. John. "Apology for the Inuit High Arctic Relocation." Speaking Notes for the Honourable John Duncan, PC, MP, Minister of Indian Affairs and Northern Development and Federal Interlocutor for theMétis and the Non-Status Indians at the Apology for the Inuit High Arctic Relocation. Inukjuak, August 18, 2010, URL: http://www.ainc-inac.gc.ca/ai/mr/spch/2010/aug18-eng.asp.; **269** Indigenous Bar Association; **270** Alex Jacobs; **271** CBC News Online; **272** From One Dead Indian: The Premier, The Police and The Ipperwash Crisis by Peter Edwards © 2003.Published by McClelland & Stewart Ltd. Used with permission from the author and the publisher; "Ipperwash inquiry spreads blame for George's death,from http://www.cbc.ca/canada /story/2007/05/31/ipperwash-main.html **273** © Queen's Printer for Ontario, 2007. Reproduced with permission; **274** Mark Bonokoski, Sun Media; Toronto Police Service; **275** Criminal Code of Canada (R.S., 1985, c. C-46), Section 718.2(e), http://laws. justice.gc.ca/en/C-46/, Department of Justice Canada, September 2010, Reproduced with the permission of the Minister of Public Works and Government Services Canada, 2010; Jean-Paul Restoule; **278** Raymond Mason; Excerpt from "Stolen from Our mbrace", by Suzanne Fournier & Ernie Crey, published 1997 by Douglas & McIntyre Ltd (now Douglas & McIntyre: an imprint of D&M Publishers Inc). Reprinted with permission from the publisher; **279** Chief Stan Beardy, Dibaajiomowin Newsletter; Keith Lickers; **280** Don Worme; Jennifer Ashawasegai receives Debwewin Citation for journalism excellence http://www.newswire.ca/en/releases/archive/November2008/ 29/c4719.html; From One Dead Indian: The Premier, The Police and The Ipperwash Crisis by Peter Edwards © 2003.Published by McClelland & Stewart Ltd. Used with permission from the author and the publisher; John Miller Professor of Journalism, Ryerson University; "Reprinted with permission Torstar Syndication Services"; Chapter 9 **286** National Chief Shawn A-in-Chut Atleo, AFN; Paul Okalik; France Picotte; **291** with permission of Andrew Koostachin, Attawapiskat First Nation Chief & Council/Education Authority; Dr Marie Battiste; **292** Excerpt from "Stolen from Our Embrace", by Suzanne Fournier & Ernie Crey, published 1997 by Douglas & McIntyre Ltd (now Douglas & McIntyre: an imprint of D&M Publishers Inc). Reprinted with permission from the publisher; France Picotte; **293** Sitting Bull; **294** National Chief Shawn A-in-Chut Atleo, AFN; **295** Redefining Success in Inuit Learning Workshop, May 2–3, 2007, Workshop Report, The Canadian Council on Learning; **296** Annie Aningmiuq; **307** Amos Key Jr.; **307** "People to People, Nation to Nation:Highlights from the Royal Commission on Aboriginal Peoples." 1996, pp. 91–02. Reproduced with the permission of the Minister of Public Works and Government Services, 2010, and Courtesy of the Privy Council Office; Blue Quills First Nations College; **309** Acknowledgment: Chart adapted from "Aboriginal languages of Canada" by Eung-Do Cook & Darin Flynn in Contemporary linguistic analysis: An introduction, 6th ed., pp. 318–333 (Toronto: Pearson Longman 2008), revised by Darin Flynn (p.c., Sept. 2, 2010)"; **310** Tomson Highway; **311** Isadore Toulouse; **314** Environics Institute; **315** Environics Institute; France Picotte; **316** "Our Languages, Our Selves," by Alexina Kublu and Mick Mallon; **318** Rebecca Pratt; Tim Thompson; Jordin Tootoo; James Bartleman; France Picotte; Tracy Boese/Métis Voyageur Magazine; **319** Jennifer Podemski; Call to Action **322** Don Worme

©P